Multivariate statistical analysis in geography

Multivariate statistical analysis in geography

A primer on the general linear model

R. J. Johnston

Longman
London and New York

Longman Group Limited London

*Associated companies, branches and representatives
throughout the world*

*Published in the United States of America
by Longman Inc., New York*

First published 1978
First paperback edition 1980

British Library Cataloguing in Publication Data

Johnston, Ronald John
    Multivariate statistical analysis in geography.
    1. Geography–Statistical methods.
    2. Multivariate analysis.
    I. Title.
    910'.01'51953   G70.3   79-42722

ISBN 0-582-30034-7

Printed in Great Britain by
Richard Clay (The Chaucer Press) Ltd, Bungay, Suffolk

Contents

for Rita

List of figures

List of tables

Preface

The use of statistics in geographical research has increased rapidly during the last two or three decades. Most students being trained in geography at tertiary educational institutions receive some instruction in statistical methods; all are given things to read, particularly research reports in journals, in which statistical procedures form a basic part of the reasoning. And yet relatively few geography students have a strong background in school mathematics, and even fewer continue with mathematical studies in parallel with their geography. How, then, can they obtain sufficient knowledge of statistical methods in order to appreciate the arguments which they must read and digest?

Two main approaches to this problem have been suggested and applied. The first is generally known as the 'cookbook', which outlines the computational procedures involved in using a statistical method and, by way of examples, illustrates the method's application within the general contexts of hypothesis-testing and statistical inference. The focus is on 'how' and 'what for'. The other approach is based much more firmly on 'why', arguing that in order to use a method it is necessary to understand how it works. Some detailed mathematical and statistical grounding is required for this.

The major texts written specifically for geographers to date have been concerned with relatively simple and straightforward statistical techniques, and they have largely been based on the 'cookbook' approach. Notable among these are the texts by Gregory (3rd ed, 1973) and by Hammond and McCullagh (1974). Two other volumes, by King (1969) and by Yeates (1974), have essayed a stronger 'why' component, but seem to have fallen between the two approaches: in addition, both aim to cover a very wide range of material in a relatively small space, a feature of the later chapters of a recent text by Smith (1975), also.

The present book follows introductory texts, such as Gregory's and Hammond and McCullagh's, both of which have twin purposes of introducing students to the fundamentals of statistical analysis and of outlining in some detail the computational procedures by which relatively simple analyses may be conducted. But many of the research reports which students must read use much more complex techniques, because the world being studied is more complex than is allowed for by the simple procedures covered by introductory texts. These more complex techniques are based on the simple ones, but students are given no introduction to them which crosses what is basically the gap between bivariate — or single cause — and multivariate — multiple cause-relationships. The present volume attempts to build a bridge over that gap with respect to one main family of techniques, the general linear model.

This is not a 'cookbook', for two reasons. First, it is impractical to attempt the use of most of the methods discussed here by hand calculations, or even with calculators of the type many people can now afford. Computers are needed, and without them many of the procedures, especially those introduced in the later chapters, cannot be employed. Secondly, the book is not aimed to help those who would make considerable use of the procedures in their own research: for that purpose, much more intensive mathematical and statistical background work is necessary, and students would need to graduate from this volume to the more detailed statistical texts relating to particular procedures. The target here is appreciation. If students must read about multiple regressions and factor analyses, dummy variables and linear discriminant functions, then they must have a general knowledge of what those procedures do. Just as appreciation of a good meal does not need understanding of the recipe, so appreciation of a research paper by someone who wishes to use its findings does not require a mathematical understanding of the calculations undertaken. The general student needs to know what in broad terms the adopted procedure does and how its results should be interpreted.

There are dangers in the approach adopted here. The wide availability of computer programs invites the 'number-crunching' of ill-assembled data sets through partly-comprehended statistical routines, and those intending research using the methods outlined here are advised that further reading is necessary before they start their analyses. But for those who only wish to know what it was that X did, whether it was relevant, and what his results mean, have a more basic requirement, which is a general appreciation of the method. It cannot be obtained without equations and formulae, but it does not demand much mathematics, beyond simple arithmetic, geometry and algebra; matrix algebra, however, is a necessity for those who would travel further. Words, diagrams, and simple examples are used here, in the hope that careful, perhaps guided, reading and study of this text will at least enable the mass of geography students to know enough about what they read to appreciate the contribution it makes to the discipline: hence the sub-title.

Statistical analysis is not the only research method in geography; it is the one which is far superior to any other when the aim is to make precise and unambiguous statements about relationships and patterns in sets of numbers. The statements which the researcher wants to make, and the numbers themselves, are based in geographical theory and the purposes of geographical work. Chapter 1 briefly discusses this background to the use of statistics, and reviews some basic concepts relevant to successful reading of the rest of the book.

As indicated by the title and sub-title, discussion here is restricted to the various aspects of the general linear model, and particularly to multivariate analyses. Most students will have encountered the bivariate aspects

— simple regression and correlation; one-way analysis of variance — prior to using this book, but as understanding of these is basic to later discussion of multivariate procedures, they are covered in some detail in Chapter 2, to provide the necessary foundation. From them, Chapters 3 and 4 develop the multivariate extensions, showing how multi-causal hypotheses can be tested with independent variables that are either interval/ratio measured, or nominally measured, or both.

Of the seven substantive chapters the first three deal with hypothesis-testing when causal and effect variables have been specified. In the other four, the process is reversed somewhat, with attention on those procedures which create new variables and test more complicated hypotheses with them. Chapters 5 and 6 deal with this topic for data measured on interval and ratio scales, with the former treating the procedures — principal components analysis and factor analysis — which are used to create new variables and the latter concentrating on methods, such as canonical correlation analysis, which test for relationships between hybrid variables. In Chapters 7 and 8 the focus turns to independent variables which are measured on nominal scales: classification of observations into categories is discussed in Chapter 7; testing of hypotheses with and about such categories by linear discriminant analysis is treated in Chapter 8. Perhaps paradoxically, these later chapters are about the more complex procedures, but they are also the shorter ones, reflecting the detailed basis given earlier.

Throughout the book, the various methods are illustrated with geographical examples. The assumption is always that there are no problems in the wholesale adoption of the methods to the research aims and data of the geographer. This is not necessarily so, and in the final chapter some of the problems raised by geographical data are discussed.

There is continuing debate within the geographical discipline concerning the methods discussed here. This has two strands. The first contends that statistical analyses of the types discussed here are invalid for much geographical work, certainly in human geography. This is a philosophical, sometimes ideological issue, whose discussion lies outside the present context. The assumptions here are (1) that the methods discussed are valuable in certain circumstances, and (2) that because the methods are widely used and reported in the geographical literature at present, it is a necessary part of a geographer's training to obtain some general comprehension of what is being done and why. The second strand is not a debate about the value of statistical techniques, but about the validity of using those discussed here in geographical research. As with the other strand, there is validity in parts of the argument against the techniques but the general case is far from proven and the previous argument still holds; the techniques are being widely used and geographers should be aware of them, thus enabling an informed assessment of their value.

The tricky issues are avoided here, therefore. The philosophy of this book is that a family of techniques that is widely used in geographical research should be appreciated — if not entirely understood — by all geographers. The book has been written in an attempt to provide such an appreciation, with as few constraints on required numeracy and mathematical skills as possible.

Acknowledgements

This book is the result of attempts to teach aspects of multivariate statistical analysis in three separate continents, largely to students with little mathematical background, let alone statistical. The methods developed during more than a decade of such teaching, based on verbal and pictorial representation of algebraic arguments, are now presented here for a wider audience, in the hope that they are useful to those who, like me, have little of the background in depth necessary to an appreciation of what is being done in so much geographical research today.

In developing the teaching method outlined here, I am grateful to those classes of students who have persevered with my attempts to help them understand the methods covered, and whose comments helped me to improve the presentation. Two 'students' in particular deserve special mention, my colleagues Stan Gregory and Alan Hay, with whom I have participated in a course involving this material. Stan Gregory encouraged me to write this book, and both he and Alan Hay read the full manuscript and made many valuable comments on it, for which I am extremely grateful. Arthur Hunt, too, read and commented on the draft and Keith Beavon provided a very meticulous critique of the whole manuscript in its penultimate form, which was extremely rewarding for me. To all of them, my thanks, whilst of course absolving them from any responsibility for the contents.

Technical preparation of a volume of this nature is a major task, and I am deeply indebted to several persons for their assistance. Joan Dunn performed marvels in transforming the manuscript into a typescript; Stephen Frampton provided an excellent set of diagrams; and the staff at Longman have translated both into an excellent book. My wife Rita meticulously checked everything in the script, a task which nobody should be asked to do. To all, my sincere thanks.

This book is dedicated to my wife, as a measly token of thanks for her fantastic support, in so many ways, throughout my career. Since no thanks could be sufficient, I trust this small mention at least records the depth of my gratitude.

R. J. Johnston
May, 1977.

We are grateful to the following for permission to reproduce copyright material:

Cambridge University Press for an extract from Table 4.23 in *The Urban Mosaic* by Timms; Geographical Analysis for Table 2 in 'On Structuring a Migration Model' by J. B. Riddell from *Geographical Analysis*, Vol. 2; the author for his Figure No. 8 by Peter Goheen from *Victorian Toronto*; Journal of Ecology for Figure 1 by Norris and Barkham from *Journal of Ecology*, 58; the author for his Figure No. 28 by R. A. Murdie from *Factorial Ecology of Metropolitan Toronto*; New Zealand Geographer for Figure 1 by W. A. V. Clark from 'The Use of Residuals for Regression' in *New Zealand Geographer*, 23, 1967; the authors for a table from 'Canonical Correlation in Geographical Analysis' by D. M. Ray and P. R. Lohnes in *Geographia Polonica*, XXV, 1973; Regional Science Association for Figure 5A by P. Haggett 'Trend-Surface Mapping in the Interregional Comparison of Intra-Regional Structures' from Haggett *Papers RSA*, Vol. 20; Regional Studies Association for Table 5 by Willis from *Regional Studies*, 6, 1972; Economic Geography for an extract from Table III by J. Morrison, M. W. Scripter and R. H. T. Smith 'Basic Measures of Manufacturing in the U.S.A. 1958' from *Economic Geography*, 44, 1968; University of Chicago Press for Figure 2 by O. D. Duncan 'Path Analysis — Sociological Examples' from *American Journal of Sociology*, 72, 1966.

Chapter 1

Introduction

This is a book about statistical methods; how they operate, what their results indicate, and how they are used in geographical research. The focus throughout is on methods and procedures for handling data. Manipulation of numbers is not a worthwhile end in itself, however; it must be directed towards a particular goal. The nature of that goal is a major concern in this introductory chapter.

In one sense, this is a book for beginners, as its sub-title suggests; its purpose is to introduce a range of widely-used statistical methods. But it is not for absolute beginners, as it assumes prior knowledge of the material usually presented in introductory courses and texts on statistical methods. Many aspects of that material are used as basic concepts here, and so the later sections of this chapter present a brief résumé of the relevant topics.

Geographical research

There are many definitions of geography, and many geographers eschew any formal definition of their subject. Increasingly, scholars are becoming convinced that strictly-drawn boundaries hinder the paths of understanding and education, and the differences between disciplines are becoming blurred as geographers, like all other scientists and social scientists, seek widely for answers to their problems. Philosophies and methodologies are shared, therefore, but each discipline has its major substantive and procedural foci.

The major topics addressed by geographers concern, as they have always done, the interactions between human societies and their environments. Within this broad field there are many particular specialisations, some on 'physical environments', some on 'social environments', and some on 'built environments'. But these are differences of emphasis within a broad common theme.

The ways in which geographers frame research questions vary enormously. Some differences reflect ideologies and philosophies; others represent various methodological preferences. Yet whatever the details of the approach, in almost every case it can be classified into one of two ways of asking the research question, and these two fundamental questions are the foundations of this book.

Question One: Are there relationships between phenomena in various locations?

Geographers are concerned with places as the locations of the man—environment inter-relationships. Delimiting a 'place' is often difficult, as the voluminous literature on the nature of a 'region' testifies, but if such definition is feasible, it is then possible to characterise each place in a great number of ways. A valley, for example, can be characterised by the percentages of its area occupied by different land uses, by the type of weather it experiences at different times of the year, by its settlements, and by the occupations of its inhabitants; a town can be identified by its area, the density of buildings in it, the percentage of its population who are children, the types of shops in its commercial centre, and the political orientation of its governing body; a segment of a stream can be characterised by the shape of its cross-section, the stability of its banks, and the variability in its water depth over the year.

A great encyclopaedia of information can be gathered together for every 'place' we can define, therefore, at any spatial scale. A major function of geography has always been the collection and dissemination of 'relevant' facts about places (Freeman, 1961). But collection alone is not the basis for a scholarly discipline. Facts are required for a purpose, which defines their 'relevance'. In geography the purpose is understanding man—environment inter-relationships, hence our first question.

To understand something implies knowledge of its origins and operations. To understand a slope is not only to know its length and its angle, but also how it was formed, what is happening to it now, and how it influences other environmental processes and forms; to understand a town is not only to know how many people live there, their occupations and their life styles, but also why they are there, and how their existence in that place influences the lives of others who live elsewhere.

We cannot understand anything by focusing on it alone; we need general concepts, laws, and languages, otherwise we cannot even describe, let alone explain. Our research project may be into the movement of material on a particular slope, but measurement of this movement, identification of its causes, even the concept of a slope itself, requires using terms and categories whose definitions are based on many observations of the same thing. If we wish to explain what is happening on our particular slope, then undoubtedly we also wish to transmit our explanation to others, and to do this successfully we must use the accepted terms and categories, otherwise we will not be understood. Such accepted terms and categories include those of measurement; metres per annum is a universally-understood index of movement, but very fast is not.

The cause of a particular phenomenon can only be discovered in terms of general understanding about the operation of events. This involves us studying the same type of phenomenon in many places, perhaps informally, even only subconsciously, in order to develop our understanding of the particular unique example we may be focusing on. It might seem from our observations, for example, that the movement of material on our slope results from the removal of protective vegetation by grazing sheep. But we could not prove that this was so without studying other slopes. Two possible procedures are open to us. In the first, we might select another slope, also with a movement problem and with grazing sheep. We measure the movement on each and then take away the sheep from our particular slope and see, after a time, whether any changes have occurred relative to those on the other slope. The results may favour our initial hypothesis that sheep cause the movement of material. Alternatively, we may select a large number of slopes, measure movement rates and sheep densities on each, and see if there is any relationship between the two variables, from which we may infer that sheep density influences movement rates.

This is a very simple example. No phenomenon which geographers study is likely to result from a single cause. The movement of material on a slope is probably related to many other partial causes; the angle of slope, aspects of the area's climate such as temperature regime and rainfall, the parent rock which is the source of the material, the type of vegetation cover, and so on. All of these variables will be acting, both separately and in combination, on every particular slope. Each slope may represent a unique combination of these variables; we will only know whether it is after a careful study of a large number of slopes, from which we can derive general principles which are applicable to unique situations.

Understanding involves knowledge of causes, which requires careful collection and use of evidence. To be valid, an explanation must be phrased in terms of known general statements concerning processes and forms. To explain the unique we must comprehend the general, and for the latter we must study many places. Hence geographical research aims to explain what places are like, and how their characteristics are created, which requires study of the relevant phenomena over a wide range of places. This is the method of Question One.

How we phrase Question One can vary considerably from problem to problem. We may start with a very simple question which assumes 'all other things being equal' or the absence of any other causal factors, such as:

> Do variations in the density of grazing sheep cause variations in the rate of movement of material on slopes?

Data can be collected to provide an answer, but this will probably be unsatisfactory, for many other factors operate to influence movement rates. Thus we might re-write the question as:

> Do variations in the density of grazing sheep, in local climate, in slope angle, in parent rock, and in vegetation cover all cause variations in the rate of movement of material on slopes?

which is much more complex, but if it can be answered the conclusion could well be satisfactory, particularly if it tells us about the relative influence of each factor in different situations.

Understanding unique phenomena involves setting them in their general context, therefore, and relating them to general processes. The research question suggests causal relationships, with variations in certain phenomena causing, or influencing, variations in others. To ask the question requires prior specification of what the causes are likely to be. The ability to do this depends on many factors, notably keen observation of what appears to be happening, comprehension of what other workers have reported from their research on the same subject, and ability to deduce the probable consequences of certain preconditions. All of these activities — the 'thinking' about research — come before the collection of relevant data and the analysis by relevant methods. The nature of the question and its proposed answer determine the statistical analysis, and not the other way round. The procedures outlined in this book, for measuring relationships between phenomena in various locations, are necessary tools for those who can first formulate valid questions.

This first question thus is an extremely wide-ranging one. The relationships which it introduces may be associational only, suggesting that where one thing is found in a certain quantity another occurs in another quantity. (An example of this would be the relationship between the size of a town and the percentage of its population living in public welfare institutions.) These are *descriptive relationships*. More likely is a suggested *causal relationship*, which says that A produces B, for example that high rainfall volumes produce flooding of rivers. In empirical work which involves the observation of events in the real world, rather than in the artificial world of laboratory experiments, cause—effect relationships are often difficult to isolate, even though associations between the relevant variables can be described. Because large cities have higher crime rates does not necessarily mean that size generates crime, but that descriptive relationship, or association, may be interpreted as evidence of a proposed causal relationship in the context of a research investigation.

Question Two: Are places different in terms of the phenomena present there?
This question is perhaps the most basic to all geography, and is the source of many people's interest in the subject. At the most fundamental level it could be considered a trivial question, for since no two places can occupy the same place on the earth's surface, they must be different in the phenomenon of location. But many argue that location is a relative and not a unique phenomenon and, in any case, location may not be a valid criterion on which to differentiate places; given that they are in different locations, do places vary in other ways?

As in the previous question, this major geographical question can be phrased in terms of simple or complex relationships. Of the former, for example, we may have:

Do Scottish towns have more people per hectare of residential land than English towns?

Do cities with Labour councils spend more per child on educational services than cities with Conservative councils?

whereas of the latter we may cite:

> Do clay soils produce lower yields of potatoes than sandy soils, assuming no variations in climate and in fertiliser applications?

> Does a greater proportion of rainfall run off directly into streams in sandstone than in limestone areas, and in clay than in sandstone areas, assuming the same vegetation cover in all areas?

(Both of these last two questions set up a common assumption; the relationship being studied is assumed to operate when all other things are equal, and thus having no influence.)

Again, the ultimate objective may be the description of a particular place, in terms of its unique characteristics (this is the purpose of classical regional geography), but this can only be achieved from an understanding of what and where differences occur.

The two questions and statistical methods

To categorise the whole of geographical endeavour into only two questions is a great simplification, but a great deal of the research and writing undertaken by geographers can be cast into these moulds. Within them, the work is extremely varied. Statistical procedures are not relevant to them all, and it is no part of the aim of this book to suggest the universal applicability of the methods to be described here. Some geographers are concerned with the personality of places, for example, with nuances of the characteristics of locations and inhabitants, the description, interpretation and explanation of which is only possible using linguistic methods. Yet whatever the detail, of approach, procedures, and substantive focus, the broad methodology remains the same. Different places can only be described as different in terms of recognised criteria which involves their mapping over a range of places; particular patterns and processes can only be understood in terms of general concepts of inter-relationships between variables, applied to the particular context.

Since about the mid-1950s, an increasing proportion of geographers have been phrasing their particular examples of the two research questions in terms of causal relationships and clear-cut differences. This has led them to adopt the relevant statistical procedures developed to test such propositions, although almost all of the development has been in a non-geographical context. There can be no doubt that in the ensuing decades there has been much mis-use and even abuse of the methods. Yet they have relevance; they provide the precision often required from research, particularly applied research; and they have allowed geographers to probe more deeply than ever before into the details of causal inter-relationships.

Geographical data

A catholic description of geography might suggest that all data are geographical data, since all phenomena have spatial locations, and geography is about locations. But geographers are neither that catholic nor that arrogant; they have tended to specialise on particular phenomena and particular types of places. With the latter, there seems to be a minimal scale threshold which most geographers do not cross, for they concentrate their interest on 'places' bigger than, say, individual houses in human geography and individual plants in physical geography.

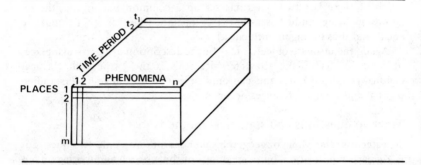

Fig. 1.1   The geographical data-cube.

Berry (1964) has suggested that the nature of geographical data can be generalised into a three-dimensional matrix, an idea taken up with enthusiasm by Chorley and Haggett (1967). The dimensions of this cube (Fig. 1.1) are places, phenomena, and time. In an end-on cross-section such as Fig. 1.1, each row is a place and each column a phenomenon, and as we move back through the cube, each separate slice is a particular time-period. For each place or row, therefore, we enter in the relevant column cell the information concerning the particular phenomenon there, whether or not it is present perhaps — as with a form of government — or the intensity of its presence — the percentage of all plants which are of that genera, for example — and this can be done for every time-period. The possible complexity of this cube almost defies comprehension, for hierarchies on each dimension are possible: on phenomena, one can have genera and species, business categories and establishments; on places, countries and cities, suburbs and street blocks; on time periods, centuries and decades, months, days and hours. The alternatives seem limitless, and each geographer assembles that data cube which is relevant to his purpose.

The data cube in Fig. 1.1 represents static patterns only, the assemblages of phenomena in particular places at particular times. But at any one time-period, unless it is extremely short, there is a great range of inter-place flows, of people, ideas, goods, plants, animals, water, etc. Thus for many phenomena one can have an inter-place matrix of flows (Fig. 1.2), in which each cell represents the interaction in that phenomenon between the relevant pair of places. And, of course, one can have a cube such as this, with a slice for every phenomenon: a fourth dimension is possible if one includes flows between places at different times.

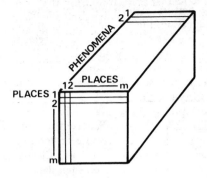

Fig. 1.2   A geographical data-cube for flows between places.

Measurement

Our interest in the geographical data cubes is not in their structure, which is more an aspect of research preparation than of research procedure, but in their contents. What form of information is entered in the cells? As we have already seen, some geographical data are not in numerical form and are thus not susceptible to statistical manipulation. They are of no interest to us, for the purposes of this book. Of the wide range of data types which we can identify, however, four general, all-embracing categories can be defined. In increasing order of complexity, they are:

1. *Nominal.* This level of measurement involves categorisation without numerical valuation. Its most basic form is the binary, or presence-absence, division of a set of objects on a given criterion, such as whether or not a city has more than a million inhabitants, whether or not a slope is cut on limestone, and so on. Any number of categories can be used, however: settlements can be divided into villages, towns, and cities; countries can be divided into regions, and so on.

Data based on a nominal scale cannot be manipulated according to the basic rules of arithmetic. If one town is in region 1 and another in region 2, you cannot say that on average they are in region 1·5! With the categorisation, however, it is possible to investigate other variables: countries with socialist governments may average annual *per capita* income growth rates of 4·5%, for example, whereas those with capitalist governments may average 3·5%.

2. *Ordinal.* On this level, the data can be placed in rank position along a continuum. Each individual place may occupy a separate position on the continuum, or places may be in ordered categories. An example of the first type is the rank ordering of British counties by people according to how much they would like to live in each (Gould and White, 1974); an example of the second is the allocation of workers to socio-economic categories (professional, managerial, skilled, manual, etc.) which are ranked in terms of their status and prestige.

All four of the basic arithmetic operations – addition, subtraction, multiplication and division – can be performed on ranked data. Thus a town spending most *per capita* on education, the second highest amount on old peoples' welfare, and the sixth highest on health services, averages third rank ((1 + 2 + 6)/3) over all three services. The 'distance' between each pair of adjacent places in the ranking is always the same, however, so that, for example, the difference between first and second place is the same as that between forty-third and forty-fourth.

3. *Interval.* At this level, each observation has a separate value on the phenomenon being measured, and differences between adjacent observations on the scale can vary. Thus a place with a temperature at noon on 30 March of 12°C is 2°C warmer than one with a recording of 10°C. Clearly, all of the basic arithmetic procedures can be conducted on such data, although some results are not as readily interpretable as are those with data in the final category.

4. *Ratio.* This is the highest level of measurement, differing from the interval scale in one respect only – it has an absolute zero. The difference is important, since it allows ratios to be calculated. For example, if it is 2 kilometres from A to B and 4 from A to C, then C is twice as far from A as B is, but if A's temperature is 10°C and B's is 20°C, B is not twice as warm as A. Distance in kilometres has an absolute zero, indicating no distance, and so kilometres is a ratio scale: 0°C is an arbitrary baseline, however, representing the freezing-point of water, and so although B is twice as far from the freezing-point of water as is A, it is not twice as warm; °C is thus only an interval scale.

For the purpose of the procedures to be discussed in this book, the difference between interval and ratio scales is of little or no importance. The two are therefore treated as the same. Special methods have been developed for handling ordinal data, particularly if they are ordinal, categorised data, but these will not be discussed here. For non-categorised ordinal data, many of the methods discussed here for interval/ratio data are applicable since they are based on the four arithmetical operations. (Spearman's rank order correlation coefficient, for example, is equivalent to a Pearson's product moment correlation coefficient calculated for ranked data.) Except in some types of research, in which interviewees are asked to rank order a set of answers in a questionnaire, ordinal data are rarely used in geography, hence they are ignored in this presentation.

The focus of this book is on statistical methods for two types of data, the nominal and the interval/ratio; nominal data are only studied where the problem also involves interval/ratio data. Analyses for which all of the measurement, i.e. the causes and the effects, is in the nominal scale are based on contingency tables, and these too are omitted.

Logarithms

In much work dealing with interval and ratio data, the recorded numerical values are transformed into logarithms, for reasons that will be described in later chapters. Logarithms are transformations of numbers which allow arithmetic operations to be conducted in different ways. Expressing the logarithm of x as log x, etc.,

$$\log x + \log y = \log (xy) \qquad (1.1)$$

or the log of a product (xy) is the sum of the logs of the numbers, and

$$\log x - \log y = \log (x/y) \qquad (1.2)$$

From this

$$\log x^m = m \log x \qquad (1.3)$$

so that

$$\log x^2 = 2 \log x$$

Logarithms can be taken to any base, the most common being base 10 (i.e. $\log_{10}$) where the logarithm is that power of the number 10 which produces the relevant number (x): thus

x = 10 $\log_{10} x = 1$ as $10^1 = 10$

x = 2 $\log_{10} x = 0.3010$ as $10^{0.3010} = 2$

x = 5 $\log_{10} x = 0.6990$ as $10^{0.6990} = 5$

x = 14 $\log_{10} x = 1.6021$ as $10^{1.6021} = 14$

x = 100 $\log_{10} x = 2.000$ as $10^2 = 100$

etc. The other common base is e, where

$$e = 2.718\ 281\ 82$$

which has important properties relative to rates of change (see Ch. 2, p. 40).

Conclusions

The two types of procedure outlined here are oriented to the two fundamental geographical questions identified earlier. For Question One — 'are there relationships between phenomena in various locations?' — we assume that all phenomena, both cause and effect, are measured on either an interval or a ratio scale. The methods of correlation and regression, and of factor, principal components, and canonical correlation analysis are all available to answer variants of the question. For Question Two — 'are places different in terms of the phenomena present there?' — the causal variable is nominal, with places being allocated to categories. The effect variable is measured on an interval or a ratio scale, however, and answers to the question using such data can be gained through analysis of variance and discriminant analysis procedures.

Two types of question and two types of analysis are the focus of this book, therefore. In effect, both types of analysis are variants of a more general one, the *general linear model*, as we shall see as we proceed through the book. This means that our two questions can be combined into one. Whenever the effect and the causes can be measured on either interval, ratio, or nominal scales, variants of the general model can be used to give precise descriptions of hypothesised relationships.

Some statistical preliminaries

Most of the discussion in the book is self-contained, in that all of the procedures are defined as they are introduced. Some basic concepts are not treated in this way, however, as it is assumed that the reader will have encountered them during introductory courses and/or reading in statistics. To provide a brief résumé, all of those procedures which are not discussed in the following chapters are mentioned here.

The normal distribution, and Z-scores

The general linear model, and thus all of the statistical methods discussed in this book, is relevant for one particular type of interval/ratio data only, that for which some aspect of the information for the set of observations forms a normal distribution. This is an ideal distribution, based on an indefinitely large number of observations, and so it can only be approximated by 'real world' data. The ideal is symmetrical and bell-shaped (Fig. 1.3A); the 'real world' approximation — such as the data for *per capita* educational expenditure used in the examples of Chapter 2 (Fig. 1.3B) — is a histogram showing the number of observations in a series of classes, and a line drawn through the central point of each bar in the histogram approximates the normal curve.

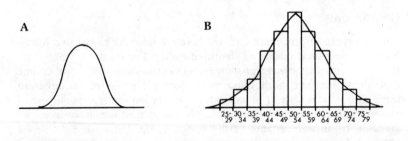

Fig.1.3   The normal distribution (left) and the distribution of values for *per capita* expenditure on education in fifty towns.

Two numerical quantities — or *parameters* — are sufficient to describe the normal curve; these are the mean, $\overline{X}$, and the standard deviation, S. The mean is the central value, having 50% of the values of the observations on each side of it; it is calculated using the formula

$$\overline{X} = \left(\sum_{i=1}^{N} X_i \right) / N \qquad (1.4)$$

In this formula

X_i is the value of X − the variable being measured − for the ith observation;
N is the total number of observations;

$\sum_{i=1}^{N}$ is the sum of all the values from i = 1 (below the sigma sign) to i = N
(above the sigma sign); and
$\overline{X}$ is the mean of all the values of X.

The standard deviation is the square root of the mean squared distance between each observation and the mean, and is calculated as

$$S_X = \sqrt{ \left(\sum_{i=1}^{N} (X_i - \overline{X})^2 \right) / N } \qquad (1.5)$$

where all the notation is as for formula (1.4), and

S_X is the standard deviation of the X values.

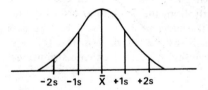

Fig. 1.4   The mean and the standard deviation in a normal distribution.

The importance of the standard deviation is that it is the basic unit of measurement along the axis of the normal curve (Fig. 1.4). It is known, for example, that in a normally-distributed set of numbers, 68·26% of them will lie within one standard deviation of the mean − 34·13% on each side; that 95·46% are within two standard deviations; and that 99·73% are within three standard deviations. The percentage within any distance (in S.D. units) of the mean can be read off from tables of the normal distribution.

The position of any particular observation on the normal distribution can be located by expressing its value of X in standard deviation units, i.e. how far it is from the mean in terms of the standard deviation of the distribution. This is the Z-score calculated as

$$Z_i = (X_i - \overline{X})/S_X \qquad (1.6)$$

where Z_i is the Z-score for observation i;
and other notation is as for formulae (1.4) and (1.5).

Full tables of the Z-scores, indicating how far any observation is from the mean, i.e. what percentage of the values are greater than it and less than it, are given in most statistics texts. The value of Z-scores is that they allow comparison between observations of unlike things in terms of their relative position in the set of observations.

The symbol representing the mean and the standard deviation of a distribution is sometimes given in Greek letters and at others in Arabic. The latter normally refer to the parameters of a sample, and the former to a population (p. 13), so that

	Mean	**Standard deviation**
Population	μ	σ
Sample	$\overline{X}$	S

In this book, little attention is paid to the separate characteristics of these two distributions and the notation for samples is used throughout. In all calculations of standard deviations, it is assumed that the data refer to populations, so that the denominator of formula (1.5) is N and not $(N - 1)$.

As stated before, the normal distribution is an ideal which can only be approximated by real world data. How close an approximation is needed? There is no hard-and-fast answer to this. Tests are available using *fractile diagrams* (see King, 1961; Hart and Salisbury, 1965), which allow an assessment of the degree to which an observed distribution approximates to the normal; the chi-square statistic (Gregory, 1973) is often used to see whether the real deviates significantly from the ideal. In most cases, however, the researcher makes a subjective judgement as to whether the data are sufficiently close to being normally-distributed; the less close they are, the less valid are conclusions from analyses which assume that distributional form.

Degrees of freedom

The degrees of freedom (df) of a set of data is the number of observations which can take on any value, within the constraint of certain calculations based on those values. For example, we have rainfall totals for four stations in California — a, b, c, and d. The mean rainfall over these four is 150 mm, so

$$\overline{X} = 150 \quad \therefore \Sigma X = (\overline{X})4 = 600 \text{ mm}$$

If we know that the rainfall at a, b and c is 150, 200 and 160 mm respectively then

$$(a + b + c + d) = 600$$

$$(150 + 200 + 160 + d) = 600 \quad \text{so}$$

$$d = 600 - (150 + 200 + 160) = 90$$

In other words, given that the mean of the four numbers is fixed, only three of them can vary; once three values are known, then the value of the fourth is determined too. The degrees of freedom in this case is thus the number of observations less one, or $(N - 1)$.

In another example, we have three samples, each of four observations of rainfall data taken at the same station in different months.

Sample	Rainfall at station					
	a	b	c	d	Σ	$\overline{X}$
I	200	300	200	500	1200	300
II	150	160	170	160	640	160
III	100	200	400	100	800	200

In each sample, there are three degrees of freedom, as in our earlier example. The total degrees of freedom for the whole population is thus $(3 + 3 + 3) = 9$, which is equal to $(N - 3)$.

The simple rule for determining degrees of freedom is that one degree is lost for every fixed value. In the first example there was one fixed value — the mean of the four observations — so one degree was lost; in the second example there were three — the mean for each of the three samples — and so three degrees were lost. This is usually written as

$$df = (N - f) \tag{1.7}$$

where f is the number of fixed values.

Hypotheses and probabilities

The questions concerning relationships between phenomena and differences between places are usually phrased in terms of hypotheses. These are statements of anticipated conclusions: thus 'there is a positive relationship between rate of movement of slope material and density of grazing sheep' states the expected result of a correlation between these two variables.

With inductive or inferential use of statistical methods (see below), the hypothesis representing the expected conclusion is usually replaced by its converse — the *null hypothesis*. For the example in the preceding paragraph, the null hypothesis is that 'there is no relationship between rate of movement of slope material and density of grazing sheep'. The reason for using a null hypothesis (often presented as H_0) rather than the original research hypothesis (H_1), is to avoid, as far as is possible, coming to a conclusion which is wrong and likely to lead to unfortunate deductions. Two forms of wrong conclusion can be made: a Type I error involves rejecting a research hypothesis when it is true; a Type II error involves accepting a research hypothesis when it is false. Of these, the latter is generally considered as the worst error, and the null hypothesis is used to try to avoid it.

Hypotheses are tested with inferential statistics when the aim of the research is to make a general statement about a population from observations taken for a sample only (for details of sampling see below). These are phrased in terms of probabilities, and are usually expressed in either proportions, 0·00 to 1·00, or percentages, 0 to 100. Before testing the hypothesis, an acceptable probability limit is set. For example, our research hypothesis may be that south-facing slopes in Derbyshire have a more rapid growth rate for grass in April than do north-facing slopes, so that the null hypothesis is of no difference between the two types of slope. A sample of slopes is taken and measurements of aspect and grass growth recorded. Before testing the hypothesis, we decide that if the evidence suggests that in more than 95% of all such samples a similar difference would occur, then we will reject the null hypothesis and accept the research hypothesis. Details of how we work out the probability of a similar result are given in later chapters (see, for example, p. 47 and p. 57). Throughout the book, the 5% probability level is always used. This is an arbitrary limit, since there is nothing magic about the 5% level. It is a conservative one, however; we are fairly sure that the pattern is not due to random sampling alone before we infer it of the population.

In this example, either there is a difference between the north- and south-facing slopes, or there is not. We want to prove that there is a difference, but want to be very sure that we are right. Thus we propose the null hypothesis and erect stringent conditions before we reject it. We will only do so if it is clear that in less than 5% of all samples that could be taken from the given population the expected difference would not occur. In other words, if there is a difference, there are only five chances in every hundred that we will reject it. The procedure is a conservative one, therefore.

Inductive statistics and descriptive statistics

The method of hypothesis-testing just discussed is a particular form of statistical procedure, and the one for which most techniques were developed. It is based on the assumptions that analyses are on a sample of observations only and that the purpose of the study is to make statements about relationships or differences not merely within the sample but in the larger population which it represents. In order to use inductive statistics, therefore, it is mandatory that the study is based on a properly-constituted sample of observations.

The major law of sampling is that every individual in the population has an equal and independent chance of being selected for the sample. If this is not the case, then the sample is biased, and some individuals will be more influential than others on the outcome of the statistical tests. In order to obey this law, the complete population must be known and must be enumerated, otherwise it is impossible to guarantee that the sampling procedure is unbiased. Once the population has been enumerated, then the sampling from it must be random; no individual in the list must have a greater chance than any other of being selected.

In the use of such data, problems arise as to how valid the conclusions from the sample are with respect to the population. The rule is that the larger the sample, the less likely one is to have an unrepresentative selection of the population. Large in this context means in absolute numbers not relative numbers: 60% of the population may seem a large sample, but if there are only 20 individuals in the population, the chances of error by omitting 8 could be quite large if the difference being sought between two groups of 10 in the population is marginal. The smaller the sample, the greater the chance of *sampling error*, of the sample being unrepresentative.

With properly-constituted samples from known populations, it is possible to test research hypotheses relating to the populations. Probability levels are set, and if the expected relationship or difference is present in the sample and is unlikely to have been observed there as a result of chance factors, i.e. the result of sampling error, then the conclusion is that the same relationship or difference probably occurs in the population.

In much geographical work, most particularly in some aspects of human geography, the ability to undertake inductive statistical analyses of this kind is very limited. Among the reasons for this are: (1) frequently the population is unknown — what, for example, comprises all the north-facing slopes in Derbyshire?; (2) often the population is known but cannot be enumerated — we may know that Sheffield has a population of about 520,000, but we have no list of those people to allow us to take a random sample of them; (3) the population may be too small for samples to be taken without sampling error being very large — there are, for example, only thirteen countries in South America; (4) random samples may be biased, because of the effects of other variables which we cannot control — if 70% of all slopes in Derbyshire are north-facing, then so should 70% of the sampled slopes; if 80% of the north-facing slopes are on limestone, however, then the sample may be biased towards limestone areas, and if lithology is also a factor influencing growth rates for grass in April, then there may be a bias towards a certain growth factor which is unknown and which will affect the results in an undetermined way; and (5) the data used in our analyses are often collected by others, and are not proper samples — many collected data sets, such as censuses, contain unknown sampling error, particularly for the small places which geographers frequently study.

If properly-constituted samples are not available, then we are dealing with data sets from which no inferences can be made regarding populations. It may be that our data are for a population — e.g. all towns with more than 200,000 inhabitants in England — but they may refer only to a selection of individuals — e.g. those who would answer a questionnaire or those places which have enthusiastic amateurs who take rainfall readings daily. In either case, all we can do with such data is to describe the relationships or differences within them: *we cannot apply statistical significance tests* (though see pp. 57-58). Such *descriptive statistics* are often extremely valuable, however; they differ from inductive statistics only in the lack of any apparent objective baseline against which the findings can be assessed to see if they are 'meaningful'.

Significance testing for inferences to populations from samples is a rationale for all of the methods to be discussed in this book. But so much geographical work cannot properly use such testing that by far the major focus here is on the use of the various methods as descriptive statistics. This represents one of the major problems facing those who wish to make geographical work more 'scientific'. At best, the most that can be hoped for from much geographical research is precise description of relationships and differences, within the context of causal hypotheses, the logic of which must be very carefully considered *before* the statistical analysis.

Geographical research and scientific method

The approach to geographical research adopted here is that of positivism, with its associated scientific method (see Harvey, 1969). This method has a logical set of procedures as outlined in Fig. 1.5. It begins with theory, which is a logically consistent set of statements comprising axioms, or 'givens' (which may be either established facts or assumptions), and deduced consequences. Such a theory is complete in itself, but if it is a theory about the real world then it must be evaluated, to see if it provides a valid description of reality.

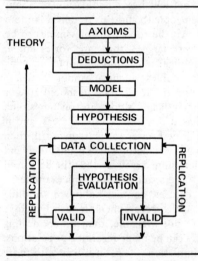

Fig. 1.5   The set of procedures comprising the positivist scientific method.

Evaluation of the theory requires its statement in an operational form, which is as a model. Thus a theory such as:

axiom — shoppers wish to minimise their transport costs;

deduction — shoppers use the cheapest available shopping centre; and

deduction — the number of establishments in a shopping centre is related to the number of people living closer to that centre than to any other;

will be put into operational form as:

model — $Y_i = f(X_i)$

where Y_i is the number of establishments in shopping centre i; and
  X_i is the number of people who live closer to shopping centre i than to any other centre.

The hypothesis is then that the two variables X and Y are related, and criteria are set for the evaluation of the truth of this expectation. Data are collected as specified by the hypothesis and the latter is evaluated as to its validity, according to the set criteria.

One test of a hypothesis, i.e. a sample of one, is not accepted as indicating its universal truth or falsehood and so, as Fig. 1.5 illustrates, replication is called for. Meanwhile, the results are fed back to the theory, to provide a growing body of evidence which either supports or refutes the deductions and which provides axioms for further deductions. (If the deductions are refuted this imples *either* bad logical thinking or invalid axioms at the theoretical level, *or* poor translation of the theory into an operational model, *or* wrong testing of the hypothesis through faulty data collection and statistical evaluation procedures.) In this, negative results (i.e. invalid hypotheses) are as valuable as positive results.

The process outlined in Fig. 1.5 would appear to be clear and un-ambiguous, but geographers have suggested that it has not been very successful in providing a set of scientifically valid general statements and theories, which are empirically tested. (Some argue that this is more true of human geography than of physical geography; a debatable point which will be avoided here!) Two reasons are suggested for this. The first is that this method is not particularly apt for the study of phenomena and events with which man is associated, and that in any case geographers have been unable to state with any clarity the grounds on which they will accept their hypotheses as valid (Guelke, 1971). This is a substantive rather than a statistical argument. It may well be that accepted criteria are met whereby a hypothesis is tested for a particular sample of observations and is found valid for the population from which the sample was drawn. But is the relationship thus established in any way real, particularly in a causal sense? To use our earlier, simple example; does the fact that the number of establishments in a shopping centre and the population of the area closer to it than to any other are statistically related in any way validate the assumed causal relationship, which concerns why people shop where they do?

This first reason for the failure of the positivist scientific method in geography is a philosophical one, related to questions of epistemology and ontology; although it is crucial to the whole development of the subject, it is irrelevant here, where we assume the value of the method outlined in Fig. 1.5. The second reason is of more importance in the present context. The positivist method just outlined assumes a body of axioms for theory-building and, if the theory is to be about the real-world, then the axioms should be accepted statements (generalisations; laws even) that have been verified empirically. Most academic disciplines, and especially those in the social and environmental sciences, are immature; they have very few axioms on which to base theoretical developments. As a consequence, much of their work involves making assumptions and then testing their validity before deductions can be made: Cattell (1966) calls this the inductive-hypothetico-deductive (I.H.D.) spiral. True scientific theory, based on well-established facts, is still the distant goal for most geographical study.

The notion of the I.H.D. spiral is important in this book since it relates to the methods discussed here. Some critics have attacked use of certain techniques (notably those discussed in Chapters 5–8), because these are not used to test hypotheses, but only to answer very vague questions about relationships and differences. The answer offered to this attack is that in a state of immaturity, use of these methods in a sensible way allows geographers to crystallise their ideas and so to move slowly towards the adoption of the formal methodology. At present our notions of causes and relationships are vague and data are being processed to improve on this vagueness, to provide useful foundations for scientific analysis. It is within such an ethos that most of the methods are introduced here.

Chapter 2

Bivariate analyses

Although it has been assumed in preparing this book that readers have some background in the simpler statistical methods and their use in geographical research, two of these methods are reviewed in the present chapter. Bivariate correlation and regression and the one-way analysis of variance are the simplest cases of the family of procedures which are covered in the rest of the book so treatment of them allows development of a series of building-blocks which are used throughout the remaining chapters.

Correlation and regression

The geographer's question 'Are there relationships between phenomena in various locations?' is typical of the more general statistical question enquiring into relationships among *variables* (characteristics) over a set of *observations* (places). The method used to answer it depends on the form of the available data. If they are on an interval- or a ratio-scale (p. 8), then correlation and regression analysis may be used, as long as certain other conditions are met (p. 37). In the bivariate case, the regression model involves the use of an *independent variable* (usually represented by X) to estimate the values of a *dependent variable* (Y): X is thus conceived as the cause, and Y as the effect.

A hypothetical problem

In formal terms, we state a hypothesised relationship that

$$Y = f(X) \tag{2.1}$$

which is a shorthand way of arguing that the value of Y at a particular observation is some function of the value of X there. (In other words, Y might be 2X, or twice the value of X; it might be $0 \cdot 5X$, $2 \cdot 76 \log_{10} X$, and so on.) If this were a perfect function, then from knowledge of X at an observation, we could estimate the value of Y with certainty. Such functions are illustrated in Fig. 2.1.

Because the functional relationships portrayed in Fig. 2.1 are perfect, all individual observations fall on the lines representing those functions. (Only straight-line functions are shown in Fig. 2.1; non-linear relationships

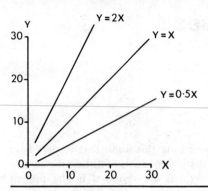

Fig. 2.1   Examples of the function Y = f(X).

are also feasible, and are dealt with later — p. 38.) The laws of nature, including those of human nature, whose effects and operations we study, very rarely, if ever, produce a completely predictable result, however. In some cases, this is because of imperfections in our measurement procedures, but in most it is because effects are usually the product of a variety of causes operating in conjunction, so that a single independent variable will not allow us to estimate the value of Y with complete certainty. And so instead we have to study general trends in our data sets, providing estimates of the relationship between X and Y implied in formula (2.1) and also of the accuracy with which the values of Y can be derived from this estimated relationship.

Table 2.1   Educational needs and spending: hypothetical data

Town	X*	Y†	Town	X	Y	Town	X	Y
1	17	27	17	47	57	34	27	31
2	42	64	18	62	70	35	52	66
3	49	52	19	45	50	36	59	69
4	35	59	20	36	54	37	33	42
5	69	77	21	48	45	38	27	43
6	48	54	22	50	68	39	33	60
7	34	50	23	30	45	40	31	46
8	43	48	24	44	58	41	49	46
9	39	49	25	24	36	42	42	52
10	56	72	26	39	40	43	40	46
11	38	52	27	64	60	44	49	58
12	43	62	28	50	64	45	42	58
13	44	50	29	41	51	46	29	40
14	57	50	30	45	36	47	43	55
15	36	40	31	37	47	48	53	63
16	22	34	32	51	38	49	39	59
			33	54	44	50	33	56

*X = percentage of the population aged between 5 and 21
†Y = *per capita* expenditure on education

To illustrate how we set about this task, a hypothetical data set has been constructed to test a hypothesis that the greater the demand for education in a place, the more the money that will be spent providing for it. To investigate the validity of this proposition, demand is measured as the percentage of the town's population aged between 5 and 21 (this is the independent variable, X) and expenditure is the amount spent per resident of the town on the education budget (the dependent variable, Y). Our expectation is that *as the percentage of the population aged between 5 and 21 increases so the amount spent per resident increases.*

Data for these two variables are available for 50 towns (Table 2.1). An immediate indication of the relevance of the hypothesis is obtained by plotting the 50 pairs of values on a scattergram (Fig. 2.2) on which, by convention, X forms the horizontal and Y the vertical axis. The general trend is as expected. For a precise statement, however, we need to know the functional relationship between X and Y, which states the increase in Y that follows from an increase in X: this is the form of the relationship, and is indicated by a regression line. We also need to know the representativeness of the relationship, or how well the regression line fits the pattern of dots on the scattergram: this is given by a correlation coefficient.

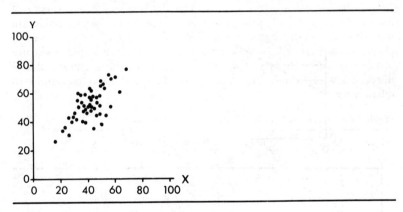

Fig. 2.2   Scattergram showing the relationship between percentage aged between 5 and 21 (X) and *per capita* expenditure on education (Y) in fifty towns (the data are in Table 2.1).

Regression — the intensity of a relationship

The amount of change in the dependent variable, Y, for a given change in the independent, X, is indicated by the parameters of a regression equation having the form

$$\hat{Y}_i = a_{yx} + b_{yx}X_i \tag{2.2}$$

where X_i is the value of X at the ith observation;

$\hat{Y}_i$ is the estimated value of Y at the ith observation; and

a_{yx}, b_{yx} are the parameters of the regression, derived by methods described below. $\hat{Y}_i$ is usually written as Y_i, omitting the circumflex.

The relative magnitude of the change is given by the steepness of a straight-line which best describes the trend in a scatter of points such as that shown in Fig. 2.2.

Different slopes are illustrated in Fig. 2.3. (Note that we can only compare different slopes in graphical form when the scales are the same on both axes of all the graphs.) In the first example (A) there is a steep slope, with values of Y increasing rapidly relative to increases in X, whereas in the second (B) the shallow slope indicates a slow rate of increase in Y relative to the rate in X. A decline in the value of Y as X increases in value is shown in the third example — Fig. 2.3C; this is termed a negative relationship, whereas an increase in Y paralleling an increase in X is a positive relationship.

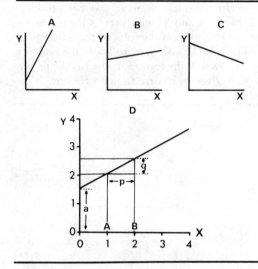

Fig. 2.3   Examples of different regression slopes for Y = f(X) (A—C); and derivation of the regression coefficient as the slope of the regression line (D).

The slope of the regression line is represented by the coefficient b_{YX} in formula (2.2). Figure 2.3D shows how this coefficient is derived. Between points A and B on the X axis the value of X increases by one unit, from 1·0 to 2·0. According to the regression line, at point A the value of Y is 2·0 and at point B it is 2·5. Thus we have

Point	X	Y
A	1·0	2·0
B	2·0	2·5

An increase of 1·0 unit in X, therefore, is associated with an increase of 0·5 in Y. Formally this is stated as:

$$b_{YX} = q/p \tag{2.3}$$

where p is the increase in X;

   q is the increase in Y; and

   b_{YX} is the slope of the regression line.

In our example

$b_{YX} = 0·5/1·0 = 0·5$

which tells us that for every increase of one unit in X, Y increases by half (0·5) that amount. Thus an increase of 5 points in X is associated with an increase of 2·5 in Y.

   The regression coefficient b_{YX} in formula (2.2) indicates the slope of the straight-line relationship between X and Y. It does not allow us to estimate what the value of Y ($\hat{Y}_i$) should be for a given value of X (X_i), however. The regression coefficient indicates the change in Y produced by a given change in X. To obtain the value of Y for some value of X we need an 'anchor point' or base, telling us the value of Y for a fixed value of X. Conventionally, this 'anchor point' is the value of Y when X = 0; this is the coefficient a_{YX}, usually known as the intercept since it is the value of Y where the regression line intercepts the vertical axis for X = 0 (Fig. 2.3D). Thus we have the expanded function

$$Y_i = a_{YX} + b_{YX} X_i \qquad (2.4)$$

in which the order of the subscripts for the parameters indicates that the first variable, Y, is the dependent and the second, X, is the independent. This formula is frequently written without subscripts as:

$$Y = a + bX \qquad (2.5)$$

   For the example in Fig. 2.3D the full regression equation is:

$$Y = 1·5 + 0·5X$$

which tells us that the value of Y is equal to half of the value of X (0·5X) plus 1·5. (The value of 1·5 is the same whatever the value of X, so the co-efficient a_{YX} is often termed the constant rather than the intercept.) From this equation we can produce an estimated value of Y ($\hat{Y}_i$ — where the circumflex indicates an estimated value, as against Y_i which is the actual value of Y at observation i). Thus

if $X_i = 5$ $\hat{Y}_i = 1·5 + 0·5X_i = 1·5 + 0·5(5)$ $= 4·0$

if $X_i = 7·3$ $\hat{Y}_i = 1·5 + 0·5X_i = 1·5 + 0·5(7·3) = 5·15$

Fitting the regression line

The regression line is the best available description, by a single straight line, of the trend in a scatter of points such as that in Fig. 2.2. How is it fitted to produce the values of a_{YX} and b_{YX}?

   The statistical aim in fitting a regression line is to place it as close as possible to all of the observations. The adopted definition of 'as close as possible' is that it should minimise the variance in the squared deviations from it on the Y axis. In formal terms the goal is to minimise

$$\sum_{i=1}^{N} (Y_i - \hat{Y}_i)^2 \tag{2.6}$$

where Y_i is the actual value of Y at observation i;
  $\hat{Y}_i$ is the estimated value of Y at observation i according to the regression equation; and
  summation (Σ) is over N observations.

This goal is achieved using the basic statistical concept of variance plus the related concept of covariance, and the procedure is known as the *least squares method* (because the smallest squared value is sought).

  The variance of a distribution is the mean squared deviation of each individual value from the mean value. The mean is

$$\bar{Y} = \left(\sum_{i=1}^{N} Y_i \right) / N \tag{2.7}$$

where Y_i is the value of Y at observation i;
  $\bar{Y}$ is the mean value of Y_i; and
  summation is over N observations;

and the variance is

$$S_Y^2 = \left(\sum_{i=1}^{N} (Y_i - \bar{Y})^2 \right) / N \tag{2.8}$$

where S_Y^2 is the variance in Y.

The standard deviation is the square root of the variance:

$$S_Y = \sqrt{S_Y^2} \tag{2.9}$$

  In a regression equation, primary interest is in the variance of the dependent variable, Y, and the relationship between this and the variance of the independent, X. Figure 2.4 illustrates the nature of this relationship, using the data of Fig. 2.2. In the diagrams, on which only some of the observations are plotted, to ensure clarity, the mean values for the two variables are indicated ($\bar{X}$ and $\bar{Y}$) and the contribution of individual observations to the respective variances (S_X^2 and S_Y^2) are computed according to the procedure indicated in Fig. 2.4A. Thus the contribution of point 1 to the variance in Y is the value p^2 (i.e. the square of the distance, p, between point 1 and $\bar{Y}$) and its contribution to the variance in X is q^2: the respective contributions of point 18 are s^2 and t^2.

  In Fig. 2.4A points 1 and 18 contribute significantly to the variances of both X and Y and point 13 contributes very little. This introduces the con-

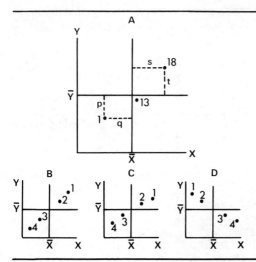

Fig. 2.4 Contributions of individual observations to the variance of X, the variance of Y, and the covariance of XY (A); and the relationship between the covariance and the slope coefficient (B−D).

cept of covariance, which is the mean of the sum of the products of the contributions of each point to the individual variances. Thus

$$COV_{YX} = \left(\sum_{i=1}^{N} ((X_i - \overline{X})(Y_i - \overline{Y})) \right)/N \qquad (2.10)$$

where $(X_i - \overline{X})$ is the difference between the mean value of X and the value of X at observation i;

$(Y_i - \overline{Y})$ is the similar difference for the value of Y at observation i; summation is over N observations; and

COV_{YX} is the covariance between Y and X.

For the example in Fig. 2.4A the contribution to the covariance from the three points − 1, 13, 18 − would be

$(X_1 - \overline{X})(Y_1 - \overline{Y}) = qp$

$(X_{13} - \overline{X})(Y_{13} - \overline{Y}) = uv$

$(X_{18} - \overline{X})(Y_{18} - \overline{Y}) = ts$

$COV_{YX} = (qp + uv + ts)/3$

(N.B. u and v are not shown on Fig. 2.4A, because of reproduction difficulties.) The ratio of the covariance to the variance in the independent variable, X, is the slope of the regression line.

Figure 2.4B, C and D illustrate the derivation of the slope coefficient, b_{YX}, as the ratio between COV_{YX} and S_X^2. In Fig. 2.4B the values are

	Point				
	1	2	3	4	
X	18	14	6	2	$\overline{X} = 40/4 = 10$
Y	18	14	6	2	$\overline{Y} = 40/4 = 10$

so that the differences from the mean are

$(X - \overline{X})$	8	4	-4	-8
$(Y - \overline{Y})$	8	4	-4	-8

and

$(X - \overline{X})^2$	64	16	16	64	$S_X^2 = 160/4 = 40$
$(Y - \overline{Y})^2$	64	16	16	64	$S_Y^2 = 160/4 = 40$
$(X - \overline{X})(Y - \overline{Y})$	64	16	16	64	

so that $COV_{YX} = 160/4 = 40$

The formula for the regression coefficient is

$$b_{YX} = COV_{YX}/S_X^2 \qquad (2.11)$$

which in this case is $40/40 = 1 \cdot 0$

For every increase in X of m units there is a similar increase in Y of m units, therefore, a regularity which is easily deduced from the raw data.

For Fig. 2.4C the values are

	Point			
	1	2	3	4
X	18	14	6	2
Y	14	12	8	6

giving

$b_{YX} = 20/40 = 0 \cdot 5$

and for Fig. 2.4D

	Point			
	1	2	3	4
X	2	6	14	18
Y	14	12	8	6

gives

$b_{YX} = -20/40 = -0 \cdot 5$

which indicates that for every increase of one unit in X, Y decreases by one-half of that value.

This definition of the slope coefficient, b_{YX}, as the ratio between the covariance of the two variables and the variance of the independent, X, can be interpreted in the following way. The individual covariance value $(Y_i - \overline{Y})(X_i - \overline{X})$ indicates the joint size of the values Y_i and X_i, whereas $(X_i - \overline{X})^2$ indicates the size of X_i alone, each value being expressed relative to the position of the relevant mean. Thus the larger the covariance relative to the variance, then the greater the increase in Y relative to a given increase in X; this is our earlier definition of b_{YX}.

The calculation of covariances and variances involves expressing the individual values of Y_i and X_i in terms of distances from their respective means, and the regressions depicted in Fig. 2.4 all pass through the point of intersection of the means. Indeed, it is a characteristic of the *least squares method* for fitting a regression line to a set of points that the line always passes through the intersection of the means. This allows for calculation of the intercept or constant value, a_{YX}, which is the estimated value $\hat{Y}_i$ when $X_i = 0$. Since, from (2.5)

$$Y = a + bX$$

and the regression line passes through the intersection of $\overline{X}$ and $\overline{Y}$, then

$$\overline{Y} = a + b\overline{X} \qquad (2.12)$$

and, by reorganisation

$$a = \overline{Y} - b\overline{X} \qquad (2.13)$$

For the three regressions in Fig. 2.4 we then get:

Fig. 2.4B

$\overline{Y} = 10 \quad \overline{X} = 10 \quad b_{YX} = 1\cdot0$

$a = 10 - 1\cdot0(10) = 0 \quad$ so $\quad Y = 0 + 1\cdot0X$

Fig. 2.4C

$\overline{Y} = 10 \quad \overline{X} = 10 \quad b_{YX} = 0\cdot5$

$a = 10 - 0\cdot5(10) = 5 \quad$ so $\quad Y = 5 + 0\cdot5X$

and Fig. 2.4D

$\overline{Y} = 10 \quad \overline{X} = 10 \quad b_{YX} = -0\cdot5$

$a = 10 - (-0\cdot5)(10) = 15 \quad$ so $\quad Y = 15 - 0\cdot5X$

Returning to the data in Table 2.1 and Fig. 2.2, we can now calculate the regression line for the relationship between educational need and provision.

The basic parameters are

$\overline{X} = 42\cdot4 \qquad S_X^2 = 120\cdot32 \quad S_X = 10\cdot97$

$\overline{Y} = 51\cdot86 \qquad S_Y^2 = 123\cdot21 \quad S_Y = 11\cdot10$

To reduce computational tedium, the b coefficient is usually worked out as the ratio of the *covariation* in X and Y, which is given by formula (2.14)

$$\Sigma(X_i - \overline{X})(Y_i - \overline{Y}) = N\Sigma X_i Y_i - (\Sigma X_i)(\Sigma Y_i) \tag{2.14}$$

to the *variation* in X, where the variation in a variable — which is the value of NS^2 is given by formulae (2.15) and (2.16)

$$\Sigma(X_i - \overline{X})^2 = N\Sigma X_i^2 - (\Sigma X_i)^2 \tag{2.15}$$

$$\Sigma(Y_i - \overline{Y})^2 = N\Sigma Y_i^2 - (\Sigma Y_i)^2 \tag{2.16}$$

The covariation and variation terms are merely the summed values rather than the mean values, therefore, and since N is the same in all computations, finding the mean is unnecessary.

Thus

$$b_{YX} = \frac{N\Sigma X_i Y_i - (\Sigma X_i)(\Sigma Y_i)}{N\Sigma X_i^2 - (\Sigma X_i)^2} \tag{2.17}$$

$$= 203\ 690/294\ 800 = 0\cdot691$$

and

$$a_{YX} = 51\cdot86 - 0\cdot691(42\cdot4) = 22\cdot56$$

so that

$$\hat{Y} = 22\cdot56 + 0\cdot691X$$

Interpreting this equation, we see that for every increase of $1\cdot0$ point in the percentage of a town's population aged between 5 and 21 the expenditure per head on education increases by 69.1 pence (£0.691). The value for the *intercept* of $22\cdot56$ literally indicates the expenditure per head when the percentage aged between 5 and 21 is zero (i.e when there is no demand for education). As a *constant*, however, it suggests a basic, or fixed, cost of £22.56, whatever the demand, whereas the regression coefficient indicates the variable cost of extra demand.

A final point to note is that this is the regression of Y on X, where Y is the dependent variable and X is the independent. If the two variables were to be reversed, the equation of X on Y would be

$$X = 7\cdot65 + 0\cdot67Y$$

which, although it passes through the intersection of $\overline{Y}$ and $\overline{X}$, is not the same as the regression line for Y on X (Fig. 2.5). Only in the special cases of a correlation coefficient of either $+1\cdot0$ or $-1\cdot0$ (see below, p. 30 ff.) will the two regression lines describe the same path.

Correlation — the strength of a relationship

The two parameters of the regression equation, a and b, indicate the form of the relationship between Y and X but say nothing about the accuracy

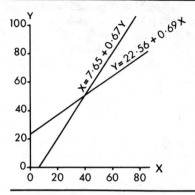

Fig. 2.5   The regressions of Y = f(X) and X = f(Y), using the data of Fig. 2.2.

of the estimates of Ŷ that are given by the regression line. For this, we use an associated parameter, the correlation coefficient.

The linear correlation coefficient, r_{YX}, relates the variance in the dependent variable Y to the reduction in that variance when the independent variable, X, is used to estimate values of Y. (Alternative names for r_{YX} are the zero-order product moment correlation coefficient and the Pearsonian correlation coefficient.) Figure 2.6 indicates how this is derived. We have a data set comprising eight observations of Y and X. The variance in Y, S_Y^2, is the mean of the squared deviations from $\overline{Y}$ indicated by the dashed lines in Fig. 2.6A. Regressing Y on X we get

$$Y = -1.86 + 1.22X$$

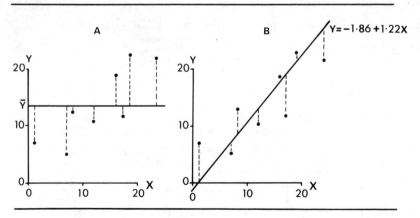

Fig. 2.6   The derivation of the correlation coefficient, showing (A) the contribution of each observation to the variance in Y — about its mean — and (B) the contribution of the same observations to the residual variance in Y — about the regression Y = f(X).

This regression line does not pass through all eight data points, so although it is as close to all of them as possible, there is still some residual variance in Y, which is the mean of the squared differences between the values of Y_i and $\hat{Y}_i$, shown by the dashed lines in Fig. 2.6B. For the whole data set, the relevant values are

X	Y	$(Y - \overline{Y})^2$	$\hat{Y}$	$(Y - \hat{Y})^2$
24	22	64	27·42	29·38
19	23	81	21·32	2·82
17	12	4	18·88	47·33
16	19	25	17·66	1·80
12	11	9	12·78	3·17
8	13	1	7·90	26·01
7	5	81	6·68	2·82
1	7	49	−0·64	58·37
Σ 104	112	314		171·70

so that $\overline{Y} = 14$ $S_Y^2 = 39\cdot25$ $S_{(Y - \hat{Y})}^2 = 21\cdot46$

The 'original' variance in Y (Fig. 2.6A) is thus 39·25, but the variance in Y around the regression line rather than around $\overline{Y}$ is 21·46. In other words by using X to estimate Y we reduce the variance in Y by $(39\cdot25 - 21\cdot46) = 17\cdot79$, which is 45·32% of the original variance in Y. Using X_i allows us to be 45% more accurate in estimating Y_i than if we just selected one of the eight values of Y at random.

The ratio between the 'explained' or 'reduced' variance (i.e. the variance in the residual values of Y) and the 'original' variance is known as the coefficient of determination. Thus

'explained' variance = 'original' variance − 'residual' variance

$$S_{\hat{Y}}^2 = S_Y^2 - S_{(Y - \hat{Y})}^2 \tag{2.18}$$

and

$$r_{YX}^2 = S_{\hat{Y}}^2 / S_Y^2 \tag{2.19}$$

where S_Y^2 is the variance in Y;

$\quad S_{(Y - \hat{Y})}^2$ is the variance in the predicted values, Y;

$\quad S_{\hat{Y}}^2$ is the 'explained' variance in Y, according to the regression Y = $a + bX$; and

$\quad r_{YX}^2$ is the coefficient of determination between Y and X.

The square root of the latter value, r_{YX}, is the correlation coefficient of Y on X:

$$r_{YX} = \sqrt{r_{YX}^2} \tag{2.20}$$

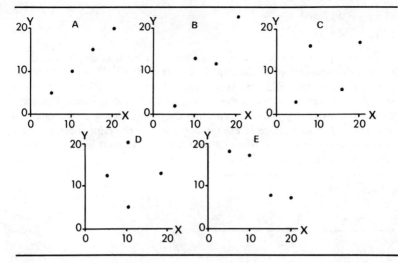

Fig. 2.7 Five examples of the relationship between covariance and correlation.

An alternative definition of the correlation coefficient to that just presented is illustrated by Fig. 2.7. The data for the scatter of points in Fig. 2.7A are

	Point			
	1	2	3	4
X	5	10	15	20
Y	5	10	15	20

from which

$\overline{X} = 12.5 \quad S_X^2 = 31.25$

$\overline{Y} = 12.5 \quad S_Y^2 = 31.25$ and $COV_{YX} = 31.25$

The correlation coefficient is the ratio between the covariance and the square root of the product of the variances; so that

$$r_{YX} = COV_{YX}/\sqrt{(S_X^2)(S_Y^2)} \tag{2.21}$$

which for Fig. 2.7A gives

$$r_{YX} = 31.25/\sqrt{(31.25)(31.25)} = 1.0$$

For the other examples we get

B $r_{YX} = 0.93$

C $r_{YX} = 0.56$

D $r_{YX} = 0 \cdot 07$ and

E $r_{YX} = -0 \cdot 93$

For any given data set, the denominator in formula (2.21) is always the same — the square root of the joint variances of X and Y — so that the size of the correlation coefficient is determined by the covariance term. The size of the latter is related to the pairing of the X and Y values. The maximum value of COV_{YX} will occur when the rank ordering of the values of Y over the N observations is the same as that for the rank ordering of the X values, and where the values of Y and X form a straight line on a scattergram. Thus where

	Point				
	1	2	3	4	
X	2	4	6	8	$\overline{X} = 5$
Y	8	16	24	32	$\overline{Y} = 20$

$COV_{YX} = 80/4 = 20$

The same values of X and Y, but differently ordered, might produce

	1	2	3	4	
X	2	4	6	8	$\overline{X} = 5$
Y	16	8	32	24	$\overline{Y} = 20$

$COV_{YX} = 48/4 = 12$

or

	1	2	3	4	
X	2	4	6	8	$\overline{X} = 5$
Y	24	32	8	16	$\overline{Y} = 20$

$COV_{YX} = -48/4 = -12$

In all cases $S_X^2 = 5$ and $S_Y^2 = 80$ so that

$$\sqrt{(S_X^2)\,(S_Y^2)} = \sqrt{(5)\,(80)} = \sqrt{400} = 20$$

and the three respective values of r_{YX} are $1 \cdot 0$, $0 \cdot 6$, and $-0 \cdot 6$.

These examples illustrate that when all of the points lie along a straight line the covariance of Y and X is at a maximum, which is the same as the square root of the joint variances of Y and X. This produces a correlation coefficient of $+1 \cdot 0$ if the regression is positive, and $-1 \cdot 0$ if it is negative: in the former case it indicates that the largest value of Y is for the same observation as the largest value of X, the next largest value of Y is for the same observation as the next largest value of X, and so on. Thus, correlation coefficients of $\pm 1 \cdot 0$ indicate 'perfect' relationships with all of the observations on the straight line. Correlations of 0·0 indicate a random scatter of points, in which $S^2_{(Y - \hat{Y})}$ is the same as S^2_Y (Fig. 2.7D). Intermediate values between 0 and ±1·0 indicate the relative strength of the relationship between these two extremes, with the value of r^2_{YX} indicating the proportion of the variance in Y which is removed by estimating $\hat{Y}$ from the equation $\hat{Y} = a + bX$ (this is usually known as the percentage level of statistical explanation).

As with the calculations for the regression equation, the formula for the correlation coefficients is reorganised, by using covariation and variation, to reduce computational tedium, as

$$r_{YX} = \frac{N\Sigma X_i Y_i - (\Sigma X_i)(\Sigma Y_i)}{\sqrt{(N\Sigma X_i^2 - (\Sigma X_i)^2)(N\Sigma Y_i^2 - (\Sigma Y_i)^2)}} \qquad (2.22)$$

For the example of Table 2.1 and Fig. 2.2, this gives

$$r_{YX} = 203\ 690/\sqrt{(294\ 800)(301\ 901)} = 203\ 690/298\ 300 = 0·683$$

By knowing the percentage of a town's population aged between 5 and 21, therefore, we can reduce the variance in the dependent variable, expenditure per head on education, by 46·6% ($0·683^2 \times 100$) by using the following equation to estimate values of Y:

$$Y = 22·56 + 0·691X$$

A more usual way of expressing this is to say that 46% of the variance in Y can be explained, statistically, by the variance in X. Whether this *statistical* explanation can be interpreted as a *causal* explanation depends on the logic of the theory from which the hypothesis was derived. It may be better to say that the variation in X *accounts for* 46·6% of the variation in Y, but the more emotive term 'explains' is widely used in the geographical literature.

Residuals

When all of the observations do not lie on a straight line, the correlation coefficient indicates the overall fit of the regression line to the scatter of points. It does not indicate either the success of the equation at estimating any particular observation or the likely variation around the estimated values of Y. To obtain the latter, we look at the residuals from the regression.

On the assumption that $r_{YX} = 1·0$, we can estimate the values of Y_i by substituting the relevant values of X_i in the regression equation. Thus in Table 2.1 the value of X for place 1 is 17 so

$$\hat{Y}_1 = 22·56 + 0·691(17) = 34·31$$

In fact, the value of Y at place 1 is 27. The *residual value of Y* (ResY) is defined as the difference between the actual and estimated values, thus

$$ResY_i = Y_i - \hat{Y}_i \qquad (2.23)$$

Formula (2.23) indicates the *absolute residual* at observation i. Interpretation of such a value may be difficult. If, for example,

(case 1) $Y_i = 104$ $\hat{Y}_i = 100$ then $Y_i - \hat{Y}_i = 4$

but also, if

(case 2) $Y_i = 8$ $\hat{Y}_i = 4$ then $Y_i - \hat{Y}_i = 4$

In both of these cases the absolute residual is +4; the estimated value is four units less than the actual. But this same difference is much less important in the first case — a difference of 4 against an expected of 100 is slight compared to a difference of 4 against an expected of 4. Thus we might define *relative residuals* (RRes) as

$$\text{RRes } Y_i = (Y_i - \hat{Y}_i)/\hat{Y}_i \qquad (2.24)$$

in which the absolute residual of formula (2.23) is expressed as a ratio of the expected value. For the two cases above,

(case 1) $Y_i = 104$ $\hat{Y}_i = 100$ $\text{RRes } Y_i = (104-100)/100 = 0.04$

(case 2) $Y_i = 8$ $\hat{Y}_i = 4$ $\text{RRes } Y_i = (8-4)/4$ $= 1.00$

which emphasises the relative importance of the differences in the latter case. In graphical terms, formula (2.24) involves the derivation of a series of lines diverging from the regression line, as in Fig. 2.8 for our hypothetical data set. (The point of divergence is where the regression line crosses the X-axis.) Clearly, for any regression, the larger the value of X, the smaller the value of RRes Y_i is likely to be.

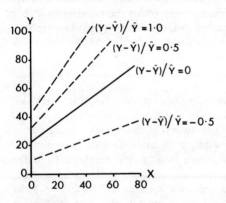

Fig. 2.8   Relative residual bands around the regression line of Y = f(X) in Fig. 2.5.

Neither the absolute nor the relative residuals defined in formulae (2.23) and (2.24) are used much in geographical research, because of the problem of the metric or scale of measurement when comparing two or more residual values. Much preferred is the *standardised residual* which expresses the values of $(Y_i - \hat{Y}_i)$ in terms of a normal distribution of residuals. (As outlined below, p. 41, such a normal distribution is assumed for valid regression analyses.) The variance of this normal distribution of residuals is

$$S^2_{(Y - \hat{Y})} = \left(\sum_{i=1}^{N} (Y_i - \hat{Y}_i)^2 \right) / N \qquad (2.25)$$

and the associated standard deviation, known as the *Standard Error of Y* (SE_Y) is

$$SE_Y = \sqrt{S^2_{(Y - \hat{Y})}} \qquad (2.26)$$

This standard error is the residual variance from the regression of Y on X. Since according to (2.19)

$$r^2_{YX} = S^2_{\hat{Y}} / S^2_Y \qquad (2.27)$$

then the residual variance is that portion of the variance in Y not accounted for by X, with its standard deviation (the Standard Error)

$$SE_Y = S_Y (\sqrt{1 - r^2_{YX}}) \qquad (2.28)$$

where S_Y is the standard deviation for Y; and
$1 - r^2_{YX}$ is the unexplained proportion of the variance in Y.

Standardised residuals (SRes) can now be defined as

$$SRes\ Y_i = (Y_i - \hat{Y}_i)/SE_Y \qquad (2.29)$$

and the location of various parameters of the distribution of residuals can be indicated by interpolating standard error bands on a scatter diagram. The +1 S.E. and −1 S.E. error bands around the regression line for our hypothetical data set are shown in Fig. 2.9. As with the standard deviation

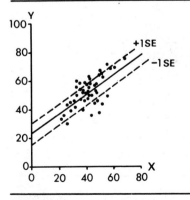

Fig. 2.9 Standardised residual bands around the regression line of Y = f(X) in Fig. 2.5.

of a normal distribution, these enclose approximately 68% of all the observations.

Compared to the relative residuals of Fig. 2.8, these standardised residuals have the twin advantages of (1) being associated with a clearly

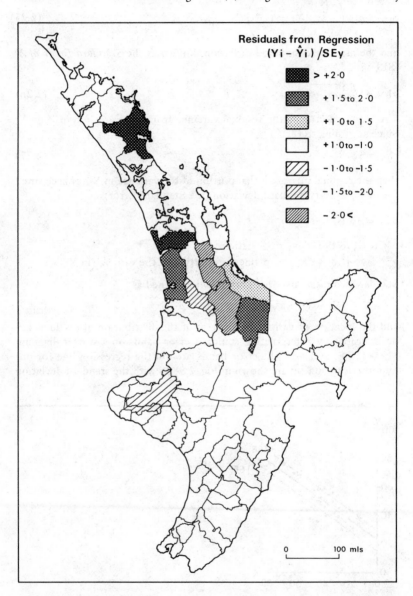

Fig. 2.10   Standardised residuals from a regression of pigs per county against cows per county in the North Island of New Zealand. Source: Clark (1967); reproduced with permission.

defined statistical distribution (the normal); and (2) comprising bands which run parallel to the regression line and therefore do not give undue emphasis to the residuals in Y related to either the large or small values of X (as do the absolute and relative residuals, respectively).

The standardised residual at 1 S.E. is often incorporated into the regression equation, to indicate its relative accuracy. Thus the full equation reads

$$Y = a_{YX} + b_{YX}X \pm SE_Y \qquad (2.30)$$

in which SE_Y is often replaced by ϵ.

For the data of Table 2.1, the full equation is

$$Y = 22 \cdot 56 + 0 \cdot 691X \pm 8 \cdot 19$$

Using this, we can estimate that if $X_i = 30 \cdot 0$

> then $\hat{Y}_i = 22 \cdot 56 + 0 \cdot 691 (30 \cdot 0) \pm 8 \cdot 19$ or $43 \cdot 29 \pm 8 \cdot 19$
> or between $51 \cdot 48$ and $35 \cdot 10$ in $68 \cdot 26\%$ of all cases of $X_i = 30 \cdot 0$
> and $\hat{Y}_i = 43 \cdot 29 \pm 16 \cdot 38$ $(16 \cdot 38 = 2\ SE_Y)$
> or between $59 \cdot 67$ and $26 \cdot 91$ in $95 \cdot 46\%$ of all cases of $X_i = 30 \cdot 0$

Note that a fairly high value of SE_Y can be associated with a high value of r_{YX}, if the original values are large: interpretation of predictive accuracy should be based on SE_Y.

Residuals are used to identify observations which lie some distance from the best-fit linear trend. They may indicate deviant cases, or they may suggest further independent variables which ought to be taken into consideration. In geographical work, the latter task is often undertaken by mapping the residuals. For example, Clark (1967) regressed the number of pigs per county in the North Island, New Zealand against the number of cows, to test the hypothesis that, since pigs are fed on skim milk, pig farming is important in areas of dairy farming. He obtained the regression

$$Y_i = 2445 + 0 \cdot 27X_i \quad r_{YX} = 0 \cdot 77$$

where Y_i is the number of pigs in county i; and
$\qquad X_i$ is the number of cows in county i,

and then mapped the standardised residuals (Fig. 2.10). The pattern displayed showed fewer pigs than expected (negative residuals) in two areas — both major dairying districts — and more pigs than expected (positive residuals) in the north of the island, particularly around the Auckland urban area. Such a map suggests reasons for the correlation of only $0 \cdot 77$, reasons which may be incorporated into a multivariate hypotheses (Ch. 3).

The assumptions involved in using correlation and regression

Apart from its general restriction to data measured on interval or ratio scales, nothing has been said so far in this chapter about the assumptions which must be met before the general linear model — of which bivariate correlation and regression is a particular case — can be used. Throughout the chapter, however, there has been considerable use of concepts such as means and variances, standard deviations and covariances; and the concept of variance, in particular, is only valid when discussing data which either fit, or approximate, the bell-shaped normal distribution. In all, there are seven basic requirements concerning the normal distribution which must be met by data to which regression methods are applied (Poole and O'Farrell, 1971); one is not relevant here, since it applies to multiple regression only (Ch. 3).

1. *Linearity.*   Regression analysis fits a straight-line trend through a scatter of data points, and correlation analysis tests for the 'goodness of fit' of this line. Clearly, if the trend cannot be represented by a straight line, regression analysis will not portray it accurately.

Non-linearity is illustrated by Fig. 2.11. There is a positive relationship between X and Y, but the trend is curvilinear, with Y increasing at a decreasing rate relative to increases in X. The 'real' trend in the data is shown by the dashed line in Fig. 2.11A; the straight-line regression is

$$Y = 15 \cdot 34 + 0 \cdot 27X \quad r = 0 \cdot 90$$

with a correlation indicating a good fit. But inspection of the regression line indicates that it overpredicts the largest and the smallest values of Y, while underpredicting those in the 'middle range': it is therefore not a very good representation of the trend.

Although regression and correlation methods cannot be applied to curvilinear trends, it is often possible to *transform* the trend into a linear form. This is most commonly done by expressing one or both of the variables as its common logarithm, as in Fig. 2.11B, where the values of X from Fig. 2.11A are replaced by $\log_{10} X$. The equation is then

$$Y = -0 \cdot 44 + 20 \cdot 11 \log_{10} X \quad r = 0 \cdot 99$$

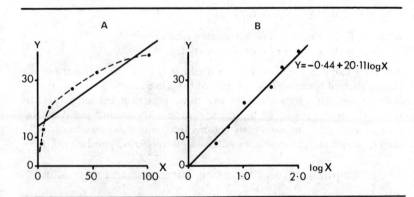

Fig. 2.11 A non-linear regression of Y on X showing (A) the trend in the points and its representation by the regression $Y = f(X)$ and (B) how the trend is more accurately displayed by the regression $\log Y = f(\log X)$.

which, as both the diagram and the correlation coefficient indicate, is a much better fit to the trend in the data than was the previous equation. Interpretation of the regression coefficient is that for every increase of $\log_{10} X$ of $1 \cdot 0$, Y increases by $20 \cdot 11$ units. An increase of $1 \cdot 0$ in common logarithms is equivalent to multiplying by 10, as follows:

$$X_i = 40 \qquad \log X_i = 1 \cdot 6021 \qquad \hat{Y}_i = 11 \cdot 67$$

$$X_i = 400 \qquad \log X_i = 2 \cdot 6021 \qquad \hat{Y}_i = 31 \cdot 78$$

$$X_i = 4000 \quad \log X_i = 3 \cdot 6021 \qquad \hat{Y}_i = 51 \cdot 89$$

so that Y increases by $20 \cdot 11$ units for every tenfold increase in X.

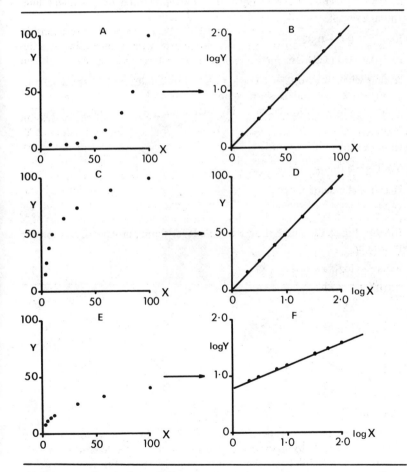

Fig. 2.12 Examples of three types of logarithmic transformation, showing: (A) an exponential relationship, better described by log Y = f(X) (B); (C) a power relationship, described by Y = f(log X) (D); and (E) a Pareto relationship, described by log Y = f(log X) (F).

For a regression line to present a faithful reflection of the trend in a data set, therefore, it is necessary to ensure that there is a linear relationship between the two variables. If this is not the case in the 'raw' data, transformation may achieve it, while at the same time introducing possible problems of interpretation. Many different transformations are available: some of the most common are illustrated in Fig. 2.12, in which the right-hand diagrams show the linear version of the curvilinear trend in the left-hand diagram. The first, Fig. 2.12A and B, shows an exponential curve, in which Y increases according to some exponent of X

$$Y = ab^X$$

$$\therefore \log_{10} Y = \log_{10} a + \log_{10} b (X) \tag{2.31}$$

In our example

$$\log_{10} Y = 0{\cdot}0 + 0{\cdot}02X$$

$$\text{or} \quad Y = 1{\cdot}0 \, (1{\cdot}047)^X$$

so that when X = 50, Y = 10 or $\log_{10} Y = 1{\cdot}0$, as indicated on the diagram.

Figure 2.12C and D show a power relationship, with Y expressed as some function of X, remembering that $2 \log_{10} X = X^2$ and $0{\cdot}5 \log_{10} X = \sqrt{X}$.

In our example

$$Y = 0 + 50 \, (\log_{10} X)$$

is a special case of

$$Y = a + b \, (\log_{10} X) \tag{2.32}$$

Finally, Fig. 2.12E and F show a double-logarithmic, or Pareto, relationship in which

$$\log_{10} Y = \log_{10} a + b \, (\log_{10} X) \tag{2.33}$$

$$\therefore 10^Y = 10^a X^b$$

$$\text{or} \quad Y = aX^b$$

In our example

$$\log_{10} Y = 0{\cdot}8 + 0{\cdot}4 \, (\log_{10} X)$$

so

$$Y = (\text{antilog } 0{\cdot}8) \, (X^{0{\cdot}4})$$

$$= 6{\cdot}31 X^{0{\cdot}4}$$

It is usual in much geographical work to use base 10 logarithms, but it may be preferable to use base e logarithms, in which the logarithm of 10 is not $1{\cdot}0$ but $2{\cdot}3026$. The benefit to be gained is that with this transformation, the coefficient b gives the *rate of increase or change* in Y per unit of X. Thus the exponential function (2.31) can be rewritten as

$$Y = ae^{bX} \tag{2.34}$$

which is the same as

$$\log_e Y = \log_e a + bX \log_e^e$$

but since $\log_e^e = 1$

then $\log_e Y = \log_e a + bX$

In the example of Fig. 2.11A and B

$$Y = 1 \cdot 0 \, (1 \cdot 047)^X$$

The base$_e$ logarithm of $1 \cdot 047$ is $0 \cdot 0459$ (which is the same as multiplying the base 10 logarithm of $1 \cdot 047$ by $2 \cdot 3026$). This tells us that for every increase of one unit in X, Y increases by $0 \cdot 0459$ of itself.

Thus, if

$$X = 50 \quad Y = 10$$

it follows that when $X = 51$

$$Y = 10 + 10 \quad X \; 0 \cdot 0459 = 10 \cdot 459$$

A major use of this sort of relationship is in studies of distance-decay, or the decline in the value of a variable with distance from a basing point. The population density of parts of a city is often related to the density in the central area by such an equation (Rees, 1970, p.277), where

$$d_x = d_0 e^{-bx} \qquad \qquad (2.35)$$

or

$$\log_e d_x = \log_e d_0 - bx$$

where d is population density;
        x is distance from the city centre; and
        o is the city centre.

The value of b in this equation indicates the rate of change in population density with a unit change in the distance variable. For Chicago in 1960, with density expressed as hundreds of persons per square mile, Rees obtained the equation

$$\log_e d_x = 4 \cdot 5195 - 0 \cdot 0559x$$

which he compared with similar equations for many other cities.

2. *Normality*.   It is widely assumed that use of the linear regression model requires that the variables have normal distributions. In fact, the requirement is not that the raw data be normally distributed; it is that the conditional distributions of the residuals are normal. The conditional distributions are the values of $(Y_i - \hat{Y}_i)$ for every value of X. If these conditional distributions are normal, then it is almost certain that the distributions of Y and of X — known as the marginal distributions — are also normal, but the converse is not necessarily the case. Thus although many authors test to see if their data are normally distributed (see, for example, Hart and

Salisbury, 1965), they are only inquiring as to whether a necessary pre-requisite for normal conditional distributions exists. Of course, one rarely if ever has enough values of Y for every value of X to see if there is a normal conditional distribution; the theory is based on an ideal of very large samples.

3. *Means of conditional distributions.*   For every value of X, the mean of $(Y_i - \hat{Y}_i)$ must be zero. If it is not, the coefficients of the regression equation (a_{YX} and b_{YX}) may be biased estimates. Figure 2.13A shows a simple example of this where the means of $(Y_i - \hat{Y}_i)$ for each of several values of X are not zero. The interpretation of a major departure from this assumption is that the trend in the scatter of points is not in fact linear — as can be inferred from Fig. 2.13A, where the (real) trend between the second and third groups is steeper than that between both the first and the second and the third and the fourth. (Such a trend could not easily be made linear by transformation.) Where deviations from this assumption are relatively small, however, they are not considered serious.

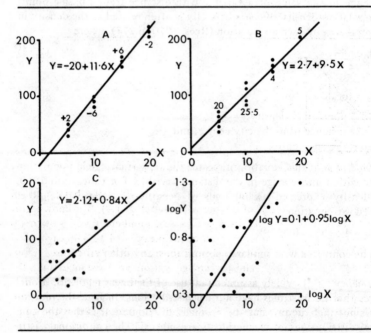

Fig. 2.13 Some of the assumptions of the general linear model, showing: (A) non-normal conditional distributions of residuals; (B) heteroscedastic conditional distributions of residuals, with different variances for each value of X; (C) a heteroscedastic relationship; and (D) logarithmic transformation of (C) to achieve homoscedascity.

4. *Homoscedascity*.   This frightening word means equal variances in the conditional distributions. If these are not equal, which is the case with the conditional variances in Fig. 2.13B, then heteroscedascity (the opposite of homoscedascity) is said to exist.

This assumption is an important one, for if there is considerable variation in the values of $\Sigma(Y_i - \hat{Y}_i)^2/N$ for each value of X, then the regression equation coefficients may be severely biased. Unfortunately, heteroscedascity often occurs with geographical data sets containing a large number of observations with small values of X relative to those with large values: examples include town sizes and streams of various orders in a river basin. Figure 2.13C shows such a hypothetical set: X is the population of each town (in thousands) and Y is the percentage of its workforce employed in services. For all fifteen towns, the regression equation is

$$Y = 2 \cdot 12 + 0 \cdot 84X \pm 2 \cdot 68 \quad r = 0 \cdot 81$$

for all but the largest (i.e. N = 14) it is

$$Y = 2 \cdot 92 + 0 \cdot 68X \pm 1 \cdot 90 \quad r = 0 \cdot 57$$

and for all but the three largest (N = 12) it is

$$Y = 5 \cdot 89 - 0 \cdot 03X \pm 2 \cdot 52 \quad r = -0 \cdot 02$$

Clearly the three coefficients (a, b, r) are very much affected by removal of a few observations only, if these are the large ones. This is because of the heteroscedascity.

Logarithmic transformation can be used to remove heteroscedascity if the variances are related to X (i.e. their differences are not randomly located with respect to X); the data from Fig. 2.13C are plotted in Fig. 2.13D on logarithmic coordinates to illustrate this. Inspection of the scatter diagram shows that variances are still far from equal for all values of X, but the regression equations are much more stable. Thus

$N = 15, \log_{10} Y = 0 \cdot 1 + 0 \cdot 95 \log_{10} X \pm 0 \cdot 12$ $\qquad r = 0 \cdot 90$
$N = 14$ (omitting the largest town),
$\log_{10} Y = 0 \cdot 07 + 0 \cdot 98 \log_{10} X \pm 0 \cdot 12$ $\qquad r = 0 \cdot 87$
and $N = 12$ (omitting the three largest towns),
$\log_{10} Y = 0 \cdot 57 + 1 \cdot 02 \log_{10} X \pm 0 \cdot 13$ $\qquad r = 0 \cdot 81$

The closer one gets to homoscedascity, therefore, the greater one's faith that the regression coefficients are not biased by the influence of one or a few observations only, because the means and variances of the distributions of X and Y are not affected very much by the values at one or a few 'deviant' cases.

5. *Autocorrelation*.   The crux of this assumption is that the value of each observation on the independent variable is independent of all of the values of all others, so that one cannot predict the value of X for observation 7, for example, if one knows the value for observation 6. There are two

interpretations as to the importance of this assumption: one is substantively logical and the other is statistically logical.

The substantive account of autocorrelation can best be seen for the study of time series data, in which it is frequently termed serial correlation. Take, for example, the relationship between time and the population of England. Most of the people alive in England in 1976 were also alive in 1975, and so the population in the year 1976 is not independent of that in the preceding observation, 1975. If one regressed population on time using years as the independent variable, therefore, the same people would appear not once but many times: the observations would not be independent of each other, and by enumerating the same people several times, the regression coefficient could be biased.

Serial correlation also occurs in geographical data. For example, study of a soil catena may show a strong relationship between distance from the top of a slope and soil depth and an investigation of the volume of pollutants in a river may find a positive relationship between pollution and distance from the river source. But pollutants move downstream, so what is measured at one point will be very much influenced by what is measured at the previous point upstream. Again, we might be measuring the same thing many times.

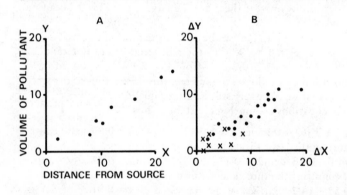

Fig. 2.14 Serial autocorrelation showing: (A) the relationship between distance from a river's source (X) and volume of a pollutant in the river (Y); and (B) the relationship of differences between observations on these two variables.

Figure 2.14A illustrates this. Measurement of the volume of a pollutant at irregularly spaced sampling points along a river indicates that the volume of pollution increases with distance from source. But does it indicate that the increase in the volume is constant? To test for this we replace X and Y by ΔX (the change in X) and ΔY (the change in Y); ΔX is the distance between two stations, ΔY is the difference in pollutant level between those two, and we measure not only between adjacent pairs of stations but

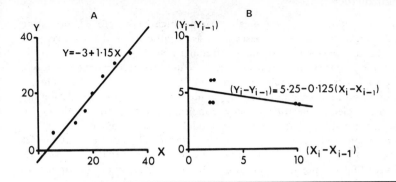

Fig. 2.15 An autocorrelated distribution of residuals (A), as indicated by the regression of differences between adjacent observations (B).

between all possible pairs. A scattergram relating these (Fig. 2.14B) indicates quite a lot of variability; the same change in distance can produce quite different changes in pollutant volume (see, in particular, the changes between adjacent stations only, indicated by crosses).

The statistical interpretation of autocorrelation relates to the linearity assumption. If the residuals from a regression equation are not independent of each other on the X variable, then adjacent values of X may have similar residuals. Figure 2.15A shows a hypothetical example of this, in which the negative residuals are clustered in the values of X between 10 and 20, and the positive residuals in the values between 20 and 30. The high correlation coefficient ($r_{YX} = 0.93$) for the regression equation indicates a very close relationship, suggesting that every unit increase of X would produce a similar response in Y. Regression of the difference between adjacent values of X ($X_i - X_{i-1}$) with that for Y ($Y_i - Y_{i-1}$) suggests the contrary, however (Fig. 2.15B), for the correlation of these two is -0.5. The positive correlation between Y and X in Fig. 2.15A thus indicates that the adjacent values on the X axis are not independent in their values of Y, the reason being that the true relationship, as suggested by the scatter of points, is S-shaped and not linear.

Auto- or serial correlation, as discussed here, concerns interdependence in one direction only, along the X axis. In much geographical work, however, the interdependence may be in all directions on a two-dimensional plane, which can cause immense problems. A brief consideration of these is provided in the final chapter.

6. *Lack of measurement error.* This final assumption assumes that X and Y are both measured without error. If this is not the case, and the magnitude of the error is unknown, then the coefficients of the regression equation may be biased, to an extent that cannot be estimated.

Significance

In many reports of geographical research which has employed correlation and regression analyses, phrases such as 'significant at the 5% level' will be encountered. Such statements often mean very little. As pointed out in Chapter 1, statistical significance tests are used to infer characteristics of a population from a sample and are validly employed only when: (1) the sample is a random one from the population; and (2) the population has been completely specified. If these conditions are met, and the data meet the requirements of the regression model, then a statement such as 'this correlation coefficient, r_{YX}, of +0·89 is statistically significant at the 5% (or 0·05) level' may be made. It would probably mean that 'there is a 95% chance that the positive relationship observed in the sample also applies to the population'.

Significance testing, then, relates to the probability of the result observed in the sample not also being true for the population. In regression analysis, we have a model for the population that

$$Y = \alpha + \beta X \quad \rho = \text{correlation}$$

which we estimate in the sample as

$$Y = a + bX \quad r_{YX} = \text{correlation} \tag{2.36}$$

and we want to know whether the relationship in the sample holds for the population.

Assume a data set comprising only three observations, for which we have measurements of X and Y. There are six different ways in which the various values of X and Y can be paired, as follows:

		Value of Y in pairing					
Observation	X	1	2	3	4	5	6
1	4	8	8	15	15	16	16
2	6	15	16	8	16	8	15
3	8	16	15	16	8	15	8
	r_{YX}	+0·92	+0·80	+0·11	−0·80	−0·11	−0·92

Each set of pairings produces a different correlation between Y and X, and these correlation coefficients form a distribution known as the *sampling distribution*. The location of any particular correlation within this distribution can then be identified, to inquire into the probability of getting a value of that size and direction in a random sample of all the possible pairings of X_i and Y_i. For data sets with large numbers of observations, there is a very large number of possible sets of pairings. If the data themselves have normal marginal distributions, then the sampling distribution of the possible correlation coefficients is normal, and usual inferential tests based upon the properties of the normal distribution can be used to suggest the likelihood of a particular correlation occurring through random pairings.

The usual way of testing the significance of a correlation coefficient employs the Snedecor's F-ratio, which is treated in more detail in the later section on the analysis of variance. Remember that the total variance in the dependent variable is

$$S_Y^2 = \left(\sum_{i=1}^{N} (Y_i - \overline{Y})^2 \right)/N \tag{2.37}$$

The portion of this variance explained by the regression of Y or X is

$$(r_{YX}^2)(S_Y^2) \tag{2.38}$$

so that the unexplained portion is

$$(1 - r_{YX}^2)(S_Y^2) \tag{2.39}$$

In the data of Table 2.1 $S_Y^2 = 123 \cdot 21$, so that

portion accounted for = $0 \cdot 683^2 (123 \cdot 21) = 0 \cdot 466 (123 \cdot 21) = 57 \cdot 42$

portion unaccounted for = $(1 - 0 \cdot 683^2)(123 \cdot 21) = 0 \cdot 534 (123.21) =$ $65 \cdot 79$

To conduct the Snedecor's-F test we correct these values — known as the variation estimates — according to degrees of freedom (see p. 12), to give variance estimates. There are $(N - 1)$ degrees of freedom in the total variance estimate, one degree having been lost in computing $\overline{Y}$; after fitting the regression line, two degrees are lost — in computing a_{YX} and b_{YX} — so $(N - 2)$ are the degrees of freedom for the estimate of the portion of the variance unaccounted for: this leaves one degree $((N - 2) - (N - 1))$ for the estimate of the portion accounted for. The F ratio is

$$F_{YX} = \frac{\text{Estimate of the variance accounted for}}{\text{Estimate of the variance unaccounted for}}$$

which is

$$F_{YX} = \frac{((r_{YX}^2)(S_Y^2))/1 \cdot 0}{((1 - r_{YX}^2)(S_Y^2))/N - 2} \tag{2.40}$$

Substituting formula (2.39) for S_Y^2 and cancelling out, this becomes

$$F_{YX} = \frac{r_{YX}^2 (N - 2)}{(1 - r_{YX}^2)} \tag{2.41}$$

For the data in Table 2.1,

$$F_{YX} = \frac{(0 \cdot 683^2)(50 - 2)}{(1 - 0 \cdot 683^2)}$$

$$= 0 \cdot 466(48)/0 \cdot 534 = 22 \cdot 368/0 \cdot 534 = 41 \cdot 89$$

Conventional tables of the F-distribution indicate the probability that a ratio between the variance estimates of a given value would occur by chance. A value of 41·89, with 48 and 1 degrees of freedom, would occur in less than one random sample in a thousand. If our 50 towns were a random sample from a specified population, therefore, we could conclude that it is extremely likely that there is a positive correlation in the total population, since the observed correlation is very unlikely to occur in a random pairing of the X and Y values: the null hypothesis of no correlation is rejected in favour of the research hypothesis of a positive correlation, *but* nothing is said about the size of the correlation.

The other coefficient whose statistical significance is frequently tested is the regression coefficient, b_{YX}. This is done using the Student's t test. It is assumed that all of the possible b_{YX} values for the data set are normally distributed with a mean $\bar{b}_{YX} = 0$ (as with all of the correlation coefficients in the three observation examples above). The standard error for the distribution of regression coefficients (SE_b) is obtained as the ratio between the residual standard error from the regression — SE_Y, formula (2.28) — and the standard deviation of X, corrected for the two degrees of freedom lost in calculating the regression equation. Thus

$$SE_b = \frac{SE_Y}{S_X\sqrt{N-2}} \qquad (2.42)$$

The t ratio then expresses the difference between the observed value of b_{YX} and the mean, $\bar{b}_{YX}$, as a ratio of the standard error, so that

$$t = \frac{b_{YX} - \bar{b}_{YX}}{SE_b} \qquad (2.43)$$

which, since $\bar{b}_{YX} = 0$, becomes

$$t = b_{YX}/SE_b \qquad (2.44)$$

For the data in Table 2.1

$$SE_b = 8·19/(10·97) \; (\sqrt{48})$$
$$= 8·19/(10·97) \; (6·93) = 8·19/76·02 = 0·11$$

and

$$t = 0·691/0·11 = 6·282$$

Reference to tables of t indicate that such a value would occur by chance in less than one sample in a hundred, so we would conclude that a positive value of b_{YX} almost certainly existed in the population.

Similar t ratios can be calculated for r_{YX} and a_{YX}, to test whether these too are significantly different from zero. The standard error for r_{YX} is difficult to obtain, however, which is why the F-test is generally used.

In all of this discussion of statistical testing, it has been assumed that the null hypotheses are that

$$r_{YX} = 0·0 \quad b_{YX} = 0·0 \quad a_{YX} = 0·0$$

so that if they are rejected, the conclusion is that there is probably a coefficient with the given sign in the population. This is how significance testing is almost always used in regression analysis in geography. One can, however, set a null hypothesis of, for example,

$$b_{YX} = 2 \cdot 0 \text{ or } r_{YX} = +0 \cdot 7$$

and test whether it is probable that these values are exceeded in the population (see Davis, 1973). Such tests would be stronger than those presently used, but are in fact not employed.

Prediction

Regression equations may be computed as tests of a hypothesis, as descriptions of relationships, or as vehicles for predicting unknown values of Y. For the latter purpose, we need to know the accuracy of our predictions, and for this use an expanded concept of standard errors.

The *standard error of the estimate* — formulae (2.27) and (2.28) — describes the variation about the regression line in terms of the distribution of the residuals for the sample points used to produce the regression equation. To forecast the value of Y for an observation of X not included in the original sample we use the *standard error of the forecast*, which is a combination of the following three variance sources:

1. The standard error of the estimate:

$$SE_Y = S_Y \left(\sqrt{1 \cdot 0 - r_{YX}^2} \right) \tag{2.45}$$

2. The standard error of the mean of the dependent variable. As $\overline{Y}$ is the mean for a sample from the population of Y values, it is subject to sampling error, defined as

$$SE_{\overline{Y}} = S_Y / \sqrt{N} \tag{2.46}$$

3. The standard error of the regression coefficient, b_{YX}:

$$SE_b = SE_Y / (S_X (\sqrt{N - 2})) \tag{2.47}$$

The standard error of $\overline{Y}$ is the error we can expect at the intersection of the regression line with $\overline{Y}$ and $\overline{X}$. The further one gets from $\overline{Y}$, the greater the likely error in Y because of the variability in the slope.

To illustrate this with an analogy; when climbing a hill, you may estimate its slope as a vertical increase of 5 feet for every 10 feet in the horizontal, with a standard error of ±2 feet. After 10 feet, therefore, the height is probably between 3 and 7 feet (Fig. 2.16). After another 10 feet, the range of possible estimates of the height is 6 to 14 feet: if one had underestimated the height by 2 feet in the first ten, and did the same again, you would have underestimated by 4 feet in all, as Fig. 2.16 suggests. The further from the origin, the greater the likelihood of error, and with a regression slope, the further from $\overline{X}$ the greater the error. Thus the standard error of the regression coefficient is different for every value of X (with the origin as $\overline{X}$), as

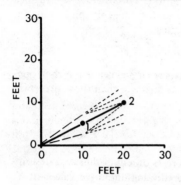

Fig. 2.16   The hill-slope analogy to the problem of forecasting. Forecasts are made every 10 feet. After 10 feet, the range of error is 2 feet; after 20 feet, the range is 4 feet.

$$SE_b = ((SE_Y/(S_X (\sqrt{N-2}))) (X_i - \overline{X})^2) \qquad (2.48)$$

For any value of X, the standard error of the forecast is then

$$SE_{\hat{Y}} = \sqrt{SE_Y^2 + SE_{\hat{Y}}^2 + SE_b^2} \qquad (2.49)$$

With the data of Table 2.1

$$SE_Y^2 = 67\cdot08 \quad SE_{\hat{Y}}^2 = (123\cdot21/\sqrt{50})^2 = 303\cdot62$$

and for X = 60

$$SE_b^2 = (8\cdot19/(10\cdot97) (\sqrt{48})) (60 - 42\cdot4)^2 = 33\cdot45$$

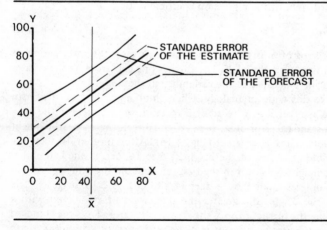

Fig. 2.17   The error bands for the standard error of the forecast and for the standard error of the estimate in the regression of Y = f(X) in Fig. 2.5.

so that

$$SE_{\hat{Y}(X = 60)} = \sqrt{67 \cdot 08 + 303 \cdot 62 + 33 \cdot 45} = 20 \cdot 1$$

For $X = 60$ $\hat{Y} = 22 \cdot 56 + 0 \cdot 691 \,(60) = 64 \cdot 02 \pm 20 \cdot 1$,

indicating that in about 68% of the forecasts with $X = 60$, $\hat{Y}$ will be within the range $44 \cdot 01 - 84 \cdot 03$.

Calculating the value of $SE_{\hat{Y}}$ for every value of X is a tedious task, and the error bands for the standard error of the forecast are usually interpolated from a few estimates. This has been done for the Table 2.1 data in Fig. 2.17. The main features to be noted are: (1) that $SE_{\hat{Y}}$ has a greater range than SE_Y; and (2) that the further one moves from $\overline{X}$, in either direction, the wider the bands for $SE_{\hat{Y}}$, and thus the less certain the forecast. If we selected two more towns with their percentages of the population aged between 5 and 21 as 50 and 70, therefore, our forecasts of the expenditure per head on education would be:

$X = 50$ $\hat{Y} = 57 \cdot 11 \pm 19 \cdot 26$ and

$X = 70$ $\hat{Y} = 70 \cdot 93 \pm 21 \cdot 32$

Correlation and regression: a summary

From this extended discussion, we see that bivariate regression is a procedure for fitting a straight line through a scatter of points, to provide the best description of the trend in that scatter and the best set of estimates of Y_i from X_i. Correlation analysis measures the 'goodness of fit' of this straight line to the distribution of points and, where relevant, a range of other statistics indicates the accuracy of forecasts from this trend line and the likelihood that a similar trend is also present in the larger population from which the observations have been sampled. There is a very large number of examples in the geographical literature of the use of this simple technique.

With regard to the use of significance testing with correlation and regression analysis, it should be stressed that this is only strictly valid when the data used are for a random sample of observations from a specified population. Thus if the 50 towns in the data set used for explication here were the only 50 in the area, then the correlation between Y and X of $+0 \cdot 683$ is the true correlation; with no population to infer about, significance testing would be irrelevant, as it would be for the values of a_{YX} and b_{YX} also. When a population and not a sample is being analysed, therefore, the various coefficients of the regression equation and the correlation are *exact descriptions* of the trend in a data set, within the constraints of the linear model; when a sample is being analysed, the cofficients are *estimates of the true values* and significance testing indicates the likelihood of these estimates holding for the population.

Unfortunately, many examples in the geographical literature (and in the literature of other subjects; we are not talking of a peculiar geographic vice here) are not entirely correct in the use of various aspects of the bivariate regression model. One of the problems faced by all users of these models is to estimate whether their data are sufficiently close to the requirements of the model that a regression line can be reliably fitted. Individual judgement is involved in determining when a deviation – from linearity, say – is important. The major point to note, however, is that whether the equation is being fitted as an estimator or a descriptor, it portrays a certain type of straight-line trend only, and major deviations from this mean that a biased estimate or description is being produced.

The analysis of variance

As pointed out in Chapter 1, the second of geography's basic questions – 'Are places different in terms of the phenomena present there?' – is very similar to the first, except that its independent variable, different types of places, is nominally-scaled. A wide range of non-parametric statistical tests is available for use in many situations where this question is asked (Siegel, 1956), but only situations where the dependent variable meets the requirements of the general linear model are discussed here. For these, the relevant statistical technique is the analysis of variance, briefly mentioned earlier in the discussion of significance testing for correlation coefficients (p. 47).

To outline the procedures used in this technique, a hypothetical problem is again posed. The dependent variable is that used before – the *per capita* expenditure on education by towns. In this case, however, the research hypothesis is that towns vary in their expenditure on education according to the nature of their political control, as certain political parties are more

Table 2.2   Educational spending and political affiliation: hypothetical data

Town	X*	Y†	Town	X	Y	Town	X	Y
1	F	27	17	S	57	34	F	31
2	S	64	18	S	70	35	S	66
3	F	52	19	L	50	36	S	69
4	S	59	20	L	54	37	L	42
5	S	77	21	F	45	38	L	43
6	L	54	22	L	68	39	S	60
7	L	50	23	S	45	40	F	46
8	L	48	24	L	58	41	L	46
9	F	49	25	F	36	42	L	52
10	S	72	26	F	40	43	F	46
11	S	52	27	L	60	44	S	58
12	L	62	28	S	64	45	S	58
13	F	50	29	F	51	46	F	40
14	S	50	30	F	36	47	F	55
15	F	40	31	L	47	48	L	63
16	L	34	32	F	38	49	S	59
			33	F	44	50	L	56

*Key to independent variable: F = free market capitalist; S = socialist; L = liberal
†Y = *per capita* expenditure on education

prepared to invest public money in education than are others. Thus we have a nominal-scale independent variable — political control — in which the towns are classified into three groups, entitled 'socialist', 'free market capitalist' and 'liberal'. The data are given in Table 2.2 and the research hypothesis is that these three types of towns differ in their *per capita* educational spending, which can be written as

$$\bar{Y}_S \neq \bar{Y}_F \neq \bar{Y}_L \neq \bar{Y}_T \tag{2.50}$$

where S is socialist;

       F is free market capitalist;

       L is liberal; and

       T is total.

In other words, despite the name of the test, the analysis of variance looks for differences between groups in their means on the dependent variable.

Variance decomposition

In analysis of variance, the total variance in a data set is decomposed into the proportion which is within each of the defined group of observations and the proportion which is between them. (Note that most of the computation is on the variation — defined below — in attempts to obtain 'variance estimates'.) Figure 2.18 illustrates the procedure. The first diagram (Fig. 2.18A) is the frequency distribution of Y for all 50 towns: the mean, $\bar{Y}_T$, is 51·86, and the variance, S^2_{YT}, is 123·21. The other three diagrams — Figs. 2.18B, C, and D — are the frequency distributions for the separate groups, which have parameters

$$\bar{Y}_F = 42\cdot71 \quad S^2_{YF} = 29\cdot39$$

$$\bar{Y}_S = 61\cdot25 \quad S^2_{YS} = 234\cdot17$$

$$\bar{Y}_L = 52\cdot18 \quad S^2_{YL} = 70\cdot03$$

For any one town, i, its value Y_i can be located with reference to both the total mean, $\bar{Y}_T$, and the mean for the group $(\bar{Y}_G)$ of which it is a member. Thus for town 1

$$Y_1 - \bar{Y}_T = 27 - 51\cdot86 = -24\cdot86$$

$$Y_1 - \bar{Y}_F = 27 - 42\cdot71 = -15\cdot71$$

The mean for its group can similarly be located relative to the total mean, so that

$$\bar{Y}_F - \bar{Y}_T = 42\cdot71 - 51\cdot86 = -9\cdot15$$

and the location of Y_1, relative to Y_T, is then

$$Y_1 - \bar{Y}_T = (Y_1 - \bar{Y}_F) + (\bar{Y}_F - \bar{Y}_T)$$

$$= (27 - 42\cdot71) + (42\cdot71 - 51\cdot86)$$

$$= (-15\cdot71) + (-9\cdot15) = -24\cdot86$$

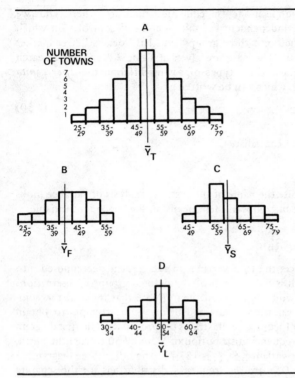

Fig. 2.18 Frequency distributions and mean values of *per capita* expenditure on education in fifty towns, showing: (A) all fifty towns; (B) those with a free-market capitalist council; (C) those with a socialist council; and (D) those with a liberal council. (The data are in Table 2.2.)

In general terms, therefore,

$$(Y_i - \overline{Y}_T) = (Y_i - \overline{Y}_G) + (\overline{Y}_G - \overline{Y}_T) \tag{2.51}$$

Figure 2.19 illustrates this for town 1.

If we square the two components of $(Y_i - \overline{Y}_T)$ in formula (2.51) we get

$$(Y_i - Y_T)^2 = (Y_i - \overline{Y}_G)^2 + 2(Y_i - \overline{Y}_G)(\overline{Y}_G - \overline{Y}_T) + (\overline{Y}_G - \overline{Y}_T)^2 \tag{2.52}$$

and summing this for all towns produces the *total variation*,

$$\sum_{i=1}^{N} (Y_i - \overline{Y}_T)^2 = \sum_{i=1}^{N} (Y_i - \overline{Y}_G)^2 + \sum_{i=1}^{N} 2(Y_i - \overline{Y}_G)(\overline{Y}_G - \overline{Y}_T) +$$

$$+ \sum_{i=1}^{N} (\overline{Y}_G - \overline{Y}_T)^2 \tag{2.53}$$

Because $\sum (Y_i - \overline{Y}_G) = 0$ (i.e. the positive and negative deviations around

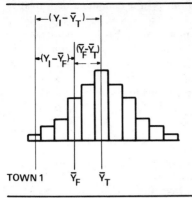

Fig. 2.19   Decomposition of the contribution of an observation to the total variance, showing the within-groups and between-groups components.

the group means cancel each other out) then the central term in formula (2.53) is zero, giving the following for the total variation:

$$\sum_{i=1}^{N} (Y_i - \overline{Y}_T)^2 = \sum_{i=1}^{N} (Y_i - \overline{Y}_G)^2 + \sum_{i=1}^{N} (\overline{Y}_G - \overline{Y}_T)^2 \tag{2.54}$$

The *total variation* (the mean of which is the variance) is thus the sum of the squared deviations of each observation from its group mean and the squared deviations (for every indiviual observation) of the group means from the total mean.

The hypothesis being tested is that the towns in the different groups have peculiar *per capita* spending patterns on education. We would anticipate relatively little variation around each of the group means, therefore, but considerable differences between the three group means themselves. The first component is the *within-groups variation*, represented by

$$\sum_{i=1}^{N} (Y_i - \overline{Y}_G)^2 \,;$$

the second is the *between-groups variation*,

$$\sum_{i=1}^{N} (\overline{Y}_G - \overline{Y}_T)^2,$$

recalling that this is summed over all observations, not over all groups. The smaller the size of the former relative to the latter, in the formula

$$\sum_{i=1}^{N} (Y_i - \overline{Y}_G)^2 \Big/ \sum_{i=1}^{N} (\overline{Y}_G - \overline{Y}_T)^2 \tag{2.55}$$

then the greater the variation between groups — the denominator — relative to that within groups — the numerator.

The ratio in formula (2.55) can be modified so that it is comparable to the product moment correlation coefficient, r_{YX}. In a regression analysis, total variation is $\sum (Y_i - \overline{Y})^2$ and residual variation, unaccounted for by the regression, is $\sum (Y_i - \hat{Y}_i)^2$, according to formula (2.18). The proportion of the variation unaccounted for by the independent variable is thus

$$\sum_{i=1}^{N} (Y_i - \hat{Y}_i)^2 \bigg/ \sum_{i=1}^{N} (Y_i - \overline{Y})^2 = 1 - r_{YX}^2 \tag{2.56}$$

In analysis of variance, the independent variable is group membership so that

$$\sum_{i=1}^{N} (\overline{Y}_G - \overline{Y}_T)^2 \bigg/ \sum_{i=1}^{N} (Y_i - \overline{Y}_T)^2 \tag{2.57}$$

is the proportion of the variation in Y accounted for by the classification of observations into types, whereas the ratio of the within groups to total variation

$$\sum_{i=1}^{N} (Y_i - \overline{Y}_G)^2 \bigg/ \sum_{i=1}^{N} (Y_i - \overline{Y}_T)^2 \tag{2.58}$$

is the residual or unaccounted for variation. The equivalent of $(1 - r_{YX}^2)$ in correlation analysis is thus given by formula (2.58), whereas formula (2.57) presents an equivalent to the squared correlation coefficient, r_{YX}^2.

Applying these formulae to the data of Table 2.2 produces

$\sum (Y_{iF} - \overline{Y}_F)^2 = 945 \cdot 46$

$\sum (Y_{iS} - \overline{Y}_S)^2 = 1036 \cdot 10$

$\sum (Y_{iL} - \overline{Y}_L)^2 = 1219 \cdot 44$

(in all these cases summation is over the relevant group memberships only), so that

$$\sum_{i=1}^{N} (Y_i - \overline{Y}_G)^2 = 3201 \cdot 00$$

which is the within-groups variation.

$$\sum_{i=1}^{N} (Y_i - \overline{Y}_T)^2 = 6038 \cdot 02$$

is the total variation, so that between groups variation is $(6038 \cdot 02 - 3201 \cdot 00) = 2837 \cdot 02$. The ratio of between groups to total variation is then $2837 \cdot 02/6038 \cdot 02 = 0 \cdot 47$, indicating that 47% of the variation in *per capita* expenditure on education among towns can be accounted for statistically by the political party of their government: this is equivalent to a product moment correlation coefficient of 0·686 (i.e. 0·47 = 0·686^2).

Variance estimation and the F-test

Snedecor's ratio was introduced in the section on significance testing in correlation as a means of enquiring whether an observed relationship in a sample was likely to occur in its parent population. The same ratio, which is based on variance estimates, can be used in the present situation.

To compute the F-ratio the variation components must be standardised according to the degrees of freedom involved in their estimation. For the total variation, based on $\overline{Y}_T$, one degree of freedom is lost in calculating the mean, so $df_T = N - 1$. For between groups variation, the degrees of freedom are the number of groups less one for the calculation of the total mean from them, so if the number of groups is K, $df_B = K - 1$. Finally, within groups one degree of freedom is lost in the calculation of each group mean, so $df_W = N - K$. For the data from Table 2.2 we then get:

Component	Variation	Degrees of freedom	Variance estimate
Between groups	2837·02	K − 1 = 2	1418·51
Within groups	3201·00	N − K = 47	68·11
Total	6038·02	N − 1 = 49	

The formula for the F ratio is

$$F = \frac{\text{Between-groups variance estimate}}{\text{Within-groups variance estimate}} \qquad (2.59)$$

which for our example is

1418·51/68·11 = 20·83

Checking in the tables of the F distribution (as in Blalock, 1960, pp. 453–5) shows that for 2 and 47 degrees of freedom a value of 20·83 would occur less frequently than once in 1000 random samples (i.e. of all the possible allocations of the 50 towns to three groups of 17, 17, and 16, less than 1 in 1000 would give an F-ratio this large). We could conclude, therefore, that the differences between the three groups did not occur because of sampling error and that their three means are almost certainly not equal in the parent population.

As has been stressed already in this chapter, significance tests are designed to allow inferences to be made about populations when the data being analysed refer to a properly-taken random sample. But the F-ratio may be used by researchers not using sample data, as a check on the validity of the classification which forms their independent variable. The argument in parentheses in the previous paragraph indicates what it is that the F-ratio tests in such circumstances and it could be argued that its use allows a researcher to decide whether the division of his data into groups has produced a between/within-groups separation of the variance which is unlikely to have occurred with a random allocation. The 'proportion of variation accounted for' statistic − formula (2.57) − provides a similar type of service, however, without involving any of the problems of statistical inference.

Assumptions of the analysis of variance procedure

Like correlation and regression analysis, the analysis of variance is based on certain assumptions about the data, in addition to those concerned with the relationships between samples and populations.

1. *Normality*. As this test is based on the concept of variance, which is relevant to normal distributions only, then the data being analysed should fit this requirement. This applies not only to the total sample but also to each particular group, since the null hypothesis is that each group is a random sample from a normally-distributed population.

2. *Homoscedascity*. Following from the previous assumption, if it is assumed for the null hypothesis that each group is a random sample from a normally-distributed population, then it follows that each group should have the same variance, i.e. that the value of $\Sigma (Y_i - Y_G)^2/N_G$ should be the same. If this is not the case, then a biased estimate of the F-ratio will be produced, in exactly the same way as a heteroscedastic distribution of residuals from regression can lead to biased regression coefficients. It may be that, again as for regression, the values of Y should be transformed − base 10 logarithms are widely preferred − in order to meet this requirement.

3. *Group size*. In analysis of variance, if one group is much larger than another, this could lead to a biased interpretation of the importance of the independent variable. In our example, instead of 16 towns in the socialist class, let us suppose that there were 32 and that each of the original 16 were duplicated by an extra representative in the expanded group with the same value of Y. The group means would remain the same (p. 53) but the variation components would be

$$\Sigma (Y_{iF} - \overline{Y}_F)^2 = 945 \cdot 46$$

$$\Sigma (Y_{iS} - \overline{Y}_S)^2 = 2072 \cdot 20$$

$$\Sigma (Y_{iL} - \overline{Y}_L)^2 = 1219 \cdot 44$$

giving as the within-groups variation

$$\sum_{i=1}^{N} (Y_i - \overline{Y}_G)^2 = 4237 \cdot 10$$

The total variation would be

$$\sum_{i=1}^{N} (Y_i - \overline{Y}_T)^2 = 8488.82$$

and the between-groups variation

$$\sum_{i=1}^{N} (\overline{Y}_G - \overline{Y}_T)^2 = 4234.6$$

From this, the ratio of between to total variation would indicate a 'correlation equivalent' of 0.707, compared with 0.686 in the original data, and an F-ratio of 32.85 compared with 20.76.

As descriptive devices, the 'correlation equivalent' and the F-ratio faithfully portray the differences between the groups. In the case of twice as many socialist towns as before, therefore, the higher values merely indicate the clear-cut differences between the groups. But if the data are samples, unequal representation of the different groups in the population can, *ceteris paribus*, lead to biased estimates of the differences within the population.

Summary

This has been a long chapter, about bivariate analyses and not about multivariate analyses, which are the focus of the book. For many readers, much of the subject matter dealt with here may not have been new. The multivariate methods to be discussed in the rest of the book are all based on the concepts introduced here, however, and these concepts are most readily described for the bivariate case. Hence the lengthy introductory revision.

One final comment may be in order. All of the analyses discussed, both in this chapter and in the rest of the book, assume certain features about the data being studied. What if these assumptions are not met? If they are not, then the analysis is at worst completely invalid and at best it is providing but a biased estimate of the real answer to the question. If research is a search for 'objective truth', then one should not employ methods which are bound to tell only half-truths. But how do we know if the assumptions are met? Clearly the normal distribution and the straight line relationship are ideals and slight deviations from them are not going to produce major biases in results. There is, then, some subjective judgement involved in deciding whether a particular data set should be analysed in a particular way; the best advice is to be cautious and conservative.

Chapter 3

Multiple correlation and regression

The world is a complex place. Very few of its patterns can be described or accounted for by a single independent variable. In our example of education spending used in the previous chapter, only 46·65% of the variance in Y could be accounted for by its statistical relationship with the independent variable expressing educational need, and a similar percentage was associated with the analysis of variance based on a division of the towns into three groups according to their political affiliations. Thus we have to think in terms of multiple causation, or patterns in the dependent variable resulting from the influence of several separate independents. Analysis of such multiple causation by regression and correlation methods is the focus of this chapter; the following one deals with multivariate analyses of variance.

Partial and multiple correlation

Regression analysis of the data in Table 2.1 produced an equation accounting for 46·65% of the variance in Y by the variance in X. (From now on, because we are discussing more than one independent variable, this first one — percentage aged between 5 and 21 — will be termed X_1.) To improve on this statistical explanation we might seek other relevant independent variables. One which suggests itself is the relative affluence of the towns; richer communities should be able to afford greater spending on education. To index this new variable we define X_2 as the *per capita* value of property in the town, in hundreds of pounds: the data are given in Table 3.1. The dependent variable is the same, but in multiple regression is conventionally termed X_0 not Y, and the independents $X_1 X_2 X_3 \ldots X_n$.

Regressing X_0 on X_2 we get

$$X_0 = 21 \cdot 02 + 0 \cdot 594\ X_2 \pm 8 \cdot 68 \quad r_{02} = 0 \cdot 592$$

which suggests that 40·07% of the variance in education spending is a function of the affluence of the town. We already know that

$$X_0 = 22 \cdot 50 + 0 \cdot 691 X_1 \pm 8 \cdot 19 \quad r_{01} = 0 \cdot 683$$

Together, these two equations suggest that X_1 and X_2 account for (34·93 + 46·65) = 81·58% of the variation in X_0. But another regression equation

$$X_2 = 31 \cdot 01 + 0 \cdot 485 X_1 \quad r_{21} = 0 \cdot 475$$

Table 3.1 Educational needs and spending: hypothetical data

Town	Variable* X_0	X_1	X_2	Town	Variable X_0	X_1	X_2
1	27	17	44	26	40	39	37
2	64	42	45	27	60	64	63
3	52	49	66	28	64	50	45
4	59	35	64	29	51	41	58
5	77	69	74	30	36	42	28
6	54	48	47	31	47	37	48
7	50	34	52	32	38	51	35
8	48	43	48	33	44	54	61
9	49	39	53	34	31	27	42
10	72	56	69	35	66	52	58
11	52	38	54	36	69	59	78
12	62	44	40	37	42	33	44
13	50	44	50	38	43	27	33
14	50	57	74	39	60	33	53
15	40	36	60	40	46	31	39
16	34	22	46	41	46	49	55
17	57	47	51	42	52	42	48
18	70	62	59	43	46	40	43
19	50	45	41	44	58	49	48
20	54	36	52	45	58	42	55
21	45	48	33	46	40	29	45
22	68	50	68	47	55	43	64
23	45	30	52	48	63	53	60
24	58	44	56	49	59	39	52
25	36	24	52	50	56	33	53

*X_0 = *per capita* expenditure on education
X_1 = percentage of the population aged between 5 and 21
X_2 = *per capita* value of property

indicates that 22·56% of the variance in X_2 is related to the variance in X_1. By regressing X_0 on X_2, therefore, we are in part regressing it on X_1, since part of X_2 is related to X_1. Thus the correlations r_{01} and r_{02} are not independent of each other and we cannot isolate either what portion of the variance in X_0 is associated with X_1 and X_2 separately or what portion of the variance in X_0 is associated with both X_1 and X_2. Our calculation above that together X_1 and X_2 account for 81·58% of the variance in X_0 is wrong, since it involves some double counting (i.e. the effect of X_1 is in the correlation r_{02} and that of X_2 is in the correlation r_{01}; the actual joint 'explanation', using the methods outlined below, is 56·2%). To avoid such problems, and to enable a full evaluation of the relative influence of the independent variables, we use the techniques of partial and multiple correlation.

Partial correlation

Partial correlation analysis is an analyst's answer to the problems of not being able to conduct a controlled experiment, which is almost always the case in geographical work. For example, we may hypothesise that the spatial variance in crop yields (X_0) over a sample of wheat farms in an American state is related to the spatial variance in both rainfall amount (X_1) and sunshine hours (X_2) during the growing season. Clearly it would not be possible to find either (1) a random sample of farms with the same rainfall, so that we could study the independent influence of sunshine hours, or (2) a random sample of farms with the same sunshine hours so that we could study the independent influence of rainfall. Partial correlation analysis handles the data in such a way, however, that we can identify the effect of one variable, *as if the other were not there*. (This is known as holding the latter variable constant.)

The partial correlation coefficient $r_{01\cdot23-n}$ indicates that this is the correlation between the dependent variable (X_0) and one independent (X_1), holding constant the effects of other specified independent variables (X_2, X_3 and all others to X_n). Any number of independent variables can be held constant; they are listed after the point in the subscript. Of the two before the point, the first is the dependent variable and the second is the 'active' independent, that being studied.

In a partial correlation analysis, the effect of variables being held constant is removed from both the dependent and the 'active' independent. Thus $r_{01\cdot2}$ indicates the correlation between X_0 and X_1 having removed the effects of both the relationship $X_0 = f(X_2)$ and the similar relationship $X_1 = f(X_2)$. These removals are undertaken by regressing X_0 on X_2 and X_1 on X_2 and then regressing the residuals from these two analyses on each other.

The data in Table 3.2 are used to illustrate this procedure. We have three variables:

X_0 is the percentage of the workforce employed in offices;

X_1 is the population of the town, in thousands; and

X_2 is the percentage of the women aged 16–25 who are unmarried;

Table 3.2   Urban size, female labour force and office employment: hypothetical data

Town	Variable* X_0	X_1	X_2	Town	Variable* X_0	X_1	X_2
1	12	45	58	9	7	12	55
2	9	40	61	10	13	34	47
3	16	47	68	11	21	68	73
4	15	62	62	12	4	25	49
5	9	36	42	13	13	44	58
5	5	38	50	14	12	50	50
7	14	58	53	15	18	75	62
8	10	28	57	16	17	55	69

*X_0 = percentage of the workforce employed in offices
 X_1 = population (in thousands)
 X_2 = percentage of the women aged 16–25 who are unmarried

Data on these have been collected for a sample of 16 towns, to test the hypotheses that office employment is most important in the largest towns and also in those towns with a relatively large supply of unmarried female labour.

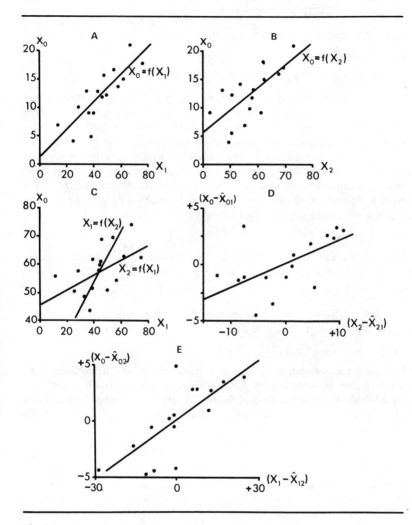

Fig. 3.1 Computing the partial regression coefficients for the regression of $X_0 = f(X_1, X_2)$ for the data of Table 3.2, showing the various regression and partial regression relationships.

The general validity of the two hypotheses is shown by the equations (Fig. 3.1A and B)

$$X_0 = 1·612 + 0·236X_1 \pm 2·748 \quad r_{01} = 0·826$$

and

$$X_0 = -10.34 + 0.394X_2 \pm 3.406 \quad r_{02} = 0.715$$

But the two independent variables are themselves interrelated, as indicated by the regressions (Fig. 3.1C)

$$X_1 = -15.525 + 1.056X_2 \pm 14.260 \quad r_{12} = 0.548$$

and

$$X_2 = 44.383 + 0.284X_1 \pm 7.400 \quad r_{21} = 0.548$$

Thus part of the correlation between X_0 and X_1 is a function of the correlations between both of them and X_2, so that we cannot identify the independent influence of urban size (X_1) on office employment (X_0), assuming that all towns have the same relative availability of female labour.

Computing partial correlation coefficients involves taking the absolute residual — formula (2.23) — from the regression of the dependent and the 'active' independent on the independents being held constant, and then correlating these residuals. For the partial correlation $r_{02 \cdot 1}$, therefore, the dependent variable is $(X_0 - \hat{X}_{01})$ where

$$\hat{X}_{01} = a_{01} + b_{01}X_1 \pm \epsilon \tag{3.1}$$

in which $\hat{X}_{01}$ is the value of X_0 estimated from the regression of X_0 on X_1 and the independent variable is $(X_2 - \hat{X}_{21})$ where

$$\hat{X}_{21} = a_{21} + b_{21}X_1 \pm \epsilon \tag{3.2}$$

in which $\hat{X}_{21}$ is the value of X_2 estimated from the regression of X_2 on X_1. These two sets of residuals are then regressed against each other

$$(X_0 - \hat{X}_{01}) = a_{02 \cdot 1} + b_{02 \cdot 1} (X_2 - \hat{X}_{21}) \pm \epsilon \tag{3.3}$$

for which the correlation is $r_{02 \cdot 1}$. This regression relates the variance in X_0 which is not associated with X_1 to the variance in X_2 which is not associated with X_1. For the data of Table 3.2, and first fitting the equations relating to the diagrams in Figs. 3.1A and B, we get Fig. 3.1D, with the equation

$$(X_0 - \hat{X}_{01}) = -0.004 + 0.207 (X_2 - \hat{X}_{21}) \quad r_{02 \cdot 1} = 0.555$$

The partial correlation indicates that of the variance in X_0 not associated with X_1, a portion — 0.308 (0.555^2) — is associated with the variance in X_2 not associated with X_1. If there were no variation in town size, therefore, the correlation between office employment and female labour supply would be 0.555. A similar regression equation can be computed for the relationship between X_0 and X_1, holding constant X_2 (Fig. 3.1E)

$$(X_0 - \hat{X}_{02}) = 0.017 + 0.177 (X_1 - \hat{X}_{12}) \quad r_{01 \cdot 2} = 0.742$$

Comparing the results of the simple correlation analyses with those of the partial correlations, produces

$$r_{01} = 0.826 \quad r_{01 \cdot 2} = 0.742$$

so that

$r_{01}^2 = 0.682 \qquad r_{01 \cdot 2}^2 = 0.550$

and

$r_{02} = 0.715 \qquad r_{02 \cdot 1} = 0.555$

so that

$r_{02}^2 = 0.465 \qquad r_{02 \cdot 1}^2 = 0.308$

Part of the original correlation between each of the independent variables and the dependent variable is a function of the inter-relationship between the two independents ($r_{12} = r_{21} = 0.548$; $r_{12}^2 = 0.300$). Once this inter-relationship has been controlled for, we find that city size (X_1) accounts for more than half of the variance in office employment rates not associated with female labour force supply, but that the latter variable accounts for less than a third of the variance remaining in X_0 once the effects of size have been removed.

The procedure outlined here for holding constant the effect of one independent variable can be extended to partial correlations involving several. Thus $r_{04 \cdot 235}$ would indicate the correlation of X_0 on X_4, with the effects of X_2, X_3, and X_5 having been held constant. This would involve regressing the residual variance in X_0 not associated with X_2, X_3, and X_5 against the residual variance in X_4 not associated with the same three variables. The interpretation of the partial correlation coefficient would remain the same. It indexes the correlation between two variables, when there is no variance in any of the other variables being held constant, and it can vary between $+1.0$ and -1.0, with the extreme values indicating complete correlation among the residuals.

Computation of partial correlation coefficients does not involve obtaining the relevant residuals and regressing them, although this is the meaning of the result. First-order partial correlation coefficients, those holding constant only one other independent variable, can be derived by the following formula, which involves use of the product moment, zero-order correlation coefficients:

$$r_{01 \cdot 2} = \frac{r_{01} - (r_{02})(r_{12})}{\sqrt{1 - r_{02}^2}\sqrt{1 - r_{12}^2}} \qquad (3.4)$$

and similar, though longer, formulae can be derived for partial coefficients with more than one independent variable being held constant.

Multiple correlation

Partial correlation coefficients indicate the strength of the relationship between two variables once the effects of others have been held constant; their squared values indicate the proportion of the residual variance in the dependent (i.e. that variance not associated with the variables held constant) which is associated with the residual variance in the independent variable. But what proportion of the total variance in the dependent variable can be accounted for by all of the independent variables together? Clearly it is not the sum of the squared zero-order correlations since, as indicated at the beginning of the chapter, this would involve double counting. For the example on office employment

$$r_{01}^2 = 0 \cdot 682 \text{ and } r_{02}^2 = 0 \cdot 465$$

and the sum of these would suggest the ludicrous result that $1 \cdot 147$ (or $114 \cdot 7\%$) of the variance in X_0 was 'explained' by the variance in X_1 and X_2!

The sum of the squared partial correlation coefficients does not provide the information on the total variance in X_0 associated with X_1 and X_2 either. In the example

$$r_{01 \cdot 2}^2 = 0 \cdot 550 \text{ and } r_{02 \cdot 1}^2 = 0 \cdot 308$$

but the former value relates to the variance in X_0 not associated with X_2 and the latter to the variance in X_0 not associated with X_1. Since X_1 and X_2 are correlated, some of the variance in X_0 is associated with the joint variance of X_1 and X_2, and this is omitted from the partial correlations.

The multiple correlation coefficient, R, indexes the strength of the relationship between a dependent and a set of independents. With subscripts, $R_{0 \cdot 12}$ indicates the multiple correlation between X_0 (before the point) and both X_1 and X_2 (after the point). $R_{0 \cdot 12}^2$ is the proportion of the variance of X_0 accounted for by the two independent variables, both jointly and separately.

$R_{0 \cdot 12}^2$ can be built up using the zero-order and partial correlation coefficients. In the example $r_{01}^2 = 0 \cdot 682$ leaving $(1 \cdot 0 - r_{01}^2) = 0 \cdot 318$ unaccounted for. The partial correlation $r_{02 \cdot 1}$ relates that proportion of the variance in X_0 not associated with X_1 to the similar proportion for X_2. Since

$$r_{02 \cdot 1}^2 = 0 \cdot 308$$

and

$$(1 \cdot 0 - r_{01}^2) = 0 \cdot 318$$

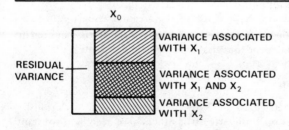

Fig. 3.2   Decomposition of the multiple correlation (R^2) into its various components.

then

$$(r_{02 \cdot 1}^2)(1 \cdot 0 - r_{01}^2) = (0 \cdot 308)(0 \cdot 318) = 0 \cdot 098$$

In other words, X_2 holding constant X_1 accounts for $0 \cdot 308$ of the variance in X_0 holding constant X_1. The latter value is $0 \cdot 318$; multiplied by the proportion explained we find that X_2 accounts for $0 \cdot 098$ of the total variance in X_0, or just under one-third of that not accounted for by X_1. Thus

$$R_{0 \cdot 12}^2 = r_{01}^2 + r_{02 \cdot 1}^2 (1 - r_{01}^2) \tag{3.5}$$
$$= 0 \cdot 682 + 0 \cdot 308 (0 \cdot 318) = 0 \cdot 682 + 0 \cdot 098 = 0 \cdot 78$$

and

$$R_{0 \cdot 12} = \sqrt{R_{0 \cdot 12}^2} = \sqrt{0 \cdot 78} = 0 \cdot 883 \tag{3.6}$$

The order in which the independent variables enter formula (3.5) is irrelevant; the same result would ensure from

$$R_{0 \cdot 12}^2 = r_{02}^2 + r_{01 \cdot 2}^2 (1 - r_{02}^2) \qquad \qquad \qquad \bullet \tag{3.7}$$

For three independent variables, another term would be added to formula (3.5) to cover the variance in X_0 not associated with either X_1 or X_2 and the related variance in X_3 not associated with the other two independents variables, viz.

$$R_{0 \cdot 123}^2 = r_{01}^2 + r_{02 \cdot 1}^2 (1 - r_{01}^2) + r_{03 \cdot 12}^2 [1 - (r_{01}^2 + r_{02 \cdot 1}^2 (1 - r_{01}^2))] \tag{3.8}$$

Why is the multiple correlation coefficient not equal to the sum of either the zero-order or the partial correlation coefficients? For the first, as we have seen, it is because of double counting; for the second it is because of the omission of the joint variance. Figure 3.2 illustrates this latter point. The variance in X_0 is represented by a square of a given size. Of this, $0 \cdot 78$ is associated with X_1 and X_2 ($R_{0 \cdot 12}^2 = 0 \cdot 78$), so that $0 \cdot 22$ remains as the residual variance. The relationships between X_0 and X_1 and X_2 within the explained variance are indicated $- r_{01}^2 = 0 \cdot 682$ so $0 \cdot 682$ of the total area is indicated by lower left to upper right cross-hatching and $r_{02}^2 = 0 \cdot 46$ so $0 \cdot 465$ of the total area is indicated by upper left to lower right cross-hatching. Inevitably, these two areas overlap. The area associated with X_1 but not X_2 is $0 \cdot 55$ of the area not associated with X_2 (i.e. the residual variance plus the area just nominated): $0 \cdot 550 = r_{01 \cdot 2}^2$. The area associated with X_2 but not X_1 is $0 \cdot 308$ of the area not associated with X_1 (i.e. the residual variance plus the area just nominated): $0 \cdot 308 = r_{02 \cdot 1}^2$. This leaves $0 \cdot 39$ of the variance of X_0 associated with X_1 and X_2 together. Thus half of the multiple correlation of X_0 on X_1 and X_2 is associated with their joint action ($0 \cdot 39/0 \cdot 78$), and cannot be attributed to either.

If the independent variables are themselves correlated, therefore, it is not possible to allocate all of the 'explained' variance of the dependent variable between them. The partial correlations relate only to those proportions of the variance which are not jointly accounted for. Thus for our example:

1. 78% of the variance in office employment percentages can be accounted for by urban size and female labour force supply;
2. 37% of this explained variance (29% of the total) can be accounted for by variations in urban size alone;
3. 13% of this explained variance (9·8% of the total) can be accounted for by variations in the supply of female labour alone; and
4. 50% of this explained variance (39% of the total) can be accounted for by the joint effects of size and female labour force supply, in that larger towns tend to have larger female labour forces.

Multiple and partial correlation: a summary

Multiple and partial correlation coefficients are very frequently used in reports of geographical research, as statements of the effects of independent variables on a given dependent. As such, like the zero-order correlation coefficients described in the previous chapter, they relate to straight-line trends only, for data which meet the requirements of the general linear model. The square of a multiple correlation coefficient — the multiple coefficient of determination — indicates the proportion of the variance in the dependent variable associated with all of the independent variables; the square of a partial correlation coefficient indicates the proportion of the variance in a dependent variable, excluding that associated with the other independent variables being analysed, which is associated with that portion of the variance of an independent variable also unassociated with the remaining independent variables. Not indexed is that proportion of the variance in the dependent variable which is associated with the joint effect of two or more independents.

As with zero-order correlation coefficients, multiple and partial correlations may be used to describe the goodness-of-fit to a linear trend, or they may be used to infer the probable relationships in a population from a properly-selected sample. For the latter purpose, Snedecor's-F test can be used, as described in Chapter 2 (p. 47), except that the degrees of freedom lost in producing the explained variance will be the number of independent variables, and not 1 — see formula (2.40). A statistically significant value of $R_{0\cdot 12}$ would indicate that a correlation with the observed sign almost certainly occurs in the population.

The multiple regression equation

The multiple correlation coefficient indexes the goodness-of-fit of an equation relating a dependent variable to a set of independent variables. Its general form is

$$X_0 = a_{0\cdot 1} - n + \sum_{i=1}^{n} b_{oi\cdot -n} X_i \pm \epsilon \qquad (3.9)$$

so that for a two-independent variable analysis, such as that using the data of Table 3.2, the multiple regression equation would be

$$\hat{X}_{0 \cdot 12} = a_{0 \cdot 12} + b_{01 \cdot 2} X_1 + b_{02 \cdot 1} X_2 \pm \epsilon \qquad (3.10)$$

where $a_{0 \cdot 12}$ is the intercept value – the value of X_0 when $X_1 = X_2 = 0$

$b_{01 \cdot 2}$, $b_{02 \cdot 1}$ are the partial regression coefficients, indicating the slopes of the relationships between X_0 and X_1 and X_2 respectively, with the other variable held constant;
ϵ is the error term; and
$\hat{X}_{0 \cdot 12}$ is the estimated value of X_0 from its regression on X_1 and X_2, according to the function $X_0 = f(X_1, X_2)$.

In an example of a multiple regression equation in which the independent variables are uncorrelated, or virtually so (see below, p. 74), most of the parameters of the equation in (3.10) are provided by the derivation of the partial correlation coefficients. The values of the regression coefficients, $b_{01 \cdot 2}$ and $b_{02 \cdot 1}$, are those of the regressions relating the sets of residuals, which are shown in Fig. 3.1D and E and reported above (p. 63). These are termed partial regression coefficients, since they represent the slope of the relationship between the two nominated variables – X_0 and X_1 in the case of $b_{01 \cdot 2}$ – when others – X_2 in this case – have been held constant or 'partialled out'. Thus we have the equations

$$(X_0 - \hat{X}_{02}) = 0 \cdot 017 + 0 \cdot 177 (X_1 - \hat{X}_{12}) \qquad r_{01 \cdot 2} = 0 \cdot 742$$
$$(X_0 - \hat{X}_{01}) = -0 \cdot 004 + 0 \cdot 207 (X_2 - \hat{X}_{21}) \qquad r_{02 \cdot 1} = 0 \cdot 555$$

which form the input to formula (3.10)

$$\hat{X}_{0 \cdot 12} = a_{0 \cdot 12} + 0 \cdot 177 X_1 + 0 \cdot 207 X_2 \pm \epsilon \qquad R_{0 \cdot 12} = 0 \cdot 883$$

To complete this equation the values of $a_{0 \cdot 12}$ and of ϵ (which is the same as the Standard Error of X_0) have to be calculated. The intercept value is derived by a direct extension of the formula used in simple regression – formula (2.13) – based on the rule that the plane of the relationship between X_0 and X_1 plus X_2 (i.e. in a three-dimensional diagram with X_0, X_1 and X_2 forming the axes) passes through $\overline{X}_0$, $\overline{X}_1$, and $\overline{X}_2$. Thus, from (2.13)

$$a_{0 \cdot 1-n} = \overline{X}_0 - \sum_{i=1}^{n} b_{0i. -n} \overline{X}_i \qquad (3.11)$$

where summation is over the n independent variables.

In the present example, with n = 2

$$a_{0 \cdot 12} = \overline{X}_0 - b_{01 \cdot 2} \overline{X}_1 - b_{02 \cdot 1} \overline{X}_2 \qquad (3.12)$$
$$= 12 \cdot 19 - 0 \cdot 177 (44 \cdot 81) - 0 \cdot 207 (57 \cdot 13)$$
$$= 12 \cdot 19 - 7 \cdot 93 - 11 \cdot 83 = -7 \cdot 57$$

This value of a is not directly interpretable, since a negative percentage in office employment is not possible (nor, of course, is a zero population — X_1 — and a nil percentage of unmarried females aged 16–25 is extremely unlikely). It does indicate, however, that office employment is absent from both small towns and towns with few potential female employees. We can estimate the population size necessary for office employment to appear, for given levels of female labour supply. Thus, if $X_2 = 10$ and we want to know when $X_0 \neq$ a negative number, so X_0 is set at 1·0 and

$$1·0 = -7·57 + 0·177X_1 + 0·207 (10·0)$$

$$0·177X_1 = 1·0 + 7.57 - 0·207 (10·0)$$

$$= 8·57 - 2·07 = 6·50$$

$$X_1 = 6·50/0·177 = 36·72$$

With a set female labour force (10% of all women aged 16–25 are unmarried), therefore, it will require a town of nearly 37 000 people before office employment is introduced, according to conditions in our sample of 16 towns.

Finally, we estimate the error term for formula (3.10) using the same equation as before — formula (2.28) —

$$SE_{X_0} = S_{X_0} (\sqrt{1·0 - R^2_{0·12} - n}) \qquad (3.13)$$

which in our example is

$$SE_{X_0} = 4·707 (\sqrt{1·0 - 0·883^2})$$

$$= 4·707 (\sqrt{0·22}) = 4·707 (0·469) = 2·208$$

We now have the complete regression equation,

$$\hat{X}_{0·12} = -7·57 + 0·177X_1 + 0·207X_2 \pm 2·208 \quad R_{0·12} = 0·883$$

into which we can substitute values of X_1 and X_2 to estimate X_0. For a town of 80 000 people, with 30% of the females aged 16–25 unmarried, the estimate of the percentage of the workforce in office employment is

$$\hat{X}_{0·12} = -7·57 + 0·177 (80) + 0·207 (30) \pm 2·208$$

$$= -7·57 + 14·16 + 6·21 \pm 2·208 = 12·8 \pm 2·208$$

Thus 68% of towns with those values of X_1 and X_2 should have an office percentage between 10·592 and 15·008. For prediction purposes involving towns not in the original sample, of course, we would have to determine the standard error of the forecast (p. 49).

The procedure outlined here for obtaining partial regression coefficients by regression of one set of residuals on another illustrates the interpretation of those coefficients rather than their derivation for most analyses; the usual way of obtaining them involves the solution of a set of simultaneous equations (see Yeates, 1974, pp. 103–4). For the data set analysed, the conclusions to be drawn are:

1. That at any given level of X_2 (i.e. holding X_2 — the percentage of

women aged 16—25 who are unmarried — constant), for every increase in town size, X_1, of one unit (= 1000 people) the office component to the work force increases by 0·177 percentage points;

2. That at any given level of X_1 (i.e. holding town size constant), for every increase of one percentage point in the number of unmarried women in the 16—25 age group the office component in the workforce increases by 0·207 percentage points; and

3. That together X_1 and X_2 account for 78% of the variance in the size of the office component — X_0 — over the 16 towns, with half of this percentage resulting from their joint influence and the other half divided between their separate influences.

The existence of a joint influence component to the statistical explanation of the variance in the dependent variable can hamper interpretation of the partial regression coefficients, because it is not incorporated in either of the partial regression coefficients. The nature and extent of this problem are discussed in more detail in the later section on collinearity (p. 74).

Standardised partial regression coefficients

A partial regression coefficient, $b_{01\cdot2}$, indicates the absolute increase in X_0 associated with a one unit increase in X_1, the effect of X_2 on both having been held constant. Comparison of b coefficients is often difficult, however, because the independent variables to which they refer are scaled in different metrics. In the example being used here, X_1 is measured in thousands of people and X_2 in percentage points and so it is not possible to say whether $b_{01\cdot2} = 0·177$ indicates a more rapid rate of change, or a relatively steeper slope, than does $b_{02\cdot1} = 0·207$. Such an indication of relative rates of change may be desirable; it can be obtained by transforming the b coefficients into beta (β) coefficients, which are standardised partial regression coefficients.

To show comparable rates of change, all of the variables must be measured on the same scale. That used is the normal curve, on which individual values are expressed as Z scores, where

$$Z_{X_i} = (X_i - \overline{X})/S_X \tag{3.14}$$

If the variables are all normally distributed, with $\overline{X}_i = 0$ and $S_{X_i} = 1·0$, then they are comparable, in that a change of one unit (the standard deviation unit) in one is equal to a similar change in any other.

With the transformation, the regression equation now reads

$$\hat{Z}_{X_{0\cdot1}-n} = a_{0\cdot1}-n + \sum_{i=1}^{n} \beta_{oi\cdot}-n Z_{X_i} \pm \epsilon \tag{3.15}$$

and as we are dealing with Z scores, the mean of every variable is 0·0, so $a_{0\cdot1}-n = 0·0$ — formula (3.11) — and the residual variance (ϵ) is 1·0, leaving

$$\hat{Z}_{X_{0 \cdot 1 - n}} = \sum_{i = 1}^{n} \beta_{oi. - n} Z_{X_i} \qquad (3.16)$$

For the office employment data this reads

$$\hat{Z}_{X_{0 \cdot 12}} = 0 \cdot 619 Z_{X_1} + 0 \cdot 376 Z_{X_2}$$

In relative terms, therefore, X_0 increases at a greater rate with a given rate of increase in X_1 than at the same rate of increase in X_2. This apparently contradicts the b coefficients of $0 \cdot 177$ and $0 \cdot 207$ respectively, but the reversal occurs because of the greater variance in X_1 ($S_{X_1}^2 = 271 \cdot 26$; $S_{X_2}^2 = 73 \cdot 10$).

Standardised partial regression coefficients, or *beta weights*, thus indicate relative changes in variables on a standard scale. They are obtained as a standardising of the b coefficient by the ratio of the standard deviations of the two variables.

$$\beta_{01 \cdot 2} = b_{01 \cdot 2} \frac{S_{X_1}}{S_{X_2}} \qquad (3.17)$$

Whether b or β is used depends on the aim of the analysis, whether it focuses on absolute or relative changes. One final point to be noted about them is that they should not be confused with the β coefficient introduced in Chapter 2 — formula (2.36) — that represents the true value of b in a population: unfortunately, the standard notation is ambiguous here.

Multiple regression has been used very widely in geographical research, and many examples can be found in the literature of the period since 1955, covering all aspects of geography. Greer-Wootten (1972) has provided a large bibliography, and several examples are quoted in later sections of the chapter.

Significance testing for regression coefficients

If the data being used comprise a properly-taken sample from a specified population, then the researcher may want to know whether the observed parameters of the regression equation are likely to have the same sign, and perhaps magnitude as well, in the population. As with bivariate analyses, the validity of such an inference is usually assessed by the Student's-t test, formula (2.43), which expresses the difference between the observed value of b and an assumed value of $\bar{b} = 0$, as a ratio of its standard error. The latter is computed — see also formula (2.42) — as

$$SE_{b_{01 \cdot 2 - n}} = \frac{SE_{0 \cdot 2 - n}}{SE_{1 \cdot 2 - n} \sqrt{N - 2}} \qquad (3.18)$$

where $SE_{0 \cdot 2 - n}$ is the standard error in the dependent variable, X_0, after the effects of all the variables being held constant ($X_2 - X_n$) have been removed;

$SE_{1 \cdot 2 - n}$ is the standard error of the independent variable, X_1, after the effects of all the variables being held constant $(X_2 - X_n)$ have been removed;

$SE_{b_{01 \cdot 2 - n}}$ is the standard error of the partial regression coefficient, $b_{01 \cdot 2 - n}$;

n is the number of independent variables; and

N is the number of observations.

In effect, the numerator of formula (3.18) is the standard error of the dependent variable in Fig. 3.1 and the denominator is the standard error of the independent variable.

For the data in Table 3.2, the standard errors are:

$$SE_{b_{01 \cdot 2}} = \frac{2 \cdot 75}{14 \cdot 26 \sqrt{16 - 2}} = \frac{2 \cdot 75}{(14 \cdot 26)(3 \cdot 74)} = 0 \cdot 052$$

$$SE_{b_{02 \cdot 1}} = \frac{3 \cdot 41}{7 \cdot 40 \sqrt{16 - 2}} = \frac{3 \cdot 41}{(7 \cdot 40)(3 \cdot 74)} = 0 \cdot 123$$

The t-ratios are obtained using the formula

$$t_{b_{01 \cdot 2 - n}} = \frac{b_{01 \cdot 2 - n}}{SE_{b_{01 \cdot 2 - n}}} \tag{3.19}$$

and for the office employment data of Table 3.2 are

$$t_{b_{01 \cdot 2}} = 0 \cdot 177 / 0 \cdot 052 = 3 \cdot 404$$

$$t_{b_{02 \cdot 1}} = 0 \cdot 207 / 0 \cdot 123 = 1 \cdot 683$$

Using the tabulated values of t with 14 degrees of freedom, for a one-tailed test the coefficient $b_{01 \cdot 2}$ is significant at the $0 \cdot 05$ level but $b_{02 \cdot 1}$ is only significant at the $0 \cdot 10$ level. Thus our hypothesised positive relationship between urban size (X_1) and office employment (X_0), holding X_2 constant, almost certainly occurs in the population, but the hypothesised positive relationship between female labour supply (X_2) and X_0, holding X_1 constant, is much less likely to be present there, and could have been observed in our sample as a result of chance ordering of the data.

In a full report of a regression equation, the t values are often given in parentheses under the regression coefficients:

$$X_{0 \cdot 12} = -7 \cdot 57 + 0 \cdot 177 X_1 + 0 \cdot 207 X_2 \pm 2 \cdot 208$$
$$(3 \cdot 404) \quad (1 \cdot 683)$$

Even if the regression does not refer to sample data, the t values may be reported, on the argument that they indicate the relative strength of a relationship. The t value is the ratio of a b coefficient to its standard error, and therefore indicates the relative scatter of points around a regression line, so that even if no inference to a population is being made, the t value does give some suggestion of the accuracy of the partial regression line (as in Fig. 3.1E) as a fit to the data points.

As indicated in Chapter 2, significance tests can be conducted on the a and R coefficients, but these are rarely reported. Also rarely reported, but potentially of considerable value, are tests which enquire not whether $b < 0 <$ in the population but whether, for example, $b > 1.0$ (see p. 49).

The assumptions of the multiple regression equation

The parameters of regression equations are valid for predictive purposes only when they refer to data collected from properly-taken samples out of a specified population; they are also valid for either predictive or descriptive purposes only when they refer to data which meet the requirements of the general linear model. Thus all six of the assumptions discussed in Chapter 2 must be met (p. 37 ff.). For each relationship, i.e. in our example, between X_1 and X_2, X_0 and X_1, X_0 and X_2, between $(X_0 - \hat{X}_{01})$ and $(X_2 - \hat{X}_{21})$ – formula (3.3) – and between $(X_0 - \hat{X}_{02})$ and $(X_1 - \hat{X}_{12})$: (1) the trend in the scatter of points should be linear; (2) the conditional distributions of the residuals of the dependent variables should have zero means and constant variances; (3) there should be no autocorrelation among the residuals; and (4) all variables should be measured without sampling error.

Testing the validity of all these assumptions is a major task, especially if the multiple regression equation contains a considerable number of independent variables. Further, it is not clear to what degree they can be violated, before the results are made completely uninterpretable. From published reports, most researchers appear to be satisfied if the relationships they are portraying are approximately linear and if each variable has a marginal distribution which is approximately normal. (No definition of approximate is given in many cases; some test for both, e.g. Thomas, 1960.) The assumption is that if these criteria are met, the more rigorous actual demands of the model probably will be.

Collinearity

In addition to the six assumptions which relate also to bivariate regression, there is a seventh which must be met in the multivariate case. This is that the residuals from each partial regression equation (e.g. those of Figs. 3.1D and E) are uncorrelated. Most researchers treat this requirement as saying that the independent variables themselves should be uncorrelated: if they are not, *collinearity* is said to exist.

Collinearity leads to biased and often difficult to interpret estimates of partial regression coefficients and their standard errors. Figure 3.3 gives an example of this, in which a dependent variable, X_0, is being regressed on two independents, X_1 and X_2. The relationships between each of the latter and X_0 are both strong and positive (Fig. 3.3B and C), with equations

$$X_0 = 4.74 + 0.63X_1 \pm 1.19 \qquad r_{01} = 0.862$$
$$(2.52)$$

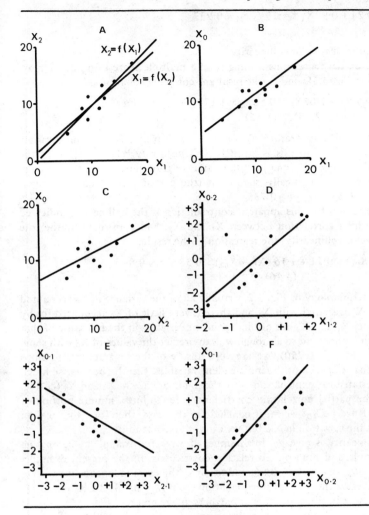

Fig. 3.3   The problem of collinearity in the regression $X_0 = f(X_1, X_2)$, showing the various regression and partial regression relationships.

$$X_0 = 6 \cdot 04 + 0 \cdot 51 X_2 \pm 1 \cdot 63 \qquad r_{02} = 0 \cdot 719$$
$$(2 \cdot 13)$$

In both cases the t value indicates that, if the eleven observations are a random sample, a similar trend very probably exists in the parent population. X_1 and X_2 are themselves very closely related, however (Fig. 3.3A)

$$X_1 = 1 \cdot 05 + 0 \cdot 91 X_2 \pm 1 \cdot 12 \qquad r_{12} = 0 \cdot 937$$
$$(2 \cdot 85)$$

$$X_2 = 0.24 + 0.97X_1 \pm 1.15 \qquad r_{21} = 0.937$$
$$(2.84)$$

which is indicative of collinearity.

The partial regressions leading to the multiple regression equation are shown in Fig. 3.3D and E: the resultant complete equation is

$$X_{0.12} = 5.93 + 1.07X_1 - 0.56X_2 \pm 1.17 \qquad R_{0.12} = 0.866$$
$$(2.55) \quad (1.56)$$

The most obvious feature of this concerns variable X_2. In the bivariate regression equation this is strongly and *positively* related to X_0; in the multiple regression equation, the same relationship is *negative*, though probably not statistically significant (the partial correlation coefficient, $r_{02.1}$, is -0.530; $r_{01.2} = +0.735$).

The reason for this apparent contradiction is the collinearity indicated by the high correlation between X_1 and X_2, and confirmed by the true measure of collinearity, the regression of the residuals (Fig. 3.3F)

$$(X_0 - \hat{X}_{01}) = 0.11 + 1.16 (X_0 - \hat{X}_{02}) \pm 0.58 \qquad r = 0.890$$
$$(4.46)$$

In the terminology of Fig. 3.2, virtually all of the variance in X_0 accounted for by X_2 is shared with X_1 and there is very little of X_0 accounted for by X_2 alone. X_1 and X_2 are not independent variables in the full sense of that term, therefore, and so although we can predict the values of X_0 with some success ($R^2_{0.12} = 0.750$), we are very unsure of the separate relationships between it and each of the independent variables. Clearly, because so much of the statistical explanation is by the joint variance of X_1 and X_2 (cf. Fig. 3.2), the partial correlation coefficients refer to but a minute portion of the variance of X_0; we must conclude in this case, therefore, that we can predict the variation in X_0, but we cannot understand it.

Collinearity is revealed in a number of ways, for example by comparing the simple and multiple correlation coefficients. In the present example, $r_{01} = 0.862$ and $R_{0.12} = 0.866$; addition of the extra independent variable, X_2, increases the statistical explanation from $r^2_{01} = 0.743$ to $R^2_{0.12} = 0.75$, or by less than three-quarters of one percentage point.

If multiple regression equations are to be interpretable, collinearity clearly should not be accepted. Several methods exist for making the independent variables uncorrelated, or orthogonal (see Ch. 5, p. 155 ff.), or alternatively some of the variables may be omitted, as by the stepwise regression procedure — see below (p. 84). As with the other assumptions of the model, however, there are problems in knowing whether collinearity is sufficiently large to impede interpretation of the regression equation. There is clearly quite considerable collinearity in the data of Fig. 3.1, for example, as indicated by the joint variance element in Fig. 3.2, and this means that the simple and partial regression coefficients differ, viz.:

$$b_{01} = 0.236 \quad \text{but} \quad b_{01.2} = 0.177; \text{ and}$$
$$b_{02} = 0.394 \quad \text{but} \quad b_{02.1} = 0.207$$

Such changes are not as marked as those shown earlier in this section. They come about because the residual variance in X_0 to be accounted for by X_2, for example, excludes that portion also associated with X_1. In this case, the consequence is a less steep regression line but, as we have seen, if nearly all of the variance in X_0 associated with X_2 is also associated with X_1, the slope of the partial regression of X_0 on X_2 could well have the opposite sign to that of the simple regression between the same two variables, because there is so little variance — other than perhaps some random error — in X_2 left to account for that in X_0 once the effect of X_1 has been held constant. The reason for this can be seen by referring back to Fig. 2.6. If the independent variables were unrelated, then the regression of X_1 on X_2 (and vice versa) would have the form shown in diagram A there; with a nil correlation, the regression line would run parallel with the horizontal axis and along the mean of the dependent variable; the residuals would be the total variance in the latter. If the two independent variables were related, however, then diagram B would be relevant. Some of the variance in the dependent variable would be lost when it became an independent variable in the partial regression, and the closer the correlation between X_1 and X_2, the more likely that this residual variance is random with respect to the association with X_0.

In regression equations involving collinear independent variables, therefore, the partial regression coefficients refer only to the residual variance in the relevant variables when all others have been held constant. As a consequence, one or more of them may be reported as statistically insignificant, despite the high overall multiple correlation. The equation may quite successfully estimate the different values of X_0, largely via the intercept ($a_{0 \cdot 1 - n}$), but the role of each independent variable in this estimation may be far from clear.

Data transformation

We saw in Chapter 2 how the assumptions of the simple regression model, particularly those of linearity and homoscedascity, can be met in many cases by transformation of the variables. Logarithmic transformation is the most popular, in multiple as well as simple regression equations. This allows proper use of the model, but may produce interpretative problems. If logarithmic transformations are used throughout, difficulties may not be too great. In his regression analyses of land values in Chicago, for example, Yeates (1965) reported that for 1960

$$\log_{10} X_0 = 3 \cdot 356 - 0 \cdot 173 \log_{10} X_1 - 0 \cdot 092 \log_{10} X_2 - 0 \cdot 146 \log_{10} X_3 -$$
$$0 \cdot 050 \log_{10} X_4 - 0 \cdot 137 \log_{10} X_5 - 0 \cdot 002 \log_{10} X_6 \qquad R = 0 \cdot 422$$

where X_0 is land value;

X_1 is distance (hundreds of feet) from the C.B.D.;

X_2 is distance (hundreds of feet) from the nearest regional shopping centre;

X_3 is distance (hundreds of feet) from the shores of Lake Michigan;
X_4 is distance (hundreds of feet) from the nearest subway system;
X_5 is population density; and
X_6 is percent non-white in the area.

For each of these, the negative partial regression coefficients indicate a decrease in land values, with greater distances from key points, with greater population densities, and with greater percentages of non-whites. Because the regression was on the logarithms of the variables, the larger the value of b, the more rapid the initial decline in values with distance from the relevant point; land values fall very rapidly immediately one moves away from the C.B.D. (X_1) or from the lakeshore (X_3), before levelling out, whereas the decline is much more gentle away from the subway (X_4).

Occasionally, transformation makes interpretation much more difficult. For example, King (1961) in a study of the determinants of the spacing of towns in the United States, used the following variables:

X_0 is the distance from a town to its nearest neighbour of the same size;

X_1 is the population of the town (hypothesised relationship—positive);

X_2 is the average size of farms around the town (hypothesised relationship—negative);

X_3 is the rural population density around the town (hypothesised relationship—negative);

X_4 is the proportion of the town's workforce employed in manufacturing (hypothesised relationship—negative, since manufacturing towns cluster for agglomeration economies);

X_5 is total population density, reflecting nearby towns in a metropolitan complex (hypothesised relationship—negative); and

X_6 is value of land per acre as an index of productivity (hypothesised relationship—negative).

All of these variables had non-normal distributions and were transformed to meet the assumptions of the regression model. The resulting equation was

$$\log X_0 = 28{\cdot}6 + 0{\cdot}13 \log X_1 - 0{\cdot}02 \log\log X_2 - 0{\cdot}14 \log X_3 - 0{\cdot}05 \arcsin X_4 -$$
$$- 0{\cdot}12 \log\log X_5 - 0{\cdot}10 \log X_6 \qquad R_{0{\cdot}123456} = 0{\cdot}50$$

in which only the regression coefficients for X_1 and X_5 were statistically significant (in part because of collinearity among the independents). Apart from it being very clear that the relationships are curvilinear, interpretation of these regression coefficients is difficult. For both X_2 and X_5, normalisation involved taking the logarithms of the logarithms, and it takes experimentation with numbers and log tables to show that where $\log X_0$ is negatively related to $\log\log X_2$ this indicates a very rapid decline in the value of X_0 for increasing values of X_2 close to zero, followed by virtually no change at all in X_0 as X_2 increases thereafter. An arcsin transformation (X_4) is generally used for angular measurements, but was used (probably in error) by King because his data for percentage employed in manufacturing had a U-shaped distribution.

With many equations, transformation of the data allows the linear regression model to be fitted, but makes detailed interpretation of the results difficult. Most transformations, especially those involving logarithms, indicate curvilinear relationships, but the nature of the curve is not always clear. Why, for example, is there such a steep curvilinear relationship between X_0 and X_5 in King's data? Thus multiple regression equations often throw up as many questions as they answer: all of the coefficients derived by King had the predicted signs, but can either the theory behind the hypotheses or the interpretation account for the form as well as the direction of the relationships?

Specific transformations. 1: Polynomials

Transformation is often required in order that the assumptions of the multiple regression model are met. In other situations, transformation is introduced for substantive theoretical reasons. It may be, for example, that a dependent variable is a function of not one but several aspects of the same independent variable.

Consider the relationship between urban size (X_1) and the percentage of the workforce in non-manufacturing occupations (X_0). Most small towns have very little manufacturing industry; their main functions are as minor central places and most of their employees are in the tertiary sector. In very large towns, too, the percentage in manufacturing is often low, as these are the important commercial, financial and political centres. Thus manufacturing is often strongest in medium-sized towns, where the tertiary sector is relatively weak.

Figure 3.4A shows an example of this hypothesised U-shaped relationship between town size $(X_1 -$ population in tens of thousands) and percentage employed in tertiary occupations (X_0). The regression between the two

$$X_0 = 27 \cdot 91 - 0 \cdot 51 X_1 \pm 7 \cdot 60 \qquad r = -0 \cdot 37$$
$$(0 \cdot 58)$$

indicates the lack of any marked linear trend. To capture the upturn in X_0 at $X_1 = 12$ one might hypothesise that X_0 increases with X_1^2 (Fig. 3.4B) but

$$X_0 = 24 \cdot 34 - 0 \cdot 011 X_1^2 \pm 8 \cdot 57 \qquad r = -0 \cdot 18$$
$$(0 \cdot 44)$$

If X_1 and X_1^2 are combined in a multiple regression equation, however — the partial equations for this are in Fig. 3.4C and D —

$$X_0 = 41 \cdot 57 - 5 \cdot 43 X_1 + 0 \cdot 25 X_1^2 \pm 1 \cdot 5 \qquad R = 0 \cdot 985$$
$$(13 \cdot 58) \quad (13 \cdot 16)$$

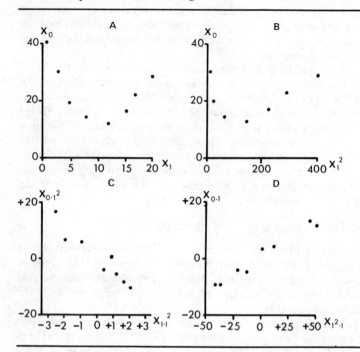

Fig. 3.4   A polynomial relationship between X_0 and X_1 (A) showing its transformation to a linear relationship with the partial regressions (C, D) $X_0 = f(X_1, X_1^2)$.

which provides an excellent fit to the trend in the data.

A U-shaped curve can be represented by an equation with the form

$$X_0 = a - b_1 X_1 + b_2 X_1^2 \pm \epsilon \qquad (3.20)$$

therefore, and an inverted-U by

$$X_0 = a + b_1 X_1 - b_2 X_1^2 \pm \epsilon \qquad (3.21)$$

In formula (3.20) the negative coefficient for X_1 indicates an initial fall in the values of X_0, and the positive value of $b_{02 \cdot 1}$ indicates a later upturn (Fig. 3.4A). The location of the upturn is a function of the relative size of the two coefficients: the larger the value of $b_{01 \cdot 2}/b_{02 \cdot 1}$, the larger the value of X_1 at which the upturn occurs.

The relationships in formulae (3.20) and (3.21) are known as second-order polynomials, because the dependent variable, X_0, is being regressed against the first- and second-order values of X_1 (i.e. against $X_1^1 = X_1$ and X_1^2). Polynomials of any order can be derived by the addition of extra terms, so that a third-order polynomial is

$$X_0 = a + b_1 X_1 + b_2 X_1^2 + b_3 X_1^3 \pm \epsilon \qquad (3.22)$$

Examples of such high-order polynomials are shown in Fig. 3.5: in the

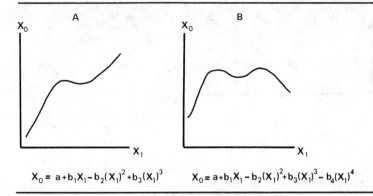

$$X_0 = a + b_1X_1 - b_2(X_1)^2 + b_3(X_1)^3$$

$$X_0 = a + b_1X_1 - b_2(X_1)^2 + b_3(X_1)^3 - b_4(X_1)^4$$

Fig. 3.5 More complex polynomials and the linear equations representing them.

third-order trend displayed, the positive coefficient for X_1 indicates an initial increase in X_0 as X_1 increases, the negative coefficient for b_2 suggests a decrease in X_0 as X_1^2 increases, whereas the positive value of b_3 shows a later upturn in the relationship of X_0 to X_1 (i.e. when X_1^3 becomes much bigger relative to X_1^2).

Higher-order polynomials are rarely fitted to geographical data, since there is little basis for such patterns in the available theory. They are not easy to interpret, also, although they are widely used in the multivariate form (see below on trend surface analyses).

Specific transformations. 2: Interaction terms

A basic assumption of the multiple regression model is that the effects of the independent variables are additive. As suggested by the equation for the multiple correlation coefficient − formula (3.5) − this implies that each independent variable accounts for a proportion of the variance in X_0 and that the sum of these proportions is R^2. (If the independent variables are collinear, the joint variance effects must also be included.) In some cases, however, the effects of independent variables may be multiplicative, indicating a joint influence extra to that which may be induced by collinearity.

Figure 3.6 illustrates the multiplicative effect of two variables, X_1 and X_2, on X_0. The separate regression equations (Fig. 3.6A and B) are

$$X_0 = 2 \cdot 43 + 0 \cdot 68X_1 \qquad r_{01} = 0 \cdot 79$$

$$X_0 = 4 \cdot 92 + 0 \cdot 30X_2 \qquad r_{02} = 0 \cdot 25$$

and the multiple regression equation is

$$X_0 = -1 \cdot 01 + 0 \cdot 82X_1 + 0 \cdot 64X_2 \qquad R_{0 \cdot 12} = 0 \cdot 94$$

In an additive equation, therefore, X_1 and X_2 together account for $0 \cdot 88$ of the variance in X_0. If a multiplicative approach is taken, however, and X_0

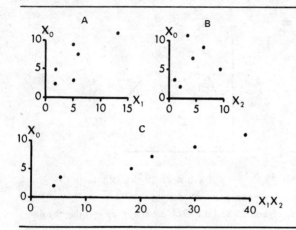

Fig. 3.6 A multiplicative relationship showing how the poor relationships (A, B) of $X_0 = f(X_1)$ and $X_0 = f(X_2)$ are combined (C) into the linear form $X_0 = f(X_1 X_2)$.

is regressed against $X_1 X_2$ (i.e. if $X_1 = 4$ and $X_2 = 3$, $X_1 X_2 = 3 \times 4 = 12$) we get a much closer fit (Fig. 3.6C)

$$X_0 = 1 \cdot 19 + 0 \cdot 25 X_1 X_2 \qquad r = 0 \cdot 99$$

The most frequent example of a multiplicative relationship in geography is the gravity model, so-called because it uses an analogy from Newtonian physics. In its 'purest' form this reads

$$I_{ij} = k \frac{P_i P_j}{d_{ij}^2} \qquad\qquad (3.23)$$

where P_i, P_j are the 'masses' at the two places involved in the interaction;

d_{ij} is the distance between places i and j;

k is a coefficient of proportionality, which scales the mass/distance ratio; and

I_{ij} is the amount of interaction between places i and j.

This model states that interaction increases with the product of the two masses ($P_i P_j$), which is a multiplicative term, rather than with the sum of the two masses ($P_i + P_j$), which is additive. This is because of an increase in interaction potential as $P_i P_j$ increases. For example, place A may have 3 persons and place B 4 persons, and the number of possible two-person friendships involving people from both places is $3 \times 4 = 12$. If place A had 10 people and place B 9, the potential number of friendships would be 90, so potential interaction is increasing with the product of the 'masses' (the population). Further, the model suggests that $P_i P_j$ should be expressed as a ratio of the square of the distance between i and j, because the greater the distance the greater the time and cost involved in movement and so the less likely it is that interaction will occur.

Formula (3.23) is the Newtonian gravity model, used by physicists. Applying it to human phenomena would not allow for variations in populations regarding their behaviour. People in one place may be less 'interaction prone' than others, and weights are fitted to account for this, giving

$$I_{ij} = k \frac{P_i^a P_j^b}{d_{ij}^c} \qquad\qquad (3.24)$$

Such variations allow better estimation of the values of I_{ij} than does formula (3.23).

Multiplicative terms are often fitted into regression equations by logarithmic transformation. Since

$$XY = \log_{10} X + \log_{10} Y \qquad\qquad (3.25)$$

$$X^a Y^b = a \log_{10} X + b \log_{10} Y \qquad\qquad (3.26)$$

and

$$X/Y = \log_{10} X - \log_{10} Y$$

then formula (3.24) can be rewritten as

$$\log_{10} I_{ij} = \log_{10} k + a \log_{10} P_i + b \log_{10} P_j - c \log_{10} d_{ij} \pm \epsilon \qquad (3.27)$$

The data in Fig. 3.6 can be regressed in this way, for

$$X_0 = 1\cdot19 + 0\cdot25\, X_1 X_2 \qquad r = 0\cdot99$$

can be written as

$$\log_{10} X_0 = -3\cdot55 + 10\cdot0 \log_{10} X_1 + 6\cdot25 \log_{10} X_2 \qquad R = 0\cdot99$$

Substituting in the latter equation for $X_1 = 2$, $X_2 = 2$ ($X_0 = 2$; Fig. 3.6C)

$$\log_{10} X_1 = \log_{10} X_2 = 0\cdot301$$

$$\log X_0 = -3\cdot55 + 10\,(0\cdot301) + 6\cdot25\,(0\cdot301)$$

$$= -3\cdot55 + 3\cdot01 + 1\cdot881$$

$$= 1\cdot341 \qquad\qquad \text{antilog } 1\cdot341 = 2\cdot19$$

There are many examples in the geographical literature of the application of the gravity model. In an analysis of migration between urban regions in the United States, for example, Schwind (1971) fitted the regression

$$\log_{10} M_{ij} = -2\cdot3 + 0\cdot64 \log_{10} P_i + 0\cdot71 \log_{10} P_j - 1\cdot11 \log_{10} d_{ij} \qquad R = 0\cdot77$$

The larger regression coefficient for P_j than for P_i indicates that the population of the destination area (j) had a greater impact on the flow pattern than did the population of the origin (i). Such an interpretation would not have been possible if a regression of the form

$$M_{ij} = f(P_i P_j) \qquad\qquad (3.28)$$

had been preferred to

$$\log_{10} M_{ij} = f(\log_{10} P_i + \log_{10} P_j) \tag{3.29}$$

Stepwise multiple regression

In many empirical studies, researchers hypothesise a number of causal influences on the variance in a dependent variable. Some of these may be valid, and others not. Their regression analyses are aimed at identifying these two groups of independent variables, isolating in particular those which do have critical causal effects (in a statistical sense) and should be retained in an equation required either to describe the variance or to predict other values of X_0. The t values can be used for this; even if 'true' significance testing is not allowed because the data do not constitute a properly collected sample, nevertheless the ratio between a partial regression coefficient and its standard error will indicate the scatter around the regression trend and whether it reduces much of the variance in X_0.

A frequent approach to the problem of which independent variables to retain in a final equation uses the technique of stepwise multiple regression. This does not feed all of the independent variables in at once, but instead builds up the equation one extra variable at a time. With 4 independent variables, there are 24 different ways in which their 'order of entry' can be arranged, however; with 5 there are 120, and with 6, 720, so clearly some rule is needed to organise the procedure. This is that variables are entered in their order of importance in reducing the variance of X_0, with the most important first, and this ordering is indicated by the partial correlation coefficients.

A paper by Wolpert (1964) exemplifies this method. He was aiming to account for spatial variations in levels of relative productivity of farms in part of Sweden, using the variables:

X_0 is relative productivity: actual productivity as a percentage of potential;

X_1 is the area of arable land per farm, in hectares;

X_2 is the area of forest land per farm, in hectares;

X_3 is the capital available per farm, in hundreds of Kronor;

X_4 is the annual labour supply per farm, in hundreds of hours; and

X_5 is the predicted potential productivity per farm, in Kronor per man-hour.

The total equation

$$X_0 = 46\cdot55 - 1\cdot52X_1 - 0\cdot14X_2 + 0\cdot99X_3 - 0\cdot09X_4 + 0\cdot63X_5$$

indicates greater relative productivity on the smaller farms, on farms with much capital available, and with high levels of potential productivity; in other words, the 'better' farms are 'better farmed'.

Were all five independent variables needed, however?

The partial correlation coefficients of

$r_{01 \cdot 2345} = -0 \cdot 57$ $r_{02 \cdot 1345} = -0 \cdot 15$

$r_{03 \cdot 1245} = 0 \cdot 74$ $r_{04 \cdot 1235} = -0 \cdot 07$

$r_{05 \cdot 1234} = 0 \cdot 50$

suggest that X_3 was the best independent predictor of X_0, and it was entered in the first equation in the stepwise procedure

$$X_0 = a + 0 \cdot 63 X_3 \qquad R^2_{0 \cdot 3} = 0 \cdot 29$$
$$(15 \cdot 75)$$

(Note that Wolpert's paper did not give the values for a.) X_1 was added at the next step, since it had the next largest partial correlation, giving

$$X_0 = a + 0 \cdot 94 X_3 - 1 \cdot 39 X_1 \qquad R^2_{0 \cdot 31} = 0 \cdot 58$$
$$(23 \cdot 5) \qquad (19 \cdot 86)$$

With this extra variable, the percentage of the variance of X_0 accounted for was doubled over the first step. At the third step, X_5 is entered, giving

$$X_0 = a + 0 \cdot 94 X_3 - 1 \cdot 47 X_1 + 0 \cdot 59 X_5 \qquad R^2_{0 \cdot 315} = 0 \cdot 67$$
$$(31 \cdot 33) \qquad (24 \cdot 5) \qquad (11 \cdot 8)$$

The increase in R^2 is still substantial, but after the fourth step, including X_2, it is much less so:

$$X_0 = a + 0 \cdot 96 X_3 - 1 \cdot 51 X_1 + 0 \cdot 59 X_5 - 0 \cdot 12 X_2 \qquad R^2_{0 \cdot 3152} = 0 \cdot 71$$
$$(32 \cdot 0) \qquad (25 \cdot 17) \quad (14 \cdot 75) \quad (6 \cdot 0)$$

Entry of X_4 at the final step produced

$$X_0 = a + 0 \cdot 99 X_3 - 1 \cdot 52 X_1 + 0 \cdot 63 X_5 - 0 \cdot 14 X_2 - 0 \cdot 09 X_4$$
$$(33 \cdot 0) \qquad (25 \cdot 33) \quad (15 \cdot 75) \quad (7 \cdot 0) \qquad (1 \cdot 5)$$

$$R_{0 \cdot 31524} = 0 \cdot 85 \qquad R^2_{0 \cdot 31524} = 0 \cdot 72$$

The value for R^2 hardly increased, and for the first time the t value for the new independent variable suggests its insignificance as an extra predictor of X_0.

Having gone through all of the steps, the researcher must then decide at which he will stop and exclude all other variables. In this case, if only significant independent variables are required, then step 4 will be accepted; stepwise procedures are not needed to aid this decision, which could be made by entering all independents and eliminating those with low t values (except where collinearity exists; see below). If prediction is the crucial issue, however, the researcher may wonder whether it is worth collecting the data for X_2 to increase the value of R^2 from $0 \cdot 67$ to $0 \cdot 71$. The predictive power of the equation is hardly affected; step 3 may be accepted as providing a reasonable fit, and data collection for prediction will be reduced by one variable.

The exact procedure for fitting a series of stepwise regression equations differs in some respects between researchers. King (1969, pp. 145–8), for example, illustrates the following procedure. Assume a problem with a dependent variable, X_0, to be regressed against X_1, X_2, X_3, X_4 and X_5. The steps are:

1. Compute the zero-order correlations r_{01}, r_{02}, r_{03}, r_{04} and r_{05} and select the largest. The relevant independent variable then enters the first step of the regression procedure so that if r_{03} was the largest of the five, the function $X_0 = f(X_3)$ would be fitted.

2. Compute the first-order partial correlation coefficients between X_0 and the remaining independent variables, holding constant the one already in the equation. Select the largest of these, and add the relevant independent variable to the multiple regression equation at the next step. In the present example, this would involve calculating $r_{01\cdot3}$, $r_{02\cdot3}$, $r_{04\cdot3}$ and $r_{05\cdot3}$. If $r_{01\cdot3}$ were the largest of these four, the new function $X_0 = f(X_3, X_1)$ would be fitted.

3. Compute the second-order partial correlation coefficients, holding constant the independent variables already in the regression equation; i.e. $r_{02\cdot13}$, $r_{04\cdot13}$, $r_{05\cdot13}$. As before, select the largest, and include the relevant independent variable in the next stage of the stepwise procedure.

The procedure outlined in step 3 continues, each time calculating a higher-order partial correlation coefficient as one further independent variable has been included, until all variables are in the regression equation.

Clearly, variations in the details of the procedure can affect the order of entry for the independent variables at the different steps. They are unlikely to affect the final conclusions to any marked extent, except in cases of extreme collinearity among two or more independent variables. Where this does occur, use of the zero-order correlations rather than the first-order partials at the first step can lead to a different variable being entered at this stage.

With only five independent variables, stepwise procedures are not always necessary. With more, they may well be useful as aids to screening out unnecessary variables. But use of a large number of independent variables will probably introduce problems of collinearity. In Wolpert's data, the correlation of X_1 and X_3 was $r_{13} = 0\cdot44$, which led to a considerable change in the regression coefficient b_{03} from the first to the second step: in the former, $b_{03} = 0\cdot63$; in the latter, $b_{03\cdot1} = 0\cdot94$. (One other change to be noted is the increase of the t values as we proceed through the steps. This is because some of the residual variance in X_0, and hence the standard error of the partial regression coefficients, is being absorbed by the new variables in the equation.) Because of collinearity, too, the ordering of the entry of variables by the partial correlation coefficients may be confusing, since the partial correlation coefficients conceal as much as they reveal.

Collinearity is responsible for instability in the regression coefficients and the t values for the relevant variables, and slight alterations in this correlation among independent variables can produce large changes in the former parameters. A hybrid data set developed by Fox (1968, see Hauser, 1974) illustrates this. He fitted the regression equation

$X_0 = a_{0 \cdot 12} + b_{01 \cdot 2} X_1 + b_{02 \cdot 1} X_2$

with $N = 20$ $r_{01} = 0 \cdot 9$ and $r_{02} = 0 \cdot 5$

but with a varying value of r_{12}

t for

r_{12}	$R^2_{0 \cdot 12}$	$b_{01 \cdot 2}$	$b_{02 \cdot 1}$
0·2	0·98	11·7	4·7
0·5	0·81	7·2	0·6
0·7	0·84	8·0	−1·9
0·8	0·94	14·6	−6·4

As collinearity increased, so the t values became more variable; those for $b_{02 \cdot 1}$ indicate that the partial regression coefficient for X_2 changed sign (see above, p. 76). In a stepwise procedure, X_1 would be entered first, but slight variations in its collinearity with X_2 could seriously influence: (1) the apparent predictive accuracy of its partial correlation with X_0, shown by the t values; and (2) whether X_2 was also included, as a significant 'independent' variable, after the next step.

As with all multiple regression procedures, stepwise regression should only be employed when there is no sizeable collinearity. If the aim is 'blind' predictive power, for which R^2 is the guide, then all one wants to pick is the best-fitting equation, within the constraints of data collection (i.e. is a further variable worth it to increase R^2 from 0·71 to 0·72?). But if the meaning of the regression coefficients is important, to aid in the understanding of causal influences, stepwise regression procedures do not produce the 'best' equation if there is collinearity.

Trend surface analysis

An increasingly popular special case of multiple regression procedures in geographical work is trend surface analysis, for which the independent variables are spatial coordinates (i.e. locations on a grid, as with the British National Grid). Figure 3.7A is a map showing the mean pebble size for the 20 nearest pebbles to each of 16 intersections on a sampling grid laid across a beach. Is there a spatial trend to these values? Regressing mean pebble size − Y − against the two coordinates − U and V, the eastings and northings respectively − gives

$Y = 1 \cdot 45 + 0 \cdot 71U$ $r_{YU} = 0 \cdot 85$

$Y = 1 \cdot 45 + 0 \cdot 71V$ $r_{YV} = 0 \cdot 85$

The first of these equations indicates a strong trend of pebble size increasing eastwards along the beach, and the contours of this relationship (i.e. the predicted values − $\hat{Y}$ − from the equation) are given in Fig. 3.7B. A similar northerly trend is indicated by the other equation (Fig. 3.7C). Inspection of the original data in Fig. 3.7A suggests that the major trend in

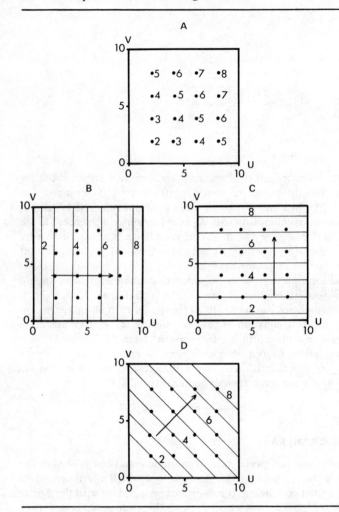

Fig. 3.7   A simple trend surface, showing: (A) mean pebble sizes at 16 beach sample locations; (B) the regression of mean pebble size on easting (U); (C) the regression of mean pebble size on northing (V); and (D) the multiple regression of mean pebble size on easting and northing.

pebble size is from south-west to north-east, and this is brought out in the multiple regression equation

$$Y = 0.0 + 0.5U + 0.5V \qquad R_{Y.UV} = 1.0$$

whose predicted contours are in Fig. 3.7D. As the two independent variables are measured on the same scale (grid units) then we can compare the partial regression coefficients and see that the two trends — easterly and northerly — are of equal strength. (If measurement of U and V were not on the same scales — e.g. for a large grid using degrees of latitude and longitude — then the partial regression coefficients would have to be converted to β coefficients — p. 71 — to allow comparison.)

A small amount of collinearity is often tolerated in multiple regression equations, so that with two independent variables X_0 is related to X_1, to X_2, and to the joint influence of X_1 and X_2. When collinearity is substantial, the partial regression coefficients are hard to interpret, which would be the case in the basic trend surface equation

$$Y = a_{Y.UV} + b_{YU.V}U + b_{YV.U}V \pm \epsilon \qquad (3.30)$$

if $r_{UV} \neq 0.0$. Trend surface analysis aims to identify the major latitudinal and longitudinal trends in a map, but with collinearity the partial regression coefficients could mean very little. This is illustrated in Fig. 3.8. In Fig. 3.8A, $r_{UV} = 0.62$ and the trend surface equation is

$$Y = -13.67 + 0.029U + 0.904V \qquad R = 0.997$$
$$(0.9) \qquad (29.1)$$

which, by the t values, suggests an insignificant easterly trend in this sample of pebble sizes. This is because much of the easterly trend is also captured in the northerly trend.

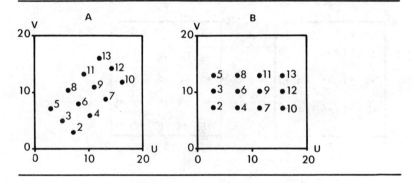

Fig. 3.8 Collinearity in trend surface analysis (A) and its removal by rotation of the axes (B).

In this example, collinearity could be removed by reorientation of the grid (Fig. 3.8B), so that $r_{UV} = 0.0$ and

$$Y = -49.5 + 0.67U + 0.63V \qquad R_{Y.UV} = 0.997$$
$$(34.3) \quad (15.6)$$

but this is only possible if the sample points are regularly distributed. If they are not, and there is some spatial clustering of the points, collinearity is inevitable and the results consequently difficult to interpret. Thus accurate trend surface mapping requires uncorrelated coordinate sets if, for example, significance tests are to be applied or the coefficients interpreted. (Often such data sets are said to contain orthogonal, or uncorrelated, independent variables.) Trend surface mapping is most applicable to studies for which data on regular grids are available, therefore, which is more the case in physical than in human geography. Where it has been applied to the latter, the trend surface coefficients probably should be interpreted with some suspicion. Further, high correlations may reflect spatial auto-correlation (see Ch. 9).

The patterns discerned by the trend surface analysis of Figs. 3.7 and 3.8 comprise undirectional trends. More complex patterns can be depicted by the use of polynomials, as already demonstrated for conventional multiple regression analyses. Thus we could have

$$Y = a + b_1 U - b_2 U^2 \pm \epsilon \qquad (3.31)$$

indicating that as one moved eastwards away from the origin of the grid the value of Y first increased and then decreased (Fig. 3.9A). Similarly,

$$Y = a - b_1 V + b_2 V^2 \pm \epsilon \qquad (3.32)$$

indicates that Y first decreases and then increases as one moves north from the origin (Fig. 3.9B). Adding together formulae (3.31) and (3.32) requires

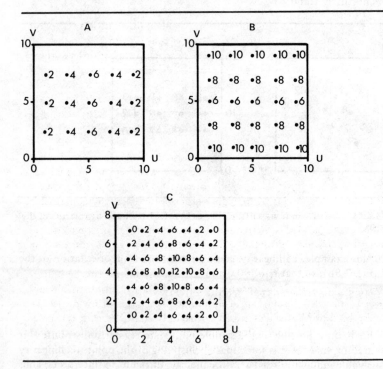

Fig. 3.9 Three more complex trend surfaces, showing: (A) a north–south trending ridge; (B) an east–west aligned valley; and (C) a dome.

that we also include a term for the interaction of U and V, so that

$$Y = a + b_1 U + b_2 U^2 + b_3 UV + b_4 V + b_5 V^2 \pm \epsilon \qquad (3.33)$$

describes a second order, or quadratic trend surface, whose characteristic shape is either a dome or a basin. Figure 3.9C shows a data set to which a quadratic surface can be fitted, with the equation

$$Y = -85 \cdot 71 + 4 \cdot 57U - 0 \cdot 57U^2 + 0 \cdot 0UV + 4 \cdot 57V - 0 \cdot 57V_2$$

$$R_{Y.UV} = 0 \cdot 96$$

$$(14 \cdot 5) \quad (16 \cdot 1) \quad (0 \cdot 0) \quad (14 \cdot 5) \quad (16 \cdot 1)$$

In this, the partial regression coefficients for U and V are the same, as are those for U^2 and V^2, indicating that the northward and eastward trends are exactly the same. The result is an almost perfect dome. If $b_1 \neq b_4$ and $b_2 \neq b_5$ in fits to formula (3.33) the shape of the dome or basin will be elliptical and not circular.

Higher-order surfaces can be fitted where the pattern is exceedingly complex. In most cases these are used to describe patterns as accurately as possible, since the meaning of the partial regression coefficients is often very difficult to interpret; not surprisingly, since in a third-order, or cubic surface, there are nine such coefficients, whereas a fourth-order, or quartic, contains fourteen. Figure 3.10A is an example of a cubic surface (from Haggett, 1968, p. 28) showing the pattern of unemployment in south-west England increasing towards the tip of the peninsula (on that map, the stippled area denotes above average unemployment). A higher-order surface (sixth degree) is shown in Fig. 3.10B, for the economic status of Toronto households in 1860 (Goheen, 1970, p. 123). The denser shading denotes two main areas of low economic status in the north-west and east of the city, separated by a ribbon of high economic status (open crosshatching) which joins the city's commercial centre to the still prestigious district of Rosedale in the north.

The production of trend surface equations and their associated maps frequently proceeds in the same way as stepwise regression analysis, starting with the simple linear trend-formula (3.30) − and successively adding further variables to create higher-order polynomials. The increasing value of R^2 − the proportion of the variance in the original map accounted for by the trend surface − is frequently used as an index of when to stop increasing the complexity of the surface; alternatively, the F test may be used to inquire whether there is a statistically significant difference between a surface and that of the next highest order. Usually the process ends after only two or three steps, because of the interpretative problems already mentioned and also because of computing difficulties (Unwin, 1975). When very high order surfaces are fitted (as in Goheen, 1970) it is usually to maximise R^2; of greater interest in such cases is often the pattern of residuals, of areas deviating from the general trend.

Statistical manipulation of mapped data, such as trend surface analyses, often produces a boundary problem, which involves interpolation of con-tours or their equivalents in the area between an observation and the

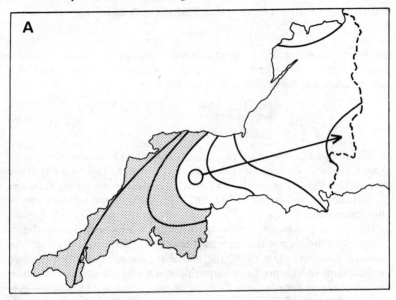

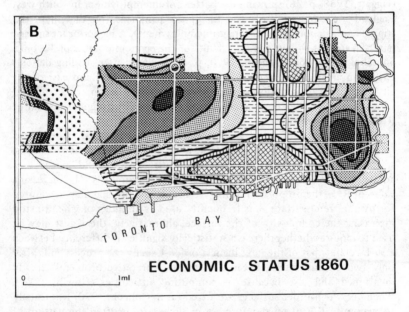

Fig. 3.10 Two examples of trend surfaces: (A) a cubic surface for unemployment rates in southwest England; and (B) a sixth-degree surface for patterns of economic status in Toronto, 1860. Sources: Haggett (1968) and Goheen (1970); reproduced with permission.

boundary, where there are no further data points. In ordinary regression this is the extrapolation problem. An equation is fitted to a set of observations and refers only to that set of values – i.e. the range of the independent variable, often known as *the domain of the variable*. Beyond that domain, it is unsafe to predict that the relationship would be the same as that observed, and indeed at the edges of the domain, where usually there are relatively few data points, interpolation is less safe than around the mean. The lesson to be learned from the boundary effect in trend surface analysis, therefore, is that one should always be conservative in interpreting patterns and trends around the edge of a data set. This is exactly the same as the problem of interpolating contour lines between a set of control points and the edge of a map.

Trend surface analysis has been used in a wide variety of geographical applications since its introduction to the discipline by Chorley and Haggett (1965). Geomorphologists, for example, have used it to analyse altitudinal data in the search for planation surfaces (King, 1969). This can involve problems, as the general linear model, of which trend surface analysis is an example, assumes a random distribution of residuals around the trend; clearly, if this were the case, it would not indicate a flat surface! (Tarrant, 1970). For human geographers, trend surface analysis has been used to 'smooth' data, to portray the general rather than the particular spatial trends in a map (e.g. Tarrant, 1969; Pyle, 1971). Problems faced in this, however, are that most human geography data refer to areas rather than points, with consequent difficulties in the location of the control points, that areas usually differ in size (Haggett, 1968), and that points are not uniformly distributed (Robinson and Fairbairn, 1969), making interpolation of the trends somewhat arbitrary.

Partial correlation and hypothesis testing

Correlation and regression methods are undoubtedly those most frequently used by geographers to test hypotheses, whether about patterns in a population which can be inferred from a sample or, more often, about the interrelationships in a total enumeration. Because of the immature development of much of the theory behind them, many of the hypotheses are relatively vague, claiming perhaps merely that X_0 should be some function of X_1 and X_2. With theoretical development, however, greater precision in hypothesis formulation is possible. To test these more specific hypotheses, methods based on partial correlation analysis are available, and the uses of two of them are reviewed here.

Causal modelling

In the development of models, theories, and hypotheses, researchers often postulate causal relationships which indicate that a dependent variable is linked to an independent by another variable. Such a situation is illustrated in Fig. 3.11, where

X_0 is the proportion of rainfall which enters the river system directly;

X_1 is vegetation cover — some measure of intensity; and

X_2 is rainfall amount.

The arrows in the diagram indicate only two expected relationships: rainfall amount determines vegetation cover, and vegetation cover determines run-off. What does this imply in terms of correlation analysis? It hypothesises a positive correlation between X_2 and X_1 and a negative one between X_1 and X_0. It also suggests that the partial correlation $r_{02 \cdot 1}$ is zero, that X_2 has no independent influence on X_0. Because of this, we can predict the value of r_{02},

if $r_{21} = 0 \cdot 7$ and $r_{01} = -0 \cdot 6$

r_{02} should equal $r_{01} r_{21} = (0 \cdot 7)(-0 \cdot 6) = -0 \cdot 42$

The reasoning for this lies in the concept of joint variance introduced earlier (see Fig. 3.2). According to our model, X_2 only affects X_0 through X_1 and so any correlation of X_0 with X_2 should represent the two correlations r_{01} and r_{12}. None of the variance of X_0 is explained by X_2 without the intervening effect of X_1, therefore. Thus if X_2 accounts for $0 \cdot 49$ of the variance in X_1 ($0 \cdot 7^2 = 0 \cdot 49$) and in turn X_1 accounts for $0 \cdot 36$ of the variance in X_0 ($-0 \cdot 6^2 = 0 \cdot 36$) then X_2 should only be accounting for, at best, $0 \cdot 49$ of the $0 \cdot 36$, or $0 \cdot 176$ ($-0 \cdot 42^2 = 0 \cdot 176$). Thus by taking the product of the two observed correlations for the model, we can predict what the other correlations should be, and test whether they indeed are. If they are not as predicted, then there are causal links operating which have not been identified in the model, with X_2 having an unexpected direct influence on X_0.

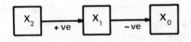

Fig. 3.11   A predicted causal chain.

An example of such hypothesis testing is provided by Taylor (1969), derived from an earlier study by Cox (1968). Two independent variables are involved, and four independents, with the hypothesised causal links as indicated in Fig. 3.12. The correlations for the links shown there are

$r_{04} = 0 \cdot 923$

$r_{12} = -0 \cdot 732$ $r_{13} = -0 \cdot 740$

$r_{23} = 0 \cdot 573$

$r_{43} = -0.340 \qquad r_{45} = -0.730$

$r_{53} = 0.582$

If the model is correct, then all of the other correlations among the six variables should be predictable from the above values. Age structure (X_5), for example, is believed to have no independent effect on percentage voting Conservative (X_0); it influences the latter only through its correlation with social rank (X_4). Thus we can predict

$r_{05} = r_{04} r_{45} = 0.923 \, (-0.730) = -0.674$

From the data, $r_{05} = -0.717$, which suggests some direct influence of age on Conservatism. Similarly, we can predict that the correlation between the two dependent variables should be

$r_{01} = r_{04} r_{43} r_{13} = 0.923 \, (-0.340)(-0.740) = 0.232$

which compares with the observed value of $r_{01} = 0.343$.

This procedure allows not only testing of the validity of certain hypotheses through direct correlations, therefore, but also enquiry into whether all of the causal links have been identified in the underlying theory. If this is the case, then all of the correlations outside those directly postulated in the model are predictable once the relationships within the model are known. Unfortunately, as Moore (1969) has shown, there is no way of assessing whether there is any significant difference between the observed and predicted values: in Taylor's data, for example, is -0.717 significantly different from -0.674? Here researcher judgement becomes important in the use of a tool which promises considerable assistance in the development of understanding.

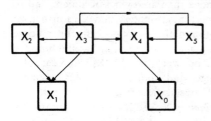

X_0 = CONSERVATIVE VOTE
X_1 = VOTER TURNOUT
X_2 = COMMUTING WORKERS
X_3 = SUBURBAN LIVING
X_4 = SOCIAL RANK
X_5 = AGE STRUCTURE

Fig. 3.12 A predicted set of hypotheses for two dependent variables (after Taylor, 1969).

Path analysis

Related to the method of causal modelling just discussed is that of path analysis, now being widely used in sociological research (Duncan, 1975). This attempts to identify the relative strengths of the various direct and indirect links between two variables. In the simplest case (Fig. 3.13A) there are no indirect links, and each of the four independent variables simply has a direct effect on the dependent, X_0.

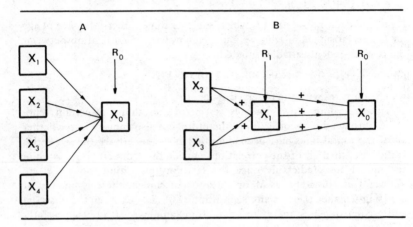

Fig. 3.13   Two examples of path analytic models.

An example of a set of direct and indirect links is shown in Fig. 3.13B. Here the dependent variable, X_0, is the mobility rate, the percentage of a city suburb's population moving home in a given year. We know that people renting homes are more likely to move than are owner-occupiers, and so predict a positive link between X_1, percentage renters, and X_0. Further we suggest that younger people are more mobile, as are poorer people, hence the positive links between X_2, percentage under 35, and X_0, and between X_3, percentage earning less than £40 per week, and X_0. X_2 and X_3 are also related to X_1, however, since younger and poorer households are more likely to be renters, hence the links between these two and X_1. Finally, we have residual variables, R_1 and R_0, affecting X_1 and X_0 – i.e. accounting for that variance in those variables not within the model (Fig. 3.13B).

The model we have just described suggests that each independent variable affects the dependent through a series of *paths*, so that each correlation is a combination of those paths. Each path is represented by a *path coefficient*, p, which shows the direct influence of a variable on another: p_{12} is the path coefficient of the effect of X_2 on X_1. For the model in Fig. 3.13B, then

$$X_1 = p_{12}X_2 + p_{13}X_3 + p_{1R}R_1 \qquad (3.34)$$

where R_1 is the residual influence on X_1; indicating that the value of X_1, at a given observation, is a function of X_2 and of X_3 at that observation, plus the residual influence; and

$$X_0 = p_{01} X_1 + p_{02} X_2 + p_{03} X_3 + p_{0R} R_0 \qquad (3.35)$$

Correlation coefficients can be decomposed similarly; thus for Fig. 3.13B

$$r_{01} = p_{02} r_{12} + p_{03} r_{13} + p_{01} \qquad (3.36)$$

where p_{02}, p_{03} are the path coefficients linking X_2 and X_3 to X_0 through X_1; and

p_{01} is the direct link of X_1 to X_0.

Thus the value ($p_{02} r_{12}$) is that component of the correlation r_{01} which is produced by the effect of X_2 on X_0 through X_1, i.e. of tenure on mobility because of the effect of age on tenure. Similarly ($p_{03} r_{13}$) is the component produced by the effect of X_3 and p_{01} is the direct path of X_1 to X_0. If $p_{01} = 0$ then tenure is not a relevant independent predictor of X_0, since it accounts for none of the variance in X_0 other than that accounted for by X_2 and X_3, for which it is an intermediary.

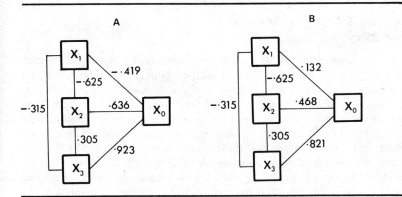

Fig. 3.14   Path analysis of patterns of intra-urban population density (X_0), showing (A) the inter-variable correlations; and (B) the inter-variable path coefficients. Source: Duncan (1966); reproduced with permission.

Figure 3.14 shows an example of this procedure, taken from the work of Duncan (1966) and Winsborough (1962). In it, the logarithm of population density by city suburb (X_0) is related to:

X_1 is the logarithm of persons per dwelling unit;

X_2 is the logarithm of dwelling units per building; and

X_3 is the logarithm of buildings per area.

The aim of the analysis is to discover the direct and indirect effects of these variables on total population density. Simple correlations between the variables are given in Fig. 3.14A, indicating, for example, that population density is negatively related to persons per dwelling unit ($r_{01} =$

−0·419) and that the strongest correlation involves buildings per area ($r_{03} = 0.923$).

The path coefficients for this problem are indicated in Fig. 3.14B. These indicate that X_3 has the strongest independent effect, and that once the negative correlations r_{13} and r_{12} are held constant, the indirect influence of X_1 is slight but positive.

Thus

$$r_{01} = p_{01} + p_{02} r_{12} + p_{03} r_{13}$$

$$= 0.132 + (0.468)(-0.625) + (0.821)(-0.315)$$

$$= 0.132 + (-0.293) + (-0.259) = -0.419$$

Path coefficients thus are somewhat similar but not identical to partial correlation coefficients. (Note that although $r_{01 \cdot 23} = r_{10 \cdot 23}$, $p_{01} \neq p_{10}$.) Solution of the simultaneous equations allows decomposition of a correlation into its components. As with causal modelling, this allows a researcher to 'get inside' his model and identify all of the links (for a much fuller outline, see Duncan, 1975).

Summary

Bibliographies of the use of quantitative methods in geographical research (e.g. Greer-Wootten, 1972) indicate the great popularity of correlation and regression methods. Particularly with the advent of computer program packages, these are easy to apply, and their output usually is easily interpreted. This chapter has outlined the bases to those interpretations, indicating the uses of the methods in geographical work, and the care which must be taken to ensure that these do not become abuses. The multiple regression model offers a great depth of analytical possibilities to the student of complex 'real worlds', with the promise of greater understanding of the matrix of direct and indirect causal links between phenomena.

Multiple regression analyses can be used to test hypotheses, and also to generate them. A researcher may predict, for example, that

$$X_0 = f(X_1, X_2, X_3) \tag{3.37}$$

but find that the multiple regression equation representing that function accounts for only 45% of the variance in X_0. Thus suggests that either there is a lot of random variation in X_0 or that he has overlooked a vital independent variable. To inquire whether the latter is indeed the case, he may map the residuals from the equation for formula (3.37), and see whether the spatial pattern of major under- and over-predictions of the dependent variable suggests the ignored cause (Haggett, 1965). This may result in him adding a new variable, X_4, to his model, and proceeding to re-run the regression analysis, and in this way the regression both asks questions of the researcher and aids in developing the answer.

Chapter 4

Multivariate extensions of the analysis of variance

Analysis of variance was introduced in Chapter 2 as a means of relating a dependent variable, measured on an interval or ratio scale, to a mutually exclusive classification of the observations, which acted as the independent variable. The analytical procedure indicated what proportion of the variation in the dependent variable could be accounted for by the classification, and the F-ratio test indicated the probability of the differences observed in a sample also being present in its parent population.

What if we have more than one independent variable, all of them classifications? In the example of Chapter 2, the 50 towns were divided into those with socialist, free-market capitalist, and liberal councils, and this classification accounted for some 47% of the variation in *per capita* expenditure on education. Other classifications might account for some of the remaining 53%, so that we need a multivariate extension of the analysis of variance, just as a multiple regression analysis incorporates more than one hypothesised causal independent variable.

Two-way analysis of variance

For the *per capita* education expenditure example, the 50 towns have now been classified into two locational groups — England and Wales — as well as into the three governmental-type groups (Table 4.1). This gives a two-way classification, with the number of towns in each cell, as follows:

Location of town (X_2)	Type of government (X_1)			
	Capitalist	Socialist	Liberal	Total
England	8	8	9	25
Wales	9	8	8	25
Total	17	16	17	50

The notation for the mean values on the dependent variable (Y — *per capita* spending on education) in each cell of this two-way classification is:

X_2	X_1			
	1	2	3	Total
1	$\overline{Y}_{11}$	$\overline{Y}_{12}$	$\overline{Y}_{13}$	$\overline{Y}_{1.}$
2	$\overline{Y}_{21}$	$\overline{Y}_{22}$	$\overline{Y}_{23}$	$\overline{Y}_{2.}$
Total	$\overline{Y}_{.1}$	$\overline{Y}_{.2}$	$\overline{Y}_{.3}$	$\overline{Y}_{..}$

Within the body of the table, the first subscript is the row identification and the second indicates the column: thus $\overline{Y}_{23}$ is the mean *per capita* education expenditure in row 2, column 3, which refers to the Welsh towns with liberal governments. A dot for a subscript indicates a summation, so $\overline{Y}_{1.}$ is the mean for row 1 over all columns − i.e. for all English towns − and $\overline{Y}_{.2}$ is the mean for column 2 over all rows − i.e. all socialist towns: $\overline{Y}_{..}$ is thus the grand mean for all 50 towns.

Decomposition of the variance

The value of Y for any observation can be expressed as its distance from the grand mean. Thus Y_i is replaced by $(Y_i - \overline{Y}_{..})$ and the total variation

Table 4.1 Educational spending, political affiliation and town location: hypothetical data

Town	Variables* Y	X_1	X_2	Town	Variables Y	X_1	X_2	Town	Variables Y	X_1	X_2
1	27	1	1	17	57	2	1	34	31	1	1
2	64	2	2	18	70	2	2	35	66	2	2
3	52	1	2	19	50	3	1	36	69	2	2
4	59	2	1	20	54	3	2	37	42	3	1
5	77	2	2	21	45	1	2	38	43	3	1
6	54	3	1	22	68	3	2	39	60	2	2
7	50	3	2	23	45	2	1	40	46	1	2
8	48	3	1	24	58	3	2	41	46	3	1
9	49	1	2	25	36	1	1	42	52	3	1
10	72	2	2	26	40	1	1	43	46	1	2
11	52	2	1	27	60	3	2	44	58	2	1
12	62	3	2	28	64	2	2	45	58	2	1
13	50	1	2	29	51	1	2	46	40	1	1
14	50	2	1	30	36	1	1	47	55	1	2
15	40	1	2	31	47	3	1	48	63	3	2
16	34	3	1	32	38	1	1	49	59	2	1
				33	44	1	1	50	56	3	2

*X_1 = type of government: key − 1 = free-market capitalist; 2 = socialist; 3 = liberal
X_2 = town location: key − 1 = England; 2 = Wales
Y = *per capita* expenditure on education

about the mean is

$$\sum_{i=1}^{N} (Y_i - \overline{Y}..)^2 \tag{4.1}$$

If we define $\overline{Y}_C$ as the mean for the column in which observation i is classified and $\overline{Y}_R$ as its row mean, then

$$(Y_i - \overline{Y}..) = (Y_i - \overline{Y}_C) + (\overline{Y}_C - \overline{Y}..) \tag{4.2}$$

and

$$(Y_i - \overline{Y}..) = (Y_i - \overline{Y}_R) + (\overline{Y}_R - Y..) \tag{4.3}$$

which decomposes the variation in two separate ways. In formula (4.2), for example, each value of Y is rewritten as its distance from the column mean, plus the distance between the column mean and the total mean.

Two-way analysis of variance looks at the separate effects of the two independent variables and also at their joint effect. It proceeds in the same way as multiple regression, in that the 'residuals' from the variation between columns are tested for between-row differences and the 'residuals' from the variation between rows are tested for between-column differences: X_1 is held constant while the effect of X_2 is investigated and vice versa. The assumption is that X_1 and X_2 are independent; if they are not, collinearity is present, with consequences described below (p. 108).

The procedure for decomposing the variation into within-class and between-class components is as follows:

$$\Sigma(Y_{ij} - \overline{Y}..)^2 = \Sigma(Y_{ij} - \overline{Y}_{ij})^2 + \Sigma(\overline{Y}_{ij} - \overline{Y}..)^2 \tag{4.4}$$

where Y_{ij} is an observation in row i, column j;

$\overline{Y}_{ij}$ is the mean for the class of observations in row i and column j;
and summations are over all N observations.

From this

$$\Sigma(Y_{ij} - \overline{Y}_{ij})^2 = \textit{within-class variation} \tag{4.5}$$

which is sometimes known as the error or residual variation (that which is not accounted for by the classification), and

$$\Sigma(\overline{Y}_{ij} - \overline{Y}..)^2 = \textit{between-class variation} \tag{4.6}$$

The latter can be subdivided into *between-row variation*, the first term in formula (4.7), and *between-column variation* (the second term), viz.:

$$\Sigma(\overline{Y}_{ij} - \overline{Y}..)^2 = \Sigma(\overline{Y}_{i.} - \overline{Y}..)^2 + \Sigma(\overline{Y}_{.j} - \overline{Y}..)^2 \tag{4.7}$$

In all of these formulae, summation is over the N observations, so that in the final term of (4.7) the value of $(\overline{Y}_{.j} - \overline{Y}..)^2$ is obtained for *each* observation in row i.

The cell means for the 50 towns in our example are

X_2	X_1			
i =	j =			
	1	2	3	Total
1	$\overline{Y}_{11} = 36\cdot50$	$\overline{Y}_{12} = 54\cdot75$	$\overline{Y}_{13} = 46\cdot23$	$\overline{Y}_{1.} = 45\cdot84$
2	$\overline{Y}_{21} = 48\cdot23$	$\overline{Y}_{22} = 67\cdot76$	$\overline{Y}_{23} = 58\cdot88$	$\overline{Y}_{2.} = 57\cdot88$
Total	$\overline{Y}_{.1} = 42\cdot71$	$\overline{Y}_{.2} = 61\cdot25$	$\overline{Y}_{.3} = 52\cdot18$	$\overline{Y}_{..} = 51\cdot86$

and the various components of the variation are:

Source	Amount
Within classes	1264·99
Between columns	2837·02
Between rows	1932·39
Total	6038·02

The between-classes variation (columns + rows) sums to 4769·41, which is 0·790 of the total variation, suggesting a correlation of $\sqrt{0\cdot790}$, which is 0·889 (see p. 56). The 'partial correlations' for the two separate variables are 0·686 for type of government (X_1, columns) and 0·566 for location (X_2, rows). Inclusion of the latter variable has increased the statistical 'explanation' of the variation in *per capita* education expenditure from 47% (p. 57) to 79%.

The interaction variance

Addition of the three components of the variation given above does not give the total variation (i.e. 1264·99 + 2837·02 + 1932·39 = 6034·40 not 6038·02). The 3·62 shortfall is a further source of variation in Y — the interaction variance component.

The nature of the interaction can be understood by reference back to Fig. 3.2 and the discussion of collinearity (p. 74). In the present case, part of the variation in educational expenditure is related to type of government, part to town size, and a third part — the interaction — to the

Table 4.2   The interaction effect: hypothetical data

Values of Y in cells where			
X_2	X_1		
i =	j =		
	1	2	3
1	10, 11, 12, 13, 14	12, 13, 14, 15, 16	14, 15, 16, 17, 18
2	12, 13, 14, 15, 16	14, 15, 16, 17, 18	30, 31, 32, 33, 34

joint effect of both variables, as a consequence of their intercorrelation. This joint effect is not associated with either of the independents, therefore, but it is still part of the 'explanation'. Added to the other components it means that 0·79 of the variation of Y is accounted for by X_1 and X_2, separately and jointly.

A clearer example of the interaction effect is given by the data set in Table 4.2; there are five observations in each cell, and the means are

X_2	X_1			
i =	j =			
	1	2	3	Total
1	$\overline{Y}_{11} = 12 \cdot 0$	$\overline{Y}_{12} = 14 \cdot 0$	$\overline{Y}_{13} = 16 \cdot 0$	$\overline{Y}_{1.} = 14 \cdot 0$
2	$\overline{Y}_{21} = 14 \cdot 0$	$\overline{Y}_{22} = 16 \cdot 0$	$\overline{Y}_{23} = 32 \cdot 0$	$\overline{Y}_{2.} = 20 \cdot 67$
Total	$\overline{Y}_{.1} = 13 \cdot 0$	$\overline{Y}_{.2} = 15 \cdot 0$	$\overline{Y}_{.3} = 24 \cdot 0$	$\overline{Y}_{..} = 17 \cdot 33$

Analysis of variance produces

Source of variation	Amount
Within classes	60·00
Between columns	686·67
Between rows	333·34
Interaction	326·66
Total	1406·67

and the interaction effect accounts for almost as much of the variation in Y as does X_2 (the row classification).

The means in this data set indicate that where $X_2 = 1$, there is a steady transition in the values of $\overline{Y}$ across the three categories of X_1. There is a similar trend in the second row between $\overline{Y}_{21}$ and $\overline{Y}_{22}$, but the final cell stands out with a much larger mean than the general trend would predict: $\overline{Y}_{23} = 32$ when one might have 'predicted' 18 from the other values. The interaction of X_1 and X_2 when $X_1 = 2$ and $X_2 = 3$ is considerable, therefore, a situation which is akin to the interaction regressions relating X_0 to $X_1 X_2$ (Fig. 3.6, p. 81).

The interaction effect thus represents a cell which stands out from the general trend; it is a part of the variation in Y which is accounted for only by a combination of X_1 and X_2 and not by either alone. It may be any cell, as the categories can be arranged in any order on the axes of the table.

As in multiple regression, therefore, collinearity among the independents can produce a joint effect which is not allocated to either. The greater the number of independent variables in an analysis of variance, the greater the number of possible interaction effects, as we shall see in a later section.

Significance testing

The proportions of the variation accounted for by the row and column classifications are interpreted in the same way as partial correlation coefficients; they are the proportions accounted for by that variable acting alone. The proportion accounted for by the classifications together is the equivalent of a squared multiple correlation coefficient, and the proportion accounted for by the interaction of X_1 and X_2 reflects their joint influence on the dependent variable. If the data refer to sampled observations, the analyst may want to know the significance of these 'correlations'.

As with one-way analysis of variance, the statistical significance of each 'correlation' can be computed using Snedecor's F-ratio between the variance estimates, which are the components of the variation standardised for degrees of freedom. Using

N is the number of observations;
r is the number of rows; and
c is the number of columns
the degrees of freedom are

for the total variance	(around $\overline{Y}_{..}$)	$N-1$
for between-rows variance	$(\overline{Y}_{.j} - \overline{Y}_{..})$	$r-1$
for between-columns variance	$(\overline{Y}_{i.} - \overline{Y}_{..})$	$c-1$
for row—column interaction variance		$(r-1)(c-1)$
for the within-classes variance	$(Y_{ij} - \overline{Y}_{.j})$	
and	$(Y_{ij} - \overline{Y}_{i.})$	$(N - rc)$

so that for the data of Table 4.1

Source of variation	Amount	df	Variance estimate
Between rows	1932·39	1	1932·39
Between columns	2837·02	2	1418·51
Interaction	3·62	2	1·81
Within classes	1264·99	44	28·75
Total	6038·02	49	123·22

Several F-ratios can be computed from these variance estimates. The first is for the Interaction (F_I)

$$F_I = \frac{\text{Interaction variance estimate}}{\text{Within-classes variance estimate}} = \frac{1·81}{28·75} = 0·063$$

Tables of the F-ratio indicate that, for 2 and 44 degrees of freedom, a value this small could have occurred more than five times in every hundred samples, and so we would accept the null hypothesis and conclude that there is probably no interaction effect of $X_1 X_2$ on Y in the parent population.

If the interaction effect is statistically insignificant, then the small amount of variation associated with it probably results from sampling error. It is therefore added to the within-classes effect (which is often known as the error or residual effect), giving

Source of variation	Amount	df	Variance estimate
Error	1268·61	46	27·58

and this new error variance estimate is used as the denominator for the F-ratios for row (F_R) and column (F_C) effects. Thus

$$F_R = \frac{\text{Between-rows variance estimate}}{\text{Error variance estimate}} = \frac{1932 \cdot 39}{27 \cdot 58} = 70 \cdot 065$$

and

$$F_C = \frac{\text{Between-columns variance estimate}}{\text{Error variance estimate}} = \frac{1418 \cdot 51}{27 \cdot 58} = 51 \cdot 433$$

Both ratios are unlikely to have occurred by chance, and so we reject the null hypothesis and conclude that the differences in Y between the categories of X_1 and between the categories of X_2 almost certainly exist in the parent population (i.e. that English towns spend less than Welsh towns per head on education, holding political affiliations constant, etc.).

In analyses where the interaction effect is statistically significant at the chosen probability level, different denominators are used to calculate F_R and F_C. Some situations require the within-classes variance estimate as the denominator, whereas for others it is the interaction variance estimate. The rules for deciding which to use are:

1. Using the within-classes estimate. If our research has been designed so that we are certain that all of the relevant independent variables are included, we would conclude that the row, the column and the interaction contributions are all 'real' influences on Y, and only random, error variance remains. The residual or error variance estimate is then the best denominator, and this is the within-classes estimate.

2. Using the interaction estimate. If we feel that other, unidentified variables are influencing Y, it may be that their effect is absorbed in the interaction. In this case, the interaction variance estimate as the denominator contrasts the chosen independent variables with the ignored independent variables.

For the example in Table 4.2, it may be that the second rule is the applicable one, since we are not certain that all of the relevant independent variables have been identified. The significance testing then becomes:

Source of variation	Amount	df	Variance estimate
Within classes	60·00	24	2·50
Between columns	686·67	2	343·34
Between rows	333·34	1	333·34
Interaction	326·66	2	163·33
Total	1406·67	29	48·51

$F_I = 163 \cdot 33 / 2 \cdot 50 = 65 \cdot 33$

which is significant at the 5% level, so that

$F_R = 333 \cdot 34 / 163 \cdot 33 = 2 \cdot 04$, and

$F_C = 343 \cdot 34/163 \cdot 33 = 2 \cdot 10$

neither of which is significant at the 5% level. Our conclusion would then be that relative to the unidentified variables obscured in the interaction

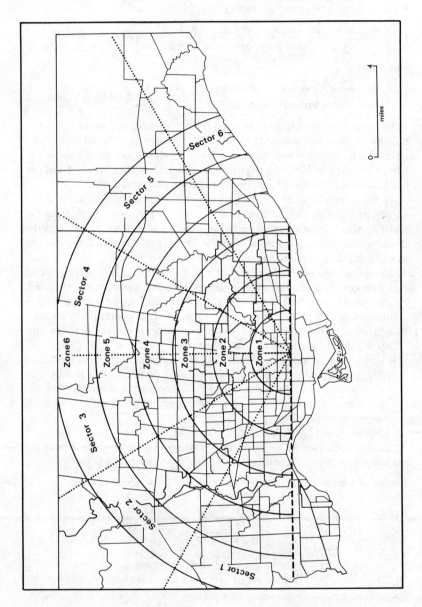

Fig. 4.1   The census small areas in Toronto classified into zones and sectors for a two-way analysis of variance. Source: Murdie (1969); reproduced with permission.

effect, X_1 and X_2 are not likely to produce the same differences in Y in the total population. On the other hand, we may argue that no other independent variables are likely to affect Y, and that the interaction effect reflects an interpretable joint influence of X_1 and X_2. In this case

$F_R = 333 \cdot 34/2 \cdot 50 = 133 \cdot 34$, and

$F_C = 343 \cdot 34/2 \cdot 50 = 137 \cdot 34$

both of which ratios are significant at the 5% level. This conclusion suggests that X_1 and X_2 almost certainly have a major influence on the values of Y in the population, and would lead to a rejection of the null hypothesis of no difference between the group means.

Just as in one-way analysis of variance (Ch. 2), use of the F-ratio for significance testing assumes that the data are a properly constituted sample from a known population. Even when this is not so, however, the F-ratio can be used in a descriptive context, to suggest the relative importance of an independent variable as an 'explanation' of variation in a dependent. Similarly, the assumptions of the one-way model — regarding sample size, normality, and homoscedascity — also apply.

Analysis of variance for spatial patterns

Two-way analysis of variance has been used by several researchers to test the significance of two models of the spatial patterning of urban residential areas (Murdie, 1976). These models suggest: (1) that certain characteristics of local populations vary zonally around the urban centre (e.g. the richer live further away), and (2) that the variation in some population characteristics is sectoral in form, with the sectors focused on the urban core.

An example of such a study is Murdie's work on the social geography of Toronto, which was divided into 6 zones and 6 sectors (Fig. 4.1); each small area for which population and housing data were available was classified into this 36 cell system. The patterns of 6 indices were investigated (there were component scores; see Chapter 5), with the following F-ratios (values significant at the 5% level are underlined):

Variable	Between sectors	Between zones	Interaction
Economic status	27·0	0·9	3·5
Italian ethnic status	23·3	9·2	4·3
Household and employment characteristics	1·0	58·5	1·9
Family status	4·6	49·2	3·8
Jewish ethnic status	20·7	2·9	4·6
Recent population growth	5·3	21·9	1·6

As samples were not involved, the F-ratios are merely guides to the descriptive power of each classification; both were clearly relevant for most of the indices. In line with the hypotheses, Toronto's residential areas were both zonally and sectorally patterned, with the zonal hypothesis obtaining the strongest support in three cases and the sectoral in the other three. Five of the F-ratios for the interaction effect were also significant, suggesting that for certain indices — zones within sectors — some cells stood out from the general spatial trends, having either very strong concentrations or very marked absences of the relevant characteristics. One could interpret these as indicating that the zonal and sectoral classification was not particularly successful and that other patterns had been ignored, but none of the five interaction ratios was very large relative to either the error variance estimate (the denominator for F_I) or the major element in the spatial pattern—zone or sector. They can be taken as indicative of particular minor deviations from the general trends, therefore.

Collinearity and interaction

In one-way analysis of variance, some differences in group size are not crucial although, as shown in Chapter 2 (p. 58), they can bias the results. In two-way analyses, such bias is often much more marked, and unequal numbers of observations in the various cells may well accentuate the interaction effect.

This last statement can be illustrated using the data of Table 4.1 except that instead of having 8 towns in the 'socialist, English' class — row 1, column 2 — we have 16. In terms of data, each of the values for the 8 original towns in this category appears twice (i.e. the 8 'new towns' are carbon copies of the first 8) so that the cell mean, $\overline{Y}_{12}$, does not change. But the row and column means do change, as follows:

$\overline{Y}$ when $N_{12} = 8$					$\overline{Y}$ when $N_{12} = 16$			
X_2	X_1				X_2	X_1		
$i =$	$j =$				$i =$	$j =$		
	1	2	3			1	2	3
1	36·50	54·75	46·23	45·84	1	36·50	54·75	46·23	48·00
2	48·23	67·76	58·88	57·88	2	48·23	67·76	58·88	57·88
	42·71	61·25	52·18	51·86		42·71	59·29	52·18	52·34

and the relevant analyses of variance produce:

N$_{12}$ = 8			N$_{12}$ = 16		
Source of variation	Amount		Source of variation	Amount	
Within classes	1264·99	(0·21)	Within classes	1452·49	(0·23)
Between rows	1932·39	(0·32)	Between rows	1388·49	(0·22)
Between columns	2837·02	(0·47)	Between columns	2669·30	(0·42)
Interaction	3·62	(0·001)	Interaction	772·85	(0·12)
Total	6038·02		Total	6283·13	

(the proportions of the total variation accounted for by each effect are given in parentheses).

The major influence of changing the number of observations in one cell has clearly been the increase of the interaction effect at the expense of the independent effects. This is because in the example where N$_{12}$ = 16, the much larger number of observations in that cell has a greater influence on the values of $\overline{Y}_{1.}$ and $\overline{Y}_{.2}$ relative to the other values in row 1 and column 2 than do the eight values in the same cell when all three cells in that row and both in that column are virtually of the same size. Thus the cell stands out in the former case, not because of a cell mean which deviates markedly from the general pattern — as in the earlier example (p. 103) — but because its mean is based on many more observations than are those for all the other cells. A stronger interaction effect is indicated, but interpretation of this in the suggested way, as a consequence of the joint influence of X_1 and X_2, would be false.

Clearly unequal cell sizes should be avoided since they can produce results which are amenable to two very different interpretations. Sampling designs are clearly crucial here, but if unequal cell sizes are inevitable, one way to avoid the problem of the induced interaction effect just described is to ignore the within-classes effect and treat each cell mean as a single observation. Whatever the number of observations in each cell, the row and column means will not be changed, since they are the means of the means and not the means of the observation. Thus for the data just analysed we would get

X_2	X_1			
i =	j =			
	1	2	3	
1	36·50	54·75	46·23	45·84
2	48·23	67·76	58·88	57·88
Total	42·71	61·25	52·18	51·80

and

Source of variation	Amount	df	Variance estimate
Between rows	232·88	1	232·88
Between columns	357·57	2	178·79
Residual	0·56	2	0·28
Total	591·01	5	118·20

Since there is no within-class effect, all of the residual variation represents an interaction effect.

The great drawback of this procedure is, of course, that it totally ignores what may be the greatest source of variation, that within classes. It avoids one problem – the production of interaction effects by unequal cell sizes – but creates what might be a much more serious one, which is the increased possibility of a type II error with the acceptance of a false hypothesis (see p. 13). Neither problem is desirable and neither will be produced if the analysis is so structured as to produce equal cell sizes. This is much more feasible in experimental work, which is why analysis of variance is more suited to some types of geographical problem than to others.

Three-way analysis of variance

Providing that the sampling is feasible, any number of independent variables can be introduced to an analysis of variance. In Table 4.3 we have a hypothetical data set for a three-way analysis, where

X_1 is type of soil (three classes);
X_2 is aspect (two classes);
X_3 is slope angle (two classes); and
Y is yields of potatoes per hectare of land.

Thus we have twelve cells ($3 \times 2 \times 2$) and in each five random samples of potato yields have been taken from fields classsified on the three variables.

In the analysis of variance, to see whether these three variables all have an independent influence on potato yields, there are eight sources of variation, as follows:

Source of variation	Amount	df	Variance estimate
Between classes of X_1	2470·0	2	1235·00
Between classes of X_2	166·67	1	166·67
Between classes of X_3	26·67	1	26·67
Interaction of X_1 and X_2	53·33	2	26·67
Interaction of X_1 and X_3	83·33	2	41·67
Interaction of X_2 and X_3	106·67	1	106·67
Interaction of X_1, X_2, and X_3	213·33	2	106·67
Residual (within classes)	120·00	48	2·50
Total	3240·00	59	54·92

Note that it is not possible to speak now of rows and columns, so the 'main sources' of variation are categorised by variables. There are also several

Table 4.3 Three-way analysis of variance: hypothetical data

Values of Y in cells where

$X_3 = 1$
X_2 X_1
$i =$ $j =$

	1	2	3
1	10, 11, 12, 13, 14	12, 13, 14, 15, 16	16, 17, 18, 19, 20
2	12, 13, 14, 15, 16	14, 15, 16, 17, 18	30, 31, 32, 33, 34

$X_3 = 2$
X_2 X_1
$i =$ $j =$

	1	2	3
1	7, 8, 9, 10, 11	9, 10, 11, 12, 13	26, 27, 28, 29, 30
2	9, 10, 11, 12, 13	11, 12, 13, 14, 15	24, 25, 26, 27, 28

separate sources of interaction, involving each possible combination of independent variables.

The F-ratios for the four interaction terms are

X_1 and X_2 10·67 X_1 and X_3 16·67 X_2 and X_3 42·67

X_1, X_2 and X_3 42·67

all of which are significant at the 5% level. Using the within-classes variance estimate for the remainder of the tests we get F-ratios of

X_1 494·00 X_2 66·67 X_3 10·67

all of which, again, are significant at the stipulated level. Thus each of the three variables — type of soil, aspect, and slope angle — makes an independent contribution to the 'explanation' of variation in potato yields, and in addition all have joint effects with each of the others.

Three-way, and further extensions to many-way, analysis of variance is a powerful tool for isolating the effects of different nominal variables, separately and in combination, on a dependent. It is particularly suited to experimental data, in which the researcher has close control over the sampling procedure, so as to ensure equal cell sizes, equal variances, and so on. It was developed for use in agricultural science, with application, for example, in the field testing of seeds under different conditions, and it has been widely adopted in experimental psychology, in which considerable methodological advances have been made. Very little geography, particularly human geography, comprises carefully controlled experimental research, however, although Haggett (1961) illustrated the possibilities in a pioneer paper. Use of the more sophisticated analysis of variance procedures is unlikely to be widespread in the subject, however, or in the social sciences in general.

Analysis of variance via multiple regression

Geography is not the only academic discipline in which much of the work is non-experimental and which therefore faces problems with regard to sampling and the structure of data sets. Fortunately, some of these problems can be overcome by conducting analysis of variance procedures within the multiple regression model.

Dummy variables

Multiple regression was presented in Chapter 3 as a method in which all of the independent variables are measured on either interval or ratio scales. But it is possible to use binary data in this framework, in which each observation is coded either 1 or 0 on the relevant independent variable; for example, town location could be entered as a binary independent variable, with a value of 1 for an English town and 0 for a Welsh town. (Values of +1, 0 and −1 are sometimes used as dummy variables also.)

In Chapter 2 an analysis of variance was conducted for the data in Tables 2.2 and 4.1, in which *per capita* education expenditure was related to a three-fold classification of the town according to the political affiliations of their governments. The means for each type are

Free-market capitalist $\overline{Y}_F = 42 \cdot 71$
Socialist $\overline{Y}_S = 61 \cdot 25$
Liberal $\overline{Y}_L = 52 \cdot 18$

and the classification accounted for 47% of the variation in *per capita* spending.

This problem could be set in the regression framework. If

X_1 is 1 if town has capitalist government, 0 if not;
X_2 is 1 if town has socialist government, 0 if not; and
X_3 is 1 if town has liberal government, 0 if not;

then we have created three independent variables measured in binary form, against which X_0 — the *per capita* education spending — could be regressed in the equation

$$X_0 = a_{0 \cdot 123} + b_{01 \cdot 23} X_1 + b_{02 \cdot 13} X_2 + b_{03 \cdot 12} X_3 \pm \epsilon \qquad (4.8)$$

In this, the partial regression coefficients indicate the change in the value of X_0 with an increase of $1 \cdot 0$ in the value of the independent variable, so that if $b_{01 \cdot 23} = 3 \cdot 5$, this indicates an increase of $3 \cdot 5$ in X_0 for each increase of $1 \cdot 0$ in X_1, holding variables X_2 and X_3 constant. But the original values of X_1 are only 0 and 1, so that $b_{01 \cdot 23}$ is the difference in the value of X_0 between a town without a capitalist government ($X_1 = 0$) and one with such a government ($X_1 = 1$). This is the same as the difference between $\overline{X}_0$ when $X_1 = 0$ and $\overline{X}_0$ when $X_1 = 1$.

In the multiple regression model, the independent variables must be uncorrelated, and if we included X_1, X_2, and X_3 in the same equation that rule would be violated. The three variables are mutually exclusive, and every observation must be in one of the three groups — it has a value of 1 on one, and one only, of X_1, X_2, and X_3. Thus if we know the values of X_1

and X_2 for a town, the value of X_3 must also be known (this is a special case of the concept of degrees of freedom).

Town	X_1	X_2	X_3
i	1	0	
j	0	0	
k	0	1	

In the above example, for town i X_3 must be 0, since the town cannot be in two groups; for j, $X_3 = 1$, and for k, $X_3 = 0$.

To avoid this interdependence problem, we omit variable X_3 and write the equation

$$X_0 = a_{0 \cdot 12} + b_{01 \cdot 2} X_1 + b_{02 \cdot 1} X_2 \pm \epsilon \tag{4.9}$$

which affects the interpretation in the following way. We usually interpret $a_{0 \cdot 12}$ as the value of X_0 when $X_1 = 0$ and $X_2 = 0$. In this case we know that if $X_1 = X_2 = 0$, then $X_3 = 1$, so that

$$a_{0 \cdot 12} = b_{03 \cdot 12} X_3 \tag{4.10}$$

which is $\overline{X}_0$ when $X_3 = 1$.

Fitting equation (4.9) to the data of Table 2.2 coded in this way gives

$$X_0 = 52 \cdot 18 - 9 \cdot 47 X_1 + 9 \cdot 07 X_2 \pm 8 \cdot 25 \qquad R_{0 \cdot 12} = 0 \cdot 69$$

The value of $a_{0 \cdot 12}$ is $\overline{X}_0$ when $X_3 = 1$ (or $\overline{X}_L$); $b_{01 \cdot 2}$ is $-9 \cdot 47$, so when $X_1 = 1$, $X_0 = 52 \cdot 18 - 9 \cdot 47 = 42 \cdot 71$, which is $\overline{X}_F$, and $b_{02 \cdot 1} = +9 \cdot 07$, so when $X_2 = 1$, $X_0 = 52 \cdot 18 + 9 \cdot 07 = 61 \cdot 25$ (which is $\overline{X}_S$). $R_{0 \cdot 12}{}^2$ is $0 \cdot 47$, which is the proportion of the variation in X_0 explained by variables X_1, X_2, and X_3 in the analysis of variance of Chapter 2 (p. 56).

Any one of the variables could be omitted. Leaving out X_2, we get

$$X_0 = 61 \cdot 25 - 18 \cdot 54 X_1 - 9 \cdot 07 X_2 \pm 8 \cdot 25 \qquad R_{0 \cdot 12} = 0 \cdot 69$$

and leaving out X_1

$$X_0 = 42 \cdot 71 + 18 \cdot 54 X_2 + 9 \cdot 47 X_3 \pm 8 \cdot 25 \qquad R_{0 \cdot 23} = 0 \cdot 69$$

In each case, the group means can be computed from the regression coefficients.

Dummy variables and 'continuous' variables

Dummy variables can be used as an alternative analysis of variance procedure, with the added advantage over the conventional method that the partial regression coefficients can be used, where relevant, to test whether each group mean is significantly different from the mean represented by the constant. (In analysis of variance one only tests for overall differences between means. With dummy variables, one can test if $b_{01 \cdot 23} \neq b_{02 \cdot 13}$, which is whether $\overline{X}_0$ for group 1 differs from $\overline{X}_0$ from group 2.) More importantly, they can also be used in combination with 'continuous' variables — i.e those measured on interval or ratio scales. This allows both conventional regression methods and analysis of variance of the residuals to be performed in a single procedure.

An example of this use of dummy variables is given in Wolpert's (1964) study of farm productivity in Sweden, which has already been quoted (pp. 84-87). For his total sample, the equation obtained was

$$X_0 = 45 \cdot 55 - 1 \cdot 52X_1 - 0 \cdot 14X_2 + 0 \cdot 99X_3 - 0 \cdot 09X_4 + 0 \cdot 63X_5$$

$$R^2_{0 \cdot 12345} = 0 \cdot 72$$

(for key to variables, see p. 84).

Wolpert was interested in whether there were spatial variations in these relationships within his sample of farms, which were classified into 5 regions on the basis of their Productivity Index (X_0). A separate equation was computed for each region: as follows

Region 1
$$X_0 = a - 1 \cdot 66X_1 - 0 \cdot 16X_2 + 1 \cdot 06X_3 - 0 \cdot 42X_4 + 0 \cdot 66X_5$$

$$R^2_{0 \cdot 12345} = 0 \cdot 89$$

Region 2
$$X_0 = a - 1 \cdot 37X_1 - 0 \cdot 21X_2 + 0 \cdot 97X_3 + 0 \cdot 12X_4 + 0 \cdot 40X_5$$

$$R^2_{0 \cdot 12345} = 0 \cdot 75$$

Region 3
$$X_0 = a - 1 \cdot 90X_1 + 0 \cdot 07X_2 + 1 \cdot 30X_3 - 0 \cdot 82X_4 + 0 \cdot 78X_5$$

$$R^2_{0 \cdot 12345} = 0 \cdot 83$$

Region 4
$$X_0 = a - 1 \cdot 76X_1 - 0 \cdot 14X_2 + 0 \cdot 97X_3 + 0 \cdot 04X_4 + 1 \cdot 00X_5$$

$$R^2_{0 \cdot 12345} = 0 \cdot 77$$

Region 5
$$X_0 = a - 1 \cdot 28X_1 - 0 \cdot 15X_2 + 0 \cdot 93X_3 - 0 \cdot 22X_4 + 1 \cdot 11X_5$$

$$R^2_{0 \cdot 12345} = 0 \cdot 80$$

(Wolpert did not provide the a values in his paper.)

There are apparently some very substantial differences between the five regions in the regression and correlation coefficients, but are these statistically significant? (Wolpert was using a sample of farms, so this question could be asked.) To answer it, four new dummy variables were created, where

X_6 is 1 if farm in region 1, 0 otherwise;
X_7 is 1 if farm in region 2, 0 otherwise;
X_8 is 1 if farm in region 3, 0 otherwise;
X_9 is 1 if farm in region 4, 0 otherwise;

and region 5's mean is in the constant term.

The resulting equation was

$$X_0 = 47 \cdot 51 - \underline{1 \cdot 42X_1} - \underline{0 \cdot 14X_2} + \underline{0 \cdot 99X_3} - \underline{0 \cdot 09X_4} + \underline{0 \cdot 63X_5} + 2 \cdot 80X_6 - 3 \cdot 31X_7 + \underline{4 \cdot 47X_8} - \underline{3 \cdot 90X_9} \pm \epsilon \quad R^2_{0 \cdot 1 \text{-} 9} = 0 \cdot 75$$

with statistically significant variables at the 5% level being underlined.

The regional classification thus accounts for 3% of the variance in farm productivity (R^2 increases from 0·72 to 0·75). The significant regression coefficients for X_8 and X_9 indicate that it is very likely that farms in region 3 have a higher average productivity as a percentage of potential — when all other variables are held constant — than farms in the 'baseline' region (5) of the constant, whereas those in region 4 have lower average productivities. The a value of 47·51 is 1·96 percentage points above the corresponding value — 45·55 — for the earlier equation without variables X_6 to X_9. This is the difference in the value of X_0 when variables X_1 to X_5 are all at zero and that of X_0 when variables X_1 to X_9 are all at zero; in other words, it is the difference between the overall mean for X_0 and the mean for X_0 in region 5.

The combination of continuous and dummy variables in a single analysis is equivalent to an analysis of variance of the residuals from a multiple regression using the continuous variables only, if the classification represented by the dummies is independent of the continuous variables. Interpretation proceeds as follows. We have the equation (Fig. 4.2A)

$$X_0 = 10·0 + 0·5X_1$$

where X_0 is *per capita* education expenditure;

X_1 is town size in thousands;

and both X_0 and X_1 are continuous variables.

A dummy variable is then introduced, such that

X_2 is 1 if the town council is socialist, 0 if not;

and the regression expanded to

$$X_0 = 10·0 + 0·5X_1 + 2·5X_2$$

Substituting in this, when

$X_1 = 0$ and $X_2 = 1$ $X_0 = 12·5$

$X_1 = 10$ and $X_2 = 1$ $X_0 = 17·5$

for which the regression line is in Fig. 4.2B. On the other hand, when

$X_1 = 0$ and $X_2 = 0$ $X_0 = 10$

$X_1 = 10$ and $X_2 = 0$ $X_0 = 15$

we get the regression line of Fig. 4.2C. This last regression line is the same as in Fig. 4.2A (i.e. $X_0 = 10·0 + 0·5X_1$); X_2 can be either 1 or 0 and when it is 0, X_2 has no influence on the value of X_0. Hence with the dummy variable there are two regression lines (Fig. 4.2D) when

$X_2 = 1$: $X_0 = 10·0 + 0·5X_1 + 2·5X_2$

and when

$X_2 = 0$: $X_0 = 10·0 + 0·5X_1$

which are parallel and divided by the distance S on the vertical scale (Fig.

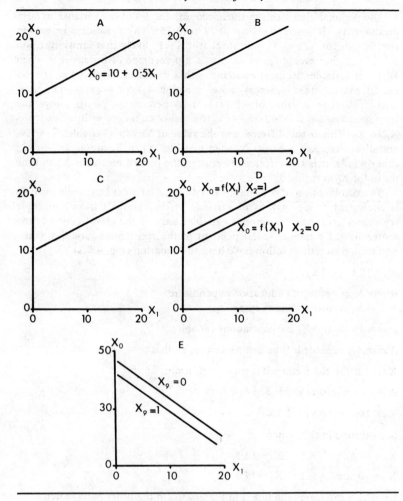

Fig. 4.2   The interpretation of dummy variables in regression equations. A–D show the regression lines for $X_0 = f(X_1)$; E shows the regression lines of $X_0 = f(X_1)$ in Wolpert's (1964) data when $X_9 = 1$ and $X_9 = 0$.

4.2D). The value of S is the regression coefficient for X_2; it is the average difference between socialist and non-socialist towns in their value of X_0 (*per capita* educational expenditure) for any value of X_1 (town size).

This same interpretation holds for equations with more variables. From Wolpert's findings (p. 114) we can extract the relationship $X_0 = 47\cdot51 - 1\cdot42X_1 - 3\cdot90X_9$ which holds true when all other variables are held constant. This implies two regression lines (Fig. 4.2E); the upper one is for farms not in region 4 ($X_9 = 0$), and the lower one for farms in that region.

Dummy variables and multiple classifications

In the examples of the previous section the dummy variables have represented one classification only. More than one can be included, however, as it was in the earlier two-way analysis of variance (p. 99) of *per capita* expenditure on education (X_0) against type of government (X_1) and town location (X_2). As the former independent variable comprised three classes and the latter two, for a regression analysis of this problem we have

X_{11} is 1 if a town with a capitalist council, 0 otherwise;

X_{12} is 1 if a town with a socialist council, 0 otherwise;

X_{13} is 1 if a town with a liberal council, 0 otherwise;

X_{21} is 1 if an English town, 0 otherwise; and

X_{22} is 1 if a Welsh town, 0 otherwise;

giving a regression equation

$$X_0 = a + b_{01}X_{11} + b_{02}X_{12} + b_{03}X_{13} + b_{04}X_{21} + b_{05}X_{22} \pm \epsilon \quad (4.11)$$

in which full subscripts have not been given for the regression coefficients, to make for simplicity of presentation.

Two of these variables must be removed following our earlier rules (p. 113). If X_{11} and X_{12} are known, then the value of X_{13} is fixed, and if X_{21} is known, the value of X_{22} is similarly fixed (not an English town = a Welsh town). Excluding X_{13} and X_{22}, therefore, we get

$$X_0 = 58.77 - 10.20X_{11} + 8.71X_{12} - 12.45X_{21} \pm 5.25 \quad R^2 = 0.790$$

From this, we can calculate the mean values of X_0 for various groups of towns. The a value, 58.77, is the value of X_0 when $X_{11} = X_{12} = X_{21} = 0$, which is when $X_{13} = X_{22} = 1$; it is the mean for Welsh towns ($X_{22} = 1$) with a liberal government ($X_{13} = 1$). Using the regression coefficients, we can then calculate the other means. For example, an English town with a liberal government will be $X_{13} = 1$, $X_{21} = 1$, so

$$X_0 = 58.77 - 12.45X_{21} = 46.32$$

and the whole table of means becomes

	X_{11}	X_{12}	X_{13}
X_{21}	36.11	55.03	46.32
X_{22}	48.56	67.48	58.77

Significance testing indicates that for all three variables in the equation the regression coefficients are significantly different from zero, which suggests rejection of a null hypothesis of no differences in the population between the various classifications on their values of X_0.

This procedure can be used in a large variety of geographical research problems. For example, Johnston (1974) used it to test the hypothesis that candidates in a multi-member election obtained a greater percentage of the vote, relative to other members of their party, in the booths close to their homes. The equation fitted was

$$X_0 = a_{0\cdot12} + b_{01\cdot2} X_1 + b_{02\cdot1} X_2 \qquad (4.12)$$

where X_0 is percentage of the vote received by the candidate at each booth;
$\qquad$ X_1 is an index of the percentage of the vote received by the candidate's party; and
$\qquad$ X_2 is a dummy variable — $X_2 = 1$ if the booth was within 2000 yards of the candidate's home, 0 otherwise.

Of 43 candidates standing in the 1971 Christchurch City Council election, the t statistic was greater than $2\cdot0$ for ten — suggesting a clear 'local effect' in the voting pattern ('pure' statistical significance testing was not valid since the analysis dealt with the total population).

Interaction variables

Analyses of variance involving more than one independent variable provide information not only on the independent effect of each on the dependent but on their joint influence, through the interaction variables. We saw how interaction variables could be introduced to regression analyses in Chapter 3 (p. 81), by replacing

$$X_0 = f(X_1, X_2) \qquad (4.13)$$

by either

$$X_0 = f(X_1 X_2) \qquad (4.14)$$

or

$$X_0 = f(\log X_1, \log X_2) \qquad (4.15)$$

and the same procedure can be used in analysis involving dummy variables. Thus our equation

$$X_0 = a + b_{01} X_{11} + b_{02} X_{12} + b_{03} X_{13} + b_{04} X_{21} + b_{05} X_{22} \qquad (4.16)$$

can be expanded, to include all possible interactions, to

$$X_0 = a + b_{01} X_{11} + b_{02} X_{12} + b_{03} X_{13} + b_{04} X_{21} + b_{05} X_{22} + b_{06}(X_{11} X_{21}) +$$
$$+ \; b_{07}(X_{11} X_{22}) + b_{08}(X_{12} X_{21}) + b_{09}(X_{12} X_{22}) + b_{10}(X_{13} X_{21}) +$$
$$+ \; b_{11}(X_{13} X_{22}) \qquad (4.17)$$

In this, the regression coefficient b_{06}, for example, relates to the interaction effect of X_{11} and X_{21}; it indicates the value of X_0, when all other variables are held constant, for a town which is both English and has a capitalist council irrespective of the separate effects of size and political orientation (i.e. if $X_{11} = 1$ *and* $X_{21} = 1$ then $X_{11} X_{21} = 1$; otherwise $X_{11} X_{21} = 0$). As variables X_{11} and X_{21} are already in the equation, this interaction variable identifies the joint effect of the two variables, when their individual effects have already been taken into account. Thus interaction effects in the regression model pick out the cells of the classification which stand out from the general trend, which is not achieved in the conventional analysis of variance.

As before, not all of the variables are required, so X_{13}, X_{22} and $X_{13}X_{22}$ are omitted to give

$$X_0 = 55 \cdot 796 + 35 \cdot 655X_{11} - 0 \cdot 710X_{12} - 12 \cdot 749X_{21} - 24 \cdot 825(X_{11}X_{21}) -$$
$$- 39 \cdot 799(X_{11}X_{22}) + 5 \cdot 871(X_{12}X_{21}) + 4 \cdot 170(X_{12}X_{22}) + 0 \cdot 257(X_{13}X_{21})$$
$$R^2 = 0 \cdot 460$$

in which, because of serious multicollinearity problems, only the regression coefficient for X_{21} is statistically significant. The procedure in this form, then, seems to offer little in the way of interpretable results.

In some analyses, the separate effects of the independent variables are omitted, and the data structured to look at each interaction as a separate variable. For our two-way classification, variables are defined as

	X_{11}	X_{12}	X_{13}
X_{21}	X_4	X_5	X_6
X_{22}	X_7	X_8	X_9

so that $X_4 = 1$ if both $X_{11} = 1$ and $X_{21} = 1$; $X_4 = 1$ for English capitalist cities. One of these variables can be omitted, and excluding X_9 we get

$$X_0 = 58 \cdot 88 - 22 \cdot 38X_4 - 4 \cdot 13X_5 - 12 \cdot 65X_6 - 10 \cdot 65X_7 + 10 \cdot 65X_8 \pm 5 \cdot 36$$
$$R^2 = 0 \cdot 790$$

where the a coefficient is $\overline{X}_0$ when $X_9 = 1$, and all the other means can be read off directly. In significance testing, four of the five regression coefficients suggested differences between their cell mean and the 'base line' mean — X_9; the exception was for X_5, suggesting that the null hypothesis of no difference between large, socialist towns and small, liberal towns should not be rejected.

Dummy variables, interaction effects and analysis of covariance

Interaction terms were introduced in the previous section to illustrate the joint effects of two dummy variables, and we saw in Chapter 3 how it is possible to combine two 'continuous' variables into an interaction term. It is also possible to combine a dummy variable with a continuous variable.

Using our educational expenditure example again, we can structure it as: when

X_0 is *per capita* expenditure on education;

X_1 is percentage of the population aged between 5 and 21;

X_2 is 1 if the town has a capitalist government, 0 otherwise;

X_3 is 1 if the town has a socialist government, 0 otherwise; and

X_4 is 1 if the town has a liberal government, 0 otherwise;

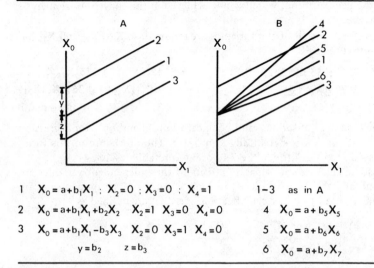

1	$X_0 = a + b_1 X_1$; $X_2 = 0$; $X_3 = 0$; $X_4 = 1$	1–3 as in A
2	$X_0 = a + b_1 X_1 + b_2 X_2$ $X_2 = 1$ $X_3 = 0$ $X_4 = 0$	4 $X_0 = a + b_5 X_5$
3	$X_0 = a + b_1 X_1 - b_3 X_3$ $X_2 = 0$ $X_3 = 1$ $X_4 = 0$	5 $X_0 = a + b_6 X_6$
	$y = b_2$ $z = b_3$	6 $X_0 = a + b_7 X_7$

Fig. 4.3   The different regression lines fitted at various stages of an analysis of covariance: (A) differences between groups in the intercept; (B) differences between groups in the slope.

then − omitting X_4 because its values are fixed by X_2 and X_3 −

$$X_0 = 30 \cdot 56 + 0 \cdot 523 X_1 - 8 \cdot 056 X_2 + 5 \cdot 861 X_3 \pm 6 \cdot 211 \quad .R_{0 \cdot 123} = 0 \cdot 840$$

In this equation, the partial regression coefficients $b_{02 \cdot 13}$ and $b_{03 \cdot 12}$ test whether the regression of X_0 on X_1 differs in its intercept between the three types of government (Fig. 4.3A; in this $b_{02 \cdot 13} = b_2$ and $b_{03 \cdot 12} = b_3$). No test is introduced regarding a research hypothesis that the relationship between X_0 and X_1 differs between the types (i.e. b_{01} when $X_2 = 1 \neq b_{01}$ when $X_3 = 1 \neq b_{01}$ when $X_4 = 1$). In order to achieve this, we could introduce interaction variables as follows:

$$X_5 = (X_1)(X_2)$$

$$X_6 = (X_1)(X_3)$$

$$X_7 = (X_1)(X_4)$$

Variable X_5 will have the value of 0 when $X_2 = 0$, and of X_1 when $X_2 = 1$, and similar values will be produced for X_6 and X_7 for when $X_3 = 1$ and $X_4 = 1$ respectively. We then get an expanded regression equation which includes separate regression lines for each group of towns. Examples of these are shown in Fig. 4.3B which represents the equation

$$X_0 = a_{0 \cdot 123567} + b_{01 \cdot 23567} X_1 + b_{02 \cdot 13567} X_2 + b_{03 \cdot 12567} X_3 + b_{05 \cdot 12367} X_5 +$$
$$+ b_{06 \cdot 12357} X_6 + b_{07 \cdot 12356} X_7 \qquad (4.18)$$

In that, regressions 2 and 3 represent the relationship of X_0 on X_1 if b_2 and b_3 are significant (as in Fig. 4.3A); lines 4, 5 and 6 assume that b_2 and b_3

are not significantly different from zero, but that b_5, b_6, and b_7 are, so that each group of towns has a different slope for its relationship between X_0 and X_1. The coefficient b_7 can be derived from the others, so the equation is fitted with five variables only, giving

$$X_0 = 27 \cdot 792 + 0 \cdot 590 X_1 - 2 \cdot 295 X_2 + 8 \cdot 224 X_3 - 0 \cdot 144 X_5 - 0 \cdot 058 X_6 \pm$$
$$6 \cdot 319 \qquad\qquad\qquad R = 0 \cdot 842$$

in which only the regression coefficient for X_1 is 'statistically significant'. Clearly the 'insignificance' of X_5 and X_6 indicates no different slopes for towns with different political orientations, and collinearity between X_5 and X_6 on the one hand and X_2 and X_3 on the other undoubtedly accounts for the 'insignificance' of the latter pair.

The hypotheses tested by such an analysis are important ones, investigating whether, in this case, towns with different types of councils differ not only in their intercepts for the function $X_0 = f(X_1)$ but also in the slope of this function. Testing the hypothesis via interaction variables can introduce difficult interpretation problems, however, particularly because of collinearity among the independent variables, and the alternative, though little used, procedure of the analysis of covariance is to be preferred.

The analysis of covariance

The fundamental question of this analysis is illustrated in Fig. 4.4. Two variables, X_0 and X_1, are being regressed over a set of observations, which is divided into two groups, A and B. In Fig. 4.4A the regression line $X_0 = a_{0 \cdot 1} + b_{01} X_1 \pm \epsilon$ is shown passing through the mean of all the observations in the two variables ($\overline{T}$), as is the case with all linear regressions; it does not pass through the separate means for the two groups ($\overline{A}$ and $\overline{B}$). In Fig. 4.4B are two regression lines with the same slope but different intercepts, one for the group A observations and passing through $\overline{A}$ and the other for the group B observations and passing through $\overline{B}$. Finally, in Fig. 4.4C two regression lines are again shown, one each for groups A and B, but this time they have different slopes as well as intercepts.

Which of the three diagrams in Fig. 4.4 represents the best fit to a set of data in which the observations are divided into two groups? Analysis of covariance provides the answer to this in the following way.

If the first case (Fig. 4.4A) is the best representation of the variation in the data, the variance in X_1 is sufficient to account for the variance in X_0, and the classification into groups A and B adds nothing to the 'explanation'. ($\overline{A}$ and $\overline{B}$ will then equal $\overline{T} \pm \epsilon$.) In the second, part of the residual variance from $X_0 = f(X_1)$ can be accounted for by the division into the two groups, whereas in the third the residual variance can be accounted for both by the division into two groups and by the variation within each group.

Analysis of covariance tests whether the second and third cases are necessary, or whether the first accounts for all of the 'explainable' variance in X_0. It proceeds in the same way as the analysis of variance, except that because it is dealing with the covariation between two variables rather than

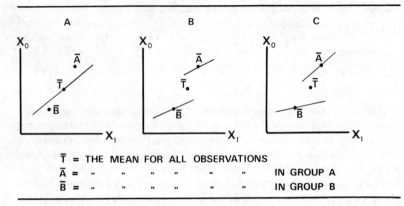

$\overline{T}$ = THE MEAN FOR ALL OBSERVATIONS
$\overline{A}$ = „ „ „ „ „ „ IN GROUP A
$\overline{B}$ = „ „ „ „ „ „ IN GROUP B

Fig. 4.4 The three hypotheses of the analysis of covariance: (A) groups are the same; (B) groups have different intercepts but similar slopes; (C) groups have different intercepts and slopes.

the variation in one (the latter is the analysis of variance) it deals with components of the covariance not the variance. In the analysis of variance (p. 53), total variation is decomposed into between- and within-groups variation, and the latter is

$$\sum_{i=1}^{N} (X_i - \overline{X}_G)^2 = \text{within-groups variation} \qquad (4.19)$$

where $\overline{X}_G$ is the mean value of X for the group to which individual i belongs.

In analysis of covariance, the within-groups covariation of $X_0 = f(X_1)$ is

$$\sum_{i=1}^{N} (X_{i0} - \overline{X}_{0(G)})(X_{i1} - \overline{X}_{1(G)}) \qquad (4.20)$$

where $\overline{X}_{0(G)}$ is the mean of X_0 for the group to which individual i belongs; and
$\overline{X}_{1(G)}$ is the mean of X_1 for the group to which individual i belongs.

Total covariation is

$$\sum_{i=1}^{N} (X_{i0} - \overline{X}_{0(T)})(X_{i1} - \overline{X}_{1(T)}) \qquad (4.21)$$

and between-groups covariation

$$\sum_{i=1}^{N} (\overline{X}_{0(G)} - \overline{X}_{(0)T})(\overline{X}_{1(G)} - \overline{X}_{1(T)}) \qquad (4.22)$$

in both of which equations $\overline{X}_{.(T)}$ refers to the total mean on the relevant variable. There may be interaction between the groups so

Total covariation = Within-groups covariation + Between-groups covariation
$$+ \text{ Interaction} \qquad (4.23)$$

and significance tests are conducted to inquire whether the various components of the covariation are statistically significant in their contribution to the variation of X_0.

The regression method of analysis of variance is usually employed. Three regression equation are calculated. The first, the within-groups regression — sometimes known as the saturated version — fits the model of Fig. 4.4C, and the second, the between-groups regression, fits that of Fig. 4.4B. The third fits the model of Fig. 4.4A. From each, we obtain the residual variation, that amount of the variation in X_0 not accounted for by the equation. A residual variation table is then structured

Source	Amount	df
Within-groups W	Residual variation from within-groups regression	$N - 2K$
Between-groups B	Residual variation from between-groups regression	$N - (K + 1)$

from which

Interaction I	$B - W$	$K - 1$

where N is number of observations; and
K is number of groups.

The F-ratio for the interaction is

$$F_I = \frac{(B - W)/(K - 1)}{W/(N - 2K)} \qquad (4.24)$$

In this the numerator is the interaction variance estimate, and the denominator is the error variance estimate, so formula (4.24) is equivalent to the test for an interaction component in a two-way analysis of variance (p. 103). If the ratio is statistically significant, and the null hypothesis of no interaction component can be rejected, it means that the different slopes model (Fig. 4.4C) has considerably more power over the common slopes model (Fig. 4.4B), relative to the residual error.

This procedure can be illustrated by the data set on variations between towns in their educational spending according to both needs — X_1 — and political orientations of governments — X_2, X_3, X_4 (full notation is on p. 119). Using the procedures discussed above, the equations fitted are

for Fig. 4.4A $X_0 = f(X_1)$ $\qquad$ (4.25)

for Fig. 4.4B $X_0 = f(X_1, X_2, X_3)$ $\qquad$ (4.26)

for Fig. 4.4C $X_0 = f(X_1, X_2, X_3, X_1X_2, X_1X_3)$ $\qquad$ (4.27)

The residual variation from (4.27) gives the value of W, and the residual variation from (4.26) gives B, allowing formula (4.24) to be applied.

For the education provision data the equations are

$X_0 = 22 \cdot 56 + 0 \cdot 691 X_1 \quad r_{01} = 0 \cdot 638$

$X_0 = 30 \cdot 56 + 0 \cdot 523 X_1 - 8 \cdot 056 X_2 + 5 \cdot 861 X_3 \quad R_{0 \cdot 123} = 0 \cdot 840$

$X_0 = 27 \cdot 794 + 0 \cdot 590 X_1 - 2 \cdot 295 X_2 + 8 \cdot 224 X_3 - 0 \cdot 144(X_1 X_2) -$
   $- 0 \cdot 058(X_1 X_3) \quad R = 0 \cdot 842$

The total variation in X_0 is $6038 \cdot 02$ so that

$W = 6038 \cdot 02 \, (1 - 0 \cdot 842^2) = 1757 \cdot 28$

$B = 6038 \cdot 02 \, (1 - 0 \cdot 840^2) = 1777 \cdot 59$

and

$$F_I = \frac{(1777 \cdot 59 - 1757 \cdot 28)/(3 - 1)}{1757 \cdot 28/(50 - 6)}$$

$$= \frac{20 \cdot 31/2}{39 \cdot 94} = 10 \cdot 155/39 \cdot 94 = 0 \cdot 254$$

This is statistically insignificant at the 5% probability level, leading to the conclusion that there is no interaction in the system; the three groups have the same slope for the relationship between X_0 and X_1. (One further point to note is the change in the regression coefficients for X_2 and X_3 between the equations above for formulae (4.26) and (4.27); this is a clear example of the effect of collinearity on regression coefficients, in this case the collinearity between X_2 and X_3 and the interaction variables.)

Within-class correlation

This final aspect of the analysis of covariance is illustrated by Fig. 4.5. In the first example (Fig. 4.5A) there is a positive, but weak relationship in the total set of observations between X_0 and X_1, but within each of the two groups of observations – A and B – there is a strong negative cor-

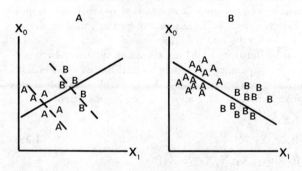

Fig. 4.5 Within-class correlation.

relation between the two variables. The overall positive relationship occurs because of the relative locations of the two group regressions. In the second example (Fig. 4.5B) the set of observations is again divided into two groups — A and B — but this time there is a fairly strong relationship between X_0 and X_1 over all observations (a negative one: Fig. 4.5B) but a weak negative relationship within each group.

Description of differences such as these can be achieved if there is no significant interaction effect, so that the slope of $X_0 = f(X_1)$ is the same in every group. We can then investigate whether the within-group (or within-class) correlations are significantly different from the total correlation, proceeding as for the earlier test for interaction. (This is a way of testing whether dummy variables representing the groups add to the 'explanation' of X_0 by X_1.)

Source of variation		Amount	df
Covariate	G	Residual variation from $X_0 = f(X_1)$	$N - K$
Between-groups B		Residual variation from between-groups regression	
Between-groups − covariate		$G - B$	1
Error	W	Residual variation from within-groups regression	$N - (K + 1)$

and an F-ratio for within-class correlation is

$$F_W = (G - B)/(W/N - (K + 1)) \qquad (4.28)$$

As with the two-way analysis of variance, having found that there is no significant interaction, we now test with formula (4.28) whether the classification of the observations into groups adds any more to the 'explanation' of the variance in X_0 than does the other independent variable — the covariate, X_1.

For the educational provision data set, the equations are given above (p. 124) and our previous test has already indicated an insignificant interaction effect. As

total variation is $X_0 = 6038 \cdot 02$ and $r_{01} = 0 \cdot 638$

$G = 6038 \cdot 02 \, (1 - 0 \cdot 638^2) = 3580 \cdot 28$

and

$F_W = (3580 \cdot 28 - 1777 \cdot 59)/(1757 \cdot 28/50 - 4)$

$\qquad = 1802 \cdot 69/38 \cdot 20 = 47 \cdot 19$

which is statistically significant at the 5% level. In other words, classification of the observations into groups adds significantly to the explanation of X_0 by X_1, indicating that we have covariation but not interaction.

The analysis of covariance has not been made much use of by geographers, because of the assumptions that the variance of X_0 is the same in each group and that $\overline{X}_1$ is the same for each group. In what was probably the first published use, King (1961), in his paper already referred to (p. 78), only employed the within-class correlation part of the procedure; he argued that only when the regression lines for the various groups were parallel could tests for the significance of the classification be made, but said nothing about the test for interaction. He had hypothesised that classification of the towns would add to the explanation of their distance to nearest neighbour of the same size (X_0 – see p. 78) and he introduced three such classifications according to: (1) whether or not they were central places; (2) whether or not they were 'on level land'; and (3) whether or not they were in one of five 'type of farming' regions. Only for the second of these could the within-class correlation test be undertaken, showing that the classification increased the value of R^2 significantly, from 0·25 to 0·36. Kariel (1963) followed King's procedure exactly in his analysis of the rate of population growth due to migration among United States' counties; the within-class correlation test indicated that classification of the counties into those whose mean winter temperature exceeded 45°F and those whose mean was less than 45°F increased the value of R^2 from 0·47 to 0·53.

Conclusions

The relative infrequency with which analysis of variance has been used by geographers was noted in a review written in the late 1960s (Gould, 1969). Since then, use has increased somewhat, particularly in the regression format involving dummy variables. The assumptions of the model are such that it is not particularly relevant to many types of geographical research, however, for it has been constructed as a way of analysing carefully specified experimental data. Nevertheless, analysis of variance has been used in a variety of forms and, particularly in its regression form, will probably receive greater attention from geographers in the future.

Chapter 5

Principal components analysis and factor analysis

So far in this book we have looked at the relationships among sets of variables in which (1) all of the variables have been defined prior to the analysis, and (2) the direction of the relationships between independent and dependent variables has been specified. In this chapter, we look at relationships involving one set of variables that has been defined prior to the analysis and another set which is generated from the first. Thus we take a group of variables measured over a sample or population of observations, and look at the inter-relationships among them. In a sense, every variable is both an independent and a dependent at the same time, being related to every other variable and perhaps, depending on the procedure adopted, to itself as well. The output from such analyses is a new set of variables, replacing the original set; the relationships between these two are the focus.

Why should we want to replace one group of variables by another? Three basic reasons are suggested.

1. *To identify groups of inter-correlated variables.* This may be a 'blind', inductive process, searching for order in a large data set. For example, a researcher may have information on the species composition of a sample of woodlands, giving a data matrix whose n variables are the species with the number of different specimens of each recorded for each of the N observations. He wishes to know whether there are groups of species which tend to occur in the same woodland communities, and by correlating the distribution of one species with that of another he can see to what extent their distributions are similar. But if he has 13 species as variables, the correlation matrix comparing each pair of distributions will contain 78 different values. (The matrix is symmetrical since $r_{AB} = r_{BA}$, and r_{AA}, r_{BB}, etc. are of no interest, so the number of different correlations is $((n^2 - n)/2)$. Discerning patterns in such a large set of numbers is difficult, and a means is required which identifies groups of species whose distributions are inter-related.

More usually, since statistical analysis is organised in scientific work on the basis of underlying theories, the search for groups of variables may be a deductive, hypothesis-testing procedure. For example, research into the differences between areas within cities according to their population and housing characteristics suggest that there are three major patterns, representing socio-economic status, life style, and segregation processes

(Johnston, 1971; Timms, 1971). There are no direct means of measuring the outcome of these processes, however, and so researchers must select various indicants of each, such as occupation, education and income for socio-economic status. Their hypothesis is that these variables are closely inter-related with each other across a set of areas, and separate from groups of indicants representing other concepts; they wish to test for the existence of such groups, and to provide a composite index of each concept.

2. *To reduce the number of variables being studied.*   A physical geographer may be interested in the spatial patterns of various soil characteristics in a tract of land, and so lays down a sampling procedure. At each point he collects a soil sample which is taken to a laboratory for analysis. Forty different characteristics of each sample are measured, the whole procedure taking 1 week per sample. Clearly, this time for analysis limits the number of samples that can be taken. But is it necessary to measure all 40 characteristics? If these are clearly inter-related so that several variables all have very much the same spatial pattern, then it is hardly sense to do what is tantamount to measuring the same thing several times. An analysis of a trial sample of his whole set of sample points may indicate much redundancy among the 40 characteristics, suggesting that only 20 need be measured, thereby halving the laboratory work.

3. *To rewrite the data set in an alternative form*, with characteristics not possessed in its original state. In Chapter 3, for example, we saw the problems of relating a dependent variable to several independent variables when the latter were characterised by severe collinearity. Reorganisation of the independent variables to remove this collinearity could be a considerable aid to interpretation of the regression equation.

Segments, components and factors

The three tasks just outlined can be tackled by using either principal components analysis or factor analysis, two related techniques which have become extremely popular as geographical research tools since about 1960. Both of these operate on the same general principles as path analysis (Ch. 3, p. 96), which are that each variable can be subdivided into several independent parts in terms of its association with other variables, and that each correlation coefficient similarly is made up of different segments.

These segments may be completely independent of each other, so that we can identify groups of variables within each of which correlations are high but between which correlations are near-zero. More often, however, the groups are not as clear cut as this. In our example of the distributions of 13 plant species over a sample of woodlands, it may be that there are three main types of woodland but that no particular species is found in only one type. For each species, therefore, we might categorise its distribution in the following way:

Ash = 50% Type A pattern + 20% Type B pattern + 20% Type C pattern

Beech = 80% Type A pattern + 10% Type B pattern + 5% Type C pattern

Willow = 5% Type A pattern + 70% Type B pattern + 20% Type C pattern

etc. These 'equations' tell us the extent of the agreement between a hybrid distribution — Type A — and the distribution of each of the original species. For none of the latter does the total sum to 100%, showing that, in the terminology of the regression model, there is an error or residual term in the distribution of each species which is not related to any of the general patterns.

Each of these general patterns we can call a *segment*, and we want to discover what they are. Thus we are formulating a regression model in which

$$X_1 = f(S_1, S_2 \ldots S_n) \pm \epsilon \tag{5.1}$$

where X_1 is one of the original variables; and $S_1 \ldots S_n$ are the segments, which are composites of the original variables.

Our regression model has as many equations as variables, however, so that if we have five variables ($X_1 \ldots X_5$) then we have five equations:

$$X_1 = f(S_1 \ldots S_n) \pm \epsilon$$
$$X_2 = f(S_1 \ldots S_n) \pm \epsilon$$
$$X_3 = f(S_1 \ldots S_n) \pm \epsilon$$
$$X_4 = f(S_1 \ldots S_n) \pm \epsilon$$
$$X_5 = f(S_1 \ldots S_n) \pm \epsilon \tag{5.2}$$

Our aim is to solve these equations, to discover the importance of each segment to each variable. If we found that X_3, X_4, and X_5 all were similarly related to S_2, we would be identifying a group of inter-related variables: if ash, beech and willow all were similarly related to the various woodland segments, we would have identified a group of species which tend to be found in the same environments.

The two methods of solving the equations of formula (5.2) differ in their treatment of the error term. In the first, *principal components analysis*, the error terms are treated as segments. Each variable is then being related to a series of *components*, one of which may well be its own error term (or a part of it; see p. 161). Thus the components model is often termed a closed system model, in that all of the variance in the original variables is being investigated. The result is a set of components whose number equals the number of variables, so that for a four variable system

$$X_1 = f(C_I, C_{II}, C_{III}, C_{IV})$$
$$X_2 = f(C_I, C_{II}, C_{III}, C_{IV})$$
$$X_3 = f(C_I, C_{II}, C_{III}, C_{IV})$$
$$X_4 = f(C_I, C_{II}, C_{III}, C_{IV}) \tag{5.3}$$

where $C_I \ldots C_{IV}$ are the four components

Comparison of the importance of each component to each variable will indicate the extent of any common pattern among the variables.

The second method of treating formula (5.2) is *factor analysis*, which puts the error term outside its equations. In this, each variable is first split into two parts: its common variance is that part of its pattern which is related to the other variables in the system; its unique variance is the residual from that multiple relationship. The common variance is then divided into a set of *factors*, in much the same way as the total variance is divided into components by principal components analysis, so that with four variables we get a set of equations

$$X_1 = f(F_I, F_{II}, \ldots F_n) + U_1$$
$$X_2 = f(F_I, F_{II}, \ldots F_n) + U_2$$
$$X_3 = f(F_I, F_{II}, \ldots F_n) + U_3$$
$$X_4 = f(F_I, F_{II}, \ldots F_n) + U_4 \tag{5.4}$$

where $F_I \ldots F_n$ are the set of factors; and
$U_1 \ldots U_4$ are the unique variances for each variable.

Since factor analysis is normally based on correlation coefficients, the variance of each variable is standardised to $1 \cdot 0$. Thus unless $U_1 = U_2 = U_3 = U_4 = 0 \cdot 0$ (which is what is assumed for principal components analysis) then the number of factors must be less than the number of variables, n: the number of components is always the same as the number of variables, though some of the former may be trivial, as we shall see below.

Development of these two methods of solving large blocks of simultaneous equations was achieved without the aid of calculators and computers. Today, solution is usually via matrix algebra, but to illustrate the process of determining components and factors we will use a geometrical analogy.

Geometrical representation of correlations

The product moment correlation coefficient, r_{12}, is the square root of the proportion of the variance in X_1 related to the variance in X_2 (and vice versa). Because these variables are normally distributed, in standardised form, they have means of zero and standard deviations of $1 \cdot 0$, so that

$$S_1 = 1 \cdot 0 \qquad S_2 = 1 \cdot 0$$

and, for our example, $r_{12} = r_{21} = 0 \cdot 75$

We can represent the standard deviation of X_1 by a line of a given length, along which we mark off its correlation with X_2 (Fig. 5.1A). A similar line could be drawn to represent the proportion of the length of X_2 associated — as indicated by r_{21} — with X_1.

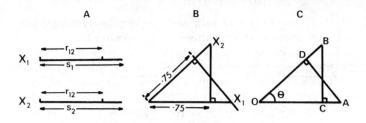

Fig. 5.1 The geometrical representation of the correlation coefficient, r_{12}.

To place these two lines in the same diagram, they must emanate from the same origin. What would be the angle between them? Remember that both lines are of the same length, and that the correlation of X_1 on X_2 accounts for three-quarters of the length of X_1, as does the correlation of X_2 on X_1 for X_2. The rule applied is that a perpendicular from the three-quarters point (represents a correlation of 0·75) on X_1 must meet the end of the line representing X_2, and a perpendicular from the three-quarters point on X_2 must meet the end of the line representing X_1. In other words, each variable is casting a shadow on the other whose length represents the value of the correlation between them. Figure 5.1B shows this.

The angle between the two variables in Fig. 5.1B can be found using simple trigonometry. Classifying the sides as in Fig. 5.1C, then

$$\text{cosine } \theta = \frac{OC}{OB} = \frac{OD}{OA} \tag{5.5}$$

Since, from Fig. 5.1B

$$OC = OD = 0·75 \quad \text{and} \quad OA = OB = 1·0$$

then

$$\text{cosine } \theta = 0·75/1·00 = 0·75 \quad \text{and} \quad \theta = 41°24'$$

We have devised a system, therefore, in which *the cosine of the angle between the lines representing two variables equals the correlation between those two variables.* More formally, if

$$OA = S_1 = 1·0 \quad \text{and} \quad OB = S_2 = 1·0$$

then

$$\text{cosine } B\hat{O}A = r_{12} = r_{21}$$

Cosines, like correlation coefficients, vary between +1·0 and −1·0. A cosine of 0·0 represents an angle of 90°, so two variables which are uncorrelated ($r_{12} = 0·0$) are represented by lines (the technical term is vectors) which are at right angles to each other (Fig. 5.2A); this is often called an orthogonal relationship. The cosine of 180° is −1·0, so negative correlations are shown by obtuse angles, and complete negative correlations by a

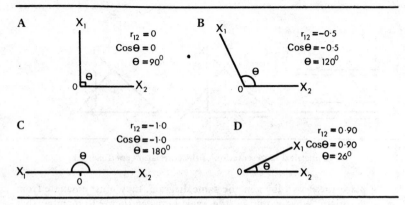

Fig. 5.2   The cosine and the correlation; four examples.

continuous line passing through the origin (Fig. 5.2B and C). High positive correlations are shown by small angles (Fig. 5.2D).

The system for portraying correlation coefficients as angles with $\cos \theta = r_{XY}$ is internally consistent, in that it obeys its own rules. It also has a clear relationship to the correlation between variables as displayed in scatter-diagrams, a point illustrated by Fig. 5.3. For each of the two variables, X_1 and X_2, the distribution of the values for the 32 observations in all three of the relationships shown is approximately normal. Together, in each case, the distributions are bivariate normal, but the form of this bivariate normal distribution varies according to the correlation between X_1 and X_2. In the first case, X_1 and X_2 are completely uncorrelated (r_{12} = 0·0; Fig. 5.3A) and the bivariate normal distribution is circular in both dimensions (i.e. the two normal distributions for X_1 and X_2 intersect at right angles). This is shown in the right-hand diagram of Fig. 5.3A, which includes the contours for the 1, 2 and 3 standard deviation distance units from the means of X_1 and X_2 (which form the point of intercept for the two axes).

With correlated variables the scatter of points is elliptical rather than circular, as indicated in Fig. 5.3B where X_1 and X_2 are positively correlated (r_{12} = 0·58). The bivariate normal distribution is thus elongated along the main axis of the scatter-diagram (from bottom left to top right) and a series of elliptical contours can be drawn to enclose all the points at the given standard deviation distances from the bivariate mean. The axes of this ellipse are separated by the angle $-\theta-$ which has a cosine of 0·58 (= r_{12}), so that the form of the set of ellipses is defined by the correlation between the two variables. In the third case (Fig. 5.3C) the correlation is much greater and the ellipse much more elongated along the axis of the correlation.

We will not go into the detailed geometry or algebra which proves that the cosine of the angle between the unique pair of vectors which define

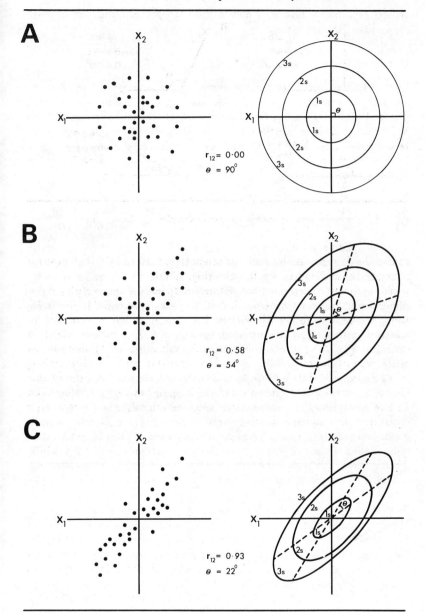

Fig. 5.3   Bivariate distributions and the derivation of the correlation coefficient.

the ellipse of the bivariate normal distribution equals the correlation co-efficient; it is sufficient for our argument to realise that the system outlined in Figs. 5.1 and 5.2 is related to the geometry of correlation coefficients.

Having established this, it is now possible to proceed with multivariate rather than bivariate systems.

Representing a correlation matrix

Figure 5.4 is a geometrical representation of the matrix of correlations among nine variables, X_1 to X_9. The angular relationships between each pair and their cosines (i.e. the correlation coefficients) are given in Table 5.1. Clearly this is an exceptional matrix, in that all of the correlations can be portrayed accurately in two dimensions. If the correlations were

	X_1	X_2	X_3	With angles X_1	X_2	X_3
X_1	1·00	0·71	0·66	0	45	49
X_2	0·71	1·00	0·81	45	0	36
X_3	0·66	0·81	1·00	49	36	0

a brief experiment with pencil and paper would indicate that this matrix cannot be represented in a two-dimensional diagram. Having drawn, for example, the correlation of r_{12} as $45°$ it would then be impossible to locate a vector for X_3 which was both $49°$ from X_1 and $36°$ from X_2. A three-dimensional diagram would be needed. The maximum number of dimensions needed to show the correlation matrix is always the number of variables, n: if we had four variables, all orthogonal (i.e. at right angles, or uncorrelated) to each other, then they would form a four-dimensional space.

The nature of such n-dimensional spaces can be visualised, although not drawn, as multivariate extensions of the diagrams in Fig. 5.3. Thus if we had three variables, all uncorrelated with the others (i.e. $r_{12} = r_{13} = r_{23} = 0·00$), then as a logical extension of the diagram in Fig. 5.3A, the trivariate normal distribution would be perfectly spherical. If, on the other hand,

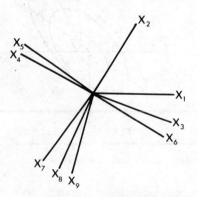

Fig. 5.4   Geometrical representation of the correlation matrix in Table 5.1.

they were all highly correlated (i.e. $r_{12} = r_{13} = r_{23} = 0.93$) then the bivariate normal distribution for each pair would be as in Fig. 5.3C and the trivariate normal involving all three would be cigar-shaped — i.e. an extension of the shape in Fig. 5.3C to three dimensions. In analyses using four or more variables, the shape of the multivariate normal distributions cannot be conceived but, just as in Fig. 5.3, the closer the correlation the more elongated the shape of the distribution (this shape is often known as the hyperspace) and the greater the constraint on the location of observations. With many variables the smaller the average correlation the closer the hyperspace is to an n-dimensional sphere (Fig. 5.3A). With high average intercorrelations, the hyperspace becomes a 'multi-dimensional cigar', with implications for the extraction of components.

Although correlation matrices cannot be drawn in two-dimensional spaces in most cases, therefore, this is a constraint in our method of illustration rather than on the procedure. It is possible to work in manydimensional spaces as an abstraction, even if these are difficult to conceive of and impossible to perceive. Our examples in the following sections thus use very simple examples, to allow visual description of the process.

Table 5.1 Angles and correlations for the matrix in Fig. 5.4

A. Angles between variables

	X_1	X_2	X_3	X_4	X_5	X_6	X_7	X_8	X_9
X_1	0								
X_2	57	0							
X_3	18	75	0						
X_4	153	96	171	0					
X_5	146	89	164	7	0				
X_6	29	86	11	178	175	0			
X_7	127	176	109	80	87	98	0		
X_8	114	171	96	93	100	85	13	0	
X_9	105	162	87	102	109	76	22	9	0

B. Product-moment correlations (= cosines of angles)

	X_1	X_2	X_3	X_4	X_5	X_6	X_7	X_8	X_9
X_1	1.0000								
X_2	0.5446	1.0000							
X_3	0.9511	0.2588	1.0000						
X_4	−0.8910	−0.1045	−0.9877	1.0000					
X_5	−0.8290	0.0175	−0.9613	0.9926	1.0000				
X_6	0.8746	0.0698	0.9816	−0.9994	−0.9962	1.0000			
X_7	−0.6018	−0.9976	−0.3256	0.1737	0.0523	−0.1392	1.0000		
X_8	−0.4067	−0.9877	−0.1045	−0.0523	−0.1737	0.0872	0.9744	1.0000	
X_9	−0.2588	−0.9511	0.0523	−0.2079	−0.3256	0.2419	0.9272	0.9877	1.0000

Principal components analysis

Principal components analysis rewrites a data matrix, comprising n variables and N observations, into another n × n form, in which the new variables are: (1) weighted representations of the original set; and (2) uncorrelated one with another. Thus the number of components is equal to the number of variables.

Extracting the components

The procedure in principal components analysis involves the production of a new set of variables, each of which in turn is as close as possible to the original set. This is very much akin to the method of finding the mean in a set of values, and so our aim in the extraction of the first principal component from the correlation matrix in Table 5.1 is to define a 'mean variable'. In our diagram (Fig. 5.4) this implies locating a new vector which is as close as possible to the nine vectors already there.

Angular closeness in a correlation diagram such as Fig. 5.4 is, as we have already seen, the equivalent of maximum correlations. So, too, is angular distance: no angle can be greater than 180° (i.e. we always measure the angle between two variables going 'round the diagram' in the shortest angular distance between the two). An angle of 180° is also a maximum correlation, of -1.0, and our aim is to locate the new variable − component I − so as to get as close to either 0° or 180° as possible with all of the vectors in the correlation diagram.

Clearly there is a finite, but very large number of locations for the first component. What we are looking for is the average location, however, so the closer any one variable is to all of the others, the closer the component will be to it − because it is the 'average variable'. If we have three variables, among which the angles representing the correlations are

	X_1	X_2	X_3
X_1	0	30	50
X_2	30	0	20
X_3	50	20	0

then intuitively, X_2 is closest to the average position. To prove this, we extract the first component. This involves: (1) converting the angles to correlations; (2) summing the correlations for each variable to see how well correlated with all of the others it is; and (3) expressing this sum as a ratio of the square root of the total correlations. Thus

Correlation matrix		X_1	X_2	X_3	
	X_1	1·00	0·866	0·643	
	X_2	0·866	1·00	0·940	
	X_3	0·643	0·940	1·00	Total sum
Sum of correlations		2·509	2·806	2·583	7·898
Sum/$\sqrt{\text{Total sum}}$		0·89	0·99	0·92	

Our intuitive judgement is correct; the sums of all correlations in each column show that X_2 does have the highest total intercorrelation with all of the other variables including itself.

In the procedure just outlined, the maximum value of the total sum of the correlations can be n^2 (n is the number of variables), which would be the case if every correlation were +1·0. By taking the square root of this value, we make it equivalent to one variable, so that if n = 3 and total sum (TS) = 9 then $\sqrt{TS} = 3$, which is the maximum sum of correlations possible for each variable. Thus $\sqrt{TS}$ is the maximum sum possible for any one variable, and is the new *average variable*, or the *principal component*. The ratio of the sum of the correlations for each variable to $\sqrt{TS}$ is thus the correlation of each variable with the component or how close it is to the average. Converting these correlations to angles allows us to locate the component in the vector diagram.

	X_1	X_2	X_3	TS
Sum of correlations	2·509	2·806	2·583	7·898
Sum/$\sqrt{TS}$	0·8929	0·9986	0·9092	
Angles	27°	3°	23°	

(The angles are taken to the nearest degree.) Since the component is equivalent to a variable, it too has a standard deviation of 1·0 and the same 'length' in a correlation diagram as one of the original variables.

The method just described is known as the centroid method for extracting components. It is not always accurate (if the correlation matrix contains many negative as well as positive entries then it provides poor estimates), and it is not generally used. The normal method, almost always performed now by computer, involves the use of matrix algebra and the extraction of the principal eigenvector of the correlation matrix. The result is the same, however; a new variable is located in the vector space by its correlations with the original variables (see Gould, 1967).

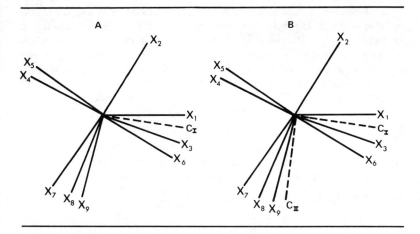

Fig. 5.5 The first (A) and second (B) principal components of the correlation matrix in Fig. 5.4 and Table 5.1.

Extraction of the first principal component thus involves location, in the n-dimensional vector space of the correlation diagram, of a new variable which is as close as possible to all of the original variables. This position for our correlation matrix of Table 5.1 is shown in Fig. 5.5A. What are the relationships between this component and the original variables? Three separate, though related, indices can be extracted: (1) the angle between the component and each of the original variables; (2) the correlation, which is the cosine of that angle; and (3) the squared correlation, which indicates the proportion of the variance associated with the component. For Fig. 5.5A, these are

Variable	Angle	Correlation (Component loading)	Squared correlation
X_1	7	0·9925	0·9851
X_2	64	0·4384	0·1922
X_3	11	0·9816	0·9635
X_4	160	−0·9397	0·8830
X_5	153	−0·8910	0·7939
X_6	22	0·9272	0·8597
X_7	120	−0·5000	0·2500
X_8	107	−0·2924	0·0855
X_9	98	−0·1392	0·0194

These correlations between the variables and the component are known as the *component loadings*. They are interpreted in exactly the same way as product moment correlation coefficients, so that the squares of their values indicate the proportion of the variance in the individual variable which can be associated with the component: for X_2, therefore, 19·22% of its variance is associated with the variance of C_I (the first component) whereas for X_4 the percentage is 88·30.

Each squared component loading indicates the degree to which the new variable — which is the average of all the original variables — subsumes or replaces an original variable (i.e. what portion of the original variable is correlated with the component). The sum of these squared loadings therefore indicates the total variance accounted for by the component. This value is known as the *eigenvalue*, often represented by the Greek letter lambda, λ, and it is calculated as

$$\lambda_i = \sum_{j=1}^{n} L_{ij}^2 \tag{5.6}$$

where L_{ij} is the loading for variable j on component i; and
$\qquad \lambda_i$ is the eigenvalue for component i.

In our case this is $(0·9851 + 0·1922 + \ldots 0·0194)$, so

$\lambda_i = 5·0323.$

To appreciate the relative importance of an eigenvalue, we must relate it to the total variance in the correlation matrix. This is the number of variables, n, which in the present example is 9. Because the matrix is made up of correlations among variables each of which has a standardised variance of $1\cdot0$ (p. 130), then the potential is there for the component to account for all of their variances, which is $n \times 1\cdot0^2 = n$. (If the component did account for all of the variance, then all of the coefficients in the matrix would be either $+1\cdot0$ or $-1\cdot0$.) Thus, if the eigenvalue, λ_I, is expressed as a percentage of n, we have the percentage of the variance in the set of variables which is correlated with component I: in our case $100\,(\lambda_I/n) = (5\cdot0323/9)\,100 = 55\cdot91$. This is frequently known as the *percentage of the trace*. The trace is the sum of the values on the principal diagonal (i.e. from top left to bottom right) of a matrix: in a correlation matrix each of these values is $+1\cdot0$, which is the correlation of a variable with itself, and so the trace is equal to n.

We can now briefly summarise the results so far from the components analysis of the correlation matrix in Table 5.1 and Fig. 5.4. The first component, C_I, represents the average variable in this matrix, and the percentage of the variance of the nine variables associated with this average is $55\cdot91$. Some variables are closer to the average than others, as is indicated by the component loadings, which are equivalent to correlation coefficients. The squares of these loadings indicate that variables X_1, X_3, X_4, X_5, and X_6 are all fairly close to the average; in each case over three-quarters of the variance is associated with the component. (Note that for variables X_4 and X_5 the negative sign for the component loadings shows an inverse relationship between their own patterns and the average pattern.) If the purpose of the components analysis were to identify groups of inter-correlated variables, therefore, we might conclude that these five variables, X_1, X_3, X_4, X_5 and X_6, are all very closely related to the average pattern as isolated by the principal component. This is confirmed by Fig. 5.5A, which shows small angles between C_I and X_1, X_3, X_6 and large angles (remembering that $180°$ represents a correlation of $-1\cdot0$) between C_I and both X_4 and X_5.

The first component accounts for over 55% of the variance in the set of nine variables by the average pattern, therefore, but what of the remaining 45%? Is there some general pattern in the residuals, in those portions of the variables not related to the average pattern? To answer this we extract a second component. From the original correlation matrix (Table 5.1) we subtract all of the proportions of the inter-correlations which are a function of the correlations of the individual variables with the component. Thus, for example, $r_{12} = 0\cdot5446$, L_{I1} (the loading of X_1, on component I) = $0\cdot9925$ and $L_{I2} = 0\cdot4384$. L_{I1}^2 (= $0\cdot9851$) is part of the correlation r_{11} (i.e. the variance of X_1) associated with the component, L_{I2}^2 is the part of r_{22} associated with the component, and $(L_{I1})(L_{I2})$ is the part of r_{12} associated with the component. Since

$$r_{12} = 0\cdot5446$$

and

$$(L_{I1})(L_{I2}) = (0\cdot9925)(0\cdot4384) = 0\cdot4351$$

then

$$r_{12} - (L_{I1})(L_{I2}) = 0.5446 - 0.4351 = 0.1095$$

This last value is the correlation between X_1 and X_2, once the influence of component I has been removed. It is the equivalent of the partial correlation $r_{12 \cdot I}$.

Having extracted the first component, we produce a residual correlation matrix containing all the values of

$$r_{ij} - (L_{Ii})(L_{Ij}) \tag{5.7}$$

where i and j are variables. These are the correlations between the variables once the effect of the first component has been removed. We then extract the average pattern — i.e. the principal component — from this matrix of partial correlation coefficients, to form the second component — C_{II} — of the total analysis. Two features of this are worthy of note. First, in the residual correlation matrix, none of the values on the principal diagonal (the trace) will be 1·0, apart from in exceptional cases when a variable is orthogonal to the first component. As we have already suggested,

$$r_{11} = 1.0 \quad \text{and} \quad L_{I1} = 0.9925 \quad \text{so}$$
$$r_{11} - (L_{I1})(L_{I1}) = 1.0 - 0.9851 = 0.0149$$

In other words, very little of the variance of X_1 (= r_{11}) remains to be accounted for, whereas for X_7

$$r_{77} = 1.0 \quad \text{and} \quad L_{I7} = -0.500 \quad \text{so}$$
$$r_{77} - (L_{I7})(L_{I7}) = 1.0 - 0.2500 = 0.7500$$

Thus the vectors in the correlation diagram representing the residual correlation matrix will not be of equal length. The larger the loading of a variable on the first component, the shorter its vector in the residual correlation matrix from which the second component is extracted. Since the component is located to be at the average position of the matrix, the longer the vector — i.e. the greater the proportion of the variance in a variable remaining to be explained — the more influence it will have on the component's location. (This argument is developed in the later section on factor analysis, p. 158.) The second component, then, is located as close as possible to the residual variance, to the partial correlations among the variables holding constant the first component.

The second feature of the residual correlation matrix stems from a general characteristic of residuals from properly specified linear regressions (i.e. meeting all six of the requirements: p. 37 ff.). This is that the residuals are uncorrelated with the independent variable. In this case, the first component is the independent variable, and so the average of the residuals from its regressions on the original variables must be uncorrelated with the first component. Zero correlation is shown by orthogonal vectors in a correlation diagram, and so components are orthogonal.

The second component from a correlation matrix is thus the average pattern among the portions of the variables not related to the first component, and is orthogonal to the latter. Its position for our nine-variable example is shown in Fig. 5.5B. The related angles, loadings, squared loadings, and eigenvalue are:

Variable	Angle	Loading	Squared loading
X_1	97	−0·1219	0·0149
X_2	154	−0·8988	0·8078
X_3	79	0·1908	0·0364
X_4	110	−0·3420	0·1170
X_5	117	−0·4540	0·2061
X_6	68	0·3746	0·1403
X_7	30	0·8660	0·7500
X_8	17	0·9563	0·9145
X_9	8	0·9903	0·9807

$$3·9677 = \lambda_{II}$$

In this case, we see that the component accounts for 44·09% of the total variance − (3·9677/9·0) 100 − and that its main associations are with variables X_2, X_7, X_8 and X_9. Note that λ_{II} is less than λ_I − the main pattern in the residual variance always being less important than that in the original variance: successive eigenvalues are always smaller than those preceding them.

If we sum the eigenvalues for the two components extracted we get

$$\lambda_I + \lambda_{II} = 5·0323 + 3·9677 = 9·0 = n$$

which indicates that all of the variance in the nine original variables has been replaced by only two new variables, representing the average pattern plus the average pattern in the residuals from the first average. We can now write out the full set of equations of formula (5.4) as follows:

$$X_1 = 0·9925C_I − 0·1219C_{II}$$
$$X_2 = 0·4384C_I − 0·8988C_{II}$$
$$\cdots$$
$$\cdots$$
$$\cdots$$
$$X_9 = −0·1392C_I + 0·9903C_{II}$$

The coefficients in these equations are the loadings and their squared values indicate the relative weight of each of the components in accounting for the variance in the relevant variable.

The equations above are usually presented in tabular form, an example of which is given in Table 5.2, for the data in Fig. 5.5. In this, one new index has been introduced − the *communality*. This is the sum of the squared loadings for a variable, so that

$$h_j^2 = \sum_{i=1}^{k} L_{ij}^2 \tag{5.8}$$

Table 5.2   Principal components analysis of the data in Table 5.1

Variable	Component loading Component I	II	Communality h^2
X_1	0·9925	−0·1219	1·0000
X_2	0·4384	−0·8988	1·0000
X_3	0·9816	0·1908	0·9999
X_4	−0·9397	−0·3420	1·0000
X_5	−0·8910	−0·4540	1·0000
X_6	0·9272	0·3746	1·0000
X_7	−0·5000	0·8660	1·0000
X_8	−0·2924	0·9563	1·0000
X_9	−0·1392	0·9903	1·0001
Eigenvalue	5·0323	3·9677	
% trace	55·91	44·09	

where L_{ij} is the loading for variable j on component i;
    k is the number of components ($\leqslant$ n); and
    h_j^2 is the communality for variable j.

The communality is thus the proportion of the variance for each variable accounted for by all of the components, the square of each individual loading being the proportion of the variance accounted for by the particular component. In Table 5.2 the communalities are all 1·0000 (allowing for rounding error at the fourth decimal place), indicating that the two components depicted in Fig. 5.5B account for all of the variance in every variable. As we shall see below, this is an extremely rare, if not impossible, occurrence: the communalities are usually less than 1·0 unless the number of components extracted equals the number of variables.

Having illustrated the extraction of components, using Fig. 5.5, according to the system of Fig. 5.1 and 5.2, we can return to Fig. 5.3 and see how the components relate to the bivariate normal distributions of correlated variables. Figure 5.6 repeats the correlation of Fig. 5.3B in which the angle of the axes of the ellipse is 54° (cos 54° = r_{12}). In a two-variable matrix, the principal component bisects the angle between those vectors 'enclosing' the correlation and so, by definition, it must follow the longest axis of the bivariate normal ellipse or hyperspace. Following from this, the second component, orthogonal to the first, must follow the shortest axis of the ellipse, as indicated by the figure. The length of those axes is equivalent to the relevant eigenvalues, so that in Fig. 5.6 OA = λ_I and OB = λ_{II}. The more elongated the hyperspace, therefore, the larger the first eigenvalue relative to the second, a relationship which holds for n-dimensional hyperspaces also. Thus successive principal components represent the axes, in descending order of length, of the hyperspace.

At the outset of this chapter we noted three basic reasons for conducting principal components analysis. From the hypothetical correlation matrix analysed here, we would conclude, in terms of those reasons:

1. *Groups of related variables.* The two components (Table 5.2) pick out two clear groups: one comprises X_1, X_3, X_4, X_5 and X_6, with X_4 and X_5 being the inverses of the other three, and the other group is X_2, X_7, X_8 and X_9, with X_2 the inverse of the other three. These are not completely exclusive — X_7 has a loading of -0.5 on C_I, for example — but the existence of the groups is very obvious.

2. *Reducing the number of variables to study.* Given that we have identified two groups, it could be argued that we really need study only one variable from each. For the first group, X_1 would seem to be the best choice — it has the largest loading on C_I — whereas X_9 would be the best for the second group.

3. *Rewriting the data set.* The nine original variables, among which there was substantial inter-correlation (Table 5.1), have been replaced by two, which are weighted combinations of the former and are independent of each other.

The data used to produce this example are extremely artificial, having been produced so that two components only will account for all of the variance in the 9×9 matrix, thereby allowing the correlation matrix to be portrayed accurately in a two-dimensional diagram. This approach has allowed a diagrammatic as well as a verbal description of the procedures of principal components analysis as the identification of the average pattern in a matrix of correlations, and then the successive average patterns in the 'residual' matrices of partial correlations.

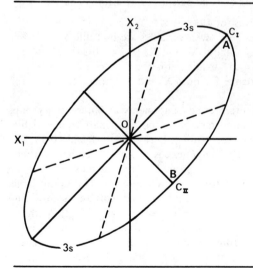

Fig. 5.6 Components as the axes of bivariate scatter-diagrams.

A 'real world' example

As stressed previously, the maximum number of components that can be extracted from a correlation matrix is the number of variables, n, the limiting case being when all n variables are uncorrelated, and thus orthogonal to each other. (An exception to this rule occurs when the number of observations, N, in the data matrix, from which the correlation matrix is derived, is less than the number of variables, n. The reason for this lies in the concept of degrees of freedom (p. 12): if $N < n$ the maximum number of components that can be extracted is N.) Thus a full principal components analysis should extract all n components. If the reason for the analysis is to identify groups of variables, then only the largest components (in terms of their eigenvalues) will be of interest; the smaller components will be rewritings of the specific variances in orthogonal form, which may be of value for particular purposes.

The small data set of Table 5.3 has been compiled to illustrate a full analysis. Its seven variables refer to the following aspects of educational provision in the listed outer London boroughs:

X_1 is the pupil:teacher ratio in primary schools;

X_2 is the Expenditure per 1000 persons on primary school teachers;

X_3 is the Expenditure per 1000 persons on secondary school teachers;

X_4 is the Expenditure per 1000 persons on non-teaching staff;

X_5 is the Administrative costs per 1000 persons;

X_6 is the Net expenditure per 1000 persons on secondary education; and

X_7 is the Net expenditure per 1000 persons on tertiary education.

The data refer to the estimates for 1973–74.

The correlations among these seven variables are in Table 5.4A. Some of them are closely related, notably X_1 and X_2 ($r_{12} = -0.84$), whose high correlation is confirmed by the loadings on the first component (Table 5.4B); over 70% of the variance for both X_1 and X_2 is associated with this new variable.

One of the problems of interpreting components as representing groups of variables is to assess the importance of a loading. Apart from variables X_1 and X_2, all of the others have loadings between ±0.31 and ±0.55. The average pattern indexed by the component is of some relevance to them, therefore, but if we square the loadings we find that at most 30% of the variation (for X_3) is accounted for by the component. This is not large, and interpretation of the new variable would undoubtedly focus on X_1 and X_2, stressing the bipolarity of those variables: not surprisingly, perhaps, boroughs with high pupil : teacher ratios in primary schools tend to spend relatively small amounts per 1000 inhabitants on primary school teachers. We might name this a 'level of provision of teaching resources in primary schools' component.

Turning to the second component, we find that four variables have loadings exceeding ±0.5, but that the largest of these (for X_3) accounts for only 52% of the original variance. From the signs and magnitude of the loadings we might interpret this component as a 'size of administrative sector'

Table 5.3 Aspects of educational provision in outer London

| Borough | Variable* | | | | | | |
	X_1	X_2	X_3	X_4	X_5	X_6	X_7
1. Kingston	23·7	106·6	177·6	18·0	2780	17 304	9248
2. Barking	24·9	100·2	153·2	18·8	2896	19 304	10 616
3. Sutton	26·7	96·3	167·6	13·6	3069	16 753	6274
4. Richmond	24·7	107·7	183·8	17·2	2916	13 724	8489
5. Harrow	24·6	98·1	191·5	14·8	4102	15 119	7545
6. Hounslow	23·6	105·3	170·8	18·8	1482	18 198	11 509
7. Waltham Forest	24·7	99·8	180·9	15·2	2183	17 890	5246
8. Haringey	25·0	100·6	167·9	21·6	3668	17 086	7324
9. Hillingdon	23·3	104·4	161·6	16·8	2967	18 075	6999
10. Redbridge	24·7	102·8	175·0	16·6	3073	17 408	3712
11. Havering	26·0	98·9	161·3	18·4	2390	20 975	5868
12. Enfield	26·6	93·7	159·5	17·2	1547	16 470	7692
13. Brent	23·4	106·5	168·0	17·1	2739	17 260	8053
14. Ealing	25·1	99·7	162·5	24·3	3385	16 838	10 418
15. Barnet	24·4	103·4	173·6	16·7	2765	17 979	3525
16. Bromley	27·0	97·1	163·7	12·6	2562	17 772	5314
17. Croydon	24·1	104·8	165·2	13·8	2738	19 229	7335
$\bar{X}$	24·9	101·5	169·6	17·1	2780	17 493	7363
S	1·1	4·1	9·8	2·9	657	1617	2275

* Variables X_2 to X_7 are measured in £ : X_1 is in pupils
Source: Society of County Treasurers (1975a)

Table 5.4 Educational provision in outer London: inter-relationships

A. Correlations

Variables	X_1	X_2	X_3	X_4	X_5	X_6	X_7
X_1	1·00						
X_2	−0·84	1·00					
X_3	−0·29	0·29	1·00				
X_4	−0·21	0·13	−0·25	1·00			
X_5	−0·09	0·02	0·31	0·12	1·00		
X_6	−0·01	−0·06	−0·61	0·02	−0·34	1·00	
X_7	−0·29	0·22	−0·19	0·52	−0·10	−0·11	1·00

B. Component loadings

| Variables | Components | | | | | | |
	I	II	III	IV	V	VI	VII
X_1	0·85	−0·24	0·36	−0·13	0·04	−0·08	0·25
X_2	−0·83	0·18	−0·43	0·04	0·00	−0·24	0·19
X_3	−0·55	−0·72	−0·06	−0·17	0·18	0·32	0·10
X_4	−0·31	0·60	0·57	0·18	0·43	0·01	0·01
X_5	−0·33	−0·43	0·46	0·66	−0·24	0·00	0·03
X_6	0·42	0·59	−0·48	0·40	−0·03	0·26	0·10
X_7	−0·40	0·61	0·43	−0·38	−0·34	0·15	0·06
Eigenvalues	2·24	1·89	1·27	0·82	0·40	0·26	0·12
% trace	32·06	27·00	18·14	11·71	5·71	3·71	1·71

dimension: boroughs spending relatively large amounts on non-teaching staff (X_4), and also on secondary and tertiary education in general (X_6, X_7) tend to spend relatively little on secondary teachers (X_3), and vice versa.

The other five components indicate no clear groupings of inter-relationships among the seven variables: the largest loading is 0·66 (for X_5 on component IV), and no component has more than one loading exceeding ±0·5. Thus components III–VII seem only to be redistributing the unique variances in an orthogonal manner. This is confirmed by the eigenvalues, and by these as a percentage of the trace. The first three components account for 77% of the variance among the seven variables, and the first four for 89%: certainly the last three are merely residual categories.

Interpretation of components through the loadings clearly requires attention to be paid to the signs of the latter. If all variables have the same sign for the loadings on a particular component, whether that sign is positive or negative is not particularly important (though care will be needed in the interpretation of the component scores – see below). All of the variables have the same sign for component VII in Table 5.4, for example, indicating that all seven covary in the same direction with the component (i.e. a high value on the component is associated with a high value of every variable). But on component I in the same table, some variables have positive and some have negative loadings. A high value on the component is associated with a high positive value for X_1 (remember each variable is expressed in Z-score form) and with a high negative value for X_2. Interpretation of component I focuses on its bipolar nature, therefore, whereas interpretation of one such as component VII can accept that all of the variables covary in the same direction.

Principal components analysis is most commonly used in geographical work to identify groups of related variables, which, if they exist, indicate more general patterns than particular indices might suggest. The question that then often arises is, 'How many components should I interpret as indicating such groups?'. There is no hard-and-fast rule to answer this, although many guidelines have been suggested. The most frequently used interprets only those components for which the eigenvalue exceeds 1·0. The rationale for this is that 1·0 represents the variance of the original variables, so that a component with an eigenvalue less than 1·0 accounts for less of the total variance than did any one of the original variables. This is only a convenient 'rule of thumb', however.

Three of the components extracted from our 7 × 7 correlation matrix have eigenvalues exceeding 1·0, and their loadings are reproduced in Table 5.5. As already pointed out, only the first of these has a clear interpretation as a combination of two or more variables. The communality values (h^2) show the proportion of its variance which each variable has in common with all of the others. Although in only one case (X_5) is this less than 70%, there is but the one clear group of variables, X_1 and X_2, among the seven.

This analysis of aspects of educational provision in outer London suggests that there is no general spatial correlation in the patterns of local

Table 5.5 Educational provision in outer London: three-component solution

| Variable | Component loadings Component | | | Communality h^2 |
	I	II	III	
X_1	0·85	−0·24	0·36	0·91
X_2	−0·83	0·18	−0·43	0·90
X_3	−0·55	−0·72	−0·06	0·83
X_4	−0·31	0·60	0·57	0·78
X_5	−0·33	−0·43	0·46	0·51
X_6	0·42	0·59	−0·48	0·76
X_7	−0·40	0·61	0·43	0·71
Eigenvalues	2·24	1·89	1·27	
% trace	32·06	27·00	18·14	

authority expenditure on those seven selected items. In terms of a general hypothesis that groups of variables indicating types of provision exist, we could only conclude that there is no evidence to support that suggestion. Other analyses may provide evidence of clearer groupings, of course. In Table 5.6 are the results of an analysis, for the same set of 17 boroughs, of various aspects of library provision. In this case, two components account for nearly 63% of the variance, and each component has a clear interpretation. The first, with high positive loadings on variables X_1 to X_4, indicates that the average pattern relates to the amount of library provision; the second, with high loadings for X_6, X_8 and, to a lesser extent, X_7, suggests a second dimension of library provision − expenditure per 1000 inhabitants − which is unrelated to the size of the service. In this case, we can clearly identify two groups of variables, with a single deviant (X_5) unrelated to either.

Table 5.6 Library provision in outer London

| Variables* | Component loadings Component | | Communality h^2 |
	I	II	
X_1 Library staff	0·80	0·33	0·75
X_2 Number of library points	0·75	0·19	0·60
X_3 Number of reference books	0·74	−0·38	0·70
X_4 Number of books	0·90	0·15	0·83
X_5 Number of serials taken	0·42	0·35	0·29
X_6 Book expenditure/1000 residents	−0·34	0·76	0·69
X_7 Newspaper expenditure/1000 residents	0·19	0·55	0·34
X_8 Total expenditure/1000 residents	−0·28	0·86	0·82
Eigenvalues	2·98	2·04	
% trace	37·25	25·50	

* Source of data: Society of County Treasurers (1975b)

Component interpretation

The majority of principal components analyses conducted in geography are seeking groups of variables, for confirmation of hypotheses of general patterns of spatial covariation in contrast to a null hypothesis that each variable has a unique spatial distribution. Successful components analyses indicate that every variable has some unique element to its spatial distribution, but that the general component dominates. Morrison, Scripter and Smith (1968), for example, tested the hypothesis that whichever of eleven different measures of manufacturing activity in American counties was employed, the same pattern would be mapped. A components analysis of their eleven measures, correlated over 2474 observations, clearly substantiated their hypothesis (Table 5.7); as a general index of the intensity of manufacturing activity, any one measure would seem as good as any other since all eleven have very high loadings on the first component.

Table 5.7 Manufacturing activity in the United States, 1958: principal components analysis

Variables	Component loadings Component		Communality
	I	II	h^2
X_1 Establishments	0·925	0·375	0·9965
X_2 Employees	0·995	−0·068	0·9956
X_3 Payroll	0·988	−0·118	0·9898
X_4 Production workers	0·994	−0·072	0·9938
X_5 Man-hours, production workers	0·993	−0·087	0·9935
X_6 Wages, production workers	0·984	−0·146	0·9902
X_7 Value added	0·989	−0·121	0·9926
X_8 New capital expenditure	0·873	−0·390	0·9145
X_9 Establishments, 1−19 employees	0·904	0·417	0·9912
X_{10} Establishments, 20−99 employees	0·925	0·371	0·9930
X_{11} Establishments, 100+ employees	0·970	−0·124	0·9564
Eigenvalue	10·120	0·687	

Source: Morrison, Scripter and Smith (1968, p. 300)

More detailed interpretation of Table 5.7 suggests that we should not over-interpret even the high loadings of the first component. If we plot the loadings on a two-dimensional diagram representing the two orthogonal components, we can reproduce the 98·25% of the original 11 × 11 correlation matrix that they replace. This shows that although all eleven variables are indeed close to the average, in fact there are three groups of variables (Fig. 5.7). The largest, comprising variables X_2–X_7 plus X_{11}, includes all those measures of the intensity of activity; the second, variables X_1, X_9 and X_{10}, identifies a group of measures of the number of separate establishments (it might be termed a 'small factory dimension'); and the third, comprising X_8 alone, identifies the slightly separate distribution of new investment. The message of Fig. 5.7 is clear; over-generalisation from a table of component loadings is very easy (see also Palm and Caruso, 1972). A loading as high as 0·873 indicates that only just over three-quarters of the variance in that variable is associated with the component (i.e. $0·873^2 = 0·762$). Further, two variables may have similar loadings on one component but be very dissimilar on another, and so in fact be poorly correlated. Thus

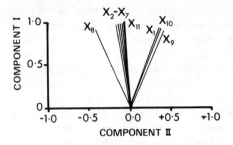

Fig. 5.7 Loadings on the first two principal components, showing the geometrical representation of the derived inter-variable correlations. Source: Morrison, Scripter and Smith (1968); reproduced with permission.

X_8 and X_9 would both seem to be close to the average of the first component with loadings of 0.873 and 0.904 respectively, but one has a positive and the other a negative loading on the second component. The angle between them — 50° — suggests that $r_{89} = 0.64$; Morrison *et al.*'s correlation matrix shows the actual correlation as 0.65, indicating a shared variance of only 42.25%. In other words, care must be taken in not making sweeping generalisations from the results (see also Meyer, 1971).

Principal components analysis can be used as a search for structure in a

Table 5.8 Migrant labour in Europe: principal components analysis

A. Data

Destination	Origin Greece	Italy	Portugal	Spain	Turkey	Yugoslavia
Austria	2	3	0	2	5	19
Belgium-Lux.	8	95	2	32	7	0
France	5	340	103	346	8	20
Netherlands	2	8	1	6	6	1
Germany	187	372	14	183	133	65
Sweden	0	5	0	0	0	5
Switzerland	7	500	1	79	4	4

B. Principal components analysis

Origin	Component loadings Component I	II	Communality h^2
Greece	0.88	0.47	0.99
Italy	0.67	−0.34	0.56
Portugal	0.41	−0.86	0.91
Spain	0.72	−0.69	0.99
Turkey	0.87	0.47	0.98
Yugoslavia	0.92	0.28	0.98
Eigenvalue	3.51	1.85	

Source: Johnston (1973a, p. 731), from Magee, 1971.

data set, according to the two major definitions of a *region* generally used in geography. A *formal region* involves a combination of areas with similar characteristics; a *functional region* combines areas with similar interaction patterns oriented on major nodes. Table 5.8 illustrates the latter. The data are the flows of labour migrants within Europe in 1965. Correlations compare countries of origin whose migrants go to similar destinations and a components analysis of the 6 × 6 matrix suggests two main functional regions. The first, component I, indicates that Greek, Turkish, and Yugoslav migrants tend to head for the same areas, and the second, component II, that Spanish and Portuguese labourers move to similar areas; Italian migrants tend to be split between the two groups. Much larger interaction matrices may be similarly analysed (e.g. Black, 1973) to identify the existence of functional regions. As yet, we have only identified one aspect of the functional region, the flow origins, however, as the next section indicates.

Component scores

The examples just given indicate that so far our discussion of components analysis has focused on rewriting the correlation matrix. Yet the latter is based on the original data for a set of observations, about which we have discovered nothing. In our labour migration analysis, full identification of functional regions requires identifying not only clusters of variables in the columns, but also clusters of observations in the rows: what areas do the migrants from each group of origins tend to move to? For this we turn to the derivation and use of component scores.

Principal components analysis replaces one set of variables by another. The original variables are measured for each of a set of observations; can one develop similar measures for the new variables, the components? Take our example relating to educational provision in Outer London. The first borough, Kingston, has a value for each of the seven variables in the original data set (Table 5.3); what are its values for the seven components (Table 5.4B)?

The components are identified in terms of the original variables; the larger the loading, the more important the variable in the interpretation of the component. Thus, if an observation has high values for the variables with large loadings on the component, then it should have a high value on the component. The component score for observation i on component k is defined to meet this requirement, using the formula

$$S_{ik} = \sum_{j=1}^{n} D_{ij} L_{jk} \tag{5.9}$$

where D_{ij} is the standardised value for observation i on variable j;

L_{jk} is the loading of variable j on component k;

S_{ik} is the score of observation i on component k; and summation is over all n variables.

In formula (5.9), the values of D_{ij} are the standardised measures, which are, of course, what the correlations are based on.

The data for the borough of Kingston upon Thames in Table 5.3 illustrate the use of this formula. The standardised values − Z-scores; see p. 10 and formula (2.25) − are

X_1	X_2	X_3	X_4	X_5	X_6	X_7
−1·09	+1·24	+0·82	+0·31	0·00	−0·12	+0·83

Solution of formula (5.9) for component I then gives

$$S_{iI} = (-1·09)(0·85) + (1·24)(-0·83) + \ldots (0·83)(-0·40) = -2·927$$

The full set of scores for each observation on each component (Table 5.9) indicates the value for every borough on all of the new variables.

Table 5.9 Aspects of educational provision in outer London: component scores

Borough	Component scores Component						
	I	II	III	IV	V	VI	VII
Kingston	−2·93	0·51	−0·38	−0·27	−0·05	0·14	0·11
Barking	0·92	3·03	0·76	0·40	−0·64	0·05	−0·01
Sutton	2·88	−2·02	0·69	−0·16	−0·44	−0·09	0·07
Richmond	−3·53	−1·94	0·67	−1·18	0·12	−0·44	0·21
Harrow	−1·83	−4·00	1·39	0·18	−0·44	0·57	−0·09
Hounslow	−1·90	3·00	−0·84	−1·61	0·07	0·30	0·01
Waltham Forest	0·61	−1·35	−1·29	−0·48	0·45	0·41	−0·07
Haringey	−0·65	0·25	1·83	1·11	0·34	−0·07	0·00
Hillingdon	−1·17	0·99	−0·95	0·74	−0·29	−0·26	−0·26
Redbridge	−0·15	−1·67	−0·81	0·81	0·47	−0·15	−0·01
Havering	3·18	1·69	−0·67	0·81	0·39	0·28	0·21
Enfield	3·88	0·58	0·99	−1·70	0·31	−0·14	−0·20
Brent	−2·23	0·79	−0·84	0·03	−0·18	−0·25	−0·10
Ealing	−0·85	2·13	3·01	0·47	0·29	−0·02	−0·01
Barnet	−0·09	−1·08	−1·38	0·74	0·58	−0·13	−0·05
Bromley	3·86	−1·51	−0·35	−0·29	−0·34	−0·19	0·15
Croydon	−0·15	0·61	−1·82	0·39	−0·64	−0·20	0·04
$\overline{X}$	0·00	0·00	0·00	0·00	0·00	0·00	0·00
S	2·25	1·88	1·27	0·82	0·40	0·26	0·12

According to formula (5.9), component scores are weighted summed values for the observations over the variables, the weights being the component loadings. The larger the value which an observation has on the variables which have high loadings on a component, the larger the score. Thus, for example, the Z scores for Bromley are

X_1	X_2	X_3	X_4	X_5	X_6	X_7
1·91	−1·07	−0·60	−1·55	−0·33	0·17	−0·90

which gives it a score on the first component of 3·862. In terms of the component, which we identified (p. 144) as indexing the level of provision of teacher resources in primary schools, Bromley with a positive score is above average on pupil : teacher ratios (indicated by positive loadings for X_1) and below average on the variables with negative loadings (the most important of which are those on expenditure): it provides a relatively poor service on this component, therefore, in comparison to the provision indicated by the negative score for Kingston (compare Table 5.9 with Table 5.3).

Component scores are values for the observations on the new variables, reflecting their values on the original variables and the contribution each component (new variable) makes to the variance of these. For k components, we have an N × k component scores matrix, and this is given in Table 5.9 for the 7 components and the 17 boroughs. In this, Richmond, for example, has a high positive loading on the first component, suggesting high pupil : teacher ratios and low expenditures in primary schools there, and a high negative score on the second component, suggesting relatively high levels of spending on secondary school teachers, but low net expenditure on secondary and tertiary education in general (variables X_6 and X_7).

One aspect of Table 5.9 to be noted is that the standard deviations of the seven-component score columns vary. (They are, in fact, equal to the eigenvalues.) The input data, the Z-scores, all had the same means and standard deviations, but in producing the component scores these have been weighted by components of different strengths, as indicated by their eigenvalues. It is often considered desirable that each of the new variables should have the same mean and standard deviation, which could be achieved by converting the scores in Table 5.9 to Z-values in the usual way. More usually the same result is achieved by making each component of the same importance; this is done by dividing each loading by the eigenvalue for that component, which expresses the loading as a proportion of the total 'explanation' and so brings all components down to a common base. Irrespective of the standardising procedure used, the result is the same − a matrix of standardised principal component scores in which the relative position of each borough on each component can be judged (Table 5.10).

Having seen how to derive component scores, we can now complete our functional regionalisation of European migrant labour flows. In standardised form, the scores for the two components outlined in Table 5.8 are:

Country	Component	
	I	II
Austria	−0·54	0·45
Belgium−Luxembourg	−0·54	0·22
France	0·67	−2·07
Netherlands	−0·71	0·28
West Germany	1·97	1·09
Sweden	−0·73	0·33
Switzerland	−0·12	−0·31

The dominant score for component I is for West Germany, indicating that migration from the countries with large positive loadings on that com-

Table 5.10 Aspects of educational provision in outer London: standardised component scores

Borough	Component scores Component						
	I	II	III	IV	V	VI	VII
Kingston	−1·29	0·27	−0·30	−0·33	−0·12	0·55	0·90
Barking	0·41	1·62	0·60	0·49	−1·62	0·20	−0·09
Sutton	1·28	−1·08	0·54	−0·20	−1·13	−0·36	0·55
Richmond	−1·57	−1·04	0·53	−1·44	0·30	−1·70	1·70
Harrow	−0·81	−2·13	1·10	0·23	−1·11	2·24	−0·69
Hounslow	−0·84	1·60	−0·66	−1·96	0·17	1·18	0·11
Waltham Forest	0·27	−0·72	−1·02	−0·58	1·15	1·60	−0·54
Haringey	−0·29	0·13	1·44	1·36	0·86	−0·26	0·01
Hillingdon	−0·52	0·53	−0·75	0·90	−0·73	−1·03	−2·12
Redbridge	−0·07	−0·89	−0·64	0·99	1·20	−0·59	−0·08
Havering	1·41	0·90	−0·53	0·99	0·99	1·08	1·72
Enfield	1·71	0·31	0·78	−2·07	0·80	−0·53	−1·66
Brent	−0·99	0·42	−0·66	0·03	−0·45	−0·96	−0·84
Ealing	−0·38	1·14	2·37	0·58	0·73	−0·09	−0·10
Barnet	−0·04	−0·58	−1·08	0·90	1·47	−0·51	−0·37
Bromley	1·77	−0·81	−0·27	−0·35	−0·87	−0·76	1·17
Croydon	−0·07	0·32	−1·44	0·48	−1·62	−0·08	0·31
X̄	0·00	0·00	0·00	0·00	0·00	0·00	0·00
S	1·00	1·00	1·00	1·00	1·00	1·00	1·01

ponent focuses on Germany. Similarly, the dominant score for component II is the negative value for France, the focus of migrations from the countries with negative loadings — Spain and Portugal. Thus we have identified two main flow types as functional regions, separately focused on the main countries of western Europe: Greece, Turkey and Yugoslavia are strongly linked with West Germany; Portugal is linked to France; Italy and Spain, with loadings on both components, are in both 'migration regions'.

In much geographical work, the observations in the data matrix are places, and so it is maps which are being correlated with each other. The component scores are then often an important part of the output of the analysis, since they provide data for a new set of maps, representing the combinations of variables which make up the components. (The number of the new maps available is the same as the number of variables, but only those on the largest components are of general interest.) Such maps are useful as representations of the general patterns in a series of maps, and they may be used, for example, as sampling frameworks for further hypothesis testing. In Fig. 5.8 are maps of the standardised scores on the first two components for our analyses of educational provision in outer London: the scores have been arbitrarily divided into four categories by their means and standard deviations. In neither case do we get a clear impression of a spatial patterning. If there are independent variables which 'explain' differences in levels of educational provision, therefore, the maps do not reveal them: they do suggest important local variations in quality of education, however, which may be of interest to parents!

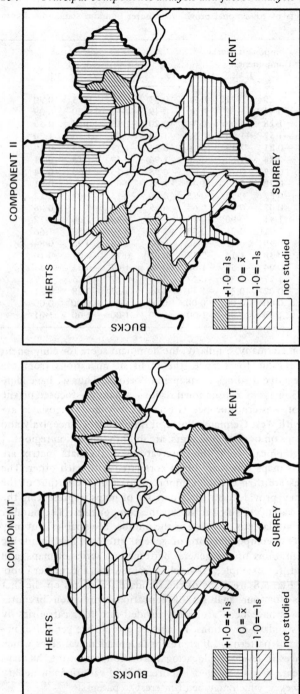

Fig. 5.8   Scores on the first two principal components of the analysis reported in Table 5.2 (see also Table 5.9).

Component scores and regression analysis

A major characteristic of components is that they are orthogonal to each other, and hence independent. They should be of particular use, therefore, in surmounting the problem of collinearity in multiple regression, discussed in Chapter 3 (p. 74), where we observed that with collinear independent variables the partial regression coefficients reflect only the residual variance in X_0 and the relevant independent variable once others have been held constant. If principal components were used as the independent variables, there should be no possible bias or ambiguity in the regression coefficients.

Use of component scores in this way was introduced to the geographical literature by Riddell (1970) in a study of migration rates to Freetown, the capital of Sierra Leone. Fifteen independent variables (identified in Table 5.11) were measured for each chiefdom and the *per capita* migration rates were regressed against them to produce the equation

$$X_0 = a - 0 \cdot 411 X_1 - 0 \cdot 324 X_2 - 12 \cdot 239 X_3 + 0 \cdot 433 X_4 - 0 \cdot 026 X_5 - 0 \cdot 003 X_6 +$$
$$\quad (-1 \cdot 19) \quad (-1 \cdot 33) \quad (-2 \cdot 74) \quad (2 \cdot 42) \quad (-0 \cdot 34) \quad (-0 \cdot 09)$$

$$\quad + 0 \cdot 491 X_7 + 0 \cdot 148 X_8 - 0 \cdot 841 X_9 - 0 \cdot 068 X_{10} + 0 \cdot 430 X_{11} + 0 \cdot 322 X_{12} +$$
$$\quad (1 \cdot 03) \quad (1 \cdot 10) \quad (-0 \cdot 19) \quad (-0 \cdot 22) \quad (1 \cdot 56) \quad (0 \cdot 66)$$

$$\quad + 0 \cdot 431 X_{13} - 33 \cdot 685 X_{14} + 0 \cdot 219 X_{15}$$
$$\quad (4 \cdot 14) \quad (-0 \cdot 80) \quad (0 \cdot 88)$$

To aid interpretation the standardised partial regression coefficients (β – p. 71) are given in parentheses; $R_{0 \cdot 1 - 15} = 0 \cdot 775$. The β values suggest that variables X_1, X_2, X_3, X_4, X_7, X_8, X_{11} and X_{13} are the most important determinants of movement to Freetown: X_{11}, for example, suggests that migration rates are highest close to Freetown, whereas X_{13} suggests that they are

Table 5.11 Migration to Freetown (Sierra Leone): principal components analysis

Variable	Component loadings Component			
	I	II	III	IV
X_1 Distance to Freetown	−0·11	−0·87	−0·19	0·04
X_2 Inaccessibility to Freetown (Road *vs.* air)	0·04	−0·79	−0·21	0·10
X_3 Date linked to national transport routes	−0·29	−0·47	−0·20	0·24
X_4 Population density	0·76	0·16	0·12	0·00
X_5 Percentage living in urban places	0·83	−0·07	−0·32	−0·12
X_6 Percentage urban growth	0·77	−0·02	−0·33	−0·28
X_7 Whether a district HQ	0·59	0·14	−0·15	0·41
X_8 Percentage in urban employment	0·89	−0·10	−0·29	−0·08
X_9 Date first primary school opened	−0·31	−0·25	−0·35	−0·37
X_{10} Percentage literate	0·68	−0·26	0·53	0·22
X_{11} Percentage children at school	0·49	−0·34	0·64	0·28
X_{12} Percentage employed in traditional sector	−0·43	−0·34	0·45	−0·47
X_{13} Distance to diamond fields	−0·34	0·69	−0·27	0·23
X_{14} Date local administration established	−0·42	−0·26	−0·52	0·39
X_{15} Size of largest town	0·90	0·00	−0·21	−0·16
Eigenvalue	5·20	2·58	1·86	1·05

Source: Riddell (1970, pp. 405, 407)

high at large distances from the other main source of employment, the diamond fields.

There is considerable collinearity among these 15 independent variables, as is shown by the component loadings in Table 5.11. The first 4 components − those with eigenvalues exceeding 1·0 − account for some 71% of the variance in the 15 variables, which is clearly indicative of non-independence among the latter. Thus the scores on the four components were derived and used as the independent variables for the following regression equation.

$$X_0 = 1·633 + 0·119C_I + 0·221C_{II} + 0·098C_{III} − 0·092C_{IV}$$

$$R_{0·I-IV} = 0·794$$

Interpretation of this equation may be difficult if the components are not unambiguously associated with groups of variables. Looking at the table of loadings, component I apparently replaces a group of variables reflecting various aspects of urbanisation; component II indexes (negatively) various aspects of distance to Freetown; component III picks out relationships among literacy and education levels, suggestive of a relatively 'advanced' population; and component IV is negatively related to the importance of the traditional sector. From this, we would conclude that migration rates increase with the level of urbanisation of the chiefdoms (component I) and with the educational level of local populations (component III) while decreasing with distance from Freetown (component II) and with the importance of the traditional sector (component IV).

The nature of the loadings may make the components difficult to interpret, in which case a regression equation in which they are the independent variables can have little interpretative value. This can be overcome by obtaining *reconstituted partial regression coefficients* which are the sums of the regression coefficients for each component weighted by the loadings of each variable on the components. For example, the component loadings for X_1 are

$$C_I \; −0·11 \quad C_{II} \; −0·87 \quad C_{III} \; −0·19 \quad C_{IV} \; 0·04$$

and the regression coefficients are

$$C_I \; 0·119 \quad C_{II} \; 0·221 \quad C_{III} \; 0·098 \quad C_{IV} \; −0·092$$

The reconstituted partial regression coefficient, b^*, is obtained as

$$b^*_{oi.-} = \sum_{j=1}^{k} L_{ij}O_{oj} \tag{5.10}$$

where L_{ij} is the loading for variable i on component j;
　　　　O_{oj} is the regression coefficient for component j;
　　　　k is the number of components; and
　　　　$b^*_{oi.-}$ is the reconstituted partial regression coefficient for variable i.

For X_1 in this case

$b_{01 \cdot 2-15}^{*} = (-0 \cdot 11)(0 \cdot 119) + (-0 \cdot 87)(0 \cdot 221) + (-0 \cdot 19)(0 \cdot 098) +$

$\qquad + (0 \cdot 04)(-0 \cdot 092) = -0 \cdot 228$

and the full regression equation becomes

$X_0 = 1 \cdot 633 - 0 \cdot 228X_1 - 0 \cdot 200X_2 - 0 \cdot 181X_3 + 0 \cdot 138X_4 + 0 \cdot 138X_5 +$

$\qquad + 0 \cdot 063X_6 + 0 \cdot 081X_7 + 0 \cdot 063X_8 - 0 \cdot 093X_9 + 0 \cdot 055X_{10} + 0 \cdot 020X_{11} -$

$\qquad - 0 \cdot 039X_{12} + 0 \cdot 063X_{13} - 0 \cdot 195X_{14} + 0 \cdot 102X_{15}$

Because component scores are standardised, these reconstituted partial regression coefficients are directly comparable — they are the same as β coefficients.

Exact interpretation of reconstituted partial regression coefficients is not altogether straightforward. For each variable they represent the sum of the regression coefficients for the components weighted by the importance of each component in accounting for the variance of the particular variable. Since the components are independent variables, therefore, these co-efficients represent the influence of the relevant original variables, incorporating their joint effect with the other independent variables with which they are collinear. Thus, if X_0 were being regressed on X_1 and X_2, and $r_{12} = 0 \cdot 80$, the joint effect of X_1 and X_2 would be absent from $b_{01 \cdot 2}$ and $b_{02 \cdot 1}$. After use of the procedure just outlined, the joint effect would be included in both $b_{01 \cdot 2}^{*}$ and $b_{02 \cdot 1}^{*}$. The reconstituted partial regression coefficients thus indicate the independent relationship between X_i and X_0, as if the proportions of the variables with which X_i is collinear had been excluded from the analysis. The reconstituted b^{*} values cannot be used to estimate values of X_0, however, since this would involve double counting.

This procedure is being used increasingly by geographers to avoid the collinearity problem (cf. Keeble and Hauser, 1972; Fuller, 1974). As employed by Riddell, with only the components whose eigenvalues exceed $1 \cdot 0$ included in the regression equation, the unique variances of the original variables, which may be related to X_0, are excluded. A full analysis should incorporate all of the components (i.e. where k = n).

Principal components analysis: a summary

The main purpose of a principal components analysis is to reorganise a data set comprising n variables and N observations, so that with k variables (k = n) and N observations the variables are all orthogonal. Its major value in geographical research is in the identification of groups of related variables — including overlapping groups which occur when variables have high loadings on more than one component — which may be used as generators of hypotheses to account for the groupings, as composite variables whose scores can be mapped as general indices, and as orthogonal independent variables for multiple regressions. Although as many components as variables can be defined in the rewritten matrix, usually only a few — those with the largest eigenvalues — are interpretable. The others are often trivial, accounting for very small portions of the original variance; in some cases, with very clear groups of variables, they may have negative eigenvalues, indicating that all of the variance has been accounted for by the earlier components.

One point stressed by many commentators on principal components analysis is that it is an inductive method; it can be used to reorganise data in a particular form (i.e. orthogonal) and to compress the main sources of variance. As such, general patterns may be clarified and ideas for further research suggested. Principal components analysis is not very useful for hypothesis-testing, however, because it confuses common and unique variance (p. 130). The search for hypothesised common patterns is best conducted via the related method of factor analysis.

Factor analysis

In the introduction to this chapter, we noted that the difference between principal components analysis and factor analysis is in the treatment of the unique variance. Factor analysis excludes this, and rewrites only the common variance as a new set of variables. For any one of the original variables, the variance is decomposed into:

$$X_i = f(F_I, F_{II} \ldots F_n) + U_i \qquad (5.11)$$

How do we estimate U_i, the unique variance of variable i?

Unlike principal components analysis, which is a single procedure, there is a variety of approaches to factor analysis, most of which have not been used by geographers and are beyond the scope of our discussion. One of the ways in which they differ concerns what is known as 'estimating the communality', which is that proportion of the variance of a variable which is its common variance (i.e. is shared with that of the other variables in the analysis). The usual procedure is to employ the squared multiple correlation coefficient of each variable against all of the others in the analysis as the estimate, since our interpretation of this is as an index of the proportion of the variance in the dependent variable accounted for by the combined variances of the independents (p. 66). These communality estimates are thus our 'guesses' of the proportion of the common variances, and they are entered in the trace of the correlation matrix (the principal diagonal); their

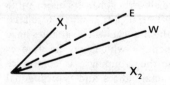

Fig. 5.9   The location of a factor (W) and a component (E) between the two variables X_1 and X_2.

sum is the total common variance to be analysed.

What this communality estimation procedure does is to weight the importance of each variable in the factor analysis according to the strength of its correlation with the other variables. In a principal components analysis for a three-variable system, the correlation matrix of

	X_1	X_2	X_3
X_1	1·00	0·60	0·70
X_2	0·60	1·00	0·80
X_3	0·70	0·80	1·00

would be replaced for a factor analysis by

	X_1	X_2	X_3
X_1	0·65	0·60	0·70
X_2	0·60	0·79	0·80
X_3	0·70	0·80	0·83

The values of the communalities are estimated using formulae (3.5) and (3.8). In terms of correlation diagrams, therefore, in factor analysis the vectors representing the variables are not of equal length, as they are for principal components analyses in which every variable has the same variance.

Having estimated the communalities, a *principal axes factor analysis* proceeds in the same way as a principal components analysis, extracting the factors from the correlation matrix in serial order of eigenvalue size. The difference between the two methods is that the variables are not of equal weight in factor analysis, so that the new variables, the factors, are pulled closer to the variables with the larger communalities. We can demonstrate this with a simple piece of geometry (Fig. 5.9). Two variables, X_1 and X_2, are 40 degrees apart in a correlation diagram. If each of these vectors were given equal weight, then a line as close as possible to both of them (the average — E) would bisect the angle, and be 20 degrees from each. But X_2 is twice as long as X_1, giving a sum of the lengths of 3 ($X_1 = 1$, $X_2 = 2$). A line as close as possible to the total lengths (i.e. the weighted average — W) would thus be only one-third of the angle from X_2 to X_1, indicating the stronger pull of X_2. (In geometry this line W is the resultant vector, which is the average position taking into account not only the angle between the two lines but also their lengths.) Principal components analysis treats X_1 and X_2 as of equal weight in a correlation diagram (at least for the first component, p. 140), and so would extract line E; factor analysis treats weighted vectors, and so would extract line W.

By application of the centroid method for extracting the principal axes of a matrix (p. 136) the component and factor loadings for the simple 3 × 3 matrix above are:

Correlations and components

	X_1	X_2	X_3
X_1	1·00	0·60	0·70
X_2	0·60	1·00	0·80
X_3	0·70	0·80	1·00

Correlations and factors

	X_1	X_2	X_3
X_1	0·65	0·60	0·70
X_2	0·60	0·79	0·80
X_3	0·70	0·80	0·83

Loadings on first component				Loadings on first factor			
X_1	X_2	X_3	λ_I	X_1	X_2	X_3	λ_I
0·86	0·90	0·93	2·41	0·77	0·86	0·92	2·18

% trace 80·33   % trace 96·04

where trace = 3·0   where trace = 2·27

In these slightly contrasting results, the rank ordering of the communalities
— $X_3 > X_2 > X_1$ — comes through in the relative size of the loadings, but
there is much greater variation in loadings for the factor than for the components analysis. In addition, the first factor is relatively more important
than is the first component (recall that the trace for factor analysis sums
the common variance only): most of the common variance can be accounted for by a single factor whereas one-fifth of the total variance (common
plus unique) remains unaccounted for by the first component.

If we square the factor loadings we discover the proportion of the
variance in a variable (its total variance, not its common variance) accounted for by the first factor. For the example above, the values are:

$$X_1 = 0·59 \quad X_2 = 0·74 \quad X_3 = 0·85$$

Compared with the communality estimates, we see that for X_1 and X_2, 91
and 94% respectively of their common variance is associated with the factor.
For X_3, the squared loading exceeds the communality estimate, emphasis-
ing that the latter is an estimate which quite frequently has to be modified
during the analysis. However many factors are extracted,.the sum of the
squared loadings for any variable cannot exceed the true communality for
that variable; only the common variance can be redistributed in a factor
analysis. If our estimate of the communality for X_1 is correct, for example,
no loading for X_1 could exceed 0·81 (= $\sqrt{0·65}$) and the sum of its squared
loadings across all factors could not exceed 0·65. Thus, the smaller the
communality estimate, the smaller the largest loading for any particular
variable can be. In terms of interpretation, this means that the variables
with relatively low communality estimates will probably not be as clearly
identified with factors. This is because, as in Fig. 5.9, the larger the communality the more a factor is drawn towards a variable: the smaller the
communality, the shorter the vector representing the variable in a correlation diagram (such as Fig. 5.11) and the further from the factor vector
the variable vector is likely to be. This does not mean, of course, that one
factor does not account for all of the common variance of a variable despite
a low loading: if the loading is 0·6 and the communality (h^2) is 0·36 then
all of the common variance is accounted for by the factor. (The actual
location of the variables in a correlation diagram for a factor analysis as in
Fig. 5.11 is determined by first setting a component diagram with vectors
of equal length, and then placing the vector for each variable relative to
that original vector according to its correlation — the square root of its
communality — with it.)

The aim of factor analysis is to produce new variables — the factors —
such that when they are held constant the partial correlations among the

original variables are all zero (i.e. $r_{12.1} = 0.0$ if all of the common variance is associated with one factor). Of the three reasons for conducting such an analysis outlined earlier in the chapter, factor analysis is the most appropriate to the search for groups in the correlation diagram. If the hypothesis is that groups of variables exist, then they will have shared common variance, and factor analysis is designed to isolate such groups. If such groups do not exist, then the communalities will be low, and the results trivial.

How many groups? There are two approaches to this question. The first is inductive, allowing the analysis to suggest how many, perhaps with the use of an arbitrary cut-off such as no factor with an eigenvalue less than 1·0 (p. 146). The success of this procedure depends on the interpretability of the results. Alternatively, a deductive approach indicates how many groups there should be and extracts that many factors. Tests are available which enquire if sufficient groups have been hypothesised, but they are rarely used (see Bell, 1955).

Factor analysis and principal components analysis

We have seen that the major difference between factor analysis and principal components analysis, as techniques, concerns the treatment of the elements of the variance (common and unique; the unique variance itself can be subdivided into error — a function of measurement problems — and specific — i.e. that which is not common). But what is the substantive differences between the two techniques? As the small example on p. 159 indicated, the major difference lies in the clarity with which inter-relationships can be identified, with factor analysis being the superior technique.

A brief résumé of principal components analysis should enlarge on this point. Some components identify inter-relationships among groups of variables; others merely indicate the unique variance of a single variable. Each variable almost certainly has a unique variance element, yet this cannot be completely separated from its common variance element — and the common variance elements of other variables. This is because the maximum number of components that can be extracted equals the number of variables, so that if each variable has some unique variance this must be confused in the component loadings with the patterns of common variance. Figure 5.5 and Table 5.1 and 5.2 illustrate this point. Variables X_2 and X_6 are virtually uncorrelated ($r_{26} = 0.0698$; Table 5.1) but X_6 has a very substantial loading (0·9272) and X_2 a loading large enough to be interpreted by many (0·4384; Table 5.2) on the first principal component. The uniqueness of X_2 relative to X_6, and also to X_4 and X_5, is being confused by the location of the principal component.

Factor analysis, on the other hand, removes this source of possible confusion by focusing only on the common variance and by weighting the variables according to their inter-relationships with the others. As stressed before, its attention is directed towards correlations and shared patterns. Principal components analysis looks at all patterns — shared and unique; it rewrites them together in an orthogonal form, but, because of the constraint on the number of components, confuses them somewhat.

Rotation

Although the purpose of factor analysis is to identify groups of variables with shared common variance, the procedure by which factors are extracted by the principal axes method somewhat contradicts this purpose. The principal axes method is identical to that used for extracting principal components; the only difference lies on the principal diagonal of the correlation matrix. It places the first factor in the average position, closest to all of the variables, which may not pick out groups of variables.

Figure 5.10A illustrates this problem for a simple four-variable example. The vectors are of equal length (to simplify presentation), and so the first factor, in the average position, bisects the major and minor angles (i.e. X_1, X_4 and X_2, X_3) in finding the average position. The second factor is orthogonal to it. The loadings are

	F_I	F_{II}
X_1	0·7660	0·6428
X_2	0·9397	0·3420
X_3	0·9397	−0·3420
X_4	0·7660	−0·6428

which do not indicate with any clarity that there are two groups of variables – X_1 and X_2, X_3 and X_4. Investigation of the signs of the two loadings for each variable suggest this (see p. 148 for the discussion of Fig. 5.7), but it would be preferable if each group were identified by a single factor.

To achieve the required identification, a hypothetical factor structure is used as an ideal to which the real data set is moved as close as possible. This ideal is known as *simple structure*, and the methods of moving towards it as *rotation of the axes*. A large number of rotation methods has been developed. They can be classified into two main types.

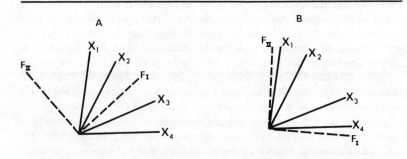

Fig. 5.10 Orthogonal rotation of two factors to find groups of related variables.

1. Orthogonal rotations

This is by far the most frequently-used group of procedures; it retains the constraint that factors be orthogonal and therefore uncorrelated. The simple structure ideal is that every variable has a loading of either +1·0 or −1·0 on one factor, and 0·0 on all others; which factor the loading of ±1·0 is with is not specified. Thus, for a three-factor structure the expected pattern may be

Variable	Factor loadings		
	Factor		
	I	II	III
X_1	+1·0	0·0	0·0
X_2	−1·0	0·0	0·0
X_3	0·0	+1·0	0·0
X_4	0·0	0·0	+1·0
X_5	0·0	+1·0	0·0
X_6	0·0	0·0	−1·0

To get as close as possible to this ideal, the factors are rotated around the origin to the best positions relative to the hypothesis. Clearly, the structure just tabulated would only be realised if the correlation matrix were

	X_1	X_2	X_3	X_4	X_5	X_6
X_1	1·00					
X_2	−1·00	1·00				
X_3	0·00	0·00	1·00			
X_4	0·00	0·00	0·00	1·00		
X_5	0·00	0·00	1·00	0·00	1·00	
X_6	0·00	0·00	0·00	−1·00	0·00	1·00

in which the communality estimates are all 1·00. Such an ideal is never attained with 'real' data: communalities very rarely, if ever, are 1·00, and groups of variables are never completely correlated among themselves and completely uncorrelated between themselves. If there are groups of variables with a lot of shared common variance, however, rotation should discover them as approximations to simple structure.

Figure 5.10B shows the results of an orthogonal rotation of the two factors isolated in Fig. 5.10A, as an approximation to simple structure. For each factor to be as close as possible to a group, F_I would be central to variables X_3 and X_4 (i.e. it would bisect the angle between them and have a correlation of 0·9848 with each) whereas F_{II} would be central to X_1 and X_2 (again with correlation of 0·9848). But the angle between F_I and F_{II} would then only be 60 degrees. The solution shown maintains the orthogonality, with loadings

Variable	Factor loadings	
	Factor	
	I	II
X_1	0·0872	0·9962
X_2	0·4226	0·9063
X_3	0·9063	0·4226
X_4	0·9962	0·0872

With a very simple correlation matrix such as that depicted in Fig. 5.10, it is possible to do the rotation by trial and error procedure using little more than a protractor. Larger numbers of variables and more-than-two-dimensional spaces require other methods. Of those which have been developed, for computer use, the most popular is Kaiser's *Varimax orthogonal rotation*. As its name suggests, its aim is maximising variance, in the cosines; the closer the loadings all are to ±1·0 or to 0·0 the greater the potential contribution of each loading to the total variance accounted for. The latter does not vary, but the contributions can. For our example in Fig. 5.10, the variance contributions (squared loadings) for the unrotated and rotated 'solution' are:

	Unrotated		Rotated	
	F_I	F_{II}	F_I	F_{II}
X_1	0·5868	0·4132	0·0076	0·9924
X_2	0·8830	0·1170	0·1786	0·8214
X_3	0·8830	0·1170	0·8214	0·1786
X_4	0·5868	0·4132	0·9924	0·0076

Comparing along the rows, we see that for X_1 and X_4 there has been a notable increase in the approximation to simple structure. For X_2 and X_3, there has been a slight movement away, but overall the trend is to clearer group identification.

With orthogonal rotation to achieve simple structure, the number of factors which has been extracted is crucial, since this determines the number of separate groups of variables which will be identified. (If only one factor is extracted, rotation is irrelevant.) We can illustrate this with the data on education provision in London (p. 145). From the two-factor solution, which accounts for just over 89% of the common variance, rotation slightly blurs the close relationship between X_1 and X_2 on the first factor, but brings into much sharper relief a group comprising X_3 and X_6 on the second factor (Table 5.12A). For the three-factor solution (Table 5.12B), the correlation between X_1 and X_2 is highlighted, but the loading of X_4 on the first factor is much smaller than in the two-factor solution. On the second factor, the loadings for X_5 and X_6 are larger when three

Table 5.12 Aspects of educational provision in outer London: factor analyses, with varimax rotations

A. Two-factor solution

Variable	Unrotated Factor loadings			Rotated Factor loadings		
	I	II	h^2	I	II	h^2
X_1	0·853	0·232	0·781	0·846	−0·254	0·781
X_2	−0·816	−0·166	0·694	−0·781	0·291	0·694
X_3	−0·475	0·688	0·700	−0·039	0·836	0·700
X_4	−0·224	−0·440	0·244	−0·423	−0·255	0·244
X_5	−0·207	0·317	0·143	−0·008	0·379	0·143
X_6	0·318	−0·577	0·434	−0·035	−0·658	0·434
X_7	−0·315	−0·457	0·308	−0·509	−0·221	0·308
Eigenvalues	1·913	1·391		1·767	1·537	
% trace	51·75	37·63		47·80	41·57	
% common variance	57·90	42·10		53·48	46·51	

B. Three-factor solution

Variable	Unrotated Factor loadings				Rotated Factor loadings			
	I	II	III	h^2	I	II	III	h^2
X_1	0·853	0·232	0·222	0·830	0·888	−0·067	−0·194	0·830
X_2	−0·816	−0·166	−0·270	0·767	−0·866	0·079	0·108	0·767
X_3	−0·475	0·688	−0·275	0·701	−0·301	0·712	−0·322	0·701
X_4	−0·224	−0·440	0·444	0·442	−0·077	−0·027	0·659	0·442
X_5	−0·207	0·317	0·228	0·196	−0·019	0·441	0·029	0·196
X_6	0·318	−0·577	−0·430	0·619	−0·023	−0·785	−0·048	0·619
X_7	−0·315	−0·457	0·443	0·504	−0·160	−0·004	0·691	0·504
Eigenvalues	1·913	1·391	0·754		1·683	1·328	1·068	
% trace	51·75	37·63	20·39		45·52	35·92	28·89	
% common variance	47·14	34·28	18·58		41·26	32·56	26·18	

factors are rotated rather than two, but that for X_3 is quite considerably smaller; the latter variable has loadings exceeding 0·3 on both factor I and factor III. The reason for these changes is the number of factors being rotated. As every additional factor is orthogonal to all of those rotated in the previous solution, those involved before are unlikely to occupy exactly the same position again. Thus eventually groups may be split, as the number of factors approaches the number of variables. Every rotation is unique, therefore, and will not be reproduced if the number of factors changes.

One point to note from Table 5.12B is that the eigenvalues for the three-factor solution exceed the trace when they are summed. This is because the initial estimates of the common variance − the squared multiple correlation coefficients − were not particularly good representations of the communalities. The coefficients are

X_1 0·769 X_2 0·721 X_3 0·615
X_5 0·227 X_6 0·559 X_7 0·444

and only for X_4 and X_5 do these exceed the h^2 values in the table. This mismatch of communalities is not serious and is to be expected, because the factors occupy different positions in the correlation diagram from those of the variables and so will have slightly different correlations with the latter. It does suggest, however, that for factor analyses rather than principal components analyses the % Trace might be replaced by the % Common Variance, which is each eigenvalue as a percentage of the sum of the communalities.

After rotation, it is incorrect to call the sum of the squared loadings of any factor the eigenvalue, since the latter term refers to the unique vector which defines the average vector in the correlation matrix it refers to (the original for the first factor; the residuals for all others). The term *sum of the squared loadings on the factor* is preferred. With these, as Table 5.12 shows, the size of the sum for the first factor is invariably less than the first eigenvalue, because the factor has been rotated away from the average position, whereas those for other factors are usually larger than the corresponding eigenvalue — although this is not the case for factor II in Table 5.12B (often, the order of the factors after rotation does not match their relative strength.) With the data in Table 5.12, note that if the general rule of extracting only factors with eigenvalues exceeding 1·0 were employed, a two-factor solution would have resulted (λ_{III} = 0·754) but that after rotation a third factor has a sum of the squared loadings exceeding 1·0. This indicates the need for experimentation, for conducting several analyses extracting different numbers of factors, in order to get the 'best' result. The latter is, of course, a function of interpreter-judgement in terms of prior expectations concerning the number of factors and groups of variables.

2. Oblique rotations

If the aim of factor rotation is to highlight groups of inter-related variables, then orthogonal rotations may not be suited to this task. There is an underlying assumption to the rotation that the factors representing the groups are independent (i.e. orthogonal), which may not be relevant in a particular

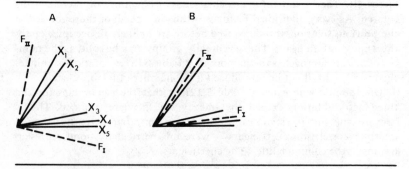

Fig. 5.11   Oblique rotation of two factors to find groups of related variables.

study. There may be two groups in a set of variables — one representing vegetation cover, perhaps, and the other indexing rainfall intensity — but these could well be inter-related. Figure 5.11A illustrates this. There are two clear groups of variables — X_1 and X_2 comprise the first, X_3, X_4 and X_5 the second — and these are identified by the rotated factors, F_I and F_{II}. The latter do not pass through the groups, however, because the orthogonality constraint requires that they be 90° apart. For accurate group identification, as in Fig. 5.11B, we remove this constraint, allowing the allocation of factors to groups of variables which are themselves inter-correlated. This requires an oblique rotation, so-called because the factors are non-orthogonal, although an oblique rotation can produce an orthogonal solution if the groups are unrelated. With such a rotation, the notion of independent factors has been replaced by one of separate factors: the simple structure hypothesis is that every variable has one loading of +1·0 or −1·0, but the other loadings need not be 0·0.

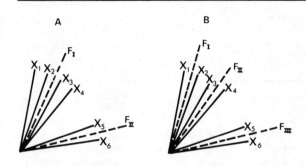

Fig. 5.12 The effect of the number of factors on the result of an oblique rotation.

Methods for oblique rotations have only been introduced in recent years and as yet they have not been widely used by geographers. As with orthogonal rotations, there are problems of how many factors to rotate, but in addition there is a difficulty regarding the degree of obliqueness between factors which is allowed, or how close to each other factors can be in the correlation diagram. In Fig. 5.12A, for example, we have a hypothetical situation in which two groups of variables have been represented by a two-factor solution, where the angle between the factors is 51°, indicating an inter-factor correlation of 0·629. A three-factor solution for the same data (Fig. 5.12B) might separate the first group into two parts, however, if the factors were allowed to be very oblique (in this case the correlation between factors I and II is 0·937). Such a solution is getting fairly close to extracting one factor for every variable and is not providing much in the way of generalisation. As with orthogonal rotations but more so, therefore, it is necessary to experiment with oblique solutions to find interpretable results, unless one has a very strong prior hypothesis.

Two factor loadings are obtained for each variable from an oblique rotation, the *structure loading* and the *pattern loading*. Figure 5.13 shows the differences between these, for a variable X_1 related to two factors which are at 60° to each other (their correlation is 0·5; other variables in the analysis are omitted for clarity). The structure loading is obtained as for orthogonal loadings. A line from the variable that is perpendicular to the factor ($X_1 - S$ in Fig. 5.13) is drawn, and the length OS as a proportion of the total length of the factor is the structure loading: in this case, the loading on factor II is 0·817. For the pattern loading, the line from the variable is drawn parallel to the other factors − in this case factor I only − bisecting factor II at P. The distance OP as a ratio of the total length of the factor is the pattern loading for X_1 on factor II; in this case it is 0·60.

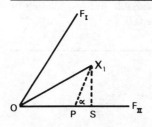

Fig. 5.13   The structure loading (OS) and the pattern loading (OP) in an oblique factor analytic solution.

For interpretation of factors, the structure loadings are the most important and they are interpreted in the same way as orthogonal loadings − as that proportion of the variance in the variable associated with the variance in the factor. In Fig. 5.13, 66·71% of the variance in X_1 is associated with factor II. The pattern loading, on the other hand, identifies the correlation between the variable and the factor, independent of the effects of other factors. In Fig. 5.13, therefore, the pattern loading for X_1 on factor II is the partial correlation between X_1 and F_{II} when the effect of factor I has been held constant. The geometry of the figure indicates this. The angle between the factors (α) is equivalent to their inter-correlation and the line $X_1 - P$ is the only one joining X_1 to factor II which would produce this angle. The distance PS thus represents that portion of the structure loading, OS, which results from the joint influence of factors I and II on X_1. So, whereas 66·71% of the variance in X_1 is associated with factor II, 30·71% of this is the product of the joint variance, since the pattern loading, 0·6, indicates that only 36% of the variance in X_1 is uniquely associated with factor II.

As an example of oblique rotations, the three-factor solution for the data set on educational provision in outer London is used again. The full output with an 'average' constraint − i.e. factors are not allowed to be very unique − is in Table 5.13A. In almost every case, the pattern loading is smaller than the structure loading, indicating the partial correlations

Table 5.13 Aspects of educational provision in outer London: factor analysis with oblique rotations

A. 'Average' solution

| | Factor structure loadings | | | Factor pattern loadings | | |
	I	II	III	I	II	III
X_1	−0·946	0·126	−0·260	−0·935	−0·032	−0·105
X_2	0·882	−0·144	0·171	0·880	0·010	0·027
X_3	0·357	−0·798	−0·364	0·287	−0·719	−0·354
X_4	0·136	0·040	0·709	0·019	−0·012	0·706
X_5	0·070	−0·397	0·000	−0·007	−0·401	0·033
X_6	−0·050	0·830	−0·020	0·121	0·860	−0·107
X_7	0·223	−0·001	0·731	0·099	−0·040	0·718

Inter-factor correlations

	F_I	F_{II}	F_{III}
F_I	1·00		
F_{II}	−0·18	1·00	
F_{III}	0·16	−0·08	1·00

B. 'Very oblique' **C. 'Less oblique'**

| | Factor structure loadings | | | Factor structure loadings | | |
	I	II	III	I	II	III
X_1	−0·946	0·167	−0·303	−0·945	0·108	−0·246
X_2	0·880	−0·183	0·211	0·881	−0·127	0·158
X_3	0·381	−0·806	−0·359	0·334	−0·791	−0·356
X_4	0·167	0·033	0·708	0·125	0·040	0·708
X_5	0·093	−0·397	−0·005	0·056	−0·397	0·007
X_6	−0·103	0·825	−0·004	−0·020	0·832	−0·036
X_7	0·256	−0·012	0·734	0·210	−0·001	0·730

Inter-factor correlations **Inter-factor correlations**

	F_I	F_{II}	F_{III}		F	F_{II}	F_{III}
F_I	1·00			F_I	1·00		
F_{II}	−0·27	1·00		F_{II}	−0·13	1·00	
F_{III}	0·26	0·08	1·00	F_{III}	0·13	0·06	1·00

between variables and factors when the influence of the other two factors is held constant. X_6 has a higher pattern than structure loading on factor II, however. (This is quite possible when there are negative correlations between factors, as Fig. 5.13 illustrates; once the effect of factor I is held constant, in that case, the correlation between X_1 and factor II is higher than the structure loading indicates.) In the table, no communalities or sums of squared loadings are given since they are uninterpretable; in some cases they involve double counting of the joint variance, whereas in others this joint variance is omitted.

Table 5.13B gives results of oblique rotations with different constraints on the degree of inter-factor correlation. Comparison of the structure loadings in the various matrices indicates that the major changes are for the variables with relatively small loadings on the factors. As obliqueness increases, these become larger. In other words, in this example at least, the

170

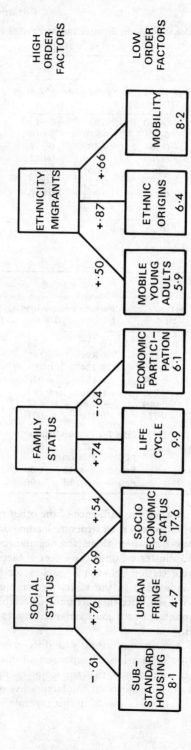

Fig. 5.14 Inter-related oblique factors; summary of a high-order factor analysis of eight factors (after Davies and Lewis, 1973).

main outlines of simple structure are as defined by the orthogonal rotation (Table 5.12B) and inter-correlation between factors is slight.

With inter-related factors, it is possible to factor analyse the inter-factor correlation matrix, producing a hierarchy of factors; the inter-related factor score vectors become the data matrix for the subsequent analysis. In a study of residential patterns in Leicester, using 56 variables, Davies and Lewis (1973) extracted eight factors, named as in Fig. 5.14. Factor analysis of these suggested a three-factor pattern encompassing the original eight, with socio-economic status related to two of the three 'higher order' factors. Interpretation suggests that the residential mosaic of Leicester comprises three major patterns, each of which is an amalgam of two or three sub-patterns. This use of oblique factors allows greater precision of conclusions, in that the researcher can specify the scale of his generalisations.

'Target' rotations

All of the rotation procedures discussed so far have been inductive searches for simple structure, on the hypothesis that groups of variables exist. A stronger hypothesis would be to state not only that groups exist but that certain variables should be members of each group. In this case, the detail of the simple structure is defined, and we see how well the data fit it.

Two main methods of rotating to a 'target' simple structure exist: Promax and Multiple Group Factor Analysis. We shall look only at the latter, with an example taken from work on spatial patterns within the residential areas of Auckland, New Zealand (Timms, 1971). From existing

Table 5.14 Residential differentiation in Auckland: factor analysis with target rotation

A. Hypothesised simple structure				B. Factor structure loadings		
Variables	**Loadings**			**Loadings**		
	I	II	III	I	II	III
Percentage aged 0–4	+1·0	0·0	0·0	0·85	−0·38	0·22
Percentage aged 65+	−1·0	0·0	0·0	−0·83	0·23	−0·03
Percent population increase	+1·0	0·0	0·0	0·87	0·06	−0·29
Percentage dwellings owned	+1·0	0·0	0·0	0·85	0·27	0·44
Percentage single-family homes	+1·0	0·0	0·0	0·88	−0·07	0·24
Percentage women with jobs	−1·0	0·0	0·0	−0·91	−0·20	−0·43
Percentage professional jobs	0·0	+1·0	0·0	−0·08	0·09	−0·62
Percentage non-manual jobs	0·0	+1·0	0·0	−0·03	0·99	−0·66
Percentage with high incomes	0·0	+1·0	0·0	0·02	0·99	−0·66
Percentage non-European birth	0·0	0·0	+1·0	−0·22	−0·65	1·00

C. Inter-factor correlations

	F_I	F_{II}	F_{III}
F_I	1·00		
F_{II}	−0·03	1·00	
F_{III}	−0·22	−0·65	1·00

Source: Timms (1971, p. 181).

theory, Timms hypothesised three dimensions to these patterns, as consequences of three different processes which allocate households to different neighbourhoods. Each of these processes should be represented by a group of variables, giving the defined simple structure of Table 5.14A.

Having hypothesised the simple structure, a factor analysis is undertaken to extract the requisite number of factors. These are then rotated to their best fit relative to the hypotheses. Table 5.14B indicates how successful Timms was. Because only one variable was related to factor III in the hypothesis, it was bound to have a loading of 1·00 on it. But the three variables for factor II all have loadings of 0·99, and for the six representing the hypothesised first factor the smallest loading is 0·83. The inter-factor correlations (Table 5.14C) show that this is an oblique factor structure; factors II and III are correlated at −0·65, suggesting that the allocation processes relating to ethnic segregation (III) and socio-economic status (II) are far from independent.

For research with well-developed hypotheses about the distribution of the common variance between factors, so that each variable can be associated with a particular factor, this approach has much to recommend it. There are no problems of experimenting with the degree of obliqueness allowed, since the obliqueness that results is a consequence of the hypothesised structure. Perhaps it is a mark of the meagre development of geographical theory, however, that this procedure has rarely been used.

Rotation of components

Simple structure is a hypothesis regarding relationships within a data set which is tested by a rotation of factors. It is not a hypothesis relevant to principal components analysis, since it refers to common variance only, and not to common plus unique variance. Nevertheless, there are many examples in the geographical literature of the rotation, usually the Varimax rotation, of components.

Strictly speaking, rotation of components is wrong; in general, it is meaningless. It is done to try to highlight groups of variables in a data set. Usually the number of components rotated (k) is not the same as the number of variables (n), and it is sometimes argued that this is then a factor analysis. The latter works on weighted variables, however, whereas components work on unweighted, total variance and part of the variance redistributed by rotation of components may be unique variance. The two procedures are not identical, therefore, but differences are often slight. Rotated components do allow better group identification, which may be desirable if, for example, the scores are to be used as independent variables in regression analyses. But if the aim of the study is to find the best approximation to simple structure, then factor analysis is preferable because it ignores specific variance.

Factor scores

Just as component scores are desirable for geographical work, relating the original observations to the new variables, so factor scores are equally in demand. Unfortunately, although component scores can be computed directly, factor scores cannot; they can only be estimated. This is because factor analysis deals only with the common variance, whereas the observed values on the original variables combine common and unique elements, in unknown proportions. Thus if we have a variable in a two-factor solution with loadings

$$F_I = 0.80 \quad F_{II} = 0.50 \quad h^2 = 0.89$$

we know that only 11% of its variance is specific, and that 72% of its common variance is associated with factor I. But these are average figures, referring to the total set of observations, and we do not know to what extent each observation on that variable conforms to the average in the explanation of its magnitude: residuals are scattered around the best-fit relationship.

In algebraic terms, the standardised value for observation i on variable $j - D_{ij} -$ is a composite of the score for i on each of the k factors, plus its score on the unique variance of j. Thus:

$$D_{ij} = \left(\sum_{m=1}^{k} S_{im} L_{jm} \right) + S_{ij} U_j \tag{5.12}$$

where S_{im} is the score for observation i on factor m;

L_{jm} is the loading of variable j on factor m;

S_{ij} is the score for observation i on variable j;

U_j is the unique variance of variable j; and

D_{ij} is the standardised value of observation i on variable j.

Since the S_{im} and S_{ij} elements cannot be separated out, however, the former have to be estimated. This is done by regressing the data matrix on the loadings matrix, thereby assuming that the average proportions for the variance distribution (i.e. the common and unique elements) are the same for each observation.

Factor scores are frequently computed and used in much the same way as component scores are in geographic research; for example, in preparing maps of the spatial patterns of the new variables. As such they are important parts of the output of a factor analysis, but there are some problems with them:

1. As already indicated, they are only estimates; and
2. If simple structure is not approximated, the resulting scores may be confounded by several interactions which impede interpretation (Joshi, 1972). For example, take a factor with loadings

X_1	X_2	X_3	X_4	X_5
+0.90	+0.85	+0.60	−0.45	−0.30

which would clearly be interpreted in terms of the high loadings for variables X_1 and X_2. But consider two observations, A and B, whose Z scores on the variables X_1 to X_5 are

	X_1	X_2	X_3	X_4	X_5
A	1·00	1·20	0·00	−0·10	−0·20
B	0·10	0·10	1·50	−1·20	−1·10

Observation A has fairly high values for the two variables by which the factor is identified; observation B has low values on those two variables, but high values on X_3 to X_5, which have medium loadings on the factor. But if we estimate the factor scores for A and B using the basic formula for component scores − formula (5.9) − we get scores of A = 2·03 and B = 1·98; two very dissimilar observations in fact produce the same score. How, then, do we interpret the scores?

A major reason for this problem is the lack of simple structure, as indicated by the factor loadings: if simple structure is not achieved, the problems are bound to appear in some form. Without detailed study of the data, therefore, it is impossible to know why an observation has the score that it does. Ways around this have been suggested. One proposal is not to derive the scores but to select a stereotype variable to represent the factor. In this case, presumably X_1 would be chosen and a geographer may produce a map of this variable as representative of the factor with which it has the largest loading. But 19% of the variation in X_1 is not associated with the factor ($0·9^2 = 0·81$; $1·0 − 0·81 = 0·19$), and so there will be about one-fifth error in the map. The smaller the loading of the chosen variable, therefore, the larger the error. And, of course, the chosen variable may be unrelated to those others (e.g. X_4) which also are related to the factor (see p. 148), introducing an error of omission to go with the error of commission.

An alternative procedure is to use only the variables with loadings above a certain threshold in the derivation of the scores (this is suggested by Joshi, 1972). Thus we might suggest a loading of 0·71 as the lower threshold, since this would indicate that 50% of the variance in the variable is associated with the factor. In this case, for our example only X_1 and X_2 would be used, and the scores would be A = 1·92 and B = 0·21. These give a clear indication of the difference between the two observations on the variables with major loadings on the factor, but whether they are acceptable depends on the interpretation of the factor structure and the relevance of the minor loadings.

Image factor analysis

One method devised to circumvent the problem of only being able to estimate factor scores is image factor analysis, which has been used in some geographical studies. This decomposes the data rather than the correlations into common and unique variance. As indicated in formula (5.12), each observation on each variable comprises common variance and unique variance elements and these can be estimated by multiple regression. Thus, in a five variable analysis, the value of variable 1 for observation i, D_{i1}, is decomposed into

$$D_{i1} = \hat{D}_{i1} + (D_{i1} - \hat{D}_{i1}) \tag{5.13}$$

where $\hat{D}_{i1}$ is the predicted value of D_{i1} from the equation

$$X_1 = f(X_2, X_3, X_4, X_5); \tag{5.14}$$

and $(D_{i1} - \hat{D}_{i1})$ is the residual from the predicted value.

The residual is taken as the estimate of the unique variance and the predicted value as the common variance component. Factor analysis thus proceeds on the correlations among the common variance components only, which allows direct computation of the factor scores, since the unique variance has been removed from the data matrix.

Image factor analysis operates on a rewriting of the data, as one way of estimating the common variance, and thus may produce different results from those of alternative factor analyses of the same data. Rees (1972) illustrates this in a comparison of separate analyses of Montreal's residential pattern.

Direct factor analysis

This final form of factor analysis to be discussed here has been used by a number of geographers. It differs from the forms previously discussed, and also from principal components analysis, in that it does not operate on a correlation matrix. Eigenvalues and related eigenvectors can be extracted from any square, symmetrical matrix. In the case of a full correlation matrix, as we have seen, the values along the principal diagonal are all +1·0, and the vectors in the correlation diagram are of equal length. In factor analysis, the values along the diagonal vary between 0·0 and +1·0. In direct factor analysis, they can take any value.

In geography, this direct method is often used to study transport networks, such as the road system of the imaginary island shown in Fig. 5.15.

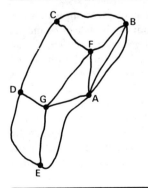

Fig. 5.15 The transport network of an imaginary island.

This network can be represented by a square, symmetrical, binary matrix (Taaffe and Gauthier, 1973) in which a 1 indicates that there is a direct connection between the two places, and a 0 indicates no direct connection (Table 5.15A). The factors of this matrix are extracted in the same way as are those of a correlation matrix (Gould, 1967), and the loadings on these are given in Table 5.15B. (The factors of Table 5.15B are, in fact, the unstandardised eigenvectors of the inter-connection matrix in Table 5.15A; as Gould shows, principal components are simply standardised eigenvectors.)

Table 5.15   Direct factor analysis of a hypothetical transport network (Fig. 5.15)

A. Inter-connection matrix

Settlement	Settlement						
	A	B	C	D	E	F	G
A	0	1	0	0	0	1	1
B	1	0	0	0	0	1	0
C	0	0	0	0	0	1	0
D	0	0	0	0	0	0	1
E	0	0	0	0	0	0	1
F	1	1	1	0	0	0	1
G	1	0	0	1	1	1	0

B. Factor loadings matrix

Settlement	Factor		
	I	II	III
A	0·83	0·15	−0·20
B	0·61	0·40	−0·21
C	0·32	0·26	0·45
D	0·29	−0·49	0·03
E	0·29	−0·49	0·03
F	0·91	0·27	0·14
G	0·82	−0·52	0·01
Eigenvalues	2·83	1·06	0·31

The loadings on the first factor in Table 5.15B provide a scaling of the seven settlements in terms of the number of direct connections which they have with other settlements; the larger the loading, the better connected the settlement is. On the second factor, two groups of settlements are identified; those with the positive loadings (A, B, C and F) form a well-connected group in the northern half of the island; those with negative loadings (D, E and G) form a southern group. The third factor, which is not very important according to its eigenvalue, isolates the link between A and B by its negative loadings and that between F and C by the two positive loadings that exceed 0·1; the interpretation of this factor is that the northern group splits into two sub-groups because C has no direct link to either A or B. Such subdivision is unnecessary in the case of the southern group.

As with most simple examples using small matrices, the results in Table 5.15B are rather obvious and could have been deduced from an inspection of Fig. 5.15. But application of the method to large matrices allows identification of the major linkage patterns in a complex transport network. For example, Garrison and Marble (1964) used it to study the 59 × 59 interconnection matrix of the Venezuelan airline services in 1958. Their first factor was a general scaling of the 59 settlements in terms of the number of cities they had direct connections to; subsequent factors identified groups of linked centres focused, respectively, on Caracas, Maracaibo, Santa Barbara, and Maturin. Similar studies by Gould (1967) and by Tinkler (1972) have also used the method to identify general and regional components to transport networks in Uganda.

Transport geographers obtain other matrices from the inter-connectivity matrix to index different aspects of the network (Taaffe and Gauthier, 1973). These involve raising the initial matrix to various powers of itself. The square of such a matrix, for example, is used to provide information on the number of two-step links between each pair of settlements (i.e. the number of routes joining A and B which pass through another place; in Fig. 5.15 there is one, via F). These matrices also could be factor analysed but, as Hay (1975) has shown, the eigenvectors of C^2 (the squared interconnectivity matrix) are the same as those of C (as also are those of C^3, C^4 - C^n), so that direct factor analysis of any one of the matrices (and it may as well be the simplest − C) will provide the required information on the structure of the transport network.

A related matrix which can be derived from one containing binary information, such as Table 5.15A, is the cross-products matrix. The cross-products are, in effect, unstandardised correlations obtained by the formula

$$CP_{ij} = \left(\sum_{k=1}^{N} C_{ki} C_{kj} \right) / N \qquad (5.15)$$

where C_{ki}, C_{kj} are the values for variables i and j (columns of the data matrix) at observation (row) k;

N is the number of observations; and

CP_{ij} is the average cross-product for variables i and j.

Since the values of C_{ki} and C_{kj} can only be either 1 or 0, and (1 × 0) = (0 × 1) = 0, the value of CP_{ij} is the average number of observations in which both i = 1 and j = 1; an alternative interpretation is as the probability of i and j both having the value of 1 in any observation.

Direct factor analysis of such cross-products matrices works on square, symmetrical matrices derived from initial matrices which need not have those characteristics. An example of these is Berry's (1967) study of the functional structure of 36 shopping centres in Spokane. (Berry's cross-products were not averaged, so that the values of $\Sigma C_{ki} C_{kj}$ were not divided by N as indicated in formula (5.15). Since N is a constant, omission of this standardisation procedure does not alter the substance of the analysis.) For each of 34 different types of retail establishment, the data matrix contained a 1 if there was an example of that type in the centre, and a 0 if not. This 36 × 34 binary matrix was used to produce two cross-products matrices. The first was a 34 × 34 matrix comparing the distribution of each retail establishment type with every other: the entries on the principal diagonal indicated the number of centres the relevant type was represented in; those off the diagonal indicated the number of centres the members of the relevant pair of types were both in. The second matrix comprised 36 × 36 cross-products comparing centres; the entries on the principal diagonal indicated the number of types represented in each centre, and the off-diagonal entries indicated the number of types which that pair of centres had in common. Joint direct factor analysis of these two matrices produced six factors. The first scaled the centres according to their numbers of types present and the types according to the number of centres they were represented in; the other five identified groups of centres with similar functional structures.

Table 5.16   Migrant labour in Europe: direct factor analysis of cross-products matrix

Origin	Loadings on factor			Destination	Scores on factor		
	I	II	III		I	II	III
Greece	42·5	6·0	56·2	Austria	0·02	−0·01	0·11
Italy	267·7	38·1	−14·6	Belgium-Lux.	0·33	0·17	−0·46
Portugal	25·5	−28·7	− 8·2	France	1·51	−2·00	−0·84
Spain	132·4	−73·6	1·2	Netherlands	0·05	−0·11	0·05
Turkey	31·6	3·0	39·7	Germany	1·48	0·21	2·17
Yugoslavia	19·0	− 2·8	17·4	Sweden	0·02	0·02	0·00
				Switzerland	1·56	1·71	−1·24

Source: Johnston (1973a, p. 733).

Direct factor analysis can be applied to any cross-products matrix. For example, instead of obtaining the correlations among the six origins in the labour migration data of Table 5.8, the cross-products matrix could be computed, and the loadings and scores derived (Table 5.16: Johnston, 1973a). Because the cross-products do not, like the correlations, vary between ±1·0 only, the loadings emphasise the absolute size of each flow as well as relative similarities and do not vary between +1·0 and −1·0 only. The first factor indexes the average pattern, and therefore the larger the flow from each place, the larger the loading, and the corresponding scores on the first factor pick out the main destinations. (Migrant labour in Europe is dominantly from Spain and Italy and to France and Germany.) The second and third factors pick out, as do those for the correlation analysis (p. 152), the two 'migration regions' respectively representing flows from Spain and Portugal to France (which is contrasted by the positive loadings/scores with Italian moves to Switzerland) and flows from Greece, Turkey and Yugoslavia to Germany: the difference between Table 5.8 and Table 5.16 is that in the latter the intensity of the flows is indicated by the loadings. For other data sets, however, which are not measured on a common scale like number of migrants, there are great problems of interpreting the results (Johnston, 1973a).

Conclusions

This is a long chapter, dealing with a suite of methods which is widely used in geography, and yet many more detailed aspects have not been discussed. Two of them need brief treatment in this conclusion.

Significance testing

Most geographical data submitted to components and factor analysis do not refer to samples of observations, and so significance testing is irrelevant. Where the latter can be used, if the data refer to a sample of observations, significance testing inquires: (1) if any one loading is significantly different from zero, and thus the variable is almost certainly related to that factor or component in the population; and (2) if any eigenvalue is significantly larger than zero, so that the factor almost certainly exists in the population.

Significance tests are occasionally reported, even when sample data are not used in the components or factor analyses. Their purpose is, it seems, to identify 'significant' loadings, indicating variables which are clearly associated with the relevant factor or component. The concept of statistical significance in this context has nothing to do with the size of the loading, which is what is usually being interpreted, but only with the probability of a loading with that sign being different from zero in the population, and this probability is very much related to the number of observations, N. As with the coefficients of regression equations (p. 49), null hypotheses other than $L_{ik} = 0.0$ could be tested, but there are no examples of these in the geographical literature.

There are two problems concerning the relevance of statistical testing to geographical analyses highlighted here. The first concerns the difference between a significant result and a substantive one. The major determinant of the significance of a finding is the size of the sample on which it is based, so that with a large enough sample it is very likely that a component or factor loading of, say, 0·20 is significant at the 5% level. In other words, there is a 95% probability of a positive loading for that variable existing in the population. Substantively, however, this finding is undoubtedly of little real value. A loading of 0·20 has a squared value of 0·04 only, which indicates that the factor or component accounts for 4% of the variance in that variable: hardly a finding of any great note (unless negative results are important!). In other words, statistical significance refers only to the probability that a finding reported for a sample applied also to the population and it should not be confused with substantive relevance.

The second problem relates to the more general issue of what is a sample. Is a census of population taken at midnight on 1 April 1971, in which every person in the country was counted, a sample? In one sense it is not, since it is a total enumeration; to some it is, since it is a sample of all possible censuses which could have been taken around that time, in which case, of course, the sample size is *one* and not the number of people enumerated. Similarly, a study of the pattern of land use by county in England may be a total enumeration, but it can be argued that it is only one of a very large number of possible subdivisions of the country into 'counties'. It may be feasible to use a complete enumeration as a single sample, therefore, although the benefits of so doing are not clear (see Meyer, 1972a and Court, 1972).

Slices of the data cube

All of the discussion in this chapter has been of the analysis of matrices with n columns (= number of variables) and N rows (= number of observations). This represents only one facet of the data cube (Fig. 1.1), and there are several other ways in which data can be structured for components and factor analyses.

Figure 5.16 shows a data cube comprising n variables, N observations, and t time slices. There are six different ways in which a data matrix can be extracted from this cube, and each of these is associated with a particular *mode* of factor or components analysis.

1. R-Mode, which is the most common way, and has been discussed here. The n variables form the columns, and the N observations the rows.
2. Q-Mode, in which the N observations form the columns and the n variables the rows.

Each of these modes holds time constant in that it looks at either the inter-variable correlations (R-mode) or the inter-observation correlations (Q-mode) at one time period only. In the former, the loadings are for the variables and the scores for the observations; loadings refer to the N observations in Q-mode.

3. O-Mode, for which the t time slices are the columns and the n variables are the rows.
4. P-Mode, with the n variables as the columns and the t time slices as the rows.

In these two modes, observations are held constant, so that the analyses refer to one 'place' only in terms of the geographical data cube. O-mode analysis emphasises inter-time period correlations, whereas P-mode emphasises inter-variable correlations, over time-periods.

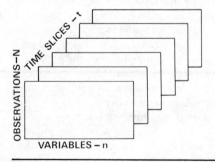

Fig. 5.16   Structure of the data-cube for the three-mode factor analysis.

5. S-Mode, for which the N observations are the columns and the t time slices the rows.

6. T-Mode, which is the transpose of S-mode, the t time-periods being the columns and the N observations the rows.

In these two final modes, only one variable or phenomenon is being studied; S-mode emphasises inter-place correlations on that variable over time, and T-mode inter-time period correlations.

As already noted, R-mode analyses are by far the most frequent in geographical work, and there are some examples of Q-mode. The other four are rarely used, in large part because of data paucity. Both S- and T-modes have been used in studies of trends in single variables, such as rainfall (Gregory, 1975; Perry, 1970) and unemployment (Casetti, King and Jeffrey, 1971). The rainfall analyses, for example, allowed the identification of stations with similar long-term rainfall trends, and also areas of precipitation anomalies; the analyses of unemployment identified groups of places with similar experiences (Jeffrey, 1974). One problem sometimes posed with analysis of some of these matrices is that the number of rows should exceed that of columns. This is a requirement for inferential purposes, however, and not for descriptive.

Finally, one can create other matrices from combinations of these basic six. For example, the Incremental-R- (or ΔR) Mode is developed as some measure of the change in each variable at each observation between time t_1 and time t_2, and analysis of this identifies groups of variables with similar patterns of change over the N observations during the particular time period, as in Murdie's (1969) work on the changing characteristics of residential areas in Toronto (see also Brown and Horton, 1970; Johnston, 1973b). If matrices for several time periods are available, these can be put together in a Three-Mode Factor Analysis, which looks at inter-variable relationships over time and over space simultaneously, but there are as yet few examples of this in the geographical literature (Cant 1971, 1975a).

Summary

Principal components analysis and factor analysis are extremely flexible tools for finding order in large geographical data matrices, either inductively or as tests of hypotheses. Because of this, it is not surprising that they have become widely used in geographical research. There are undoubtedly many examples where they have been of marginal relevance to the research problem and others where they have been mildly, if not seriously, mis-used, but their general utility for particular tasks is undoubted and will certainly continue to be recognised. Data are being made available in ever-increasing volume, often in machine-readable form, and large, fast computers for analysing such data are accessible to most researchers. As yet, the theory necessary to guide hypothesis-testing in most branches of geography is poorly developed, and inductive sifting of data via principal components analysis and factor analysis is providing useful insights for the construction of viable theory. In the end, 'number-crunching' is not a valid substitute for thinking, but many argue that the complexity of the world requires the sort of simplifying generalisations which the methods discussed here can produce, when properly handled.

In using these two methods, and in particular factor analysis, as means of describing patterns and of generating theories about their origins, it is as well to remember that the methods themselves were developed to test a particular theory in psychology. That theory concerned the independence of the different portions of the brain which control the various functions of the body. Such a theory could not be tested directly by experimenting with brains but only by examining the output of human functions. The theory was one of independence, and thus of simple structure; the method developed involved devising batteries of tests for each human function and employing factor analysis to show that (1) the tests for each function were measuring the same thing, and (2) that the test results for each group were independent of those for every other. Factor analysis was needed rather than principal components analysis because the tests were unlikely to be perfect and so there would be some element of error variance. Factor analysis tests the theory of simple structure (p. 162), therefore; whilst it may be useful to geographers in the identification of inter-relationships, its ultimate value will depend on them writing simple structure theories also. Whether such theories are likely in geography, or whether all geographical phenomena are completely inter-related, lies beyond the scope of our discussion here.

Chapter 6

Canonical correlation analysis

In the previous chapter we looked at the creation of new variables as composites of original, inter-related variables. These composite variables — principal components and factors — have a variety of uses in further research. One of them is as independent variables in correlation and regression analyses, thereby removing problems of collinearity and interpretation. Canonical correlation analysis, the main procedure discussed in this chapter, develops from that, being a method for correlation analysis when both the independent and the dependent variables are composites of several measured variables.

The canonical problem

In Chapter 2, we saw how bivariate regression analysis fits functions of the form

$$Y = f(X) \tag{6.1}$$

where Y is the dependent variable; and
X is the independent variable;

and in Chapter 3 this was extended to multiple regression with several independent variables in the function

$$X_0 = f(X_1, X_2 - X_n) \tag{6.2}$$

where X_0 is the dependent variable; and
$X_1 - X_n$ are the n independent variables.

Chapter 5 then introduced a method of rewriting the independent variables into orthogonal composite variables or components, which could then be used in a function

$$X_0 = f(C_I, C_{II} - C_n) \tag{6.3}$$

where $C_I - C_n$ are the n components representing the n variables, although usually only the most important k (where $k < n$) components are extracted.

Canonical correlation follows logically from the sequence of functions in formulae (6.1) to (6.3) by relating *sets of dependent variables* to *sets of independent variables*. The need for such a function can arise in a research problem involving several dependent variables, which are known to be inter-related. For example, Gauthier (1968) investigated the relationships between levels of economic development and accessibility in various parts of Brazil. Neither of these general concepts could be indexed by a single variable. For the independent variables, accessibility measures were derived for each of 120 locations (see p. 177 for the derivation of such measures), and for the dependent variables three indices of economic development in each of the 120 places were selected — E_1, value of industrial production; E_2, size of urban population; and E_3, value of retail sales.

Components analyses of the three 120×120 accessibility matrices produced five new variables, which we will term $I_1 - I_5$. Following the procedure outlined in Chapter 5 for the use of components as independent variables (p. 155), Gauthier could then have fitted the equations

$$E_1 = f(I_1 - I_5)$$
$$E_2 = f(I_1 - I_5) \qquad (6.4)$$
$$E_3 = f(I_1 - I_5)$$

This would assume that $E_1 - E_3$ were independent indices of the general concept of economic development, however, when a composite index seems more desirable. Thus the dependent variables require to be stated in components form, too, giving a function

$$(D_1 - D_m) = f(I_1 - I_n) \qquad (6.5)$$

where $D_1 - D_m$ are the components representing the dependent variables, up to a maximum of m, which in the number of original dependent variables; and $I_1 - I_n$ are the components representing the independent variables, up to a maximum of n, which is the number of original independent variables. The canonical equation — formula (6.5) — thus has composite variables on both sides of the functions: it is a procedure for relating inter-related groups of variables.

Canonical correlation procedures

Canonical correlation analysis is based on the same principles as those outlined in the previous chapter for the extraction of components from a correlation matrix. The data comprise a set of observations for each of which measurements are available on two sets of variables: the first set are usually known as the *predictor variables* (p) rather than the independent variables; the second, the dependent variables, are the *criteria variables* (q). These variables are intercorrelated, and from the correlation matrix orthogonal *canonical vectors* (similar to principal components) are extracted, so as to maximise the correlations between the components of the variables of the p set and those of the components of the q set. (in other words, canonical vector I is located so that the correlation between the scores on the p set for that vector and the scores on the q set is as high as possible, and each subsequent vector is similarly located among the residual correlations.) These correlations are indicated by the *canonical roots* (which are interpreted like correlation coefficients); the correlations (analogous to the component loadings) between the original variables and the canonical vectors are given by the *canonical weights*; and *canonical scores* (like component scores) are composite indices for the observations on the canonical vectors.

Comparing component structures

The methodology of canonical correlation analysis is introduced here through that of principal components analysis. For this, we have a hypothetical example of the two sets of variables, which relates aspects of urban social environments (the p set) to various crime rates (the q set) in a sample of cities. Our variables are

P_1 is town size (population); Q_1 is murder rate;
P_2 is population density; Q_2 is rape rate;
P_3 is size of police force per 1000 Q_3 is assault and battery rate;
   residents;
P_4 is degree of residential segregation Q_4 is burglary rate;
   of socio-economic groups;
P_5 is percentage of males unemployed; Q_5 is robbery rate.
P_6 is percentage males earning less
   than £1000 per annum.

These are measured over a set of towns, and expressed in standard score form. The correlations within each set of variables can then be derived, and these are shown in Fig. 6.1A and B.

Each of the correlation matrices can be resolved into a set of principal components, whose locations are indicated in Fig. 6.1A and B; the loadings are given in Table 6.1. For the crime variable set – the criteria (q) variables – the first component has fairly high loadings for all five, indicating a general criminality trend: the second separates the crimes of personal violence (Q_1, Q_2, and Q_3 – positive loadings) from the crimes against property.

The association of the environmental (p) and crime rate (q) components can be obtained by correlating the two sets of scores – i.e. C_i and C_{ii} against C_I and C_{II}. In diagrammatic terms, this involves superimposing one set of components on the other. (This is possible since both analyses refer to the same set of observations, so that in both the correlations shown in Fig. 6.1A and B are located in the same N-dimensional space, where N is the number of observations. What we have in Fig. 6.1 is in effect a cross-section of that N-dimensional space, where the orthogonal axes refer to cities a and b. Rummel, 1967, gives an elaboration of this view of correlations in 'observation space'.) The variables Q_1– Q_5 and P_1– P_6 in Fig. 6.1A and B are located relative to the axes of cities a and b, and so the relevant principal components are similarly located with reference to those axes. In Fig. 6.1C, therefore, the two previous diagrams (A and B) have been combined – with the original variables omitted for clarity. The

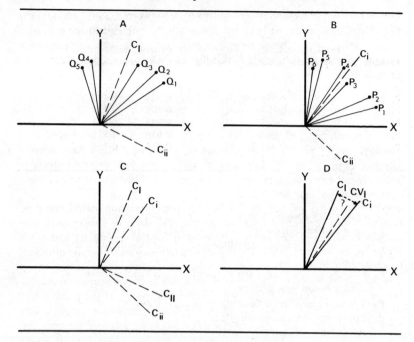

Fig. 6.1 The principal components for two data sets measured over the same observations (A, B); the comparative location of these components (C); and the location of a canonical vector (D).

cosines of the angles between those components are the inter-component correlations, which are

p set	q set	
	I	II
i	0·961	−0·276
ii	0·276	0·961

These provide the following interpretations: (1) high crime rates (C_I) are associated with towns having large police forces and a high degree of residential segregation (C_i); and (2) high rates for crimes of personal violence (positive loadings C_{II}) are related to city size and density (positive loadings C_{ii}) whereas high property crime rates are associated with high levels of poverty (negative loadings C_{II}, C_{ii}).

Canonical vectors

The inter-component correlations in the above example were obtained

Table 6.1 Urban environments and crime rates: results of separate principal components analyses

Variable	Predictor variables Component loadings		Variable	Criterion variables Component loadings	
	i	ii		I	II
P_1	0·819	0·574	Q_1	0·827	0·559
P_2	0·906	0·423	Q_2	0·905	0·423
P_3	0·996	0·087	Q_3	0·984	0·174
P_4	0·996	−0·087	Q_4	0·859	−0·515
P_5	0·906	−0·423	Q_5	0·757	−0·755
P_6	0·819	−0·574			

graphically because, as in Figs. 5.4 and 5.5, the correlation matrix could be represented in two dimensions only. With 'real' data, of course, such diagrams would be n-dimensional (where n = q for the criteria set and p for the predictor set); the inter-component correlations would then be obtained by correlating the various vectors of component scores.

Canonical correlations are also correlations between vectors of scores, but the latter are not obtained from separate analyses of the p and q sets of variables. Instead of conducting two principal components analyses, in canonical correlation analysis we extract a single set of components – the *canonical vectors* – located so as to maximise the correlation of scores between the observations on the p variables and those on the q variables. In terms of Fig. 6.1, instead of obtaining C_I and C_i as the principal components for the crime and environment variable sets respectively, we get a single vector – CV_I – located so that the scores on it for the crime set and for the environment set are maximally correlated. This canonical vector is almost certainly somewhere between C_I and C_i (Fig. 6.1D).

To emphasise this procedure, we obtain a single *canonical vector* (component) with loadings on all eleven variables. From these loadings we obtain two scores for each observation. The first is the score on the predictor set, thus

$$SP_{ik} = \sum_{j=1}^{p} D_{ij} L_{jk} \qquad (6.6)$$

where D_{ij} is the standardised score for observation i on predictor variable j;

L_{jk} is the canonical weight (loading) for predictor variable j on canonical vector k; and

SP_{ik} is the canonical score for observation i on the predictor variables associated with canonical vector k.

The second is the score on the criteria variable set, thus

$$SC_{ik} = \sum_{l=1}^{q} D_{il} L_{lk} \qquad (6.7)$$

where D_{il} is the standardised score for observation i on criterion variable l;

L_{lk} is the canonical weight (loading) for criterion variable l on canonical vector k; and

SC_{ik} is the canonical score for observation i on the criteria variables associated with canonical vector k.

These scores are obtained in exactly the same way as component scores (formula (5.9), p. 150) except that the vector of loadings is divided into two parts and a separate score computed for each. The correlation between these two vectors of scores, over the whole set of observations, is the canonical root; in its squared form (i.e. r^2) it is often known as the *latent root* and is represented by λ. The canonical vector is located to maximise the correlation (λ) between these two vectors of scores.

A simple example

The canonical vector is located in the correlation diagram, therefore, not to be as close to all of the variables as possible (which is the criterion in principal components analysis) but in that position where the correlation between the scores derived from the loadings on one group of the variables being analysed and the scores derived from the loadings on the remainder of the variables is the largest possible. This provides the best fit to the canonical equation of formula (6.5). The maximum number of canonical vectors which can be extracted is equal to the number of variables in the smaller of the two groups; in the example above, p was 6 and q was 5, so the maximum number of canonical vectors was five. Canonical vectors are orthogonal.

Table 6.2   Rainfall and stream hydrology: hypothetical data

Stream	Variable						
	P_1	P_2	P_3	P_4	Q_1	Q_2	Q_3
1	−1·16	−1·16	−0·83	−1·83	−1·49	−1·49	−0·83
2	−1·49	−1·49	−0·17	−0·17	−1·16	−1·16	−0·17
3	−0·50	−0·83	0·50	0·50	−0·83	−0·50	0·50
4	−0·83	−0·50	−1·49	−1·49	−0·50	−0·83	−1·16
5	−0·17	0·17	−1·16	−1·16	−0·17	0·17	−1·49
6	0·17	−0·17	1·16	1·49	0·17	−0·17	1·16
7	0·50	0·83	1·49	1·16	0·50	0·50	1·49
8	0·83	0·50	−0·50	−0·50	0·83	0·83	−0·50
9	1·49	1·16	0·17	0·17	1·16	1·49	0·17
10	1·16	1·49	0·83	0·83	1·49	1·16	0·83

To illustrate the full output of a canonical analysis, we take another hypothetical simple example relating three hydrological characteristics ($Q_1 - Q_3$), recorded at each of ten stream catchments, to four aspects of the rainfall intensity and distribution ($P_1 - P_4$) in those catchments.

P_1 is annual rainfall; Q_1 is mean annual flow;

P_2 is winter rainfall; Q_2 is average stream depth;

P_3 is number of 'rain days' per year; Q_3 is flow variability;
P_4 is number of 'heavy rain days' per year;

The data, in standard (Z) score form, are in Table 6.2.

Table 6.3   Rainfall and stream hydrology: canonical correlation analysis

A. Canonical weights

Variable	Canonical vector	
	I	II
P_1	0·607	−0·911
P_2	0·566	−0·930
P_3	0·974	−0·001
P_4	0·966	0·026
Q_1	0·191	−0·917
Q_2	0·153	−0·932
Q_3	0·962	0·041
Canonical correlation	0·996	0·981

B. Canonical scores

Stream	Canonical Vector I		Canonical Vector II	
	Predictors	Criteria	Predictors	Criteria
1	−0·93	−1·05	0·78	1·10
2	−0·40	−0·37	1·55	1·15
3	0·44	0·52	1·08	1·13
4	−1·54	−1·39	−0·20	−0·10
5	−1·14	−1·20	−0·74	−0·81
6	0·93	0·89	0·56	0·60
7	1·52	1·48	0·33	0·38
8	−0·21	−0·31	−1·02	−1·21
9	0·49	0·59	−1·34	−1·22
10	0·84	0·84	−1·00	−1·03

With a criteria set comprising only three variables, a maximum of three canonical vectors could be extracted. Of these, only two are 'statistically significant'. (A variety of tests is used to inquire into the 'significance' of a canonical correlation or canonical root; most common is Wilks' *lambda*, which is the reciprocal of the usual correlation coefficient and whose significance is usually tested using the chi-square distribution: see also p. 237.) The canonical weights (loadings) for these two vectors are in Table 6.3A, along with the canonical correlations. (The canonical correlation for the third vector is 0·642.) From these, we see that the first canonical vector is relating P_3 and P_4 in the predictor set to Q_3 in the criteria set, suggesting that flow variability is a function of the number of 'rain days', variously defined. The second vector relates P_1 and P_2 with Q_1 and Q_2, indicating that mean annual flow and average stream depth are both inter-related and also correlated with the inter-related measures of annual and winter rainfall amounts. (All of the important weights for this second canonical vector have negative signs, which allows a 'positive' interpretation. The signs indicate that, for P_1 and P_2, both winter rainfall and annual rainfall are negatively related to the canonical vector, so we infer that P_1 and P_2 are positively inter-related. A similar interpretation for Q_1 and Q_2 leads to an overall conclusion regarding the positive relationship between the two sets. In such cases, which occur in principal components and factor analyses also, the negative loadings for all substantive variables are much more easily interpreted by changing their signs.)

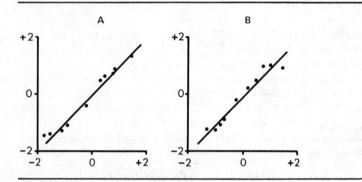

Fig. 6.2   Regressions of the canonical scores in Table 6.3.

The canonical scores for the ten streams on the two groups of variables, derived using formulae (6.6) and (6.7), are given in Table 6.3B. Regression of the scores for the criteria set against the predictor set (Fig. 6.2) illustrates the closeness of the relationships indexed by the canonical correlations. (The canonical weights, of course, are the correlations between these canonical scores and the values for the original variables. Occasionally, these weights are presented in unstandardised, and hence uninterpretable, form: Monmonier and Finn, 1973.)

Geographical applications

Canonical correlation analysis has not been widely used to date in geographical research. Those studies which have been published indicate three types of usage.

Relating groups of inter-related variables

This is the 'classical' purpose for which canonical correlation analysis was developed, as illustrated by the hypothetical examples in the previous section. Within this general type, two sub-types can be identified which differ over the specific way in which formula (6.5) is applied.

In the first of the sub-types, specific hypotheses are tested, although these do not usually predict the actual pattern of canonical weights. Corsi and Harvey (1975), for example, anticipated relationships between aspects of the population and housing characteristics of various residential areas in Cleveland, Ohio, as the predictor set and the recorded crime rates (by location of offence) in those areas. The latter, criteria, set comprised 7 variables, with 48 in the predictor set; 7 canonical vectors were extracted, with canonical correlations of 0·763, 0·586, 0·524, 0·513, 0·438, 0·283 and 0·235 respectively.

Only the first three of these canonical vectors were interpreted, as follows:

1. Large canonical weights among the predictor variables (with the same sign) were recorded for the percentage of the workforce in professional occupations and the percentage of households with above average incomes; among the criteria variables, similar large weights were reported for rates of larceny and auto theft. Together, these suggested a *property-crime—opportunity* dimension, with those crimes being most frequently reported in areas where the temptations were greatest.

2. The second canonical vector was interpreted as a *poverty/violent crimes* dimension. The largest canonical weights were for several variables indexing aspects of poverty in the predictor set and for the violent crimes (murder and assault) among the criteria variables. From this, it is clear that areas of deprivation are also areas with above average rates of violent crime (and, it could be argued, this provides evidence favouring a causal hypothesis relating the two — see p. 185). Maps of the two sets of canonical scores on this vector (Fig. 6.3) indicate a clear division between the western and eastern parts of Cleveland. Areas with positive scores in the west, south and north-east have low relative levels of both poverty and violent crime, as indicated by positive scores on both predictor and criteria set, whereas the areas with negative scores on both sets — i.e. those with concentrations of poverty and of violent crime — are in the east. Around the city centre are areas with high poverty levels (negative scores on the predictor set) but low rates for violent crime (positive scores on the criteria set). A 'classification' of areas is possible with the scores, therefore; those with 'opposing' scores — positive on one set, negative on the other for a particular canonical vector — are the areas which do not conform to the general relationship brought out by the canonical correlation.

3. Whereas the first two canonical vectors had large canonical weights, all with the same sign, the third had variables in each set with either high positive or high negative weights. Those with positive signs related areas of low status occupations with high crime rates for robbery; those with negative signs related low income areas to high larceny rates. Specific functional relationships, albeit at an aggregate scale (see p. 263 on ecological correlations), have been identified from this analysis. There were no specific hypotheses, although there is sufficient evidence of spatial associations of crime rates and certain social environments (Herbert,

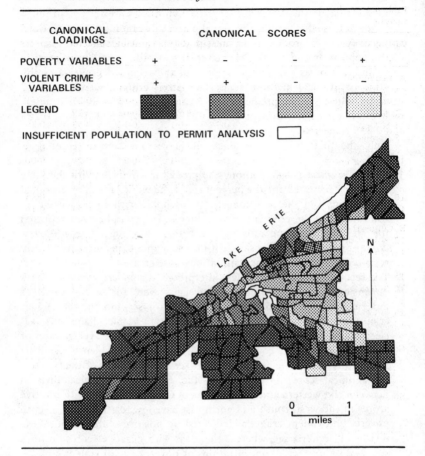

Fig. 6.3 Canonical scores for poverty variables and violent crime variables in the census tracts of Cleveland, Ohio. Source: Corsi and Harvey (1975); reproduced with permission.

1976); the method has been used only to test very generalised expectations.

The second sub-type comprises studies in which no generalised hypotheses are suggested even; the aim is merely to associate two sets of variables from different 'domains' to see if inter-relationships exist. No predictor and criteria sets are specifically defined, therefore, although they have to be identified for the operation of a computer program. Both Ray (1971) and Cant (1973), for example, have taken sets of variables referring to economic and cultural aspects of population structures (in Canada and the Philippines respectively) which they have analysed via the canonical procedures to maintain a separate identity for the two data sets rather than amalgamate them into a single factor analysis.

Table 6.4 Cultural and economic distributions in Canada: canonical correlation analysis

Variables	Canonical weights on canonical vector				
	I	II	III	IV	V
A. Economic*					
1. % managerial	−0·21	0·48	0·51	−0·44	0·17
2. % professional	−0·17	0·56	0·13	−0·25	0·51
3. % farm	0·80	−0·50	−0·05	−0·19	−0·22
4. % loggers	−0·35	−0·12	0·12	0·53	−0·20
5. % miners	0·00	0·45	−0·18	0·61	−0·24
6. % craftsmen	−0·62	0·46	−0·30	−0·19	0·15
7. % labourers	−0·63	0·11	−0·23	0·29	0·00
8. % adults in labour force	0·48	0·59	−0·01	−0·34	0·19
9. Males/females in labour force	0·11	−0·17	0·18	0·49	−0·53
10. % unemployed	−0·40	0·09	0·03	0·48	0·23
11. Average family income	0·01	0·77	−0·04	−0·51	0·16
B. Cultural†					
12. % English	0·41	0·22	0·89	−0·01	−0·31
13. % French	−0·36	−0·29	−0·81	−0·07	0·30
14. % German	0·67	0·03	0·14	−0·26	−0·22
15. % Indian and Eskimo	0·33	0·26	−0·03	0·76	−0·10
16. % Italian	−0·03	0·90	−0·11	−0·07	0·08
17. % Polish	0·75	0·34	0·03	0·06	0·11
18. % Ukrainian	0·79	−0·19	−0·02	0·21	0·25
19. % Yiddish	0·05	0·39	0·22	−0·22	0·84
Canonical correlation	0·72	0·70	0·60	0·49	0·37

* Variables 1−7 and 10 refer to the total labour force.
† Variables 12−19 refer to mother tongue of the total population.
Source: Ray and Lohnes (1973, p. 26).

Ray's data refer to the Canadian counties, and were taken from 1961 census tabulations: the first set were measures of economic activity; the second set were cultural variables (mother tongue). The aim of the analysis was to inquire: (1) whether there were cultural groups found in spatial association; (2) whether there were labour force groups similarly associated; and (3) whether there were inter-relationships between cultural and labour force groups. Five interpretable and 'significant' canonical vectors were extracted (Table 6.4), which suggest substantial, if not particularly close, correlations between the cultural and economic geographies of Canada. The first vector, for example, indicates a correlation between areas with relatively high percentages of central Europeans (German, Polish-speaking, and Ukrainian-speaking) and farming areas; the fourth vector shows a relative concentration of Indians and Eskimos in the areas where mining and logging are most important. The English-speakers, on the other hand, are not closely correlated in their spatial distribution with other cultural groups, though they have a strong dissociation with the distribution of the French, and are concentrated in areas with a large managerial workforce (vector 3); Italians (vector 2) are concentrated where incomes are high (i.e. the urban areas).

The canonical vectors isolated in the above analysis were interpreted by Ray (1971) in terms of the known cultural and economic geography of Canada, and gave him fresh insights into the developing patterns of population distributions. Similar results could have been achieved by principal components or factor analysis but use of canonical correlation analysis has a substantial advantage over those other methods if two separate groups of variables are involved. This is, that it gives the groups equal weight in the analysis. If, for example, an investigation was conducted with 15 variables in one set and 6 in the other, a factor analysis seeking the average position for the first factor among the 21 variables would almost certainly give greatest weight to those in the larger set. Canonical correlation analysis, on the other hand, emphasises correlations between groups of variables as the criterion to be maximised rather than correlations between all variables and a new one. As such, the method used by Ray ensures that the cultural/economic inter-relationships in Canada are highlighted; a factor analysis may not.

The integration of formal and functional regions

We saw in the preceding chapter (p. 149) how principal components and factor analyses can be used to identify common flow patterns — what we termed *functional regions* — in the pattern of labour migration within Europe. Similarly, we saw how *formal regions* — areas with similar characteristics (see also p. 153) — could be identified, either from the scores in an R-mode analysis or the loadings in a Q-mode analysis (p. 180). Formal and functional regions are inter-related. In Europe, for example, different origin areas and destination areas for migrants can be identified, and these are linked by the flow channels (Clout and Salt, 1976).

Studies of the inter-related formal and functional characteristics of areas may be based on two major data matrices, one relating to the 'contents' of the areas (the activities there) and the other to the flows between them. To gain an overall, synoptic view of those inter-relationships, the two matrices may be processed through a canonical correlation analysis. This was the procedure adopted by Berry (1966). His matrix for the formal regionalisation comprised 98 different variables indexing various aspects of the economy and society in each of 325 separate districts; for the functional regionalisation, he had 63 matrices, each showing the movement by rail of a separate commodity among 36 separate districts. These two data sets were brought to a common base, showing the differences between each pair of districts on both flows and formal characteristics. Canonical correlation analysis, with the flows as the criteria set, identified four vectors which could be interpreted as the major economic regions — focused on the main ports (Calcutta, Bombay, Madras) and on Delhi — of India.

Berry's analysis involved a very great volume of data, and is not without critics on various counts (Greer-Wootten, 1971; Farmer, 1973). It has been championed by Berry as a valuable method for identifying spatial order in a very complex world; a method which he later elevated into a 'general field theory' of areal organisation (Berry, 1968). It has been adopted by Freeman (1973) for a similarly ambitious attempt to identify spatial order in the flows of goods, capital and labour in the international system, and, at a smaller scale, by Clark (1973a) in analyses of the spatial structure of Wales. The latter author combined data on urban economic functions with information on inter-urban telephone calls; his predictor variable set had n columns and N rows, his criteria set (the flows) had N columns and N rows, and the canonical vectors provided a succinct description of the five main economic regions in Wales.

Comparing two equivalent data sets

In some investigations, the researcher may have two data sets referring to the same variables and the same observations, and he may wish to compare the two to see how similar they are. This might be the case, for example, in studies of changes over time, in which the data matrices may refer to the industrial structure of various cities in Great Britain in 1966 and 1976. To what extent were the structures the same? Were the same groups of industries present in the same places, at the same levels of relative importance, at the two dates? Canonical correlation analysis could be used to answer those questions, which are a verbal statement of formula (6.5).

A specific study organised along these lines deals with the comparison of a simulated and an actual pattern. Simulation is a method of prediction used to advance the understanding of how a pattern evolves. The researcher hypothesises what mechanisms produce the pattern, and then operates those processes in some way (see Morrill, 1965) to produce an estimate of the outcome. The final task is to compare the simulated pattern with the actual one, to see whether the former does reproduce the latter, at least to a large extent; if it does, then the researcher could have identified the probable genesis of the pattern.

If the simulation is of a matrix rather than of a vector, then canonical correlation analysis could be used to compare the simulated and actual matrices; Lankford (1974) has done this with work from a large study of the Chicago hospital system. The aim was to predict the home-to-hospital journey patterns of a sample of 79 178 patients, living in 206 residential areas and each using one of 49 hospitals. The simulation procedure allocated each patient to a particular hospital, giving a 49 × 206 flow matrix which was to be compared with another, having the same dimensions, which shows their actual choice of hospital. Canonical correlation analysis used the simulated flows as the predictor set (with the 49 hospitals as the variables and the 206 residential areas as the observations) and the actual flows as the criteria set. If the simulation reproduced the real pattern accurately, then similar functional regions (hospital hinterlands) should be observed in each matrix. Lankford extracted 13 interpretable canonical vectors, and showed that on each the same hospitals had large canonical weights on both predictor and criteria sets. (In fact, all Lankford identified was that the same hospitals had overlapping hinterlands in both the simulated and the actual data sets, but since the purpose of a canonical correlation analysis is to maximise the correlation between scores on the two sets of variables for each canonical vector, the existence of 'significant' canonical correlations indicates that the hinterlands are the same residential areas. Again, this demonstrates the advantage of canonical correlation analysis of the two matrices over either a principal components analysis or a factor analysis of the combined matrices.)

Two general issues

Although canonical correlation analysis has not been widely used in geographical research, there are already some problems in its application (which are not specific to geography). These are noted briefly here.

Significance

As is the case in most of this book, the uses to which various multivariate methods are being applied in geography do not fulfil all of the criteria of classic probabilistic statistics. In particular, although most of the data sets meet the normality requirements, and sometimes also those of homoscedascity, almost always they are not random samples of independent events, nor are they the results of careful experimental designs. At best, therefore, many of them are being used as simplifying — and, hopefully, clarifying — devices for large amounts of information. Statistical significance tests are usually irrelevant, and substantive interpretation is more important in the discussion of results (p. 179).

Elsewhere in this book, however, the argument has been advanced for analyses of variance that even when a population is being studied, statistical tests can validly be used to inquire whether the differences between the groups would have occurred very often in a random allocation of the individuals to that number of groups. A similar argument can be applied to several canonical correlation analyses in geography. Are the two data sets a random division of the population? In the case of Lankford's comparison of simulated and actual flows, the question would be: are those two matrices, or the major canonical vectors derived from them, random samples from the same parent population, or are they too similar for that to be the case? In Ray's study of Canada, are the cultural and economic matrices, or the major canonical vectors derived from them, two random distributions of populations over the set of counties, or are they too similar for that to be the case (except, perhaps, once in a hundred or a thousand samples)?

All principal components analyses will produce components; all factor analyses will produce factors; and all canonical correlation analyses will produce canonical vectors. The value of the output depends on the choice of the input and the interpretation of the results. For principal components and factor analyses, the eigenvalues give some indication of the importance of the derived dimensions; for canonical correlation analysis, this is given by the canonical correlations. Testing the statistical significance of the latter can aid interpretation — the degree to which hospital hinterlands are the same in both of Lankford's matrices, for example — although, of course, the final value of any analysis is a function of what was put into it, and why (Ch. 1).

'Orthogonal' canonical correlation analyses

The canonical equation — formula (6.5) — relates a set of inter-related 'independent' or predictor variables to another set of inter-related 'dependent' or criteria variables. Its distinguishing characteristic is its focus on these *three* sets of inter-relationships; the two within-groups and the one between-groups. Unfortunately, several studies using this method destroy one aspect of its major value by excluding the within-group relationships. They do this by using component scores as the predictor and criteria variables; because each set of scores comprises mutually orthogonal vectors, no within-group inter-relationships can exist.

An example of such a use of the method is Willis' (1972) investigation of migration on Tyneside. His canonical equation had aspects of the economic, social, and spatial environments of local authorities (industry types, housing tenures, district size and shape, etc.) as the predictors and the migration flows among the 23 districts as the criteria set. The former, 13 × 23, matrix was reduced to four orthogonal components and the latter, 23 × 23, matrix to nine orthogonal components; the canonical correlation analysis related the components, giving four predictor and nine criteria variables.

Table 6.5 shows the results of this canonical correlation analysis, in which two of the four correlations are substantial. The canonical weights on these canonical vectors illustrate the problems involved with such an analysis very clearly: *because within each set all of the variables are orthogonal, then only one variable in each set can have a high canonical weight on any one vector* (see Fig. 6.1). If there is a low canonical correlation, then several variables within any one set may have weights *c.* ±0·7 while still being orthogonal, but high canonical correlations almost certainly will be associated with single variables within each set only.

If the preceding principal components analyses have identified simple structure (p. 162) then the interpretation of the canonical vectors may be straightforward. If they have not, then analyses such as Willis' would seem to be obscuring as much as clarifying the complex sets of inter-relationships. Canonical correlation analysis is designed to look at three types of inter-dependence. Prior principal components analyses remove two of these types, and it would be better to run separate regression analyses using the components from the criteria set as the dependent variables and those from the predictor set as the independent variables than to submit them to canonical correlation analysis.

Table 6.5   Environment and migration on Tyneside: canonical correlation analysis

| Variables | Canonical weights on canonical vector | | | |
	I	II	III	IV
A. Environmental				
1. High socio-economic status	−0·45	−0·24	0·85	0·11
2. Size and density of population	−0·85	0·26	−0·33	−0·33
3. Area	−0·26	0·03	−0·25	0·93
4. Shape	0·13	0·94	0·31	0·09
B. Migration systems*				
5. Newcastle	−0·77	0·03	−0·18	0·45
6. South Tyne Mouth	0·05	−0·27	0·37	−0·14
7. Gateshead/Felling	0·01	0·22	−0·54	−0·08
8. North Tyne Mouth	0·22	−0·50	−0·42	0·38
9. Chester-le-Street	0·27	−0·08	−0·20	0·26
10. Blaydon/Ryton	0·26	0·69	0·01	0·42
11. Hebburn/Jarrow	0·36	0·02	−0·35	−0·15
12. Unidentified	−0·20	0·30	−0·29	−0·56
13. Unidentified	0·17	0·25	0·35	0·23
Canonical correlations	0·81	0·68	0·30	0·22

* The systems are identified by their major foci.
Source: Willis (1972, p. 79).

Comparative results from principal components and factor analyses

The canonical correlation methodology is a powerful one for investigating a variety of complex multivariate relationships. It is built on the usual assumptions of the general linear model, and in addition requires that both the predictor and the criteria sets of variables be measured over the same set of observations. It could be used in the analyses of change as already suggested; instead of the incremental-R-mode approach (p. 181), the matrix for t_1 could be the predictor set, and that for t_2 the criteria set; the canonical vectors and correlations would indicate the degree of similarity over time; and maps of the scores would indicate areas of change.

This approach has, perhaps surprisingly, not been taken up by geographers, although a variant of it has been developed (Johnston, 1973b). This may be because few data are available for such complex time series work (see p. 181). Most comparative studies involving factor and components analyses have looked at patterns over different sets of places, as with the work by Timms (1970) and Johnston (1973c) on whether the different cities of New Zealand have similar patterns of inter-relationships among the characteristics of their residential areas.

Comparisons between places are not based on the same observations, and so canonical correlation analysis cannot be used. Instead the methods of component comparison discussed with reference to Fig. 6.1A–C (p. 185) can be adopted. Two variants of this are available.

The first method, using what are generally known as *coefficients of congruence*, compare factors or components in two different matrices of loadings which refer to common sets of variables. In effect, these are correlations of the two vectors of loadings so that if one had the following results, after rotation

Variables	Town A Factor loadings			Town B Factor loadings		
	I	II	III	I	II	III
X_1	0·90	0·05	0·10	0·85	0·10	0·10
X_2	0·87	0·03	0·21	0·91	0·05	0·15
X_3	0·65	−0·25	−0·61	0·80	−0·40	−0·42
X_4	0·43	0·70	−0·32	0·10	0·90	−0·10
X_5	0·21	0·81	0·53	0·31	0·75	0·49
X_6	0·11	−0·35	0·80	0·20	−0·20	0·90
X_7	0·26	0·20	0·90	0·40	0·00	0·85

the matrix of coefficients of congruence would be

Town B	Town A		
	I	II	III
I	0·966	0·109	0·186
II	0·236	0·959	0·114
III	0·154	0·179	0·978

These coefficients, which are the cosines of the angles between the factors (Fig. 6.1C), are usually calculated as

$$G_{ij} = \frac{\sum\limits_{k=1}^{n} L_{ki} L_{kj}}{\sqrt{\sum\limits_{k=1}^{n} L_{ki}^2 \sum\limits_{k=1}^{n} L_{kj}^2}} \qquad (6.8)$$

where L_{ki}, L_{kj} are the loadings for variable k in matrix (place) i and matrix j, respectively;

n is the number of variables; and

G_{ij} is the coefficient of congruence between matrices (places) i and j.

For our hypothetical example, we see that the three factors in Town A are almost exactly matched by the three in Town B. In New Zealand, Timms (1970, p. 461) compared the four main cities. His factor analyses suggested two similar dimensions in each and coefficients of congruence showed great similarity between the cities:

	Auckland	Wellington	Christchurch	Dunedin
Auckland	—	0·991	0·962	0·918
Wellington	0·930	—	0·957	0·934
Christchurch	0·922	0·860	—	0·966
Dunedin	0·754	0·814	0·950	—

In this matrix, the coefficients above the principal diagonal compare the cities on the family status factor; those below it refer to the socio-economic status factor.

Coefficients of congruence have the disadvantage that they take the factors or components out of the context of the total structures of which they are part, so that one cannot test whether each variable has a similar pattern of loadings across all dimensions. Total loadings matrices can be compared if the variables are the same in each, however. One correlation matrix complete with its components (or factors; we will mention only components here) is superimposed on the other, and the former matrix then rotated until its components are located in the same positions as those of the other. (One structure acts as the 'target rotation' for the other, in effect: p. 171.) The *cosines of the rotation angles* indicate the amount of

Table 6.6 Comparison of the principal components of Melbourne's residential pattern: 1961 and 1966

A. Rotation cosines

1961 Component	1966 Component					
	I	II	III	IV	V	VI
I	0·86	−0·08	0·08	0·48	0·00	−0·12
II	0·02	0·99	0·06	0·13	−0·17	0·00
III	−0·09	−0·05	0·98	−0·06	0·03	−0·15
IV	−0·50	−0·09	−0·04	0·83	0·05	−0·19
V	0·02	0·09	−0·06	−0·08	0·97	−0·18
VI	0·00	0·02	0·15	0·21	0·20	0·94

B. Test correlations

Variable	Correlation	Variable	Correlation	Variable	Correlation
X_1	0·91	X_{11}	0·98	X_{21}	0·94
X_2	0·81	X_{12}	0·98	X_{22}	0·76
X_3	0·87	X_{13}	0·96	X_{23}	0·65
X_4	0·98	X_{14}	0·97	X_{24}	0·35
X_5	0·98	X_{15}	0·86	X_{25}	0·46
X_6	0·94	X_{16}	0·96	X_{26}	0·92
X_7	0·96	X_{17}	0·89	X_{27}	0·88
X_8	0·84	X_{18}	0·87	X_{28}	0·88
X_9	0·92	X_{19}	0·98		
X_{10}	0·73	X_{20}	0·92		

Source: Johnston 1973b, p. 88.

movement needed, and thus measure the inter-component correlations: after the rotation, the new loadings for the variables in the first data set are computed and correlated, for each variable, with those of the original component structure, giving a series of test correlations comparing the position of each variable in the component space with that of the same variable in the other.

Table 6.6 illustrates such a matrix comparison. Separate principal component analyses of 28 aspects of Melbourne's residential pattern were conducted for 1961 and 1966 data, and from each six components were interpreted (Johnston, 1973b). The rotation cosines indicate the closeness of the overall fit between the two dates, with very high cosines along the principal diagonal, whereas the test correlations for the individual variables suggest that only for a few variables — notably X_{23}, X_{24}, and X_{25}, all of which relate to the ethnic composition of local populations — was there any marked change in their loadings. Between the two dates, therefore, there was little change in the characteristic differences between Melbourne's suburbs, which does not mean that the characteristics of particular areas did not change but only that the same amount of change took place in related variables.

Conclusions

Canonical correlation analysis is a logical extension of the aspects of the general linear model discussed in earlier chapters, combining the characteristics of rewriting a data matrix in a new orthogonal form possessed by principal components analysis (Ch. 5) with the hypothesis-testing methodology of multiple regression analysis (Ch. 3). Its major value in geographical work, as suggested in the examples quoted above, would appear to be in the early stages of investigation into a particular topic, when vague causal hypotheses can be specified but which groups of variables within the independent (predictor) and dependent (criteria) sets are related is not particularly clear. Like principal components analysis its main use, apart from description in the manner of Berry's study and the testing of simulations, would seem to be in the generation of precise hypotheses rather than in their testing.

Chapter 7

Classification

In Chapters 5 and 6 we have seen how new variables, measured on a ratio scale, can be created as composites of other variables, when the latter are inter-related. In this chapter, we turn to look at methods of creating new variables on a nominal scale, of the type used in the analysis of variance. This involves grouping the observations into categories. Such a research procedure has a long history in geography, which has had a continuing interest in grouping similar places to form 'regions' — areas with characteristics in common, the relevant characteristics having been defined prior to the 'analysis'. Region-building is still a research theme in geography, sometimes as a didactic end in itself, often as a prelude to further research. For example, a factor analysis of 200 districts within a city may have resulted in three vectors of factor scores representing three independent aspects of districts' population composition. The researcher may, for the next stage of his work, wish to interview people in different types of 'social area', defining a social area as a group of districts with similar characteristics on all three factors. He must, then, group the original 200 districts to create social areas.

There are very many ways of grouping or classifying, as a wide literature in various disciplines testifies (Everitt, 1974; Hartigan, 1975; Jardine and Sibson, 1971; Johnston, 1976a; Smith and Sokal, 1973). As we are concerned in this book only with the general linear model, however, discussion is confined here to one widely-used technique, based on the analysis of variance.

Classification and the analysis of variance

The aim of classification is to group observations into categories comprising similar individuals, and thereby to separate dissimilar individuals into different categories. In terms of the analysis of variance, we meet the first criterion by minimising the within-group variance estimate and we meet the second by maximising the between-group variance estimate. For any set of observations, we want to find that grouping which meets both criteria, and therefore produces the largest F-ratio between them. This is, in fact, an enormous task; for more than a few observations it is computationally almost impossible.

As a simple example of our problem, we have five places whose annual rainfall averages are:

A — 100 mm   B — 80 mm   C — 120 mm

D — 70 mm   E — 110 mm

We want to group these into two categories only, producing the 'best' classification of stations with similar rainfall totals. We decide that each group must contain at least two stations, so the possible groupings are

	I	II
1.	A—B	C—D—E
2.	A—C	B—D—E
3.	A—D	B—C—E
4.	A—E	B—C—D
5.	B—C	A—D—E
6.	B—D	A—C—E
7.	B—E	A—C—D
8.	C—D	A—B—E
9.	C—E	A—B—D
10.	D—E	A—B—C

An analysis of variance has been conducted for each of these groupings, with the results shown in Table 7.1. According to the conventional test, only one — grouping 6 — produces an F-ratio which is statistically significant at even the 5% level. It is clearly the 'best', as a brief perusal of the data suggests.

The classification procedure just outlined suggests that one takes every possible grouping and evaluates each in terms of the analysis of variance model. Constraints can be set, such as the minimum number of observations per group in the above example, or the number of groups to be

Table 7.1   Classification of rainfall stations: hypothetical data

Grouping*	Sources of variation Between-groups	Within-groups	Variance estimates† Between-groups	Within-groups	F
1	120·00	1600·00	120·00	533·33	0·23
2	653·33	1066·67	653·33	355·56	1·84
3	403·33	1316·67	403·33	438·89	0·92
4	270·00	1450·00	270·00	483·33	0·56
5	53·33	1666·67	53·33	555·56	0·10
6	1470·00	250·00	1470·00	83·33	17·64
7	3·33	1716·67	3·33	572·22	0·01
8	3·33	1716·67	3·33	572·22	0·01
9	1203·33	516·67	1203·33	172·23	6·99
10	120·00	1600·00	120·00	533·33	0·23

*for key to groupings, see text;
†the degrees of freedom are: between groups df = 1; within-groups df = 3.

determined within the set of observations (e.g. 125 observations into 7 groups). But this is clearly an impossible task in most cases, even with constraints. For a data set comprising many observations, the possible number of different groupings is enormous, and beyond the capacity of even the largest computers to analyse in a short time. And, of course, it is only the large data sets which we want to classify! Furthermore, what determines the constraints? Can one be certain how many groups there should be, and how many individuals there must at least be in each?

The ideal outlined in Table 7.1 is clearly unobtainable, therefore, and we must seek an approximation to it. The one to be discussed here is based on the analysis of variance, using as its criterion the size of the within-groups variation component. Grouping proceeds hierarchically, proceeding one step at a time, and at each step minimises the growth of the within-group variation.

A univariate example

To illustrate the basic features of this procedure (which in a sense is an inverted analysis of variance) we take the simple example of seven glaciers, for each of which we know the number of metres it advanced in a single season. The values are

G_1	10	G_2	12	G_3	15	G_4	6
G_5	7	G_6	19	G_7	21		

The within-group variation is

$$\sum_{i=1}^{N} (G_i - \overline{G}_{ci})^2 \qquad (7.1)$$

where G_i is the value of G for place i;

$\overline{G}_{ci}$ is the mean value of G for group C, of which i is a member; and summation is over all N observations.

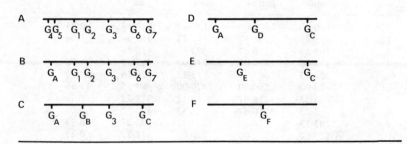

Fig. 7.1 Steps in the grouping of seven glaciers, showing the location of group means on a scale measuring annual rates of movement.

At the outset, each observation is in a separate group, so that for

$$i = 1 - N \qquad G_i = \overline{G}_{ci} \qquad (7.2)$$

There is, therefore, no within-groups variation, as each observation is also its group mean, and at a distance of 0·0 from it according to formula (7.1).

For the first step, we group together those two observations which will make the smallest increment to the within-groups variation. There are twenty-one possible groupings ($G_1 - G_2$; $G_1 - G_3$; $G_1 - G_4$, etc.), but most of these are irrelevant: we know we would not group G_1 with G_6, because G_2 and G_3 lie between these two places on the scale (Fig. 7.1A). In effect, we need look at adjacent pairs only, and the contributions to the within-group variation of combining pairs would then be

$G_4 - G_5$	0·5	$G_5 - G_1$	4·5	$G_1 - G_2$	2·0
$G_2 - G_3$	4·5	$G_3 - G_6$	8·0	$G_6 - G_7$	2·0

If, for example, we were to group G_5 with G_1, the mean value for this group would be $(G_5 + G_1)/2 = 8\cdot5$ and substituting this in formula (7.1) would give

$$(7 - 8\cdot5)^2 + (10 - 8\cdot5)^2 = 2\cdot25 + 2\cdot25 = 4\cdot5$$

Of the six possible groupings, that of G_4 and G_5 clearly produces the smallest increment in the within-groups variation (from 0·0 to 0·5) and so they are combined into a group which we call G_A. On our scale (Fig. 7.1B), G_A occupies the mean position for the group, half-way between the original locations of G_4 and G_5. None of the other five places is affected.

We now proceed to the second step. The possible groupings, and their contributions to the within-groups variation, are

$G_A - G_1$	10·37	$G_1 - G_2$	2·0	$G_2 - G_3$	4·5
$G_3 - G_6$	8·0	$G_6 - G_7$	2·0		

For the $G_A - G_1$ grouping, the mean of those three values ($G_A = G_4$ and G_5) would be $(6 + 7 + 10)/3 = 7\cdot67$, and substituting in formula (7.1) we would get

$$(6 - 7\cdot67)^2 + (7 - 7\cdot67)^2 + (10 - 7\cdot67)^2 = 10\cdot37$$

The other values are, of course, unchanged. Before this step, the within-groups variation was 0·5, involving G_A. If the $G_A - G_1$ grouping were adopted it would be 10·37, the G_A component being amalgamated into the larger group, and the extra contribution is $10\cdot37 - 0\cdot5 = 9\cdot87$. If the $G_2 - G_3$ component were adopted, however, it would be 0·5 (for G_A) + 4·5 (for $G_2 - G_3$), giving a total of 5·0.

From the values, we see that the smallest extra contribution, 2·0, will be made by two groupings, $G_1 - G_2$ and $G_6 - G_7$: these become G_B and G_C respectively, as shown on Fig. 7.1C. We now have four groups, and can work out the within-groups variations at the next step:

$G_A - G_B$	28·75	$G_B - G_3$	12·67	$G_3 - G_C$	18·67

The current situation with regard to the within-groups variation is:

contribution of G_A	0·5
contribution of G_B	2·0
contribution of G_C	2·0
Total	4·5

Thus the extra contributions are

$G_A - G_B$ less G_A G_B $= 28·75 - (0·5 + 2·0) = 26·25$

$G_B - G_3$ less G_B $= 12·67 - 2·0$ $= 10·67$

$G_3 - G_C$ less G_C $= 18·67 - 2·0$ $= 16·67$

The smallest extra contribution is made by combining G_B with G_3, creating group G_D (Fig. 7.1D).

We now work out the variance contributions for the two possible groupings that remain

$G_A - G_D$ 54·0 $G_D - G_C$ 85·20

The extra contributions are

$G_A - G_D$ less G_A G_D $= 54·00 - (0·50 + 12·67) = 40·83$

$G_D - G_C$ less G_D G_C $= 85·20 - (12·67 + 2·00) = 70·53$

Thus G_A and G_D are combined, giving G_E (Fig. 7.1E). The final grouping brings all seven glaciers into a single class (G_F), located at the mean of all their values (12·86: Fig. 7.1F), and for which the within-groups variation (194·28) is equal to the total variation.

Table 7.2   Classification of glaciers: hypothetical data

Grouping of		To form		Addition to within-groups variation	Total within-groups variation
G_4	G_5	G_A		0·5	0·5
G_1	G_2	G_B	2·0 ⎱		
G_6	G_7	G_C	2·0 ⎰	4·0	4·5
G_B	G_3	G_D		10·67	15·17
G_A	G_D	G_E		40·83	56·00
G_E	G_C	G_F		153·45	194·28

Starting with seven separate glaciers, each forming its own group, we have proceeded through five steps, at each of which a new group is formed (two at the second step because two groupings made the same contribution to the increase in the within-groups variation), until finally all seven are in a single group. The full details of this procedure are set out in Table 7.2.

Often the grouping is depicted graphically, in a diagram known variously as a dendrogram or a linkage tree. Figure 7.2 is the linkage tree for the data in Table 7.2; the order of the observations on the horizontal axis of this figure was determined so that the 'linkage branches' would not cross.

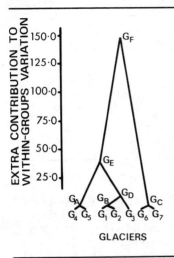

Fig. 7.2 Linkage tree for the grouping of seven glaciers.

But what is the 'best' grouping of the seven glaciers? Which of the six possibilities indicated by Table 7.2 and Fig. 7.2 should we accept? Unfortunately, there is no hard-and-fast rule that can be applied. The organisation of the grouping is such that at every step the contribution to the within-groups variation generated by the grouping is greater than it was at the preceding step, and so as the number of groups becomes smaller, the within-groups variation increases. Guidelines as to when to say 'stop' can be imposed. In Fig. 7.3, for example, the within-groups variation at each step is expressed as a percentage of the total within-groups variation (that at the last step); after the third step this percentage increases rapidly. Thus it could be that the best point to halt the grouping is at step 3, so that the seven glaciers are reduced to three groups.

$G_A = G_4$ and G_5; $G_C = G_6$ and G_7;   and $G_D = G_1, G_2,$ and G_3

But this method, and others like it such as the ratio of within-groups/between-groups variation at each step, is only a guide to sensible researcher decision-making, if the number of groups has not been predetermined by the whole research procedure.

The problem of non-dissoluble groups

The major drawback of the general procedure outlined above, which is often known as Ward's method after its designer (Ward, 1963), is that the result is not optimal at any particular step after the first. This comes about

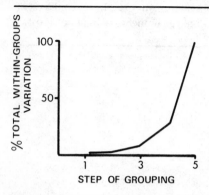

Fig. 7.3 The within-groups variation at each step of the grouping of seven glaciers.

because once a group has been formed, the next steps of the grouping act on the groups, and so no group can be dissolved and its members allocated to different 'higher order' groups. Thus if A and B form a group at step 1, at no later step can A be in one group and B in another.

The nature of this problem, and the solution to it, can be illustrated by our glacier-advance example. At the penultimate step of this classification we have two groups:

$G_C = G_6$ and G_7 $G_E = G_1, G_2, G_3, G_4,$ and G_5

Is this the 'best' division into two groups? Analysis of variance gives

Within-Groups Variation 56·00   Between-Groups Variation 138·28

If G_3 were transferred from G_E to G_C, we would get

Within-Groups Variation 41·41   Between-Groups Variation 152·87,

which is clearly a 'better' solution in terms of the variance model. We could experiment further, and transfer G_2 from G_E to G_C, getting an analysis of variance with

Within-Groups Variation 56·95   Between-Groups Variation 137·33

which is not as 'good' as the original grouping.

It would seem, therefore, that when we have decided on our grouping, we must test for its optimality, and if necessary transfer individuals from one group to another. This is usually done by finding the centroid (the central value, or mean) for each group, and calculating the distance from each individual to every group mean which is the average value for all members of the group. For G_C and G_E the means are

$\overline{G}_E = 50·00/5 = 10·00$ $\overline{G}_C = 40·00/2 = 20·00$

The distances from each individual to those means, i.e. $(G_i - \overline{G}_g)$ where G_i is an individual value and $\overline{G}_g$ is the mean for group g, are in Table 7.3A; for each individual, the shortest distance is underlined.

Table 7.3   Distance to group means: glacier data

Observation*	A Distance to mean of G_C	G_E	In Group	B Distance to mean of G_C^1	G_E^1	In Group
G_1	10·00	0·00	G_E	8·33	1·25	G_E^1
G_2	8·00	2·00	G_E	6·33	3·25	G_E^1
G_3	5·00	5·00	G_E	3·33	6·25	G_C^1
G_4	14·00	4·00	G_E	12·33	2·75	G_E^1
G_5	13·00	3·00	G_E	11·33	1·75	G_E^1
G_6	1·00	9·00	G_C	0·67	10·25	G_C^1
G_7	1·00	11·00	G_C	2·67	12·25	G_C^1
Group mean	20·00	10·00		18·33	8·75	

*The underlined value for each observation indicates the group mean that it is closest to.

Inspection of Table 7.3A shows that G_1, G_2, G_4, and G_5 are closest to the mean of the group they are allocated to (G_E) and both G_6 and G_7 are closest to the mean of the group (G_C) that they are in. Glacier G_3, however, is equidistant between the two group means. For any individual which is not closer to its group mean than to any other group mean, we transfer it to its nearest. The group composition now changes; G_3 is in G_C^1 and not G_E^1 (where G_C^1 and G_E^1 are the new groups after the first change), and so the means are recalculated, along with the distances from those means (Table 7.3B). Inspection shows that after the reallocation each individual is clearly closer to its group mean than to the other group mean, and so we accept this as the optimum two-group classification, according to our criteria based on the analysis of variance (p. 203).

It was stated from the outset that this procedure is only an approximation of the complete analysis of variance method proposed in the opening section of the chapter. As we have seen, it may not produce an optimal grouping, so that when the decision on 'how many groups?' has been made, some reallocation of individuals may be necessary to ensure that the best K-group division has been achieved.

Bivariate classification

The variance-based procedure just outlined can be extended to any number of variables. As with principal components and factor analyses, with more than two variables the classification is operating in an n-dimensional space which cannot be portrayed graphically, and so we deal here with a two-variable, two-dimensional classification problem. Data have been

collected from 8 villages on a number of variables, which were then submitted to a principal components analysis. Two components were extracted,
one with loadings on variables representing functional complexity (number
of different shop types, etc.) and the other with loadings on variables
representing aspects of population structure (percentage aged over 65, percentage born in the village, etc.). The component scores for the 8 villages
are plotted in Fig. 7.4, and the aim now is to classify the villages into types
according to their values on the hybrid variables.

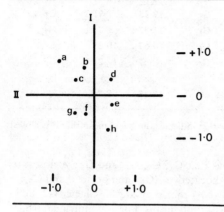

Fig. 7.4 Component scores for eight hypothetical villages.

In the procedure outlined in the previous section, the analysis of
variance base meant that the classification criterion was squared distance
from the group mean on the variable being considered. With two variables,
the procedure is exactly the same, except that the group mean is a bivariate
mean, the average position of a set of observations on two variables. Thus
in Fig. 7.4 the values for villages b and c are

component I	b = 0·8	c = 0·5
component II	b = −0·3	c = −0·5

Their means on the two variables are thus

component I	0·65
component II	−0·4

so that it they were grouped a point with these coordinates would be the
group mean (or centroid) and the within-groups variation would be calculated as squared distances around it.

The first requirement of a classification on two variables, therefore, is
to find out how close every observation is to every other one, and since
the procedure is based on the analysis of variance, similarity is measured as
the squared distance between each pair of observations. Such distances

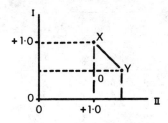

Fig. 7.5 The use of Pythagoras' theorem to measure the distance between observations on orthogonal components.

could be measured from the diagram and then squared, but the normal method involves using Pythagoras' theorem, that the square on the hypotenuse of a right-angled triangle is equal to the sum of the squares of the other two sides. Figure 7.5 illustrates this. The distance to be calculated is XY^2, and a triangle XOY is defined in which OY is the distance between X and Y on the horizontal axis (component II) and OX is the distance between X and Y on the vertical axis (component I). These lines are parallel to the axes of the graph; as the latter are orthogonal, $X\hat{O}Y$ is a right angle and so

$$XY^2 = OY^2 + OX^2 \qquad (7.3)$$

The value of X and Y on the two components are

component I	X = +1·0	Y = +0·5
component II	X = +1·0	Y = +1·5

so that

$$OY^2 = (1 \cdot 0 - 1 \cdot 5)^2 = -0 \cdot 5^2 = 0 \cdot 25 \text{ and}$$
$$OX^2 = (1 \cdot 0 - 0 \cdot 5)^2 = 0 \cdot 5^2 = 0 \cdot 25 \text{ giving}$$
$$XY^2 = 0 \cdot 25 + 0 \cdot 25 = 0 \cdot 5$$

In more general notation, the squared distance between any two points on a graph such as Fig. 7.4 is

$$d_{ij}^2 = \sum_{k=1}^{2} (X_{ik} - X_{jk})^2 \qquad (7.4)$$

where X_{ik}, X_{jk} are the values for places i and j on variable k;

k is the two variables (components), X_1 and X_2; and

d_{ij}^2 is the squared distance between observations i and j.

Application of formula (7.4) to the data of Fig. 7.4 produces the matrix of squared distances in Table 7.4A. Classification proceeds on this matrix, by selecting that pair which when grouped will make the smallest extra con-

Table 7.4   Classification of villages

A   Inter-village squared distances

| Observation | Observation | | | | | | | |
	a	b	c	d	e	f	g	h
a	0·00	0·53	0·50	2·50	3·69	2·60	2·21	5·57
b	0·53	0·00	0·13	0·73	1·64	1·45	1·48	3·38
c	0·50	0·13	0·00	1·00	1·49	0·90	0·81	2·77
d	2·50	0·73	1·00	0·00	0·49	1·30	1·81	1·97
e	3·69	1·64	1·49	0·49	0·00	0·53	1·04	0·50
f	2·60	1·45	0·90	1·30	0·53	0·00	0·09	0·61
g	2·21	1·48	0·81	1·81	1·04	0·09	0·00	1·06
h	5·57	3·38	2·77	1·97	0·50	0·61	1·06	0·00

B   Contributions to ESS   After first step

| | Observation | | | | | | |
	a	b	c	d	e	h	A
Nearest neighbour	c	c	b	e	d	e	e
ESS	0·25	0·065	0·065	0·245	0·245	0·25	0·545
Extra contribution	0·25	0·065	0·065	0·245	0·245	0·25	0·500

tribution to the within-groups variation (which initially stands at 0·0). The two points that are closest together on the graph clearly meet this criterion, since they will be closest to their group mean, and so we search the matrix for the smallest distance, which is 0·09 between villages f and g. To calculate their contribution to the within-groups variation involves finding the group mean and the squared distances to it from f and g, using the formula

$$C_l = \sum_{i=1}^{n} \sum_{j=1}^{m} (X_{ij} - \bar{X}_{lj})^2 \tag{7.5}$$

where X_{ij} is the value for observation i on variable j;

$\bar{X}_{lj}$ is the mean for group l — of which i is a member — on variable j;
C_l is the contribution of group l to the within-groups variation; and
summation is over all n observations in group l and over all m variables.

For the grouping of f and g in Fig. 7.4 we have

component I   f = −0·4   g = −0·4   so $\bar{X}_j$ where j = I = −0·4

component II   f = −0·2   g = −0·5   so $\bar{X}_j$ where j = II = −0·35

Substitution in formula (7.5) gives

	on component I	on component II
f	$(-0·4 - (-0·4))^2 = 0·0$	$(-0·2 - (-0·35))^2 = 0·0225$
g	$(-0·4 - (-0·4))^2 = 0·0$	$(-0·5 - (-0·35))^2 = 0·0225$

and

$C_1 = 0.0 + 0.0225 + 0.0 + 0.0225 = 0.045$

which is the contribution of the first grouping, of f and g, to the within-groups variation.

Calculation of this contribution is rather tedious, and it has to be done for every possible grouping after the first step. Fortunately, as the general formula for the variance of variable X is

$$\sum_{i=1}^{N} (X_i - \overline{X})^2 = \sum X_i^2 - (\sum X_i)^2/N \qquad (7.6)$$

formula (7.5) can be rewritten as

$$C_1 = \sum_{j=1}^{m} \sum_{i=1}^{n} X_{ij}^2 - \sum_{j=1}^{m} (\sum_{i=1}^{n} X_{ij})^2/n \qquad (7.7)$$

where X_{ij} is the value of observation i — a member of group 1 — on variable j;

m is the number of variables; and

n is the number of observations in group l.

This value Ward (1963) called the Error Sum of Squares (ESS). For the grouping f and g in Fig. 7.4 we get

component I   f = −0.4   g = −0.4 $\Sigma_i^2 = -0.4^2 + (-0.4)^2 = 0.32$
                                            $(\Sigma_i)^2/n = (-0.8)^2/2 = 0.32$

component II   f = −0.2   g = −0.5 $\Sigma_i^2 = -0.2^2 + (-0.5)^2 = 0.29$
                                            $(\Sigma_i)^2/n = (-0.7)^2/2 = 0.245$

$C_1 = (0.32 + 0.29) - (0.32 + 0.245) = 0.61 - 0.565 = 0.045$

As with the univariate classification, when a group is formed, the two

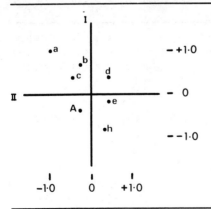

Fig. 7.6 Component scores after the first step of the grouping for the villages in Fig. 7.4. A is the group centroid replacing f and g.

or more members are replaced by the group centroid. Thus f and g are replaced in the diagram by a point midway between them (A in Fig. 7.6). A new matrix of squared distances must also be formed with group A replacing places f and g. We have seen, however, that individuals will only be grouped with their 'nearest neighbour' — i.e. individual h in Fig. 7.6 will not be grouped with a — so there is no point in working out all the distances. In Table 7.4B, therefore, only the distance from each individual to its nearest neighbour is given, along with the contribution and extra contribution that the grouping of these neighbours would make to ESS (the within-groups variation). The extra contribution which classifying group A with individual e would make (0·05) is less than the total contribution of these three, because the contribution of the members of group A (f and g; 0·045) is already present.

Table 7.5   Steps in classification of villages

Step	Observations grouped	Forming group	ESS contribution	ESS
1	f—g	A	0·045	0·045
2	b—c	B	0·065	0·110
3	d—e	C	0·245	0·355
4	a—B	D	0·322	0·677
5	A—h	E	0·590	1·267
6	C—E	F	1·045	2·312
7	D—F	G	3·042	5·354

The grouping of b and c makes the smallest extra contribution to the total ESS, and so these are combined at step 2 to form group B. The procedure is then repeated. All of the intermediate output is not given here, but a summary is provided in Table 7.5 and the linkage tree is Fig. 7.7. Testing shows that both the two-group and the three-group solutions are optimal (Table 7.6), in terms of the criterion outlined above (p. 208).

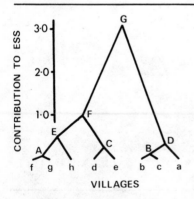

Fig. 7.7   Linkage tree for the grouping of the eight villages in Fig. 7.4.

Table 7.6   Distance to group means: village data

	A Three-group solution					B Two-group solution		
	Distance to mean of group			In group		Distance to mean of group		In group
Village	C	D	E		Village	D	F	
a	1·72	0·46	1·92	D	a	0·46	1·72	D
b	1·03	0·30	1·43	D	b	0·30	1·17	D
c	1·06	0·29	1·23	D	c	0·29	1·01	D
d	0·35	1·13	1·14	C	d	1·13	0·86	F
e	0·35	1·47	0·55	C	e	1·47	0·37	F
f	0·89	1·24	0·35	E	f	1·24	0·36	F
g	1·14	1·18	0·62	E	g	1·18	0·65	F
h	1·05	1·95	0·45	E	h	1·95	0·67	F

Multivariate classification

There are no differences between the hierarchical classification procedure just described for the bivariate case and that for the multivariate case, except that the distributions cannot be illustrated in n-dimensional space when $n > 2$. Pythagoras' theorem — formula (7.2) — can be applied in any number of dimensions, using the expression

$$d_{ij}^2 = \sum_{k=1}^{n} (X_{ik} - X_{jk})^2 \qquad (7.8)$$

where X_{ik}, X_{jk} are the values for observations i and j on variable k; n is the number of variables; and d_{ij}^2 is the squared distance separating observations i and j.

Thus if $n = 5$ the values for two observations A and B might be

	1	2	3	4	5
A	1·0	1·5	2·2	−1·0	−0·5
B	2·1	0·7	1·9	−1·5	−1·2

and the value d_{AB}^2 would then be

$$d_{AB}^2 = (1·0 - 2·1)^2 + (1·5 - 0·7)^2 + (2·2 - 1·9)^2 + (-1·0 - (1·5))^2 +$$
$$+ (-0·5 - (-1·2))^2$$
$$= 1·21 + 0·64 + 0·09 + 0·25 + 0·49 = 2·68$$

The formula for calculating ESS (formula (7.7), p. 213) can also be used in any dimensions, and so the procedure operates exactly as already described.

We might, for example, want to group our 17 London boroughs according to their scores on the components extracted from the data relating to their provision of educational facilities (Table 5.10). Classification could proceed on all 7 components, or on the most important 2 or 3 only; linkage trees for each are given in Fig. 7.8. Not surprisingly, because they are built on different data, the classifications vary; some boroughs always

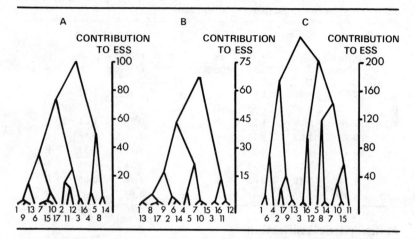

Fig. 7.8 Linkage trees for groupings of the seventeen London boroughs according to their scores on the first two components (A), the first three components (B), and all seven components (C). The scores are given in Table 5.10.

seem to fall in the same groups, as with Newham, Hillingdon and Barnet (7, 10, 15) and Sutton and Bromley (3 and 16), whereas others are closely linked in one or two of the classifications only, which is the case with Richmond and Harrow (4 and 5). Another variation between the classifications is in the size of the ESS contributions; the larger the number of variables, the greater the average distance between boroughs because whereas the first 2 and 3 components focus largely on common variance, when all 7 are employed the unique variance becomes dominant. In the 7-component classification (Fig. 7.8C), therefore, 8 groups might be selected as the best representation, whereas in the other 2 only 5 or 6 may be preferred.

Problems in classification

The procedure outlined in this chapter for classifying observations is straightforward, although with large data sets it is extremely tedious if it cannot be operated on a computer. Even with computers, large blocks of data can create problems which require short-cut procedures to save time — and thus money (Pocock and Wishart, 1969). Our focus here, however, will be on substantive rather than computational problems.

Scale

Every variable is accorded equal weight in the classification procedure, which implies a prior decision that the distance between two observations on one variable has exactly the same importance as the identical distance

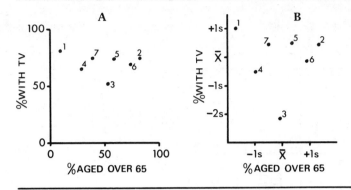

Fig. 7.9 The use of Z-scores in grouping (B) to overcome the problems of using variables with different metrics (A).

on another variable. This assumes that the variables are measured on the same scale; if their means and variances differ, then greater weight will be given to the variables with the larger values.

Figure 7.9A shows data for seven hypothetical suburbs of a city for two variables — percentage of persons aged over 65 and percentage of households with a TV. The variances for these variables are

% 65+ $S^2 = 578.6$ % with TV $S^2 = 85.7$

and so, as the figure illustrates, all of the seven suburbs are very bunched on the vertical axis (% with TV) relative to the horizontal. A classification of these data would be dominated by differences between suburbs in their age structures.

Scales can be standardised, as we have seen several times in this book, by using Z-scores (p. 10), in which each variable has a mean of 0·0 and a variance of 1·0. Figure 7.9B shows the data from Fig. 7.9A rewritten in Z-score form. The range on each of the two variables (the distance between the furthest observations) is now the same (assuming normal distributions) and classification would give both equal weight.

Data can be standardised in other ways than giving each variable the same variance, and this could be undertaken if for some reason the researcher wanted to give variables unequal weight in the classification. Very strong reasons from prior theory would probably be needed for this, however, and its use is rare (see Smith, 1973).

Orthogonal variables

Pythagoras' theorem applies to right-angled triangles, and in the present context this means that the method of measuring distances used here is only applicable with orthogonal variables. Figure 7.10 illustrates the prob-

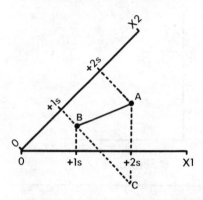

Fig. 7.10   The problem of using Pythagoras' theorem with oblique axes.

lem, which might occur when classifying observations according to their scores on a set of oblique factors.

Two observations, A and B, are located in the space defined by two correlated variables, X_1 and X_2 ($r_{12} = 0.7071$). If we were to calculate the distance between A and B with formula (7.8), the result would be

$$d_{AB}^2 = (X_{1A} - X_{1B})^2 + (X_{2A} - X_{2B})^2$$
$$= (2.0 - 1.0)^2 + (2.0 - 1.0)^2 = 2.0$$

This is an over-statement of the distance because the triangle ABC, which is equivalent to XOY in Fig. 7.5, is not right-angled. It is possible to 'orthogonalise' the variable axes, however, by multiplying each component of the distance equation by one minus the correlation. Thus d_{ij}^2 becomes

$$d_{ij}^2 = \sum_{k=1}^{m} \sum_{l=1}^{m} [(X_{ki} - X_{kj}) + (X_{li} - X_{lj})](1 - r_{kl}) \qquad (7.9)$$

where X_{ki}, X_{kj} are the values for observations i and j on variable X_k;

X_{li}, X_{lj} are the values for observations i and j on variable X_l;

r_{kl} is the correlation between X_k and X_l and

summation is over all pairs of variables.

Applying this to points A and B in Fig. 7.10 gives

$$d_{AB}^2 = [(2 - 1) + (2 - 1)] \, (1 - 0.7071)$$
$$= (2)(0.2929) = 0.5858$$

Although available, this option is rarely used (King and Jeffrey, 1972) and most researchers prefer to ensure that they are classifying with orthogonal variables.

The twin requirements of orthogonal variables and standardised measurement scales have led most researchers, especially those attempting multivariate classifications, to use scores on either principal components or orthogonal factors as their input. Except in the case of an oblique rotation, these scores meet the two requirements, and so form ideal 'variables' on which to base classifications. For example, Meyer (1972b) classified 145 metropolitan areas in the United States according to their scores on 7 factors extracted from the correlation matrix of 40 variables representing aspects of the non-white population, and their housing, in each area. The factors were labelled as: (1) socio-economic status; (2) socio-economic differences between black American-born and other non-whites; (3) stage in the life cycle; (4) size and age of housing; (5) housing type; (6) size of black population and of city; and (7) percentage of workers in service industries. The grouping produced three major types of 'black cities' according to these seven criteria: the north-eastern United States cities (New York plus several in New England); the southern cities, which comprised an amalgamation of three lower-order groups, respectively dominated by Texan, by Deep South, and by North Carolinan/Floridian plus other southern cities; and small northern industrial cities.

Is grouping valid?

The classification procedure discussed in this chapter is entirely inductive in orientation; it describes patterns within data irrespective of any prior hypotheses, much as principal components analysis merely rewrites data according to their correlations. There is a 'best' classification for any set of observations over a given assembly of variables, on the analysis of variance criterion, and this can be achieved by the 'optimalising' procedure outlined above (p. 208). But is classification justified in every case?

Figure 7.11 illustrates the background to this question, with three examples of twenty observations plotted in two-dimensional space. In Fig. 7.11A the pattern of points was generated by random numbers; that in Fig. 7.11B was generated as a uniform distribution with a random component; whereas that in Fig. 7.11C is a clustered distribution. A classification could be produced for each. But presumably classification should be based on some underlying theory about the nature of a group, even if not about the probable groups in the data set to be explored. Such a theory

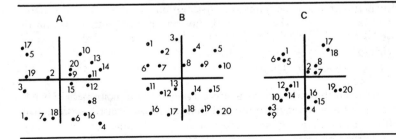

Fig. 7.11 Are groups 'real'?

might well be based on the premise that only 'real' groups are worth classifying and that where the observations are not naturally grouped, then they should remain as separate individuals. If 'natural groups' exist in the k-dimensional space being studied, then the observations should be clustered, as they are in Fig. 7.11C. A test for the existence of clustering which is widely used in geographical studies is the nearest neighbour statistic, R,

$$R = \bar{r}_A / \bar{r}_E \qquad (7.10)$$

where $\bar{r}_A$ is the mean distance from each observation in the diagram to its nearest neighbour, i.e.

$$\bar{r}_A = \sum_{i=1}^{N} d_{ik} / N \qquad (7.11)$$

where d_{ik} is the distance from observation i to the nearest other observation k;

N is the number of observations; and

$\bar{r}_E$ is the expected mean distance between each observation in the diagram and its nearest neighbour, assuming that the N observations are randomly distributed in the given area (or volume if $k > 2$), i.e.

$$\bar{r}_E = (1/2\sqrt{p}) \qquad (7.12)$$

where

$$P = N/\text{total area or volume} \qquad (7.13)$$

For the diagrams of Fig. 7.11 we have

	A	B	C
R =	1·176	1·713	0·520

The value of R ranges between 0·0 and 2·1491: 0·0 indicates a totally clustered pattern of points; 1·0 indicates a random distribution (i.e. $\bar{r}_A = \bar{r}_E$); and 2·1491 a uniform distribution. Thus the pattern in Fig. 7.11A is nearly random, that in Fig. 7.11B approaches uniform, and that in Fig. 7.11C is clustered. (There is a considerable literature on nearest neighbour analysis in geography: see King, L. J., 1969 and Yeates, 1974.)

One could argue that classification should proceed on a clustered distribution but not on a uniform distribution: random distributions may be classified, to see whether there is any evidence of grouping within the overall random patterns. And, similarly, one could argue that a nearest-neighbour test should be conducted after each step of the classification, using the lack of clustering as an index that the procedure should not be continued.

There are problems in the use of this nearest-neighbour method. One is that whereas there might be clustering in certain areas of the pattern, overall the distribution is either random or uniform. Secondly, where does one define the boundary of the area? For example, if we take the area of the diagram in Fig. 7.4 as that enclosed by the values of +1·0 and −1·0 on each coordinate, in that these surround the whole set of points, then for the eight points R = 1·49, indicative of a tendency towards uniformity. But if the area is defined by the values of +2·0 and −2·0 on each coordinate, on the argument that in standard score terms these enclose over 95% of the observations, then R = 0·73, indicating a trend towards clustering! Despite these problems, however, it is surprising that there is only one major application of the method. Berry and Garrison (1958), in their pioneering study of central place patterns in Snohomish County, Washington, classified both the types of retail and other services provided in the centres and the centres themselves. Before proceeding to the classifications, however, the nearest neighbour technique was used to show (1) that there was a clustering of types in terms of their thresholds (the size of the market needed to support one establishment) and (2) that there was a clustering of central places in terms of their variety of retail and other services and their populations.

Classification and regionalisation

As indicated in the introduction to this chapter, there is a long tradition of geographical interest in the 'region', which is usually defined as a contiguous area whose parts share similar characteristics on defined criteria. The classification procedure outlined here should be valuable as a means of defining regions except for one difficulty: the groups defined by the classification in terms of similarity on the defined criteria may not comprise contiguous units. There are two ways round this difficulty (Johnston, 1970). The first introduces contiguity constraints to the classification, so that observations are only grouped if they are spatially contiguous. The other first defines the groups in the manner described here, and then tests to see whether each is composed of contiguous units and hence also form regions. If they do not, then the grouping has produced regional types, some of which at least are represented by more than one regional example. (For further discussion, see Johnston, 1976a.)

Figure 7.12 illustrates these two alternative procedures in the classification of the 12 'counties' of diagram A. In Fig. 7.12B and C the procedure described in this chapter is applied, so that according to ESS values the first grouping is of counties 8 and 9, the second of 1 and 3, and so on (Fig. 7.12B). The grouping is halted at a certain value of ESS (the heavy dashed line across the linkage tree in Fig. 7.12B); the four resulting groups produce seven regional types (Fig. 7.12C), since the groups involving counties 2, 4, 8 and 9 and that of 1, 3 and 5 are both split into two non-contiguous blocks. According to the alternative procedure, counties are only grouped if they are contiguous (or one member of one group is contiguous with a member of another group at the later stages when groups are being grouped). This produces a very different linkage tree − Fig. 7.12D − with certain groupings based on close similarity on the relevant variables (e.g. 2 and 4, 1 and 3) being impossible because of the contiguity constraint. The resulting classification at the same ESS value (Fig. 7.12E) contains six

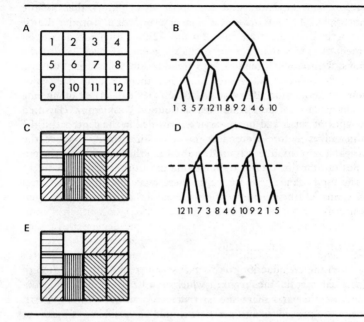

Fig. 7.12   Regionalisation as classification, showing: (A) the 16 'counties'; (B) the linkage tree for a classification of those counties without a contiguity constraint, and (C) the resulting regional types; (D) the linkage tree for a classification with a contiguity constraint, and (E) the resulting regions.

separate regions. In Fig. 7.12C, therefore, we have a classification into four regional types which form seven regions, whereas in Fig. 7.12E are seven regions, that are not the same as those in the earlier classification. Unless a contiguous regionalisation is particularly required, this clearly is sub-optimal in terms of the analysis of variance model — as suggested by a comparison of Figs. 7.12B and 7.12D — and the procedure outlined in the first three diagrams of Fig. 7.12 is generally to be preferred.

Conclusions

There are very many methods for classification. A great number of them are based upon distance matrices such as that of Table 7.4 (except that most are of d_{ij} rather than d_{ij}^2) and their procedures are very similar to that outlined in this chapter. A detailed review of them all is beyond the purposes of this book; indeed, even a general survey requires a short book in itself (Everitt, 1974). The aim here has been to introduce one method based on the analysis of variance, as an example of procedures which are widely used by geographers. The purpose of classification has not been pursued far in the discussion, which has been largely procedural. Like principal components analysis, a main feature of classification is that it reduces the amount of information, an end that may be useful for data description (as, for example, in climatic regionalisations) and hypothesis generation. The hypothesis that regions exist can be tested in this way, often as a prelude to further research such as sampling from different regions or regional types, and thus classification has a strong and undoubtedly continuing tradition in geographical work.

To some extent, principal components analysis and classification are complementary, in that the former frequently is used to provide the data for the latter; the principal components analysis — or factor analysis, if the classification is to be based on common variance only — reduces the variable complexity and the classification reduces the observational complexity. But in another sense the methods are contradictory. We may hypothesise, for example, that the vegetational structure of an area — e.g the proportional distribution of various species — is related to environmental patterns, such as slope, aspect, and climate. Using principal components or factor analysis on the vegetation data, the dependent variable could be constructed on a ratio scale — the components or factor scores — whereas a classification would reduce it to a nominal scale. The latter involves a loss of information (the within-groups variation), and its use poses a problem for the researcher regarding the value of that lost information and whether classification is a useful procedure. Occasionally it may be because precision in measurement is not possible and groups of like individuals are best employed in the ensuing analyses, but in most cases the simplicity of classifications must be weighed against the simplification that they provide.

Chapter 8

Discriminant analysis

So far in this book, all our analyses of causal systems have been concerned with dependent variables for which measurement is on either an interval or a ratio-scale. Nominally-scaled variables have been used only as independent variables, in the analysis of variance and in the regression approach to this. The focus here is reversed, to show how the general linear model can be used with nominally-measured dependent variables (as in Bayliss and Edwards, 1970).

Regression and group membership

In Chapter 2 we used a hypothetical data set to test the hypothesis that *per capita* educational expenditure in urban areas is a function of the political orientation of the town council. For this we used the analysis of variance procedures, although in Chapter 4 we saw how the multiple regression model could be used for the same purpose. Here we want to test the converse hypothesis, that the political complexion of a council can be estimated from knowledge of its *per capita* education expenditure. Thus

$$X_0 = f(X_1) \tag{8.1}$$

where X_0 is political complexion; and
$\quad\quad X_1$ is *per capita* educational expenditure.

In the particular example to be worked here, X_0 is defined as having a free-market capitalist council so that

$\quad X_0$ is 1 if a free-market capitalist council;

$\quad X_0$ is 0 if a non-free-market capitalist council; and

$\quad X_1$ is as before.

The resulting regression equation is

$$X_0 = 1 \cdot 677 - 0 \cdot 026\, X_1 \pm 0 \cdot 005 \quad\quad r_{01} = -0 \cdot 598$$

How do we interpret this equation, given that the 'real' values of X_0 are either 1 or 0? The usual way is in terms of probabilities. If we enter a given value of X_1 into the equation the resulting value of X_0 can be taken as the probability that a town with that value of X_1 would have a value of $X_0 = 1$

— in other words, that it would have a free-market capitalist council. Thus, if $X_1 = 40$

$$X_0 = 1 \cdot 677 - 0 \cdot 026 \, (40) \pm 0 \cdot 005 = 0 \cdot 647 \pm 0 \cdot 005$$

and if $X_1 = 60$

$$X_0 = 1 \cdot 677 - 0 \cdot 026 \, (60) \pm 0 \cdot 005 = 0 \cdot 117 \pm 0 \cdot 005$$

It is about 65% likely that a town spending £40 *per caput* on education has such a council, but only about 12% probable if it spends £60.

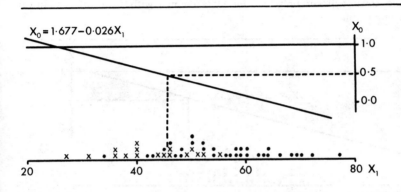

Fig. 8.1 The regression $X_0 = f(X_1)$, where X_0 is a dummy variable for free-market capitalist council. (The data are in Table 2.2.)

The regression line for this relationship is in Fig. 8.1. Along the horizontal axis are located the 50 individual towns, with those having a free-market capitalist council indicated by a cross. Clearly, the further one moves along the X_1 axis to the left, the greater the likelihood of a town being indicated by a cross. Specifically indicated on the diagram is the value of X_1 when $X_0 = 0 \cdot 5$, which can be solved as

$$0 \cdot 5 = 1 \cdot 677 - 0 \cdot 026 X_1$$

$$\therefore \quad 0 \cdot 026 X_1 = 1 \cdot 677 - 0 \cdot 5 \qquad X_1 = 1 \cdot 177 / 0 \cdot 026 = 45 \cdot 27$$

This is the point to the left of which the value of X_0 is more likely than not to be 1, whereas to the right it is more likely than not to be 0. It is the point of equal probability of being in the group, and divides the free-market capitalist from the non-free-market capitalist towns, within the error term of an equation which in any case accounts for only $0 \cdot 357$ of the variance in X_0.

Just as any value between 1 and 0 is not directly interpretable as a value of X_0 so values greater than 1 and less than 0 have no immediate meaning (see Wrigley, 1976). And yet, as Fig. 8.1 shows, the regression line does not describe the relationship of X_0, between 0 and 1 only, and X_1. By substitution we find

if $X_0 = 1 \cdot 0$ $1 \cdot 0 = 1 \cdot 677 - 0 \cdot 026\, X_1$

$\therefore$ $0 \cdot 026\, X_1 = 0 \cdot 677$ $X_1 = 26 \cdot 04$ and

if $X_0 = 0 \cdot 0$ $0 \cdot 0 = 1 \cdot 677 - 0 \cdot 026\, X_1$

$\therefore$ $0 \cdot 026\, X_1 = 1 \cdot 677$ $X_1 = 64 \cdot 50$

In other words, if $X_1 \leqslant 26 \cdot 04$, then $X_0 \geqslant 1 \cdot 0$, or the town will certainly be run by a free-market capitalist council; if $X_1 \geqslant 64 \cdot 50$, then $X_0 \leqslant 0 \cdot 0$, so the town will certainly be run by a council with some other political complexion.

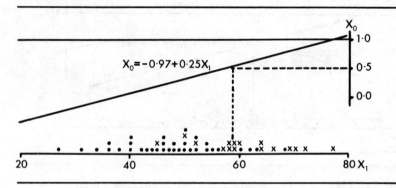

Fig. 8.2   The regression $X_0 = f(X_1)$, where X_0 is a dummy variable for socialist council. (The data are in Table 2.2.)

Three types of council were identified in Chapter 2 and 4 (Table 2.2). Separate regressions can be run for each. If

X_0 is 1 if a socialist council; and

X_0 is 0 if a non-socialist council

the resulting equation (Fig. 8.2) is

$X_0 = -0 \cdot 97 + 0 \cdot 025\, X_1 \pm 0 \cdot 005$ $r_{01} = 0 \cdot 586$

For the other grouping, however, if

X_0 is 1 if a liberal council; and

X_0 is 0 if a non-liberal council

the resulting equation (Fig. 8.3A) is

$X_0 = 0 \cdot 294 + 0 \cdot 001\, X_1 \pm 0 \cdot 006$ $r_{01} = 0 \cdot 021$

The poor fit, indicated by the correlation coefficient, occurs because in this case the values of $X_0 = 1$ (shown by an X) are clustered in the centre of the range of values of X_1. For a more accurate prediction we need a poly-

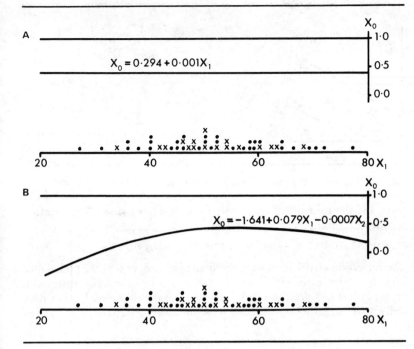

Fig. 8.3   The regressions $X_0 = f(X_1)$ and $X_0 = f(X_1, X_2)$ — where $X_2 = X_1^2$ — where X_0 is a dummy variable for liberal council. (The data are in Table 2.2.)

nomial (see Ch. 3, p. 79) relating X_0 to both X_1 and X_1^2 (Fig. 8.3B), where

$$X_0 = -1.641 + 0.079 X_1 - 0.0007 X_1^2 \pm 0.005 \qquad R = 0.241.$$

Multiple predictors

It may be that to estimate whether or not the value of $X_0 = 1$, or whether or not a particular observation is in a particular group, several independent variables are needed. In such a case, we use the multiple regression model.

Figure 8.4 shows the distribution of 16 observations on a beach, where measurement has been taken on two variables — distance from high water mark (X_1) and distance from a river mouth (X_2). At 8 of these observations the beach is composed of sandy materials, whereas at the other eight it is shingly. Thus

X_0 is 0 if a sandy beach (B on the figure); and

X_0 is 1 if a shingly beach (A on the figure)

and we are testing the hypothesis that

$$X_0 = f(X_1, X_2) \qquad\qquad (8.2)$$

such that we expect that the further an observation is from both high water

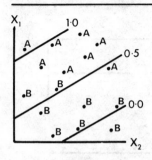

Fig. 8.4   Regression of a dummy variable on two orthogonal independent variables.

mark and the river mouth, the more likely it is to be sandy. The equation for the relationship in formula (8.2) is

$$X_0 = 0 \cdot 261 + 0 \cdot 054 \, X_1 - 0 \cdot 030 \, X_2 \pm 0 \cdot 387 \qquad R_{0 \cdot 12} = 0 \cdot 715$$

The regression coefficients have the predicted sign, in that the probability that $X_0 = 1$ increases with distance from high water mark (i.e. with an increase in X_1) and decreases with distance from the river mouth (i.e. with a decrease in X_2). Contours for this relationship are interpolated in Fig. 8.4.

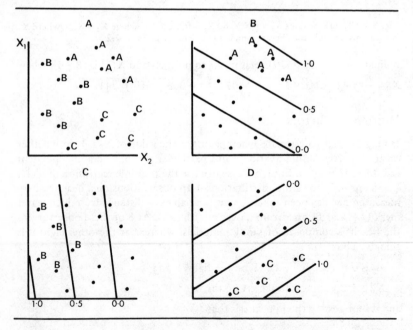

Fig. 8.5   Regression of a series of dummy variables comprising three groups on two orthogonal independent variables.

Further extensions to this method are possible. We may, for example, have three predictor variables, so that formula (8.2) would be extended to a regression equation with three independents. Or we may have our observations classified into more than two groups, as in Fig. 8.5A where the 16 beach samples of Fig. 8.4 are categorised into silt (C), sand (B), and shingle (A). In the latter, three separate regressions are reported: the first — Fig. 8.5B — where membership of group A is the dependent variable and the contours are the probabilities of being in that group; the second — Fig. 8.5C — where group B is considered (note that one member of the group is in the area of the graph where it is unexpected); and the third — Fig. 8.5D — deals with group C.

As this form of analysis is extended, particularly with respect to the number of independent variables, we soon encounter the collinearity problem. The instability of regression coefficients which this causes means that we need to turn to procedures for making the independent variables orthogonal. Linear discriminant analysis provides such a procedure.

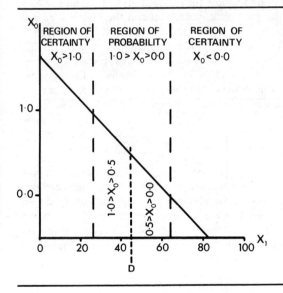

Fig. 8.6   Interpretation of regressions when the dependent variable is a dummy variable. (The regression line is that of Fig. 8.1.)

Discriminant analysis

As an introduction to this method, let us reconsider the problems discussed in the previous section, using an alternative viewpoint. Figure 8.6 suggests the following interpretation of Fig. 8.1. We have two univariate distributions on the same variable — *per capita* expenditure on education (X_1). One of these is for the 17 towns with a free-market capitalist council and the other is for the 33 with some other form of council. The regression equation estimates, for every value of the independent variable, the probability that a town spending that much on education has a capitalist council (X_0). Of particular interest to us is the value of X_1 for which the estimated value of X_0 is 0·5. This is the value of *per capita* education expenditure to the left of which towns are more likely than not to have a capitalist council ($X_0 > 0·5$), whereas to the right of it towns are more likely than not to have a non-capitalist council. This value of X_1 is the best estimate of the discriminant (D) between the two groups of towns, as suggested in Fig. 8.6. The graph can, in effect, be divided into three 'regions': that where $\hat{X}_0 > 1·0$, and we are certain that the town has a capitalist council; that where $0·0 < \hat{X}_0 < 1·0$ which is where the value of $\hat{X}_0$ indicates a probability of the town having a capitalist council; and that where $\hat{X}_0 < 0·0$ which indicates a certainty that the town has a non-capitalist council. There are two regions of certainty and one of probability, therefore, with the latter being divided by the discriminant into 'more probable than not' and 'less probable than not' (Fig. 8.6).

Similar interpretations are possible for Figs. 8.2—8.5; the values of $X_0 = 0·5$ (a single point in the univariate cases, a line in the bivariate case of Figs. 8.4 and 8.5) are the best regression estimates of the differences between two groups. These are, in effect, discriminant functions: the $X_0 = 0·5$ line in Fig. 8.4 is the discriminant function which provides the best separation between the two groups of samples — sandy and shingly. We turn now, therefore, to a more detailed investigation of discriminant functions, and their interpretation in bivariate and multivariate analyses.

The discriminant equations

The regressions of Figs. 8.1—8.5 are based on truly independent (i.e. non-collinear) variables. When collinearity exists, such regressions may need new variables with which to discriminate between the categories of the dependent variable. These new variables are the discriminant functions — which are analogous to components, factors, and canonical vectors — and the original variables have loadings on these functions. Their basic equation is

$$X_0 = f(D_I, D_{II}, - D_m) \tag{8.3}$$

where $D_I - D_m$ are the discriminant functions;

X_0 is the dependent variable — the categories into which the observations are divided; and

m is the number of categories into which the dependent variable is divided, less one.

The value of m is the salient element of formula (8.3). If, for example, the observations are divided into two groups to form the dependent variable only a single discriminant function, or new variable, can be derived.

The individual observations have scores on the discriminant functions — which are analogous to component, factor and canonical scores. These scores are usually derived in standardised form, and a mean score is computed for each group of observations. (This mean is frequently known as the group centroid.) Analyses of variance can be conducted on these scores, and the aim of the discriminant analysis is to maximise the F-ratio of the between-group to within-group variance estimates: the discriminant function is located to produce the 'best' analysis of variance.

Discriminant analysis is a method of producing hybrid variables so as to produce the best possible separation, or discrimination, between the various groups. It thus involves two sets of equations. The first relates the group membership to the discriminant functions, as in the regression discussed earlier in this chapter, so that

$$G_1 = f(D_I, D_{II} - D_m)$$
$$G_2 = f(D_I, D_{II} - D_m)$$
$$G_m = f(D_I, D_{II} - D_m) \qquad (8.4)$$

where $G_1 - G_m$ are the dummy variables representing group membership;
$\quad\quad D_I - D_m$ are the discriminant functions; and
$\quad\quad$ m is the number of groups within the set of observations, less one.

The number of equations in this set is thus one less than the number of groups for reasons suggested in our initial discussion of dummy variables (p. 112); if there are four groups, for example, once the membership of three is known, the fourth is fixed. The second set is analogous to the equations for principal components analysis, with

$$D_I = f(X_1, X_2 - X_n)$$
$$D_{II} = f(X_1, X_2 - X_n)$$
$$D_m = f(X_1, X_2 - X_n) \qquad (8.5)$$

where $D_I - D_m$ are the m discriminant functions;
$\quad\quad X_1 - X_n$ are the independent variables, which are collinear; and
$\quad\quad$ n is the number of independent variables.

The parameters of the functions in formula (8.5) are the discriminant loadings.

Some simple examples
To illustrate the derivation of these equations, particularly those in formula (8.5), Fig. 8.7 is a simple example involving only 2 variables and 2 groups of observations. There are 12 observations in the data set, divided into 2 groups; group P has 5 members and group Q has 7 members. The bivariate scatter diagram (Fig. 8.7A) shows that the members of group P are concentrated in the upper left quadrant of the distribution, with those of group Q below them and to the right. Neither of the variables — X_1 and X_2 — effectively separates the two groups, as indicated in the two univariate plots of Fig. 8.7B (in these, the observations are located on the relevant variable, with their perpendicular distance from that axis representing their value on

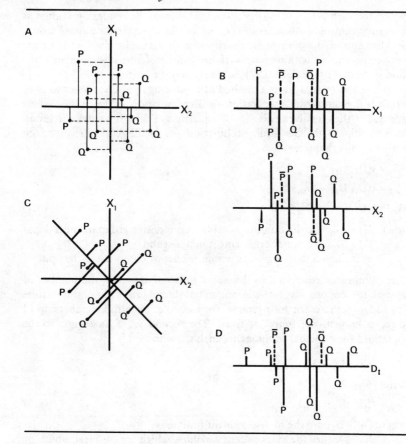

Fig. 8.7 Derivation of a discriminant function, showing: (A) the location of 12 observations, in two groups, on two orthogonal independent variables; (B) the location of members of the two groups, and the group means, on the separate independent variables; (C) location of a discriminant function which achieves maximal separation of the two groups; and (D) the location of members of the two groups, and the group means, on the discriminant function.

the other variable). Thus in the plot on X_1, for example, although there is a tendency for the group P members to be clustered at the left-hand end (i.e. below the mean, assuming the axis to be scaled in standard scores) and for the group Q members to be clustered at the right-hand end, there is some overlap of the two groups, with several individual observations being closer to the mean of the other group than to their own group mean.

The value of each of the two independent variables as an estimator of whether or not an individual observation is in group P or group Q can be assessed in two ways. The first is by a univariate analysis of variance for each (p. 52), which produces the results.

Variable	X_1	X_2
Total variance estimate	38·54	34·72
Between-groups variance estimate	169·00	154·00
Within-groups variance estimate	25·50	22·80
F-ratio	6·63	6·75

Both of the F-ratios are significant at the 0·05 level, indicating that each independent variable can reasonably be used to estimate which group an individual observation is in. The second method of assessment, however, indicates the failure rate. This is the number of misclassifications, and it is obtained by counting the number of observations closer to another group's mean (or centroid) than to their own. (In more detail, a misclassification occurs in a regression so that, for example, if members of group P are coded 1 and members of group Q are coded 0, and group membership is the dependent variable, the misclassifications are those members of P with an estimated value from the regression equation of less than 0·5 and those members of group Q with an estimated value exceeding 0·5; see p. 230.) From Fig. 8.7B, the numbers are

Variable	X_1	X_2
Number of misclassifications for		
Group P	1	1
Group Q	2	2

Although both X_1 and X_2 provide a statistically significant estimate of group membership, therefore, in each case three out of the twelve observations (25%) will be misclassified, or allocated to the wrong group.

The number of misclassifications is substantial, therefore, and some better estimator of group membership is required. This is provided by a discriminant analysis, as illustrated by Fig. 8.7C. In this, a discriminant function, D_I, which is a composite variable derived from X_1 and X_2, has been fitted to the bivariate scatter diagram so as to separate the two groups, P and Q. Figure 8.7D shows how successful a separation this is, with no group overlapping.

The summary statistics are

Analysis of variance
Total variance estimate	42·77
Between-groups variance estimate	349·24
Within-groups variance estimate	12·12
F-ratio	28·81

and

Number of misclassifications for
Group P   0
Group Q   0

Clearly, on both criteria the discriminant function, D_I, is better at separating the two groups than is either of the original independent variables from which it was derived.

The location of the discriminant function in Fig. 8.7C suggests that it is similar to a regression line. Indeed, the equation for the discriminant function − formula (8.5) − is analogous to a multiple regression equation, and for the present example has the parameters

$$D_I = 0 \cdot 0 - 0 \cdot 71\ X_1 + 0 \cdot 71\ X_2$$

Solution of this equation for any particular observation gives its discriminant score on the function (as shown in Fig. 8.7D) so that, for example, an observation with values of +1·5 and −0·5 respectively for X_1 and X_2 would have a discriminant score of 1·42. The equivalents of the regression coefficients in this equation are the correlations between the original variables and the discriminant function, which are the cosines of the angles between them in the diagrams.

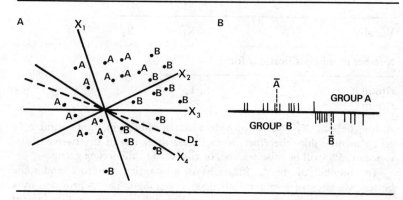

Fig. 8.8 A discriminant function separating two groups of observations according to their values on four, related variables.

The same procedure is followed when the analysis involves more than two original variables. Figure 8.8 illustrates such a situation, in which a set of 24 observations divided into two groups (A and B) of 12, has been measured on four variables (X_1 to X_4). These four variables are collinear, and so Fig. 8.8A is a two-dimensional cross-section through the non-orthogonal four-dimensional space which they form. (This space is similar to that for oblique factors − p. 166 − on which classification proceeds: p. 217.) The discriminant analysis locates a discriminant function, D_I, which separates the two groups of 12 so that there is no overlapping of the groups (or as little as possible if complete separation is not feasible).

The discriminant function in Fig. 8.8A is a hybrid variable which is a composite of the originals X_1 to X_4. The angles between D_I and those variables are (the axes are for standard scores, with the positive pole indicated by the variable label)

X_1 130° X_2 45° X_3 19° X_4 11°

for which the cosines are

X_1 −0·64 X_2 0·71 X_3 0·95 X_4 0·98

so that the equation — formula (8.5) — describing the discriminant function is

$$D_I = 0·0 − 0·64\, X_1 + 0·71\, X_2 + 0·95\, X_3 + 0·98\, X_4$$

Since the parameters of this equation can be interpreted like correlation coefficients (as are principal component loadings) then the interpretation is that of the four variables, X_3 and X_4 — which are themselves closely related — make the greatest contribution to discriminating between groups A and B.

The scores for the 24 observations on the discriminant function are located on Fig. 8.8B. As will be seen, since the values for group A are located above the axis of the function whereas those for group B are located below it, the discriminant function effectively separates the two groups. There is, however, one misclassification; one of the members of group A (that furthest to the right on the function) is closer to $\overline{B}$ than to $\overline{A}$. The interpretation of this would be that, in terms of its values on the four original variables, that individual is more like the members of group B than it is to the other eleven in group A.

Finally, Fig. 8.9A shows a hypothetical example in which 15 observations, divided into three groups of 5 (A, B, and C), are measured on three collinear independent variables (X_1, X_2, X_3). Taking a discriminant function with the parameters.

$$D_I = 0·0 − 0·45\, X_1 + 0·31\, X_2 + 0·94\, X_3$$

effectively separates groups A and B, as the discriminant scores on D_I indicate in Fig. 8.9B, but does not separate those two groups from group C. A second function, D_{II}, which must be orthogonal to the first, has the form

$$D_{II} = 0·0 + 0·89\, X_1 + 0·95\, X_2 − 0·31\, X_3$$

and this effectively separates group C from the other two. Together, as shown in Fig. 8.9C which is a bivariate plot of scores on the two discriminant functions, the two new variables D_I and D_{II} separate the three groups, with no misclassifications.

Discriminant analysis is most useful, of course, when there are many collinear independent variables and several groups of observations. The principles and procedures in such cases are exactly the same as those outlined in the simple examples of Fig. 8.7 to 8.9, however. New variables which are composites of the originals are located so as to maximise the F-ratio between the groups of observations. These new variables, the dis-

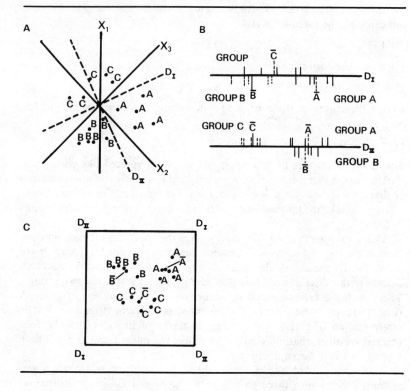

Fig. 8.9   A discriminant analysis showing the use of two discriminant functions to separate three groups of observations in a three-variable space.

criminant functions, are extracted sequentially. Thus in the example of Fig. 8.9, the full procedure for this three-variable, three-group example would have been: (1) extract the first function, and perform an analysis of variance on the discriminant scores; (2) extract the second function, orthogonal to the first, and perform an analysis of variance on distances from the group centroids in the two-dimensional space formed by both functions; and (3) compare the F-ratios from the two analyses to see whether extracting the second function adds substantially to the discriminatory power provided by the first (this is analogous to the stepwise regression procedure: p. 84). With more than three groups of observations, a further discriminant function might be extracted, and so on. Each function is located to maximise the F-ratio in the residuals from the earlier functions, within the constraint that each discriminant function is orthogonal to those previously extracted.

How substantial is the contribution of a discriminant function to the overall separation of the groups? Several statistics may be used, of which the more important are:

1. *The canonical correlation*, associating the discriminant function with the dependent variable (the grouping of the observations). This correlation is analogous to the squared product moment correlations reported for analyses of variance in Chapter 4 and in the first section of this chapter; it indicates the ratio of between-group to total variance estimates along the discriminant function.

2. *Wilks' lambda* (Λ) which is the ratio of within-groups cross-products to the total cross-products along the discriminant function. It is

$$\Lambda = \frac{\displaystyle\sum_{i=1}^{N} (X_{Di} - \overline{X}_{DG})^2}{\displaystyle\sum_{i=1}^{N} (X_{Di} - \overline{X}_{DT})^2} \tag{8.6}$$

where X_{Di} is the score for observation i on the discriminant function D;

$\overline{X}_{DG}$ is the mean score on discriminant function D for the observations in the group of which i is a member; and

$\overline{X}_{DT}$ is the mean score on discriminant function D for all observations.

The larger value of Λ, therefore, the greater is the within-groups variation as a proportion of the total, and the less successful is the discriminant function at separating the groups. In a sense, therefore, Λ is an inverse of the F-ratio; it can also be transformed into a chi-square value, and used to test the statistical significance of a discriminant function. (Wilks' lambda is also used in canonical correlation analysis: p. 189.)

The uses of discriminant analysis in geography

As with all of the other multivariate methods discussed in this book, discriminant analysis was developed to test hypotheses, in this case relating measurements on nominal scales to others on collinear interval- and ratio-scales. Once those hypotheses were shown to be valid, and the findings become part of established theory, then the discriminant functions, derived for a sample of observations, could be used to predict results in further samples from the same population. Such mature scientific work, based on properly-taken samples, is more typical of some disciplines than others. Among the latter, of which geography is one, discriminant analysis has been adapted to a number of uses, of which we shall discuss three here.

1. *Testing (and generating) hypotheses.*   This is the 'purest' use, with the method employed to investigate whether a certain set of related variables (measured on interval- and ratio-scales) successfully discriminate between groups of observations on a nominal scale. Usually, however, the form of these relationships is not clearly stated: a researcher may indicate that inner

Table 8.1   Library provision in 17 outer London boroughs

Borough	X₁	X₂	X₃	X₄	X₅	X₆	X₇	X₈	Population
	X_1	X_2	X_3	X_4	X_5	X_6	X_7	X_8	
Kingston	100	8	28	331	177	562	13·3	2787	139
Barking	109	12	31	374	435	482	11·4	2544	158
Sutton	128	9	51	431	1600	517	18·6	2830	168
Richmond	112	12	48	311	367	488	23·3	2504	171
Harrow	121	10	17	420	786	520	17·1	2691	205
Hounslow	144	10	51	464	742	505	13·9	2513	207
Waltham Forest	170	13	42	616	730	534	10·7	2444	233
Haringey	230	11	58	485	728	410	15·4	2842	235
Hillingdon	165	16	18	448	608	499	15·8	2289	235
Redbridge	164	12	29	512	441	456	16·6	2885	237
Havering	146	10	38	507	410	419	18·9	2211	245
Enfield	169	15	46	684	1008	456	21·0	2500	265
Brent	161	13	61	721	627	462	13·2	2102	275
Ealing	180	13	78	624	1422	460	16·0	2384	293
Barnet	232	16	44	720	965	646	18·8	3134	302
Bromley	209	16	75	828	722	455	25·5	2609	306
Croydon	170	14	99	623	632	358	9·2	1828	333
$\bar{X}$	159·4	12·3	47·9	535·2	729·4	484·1	16·4	2535·1	
S	39·3	2·5	21·8	149·5	363·8	64·7	4·4	320·4	

Key to variables:
X_1 = number of library staff; X_2 = number of library points; X_3 = reference books ('000s); X_4 = total books held ('000s); X_5 = serials subscribed to; X_6 = expenditure (£) per 1000 inhabitants on books; X_7 = expenditure (£) per 1000 inhabitants on newspapers; X_8 = total expenditure (£) per 1000 inhabitants. Population is given in thousands
Source: Society of County Treasurers (1975b)

suburbs (group A) and outer suburbs (group B) can be distinguished on variables relating to socio-economic status, lifestyle, etc., but is not sure either which variables are most important or which are related with which others. The discriminant analysis is exploratory only, therefore, identifying probable inter-relationships which give general support to the initial notions and which should be subjected to further scrutiny.

2. *Evaluating a classification.*   As we have seen, discriminant analysis indicates the number of misclassifications in the dependent variable. These are observations whose scores on the discriminant functions suggest that,

according to the relevant characteristics identified by the loadings, they are more like the members of another group than they are like those in the group they belong to. Such information is useful in terms of isolating deviant observations from a general pattern, and perhaps also suggesting further hypotheses which would account for such deviance. A particularly valuable use of discriminant analysis in this way is to see whether a classification, perhaps obtained by the method outlined in Chapter 7, is optimal.

3. *Estimating values for other observations.* If a discriminant analysis is successful in isolating differences between groups, it can then be used to predict values on the dependent variable for observations not in the original sample. Such a general predictive methodology could be valuable in allocating new observations to an existing classification: a new weather station, for example, could be entered into an existing climatic classification in this way.

There are few examples of these three types of use in the geographical literature. To illustrate them, a review of selected studies is provided at the end of the chapter. First, however, discriminant analysis is applied to a single data set, to show its uses and to indicate the variety of detailed procedures associated with it.

Discriminant analysis of London borough data

To illustrate the output of discriminant analyses, we return to some of the data for London's outer boroughs. These refer to their library provision, information on various aspects of which was used in Chapter 5 to illustrate aspects of principal components and factor analysis. There are eight variables, and the full data set is given in Table 8.1.

Testing a hypothesis

In this first example, the 17 boroughs have been divided into two groups according to their size -- as indicated by their populations. The 8 smallest (from Kingston to Haringey in Table 8.1) form group A, and the other 9 form group B. The hypothesis is that aspects of library provision can be used to estimate whether or not a borough has a large or a small population.

Only one discriminant function can be extracted for this analysis of two groups.

$$X_0 = -0.128\,X_1 - 0.527\,X_2 + 0.566\,X_3 - 1.081\,X_4 + 0.006\,X_5 + 0.409\,X_6 - 0.287\,X_7 + 0.508\,X_8$$

for which the canonical correlation is 0.807. Wilks' *lambda* is 0.348, for which the chi-square value of 12.653 with 8 degrees of freedom (the number of variables) has a probability of 0.124 of not appearing by chance in a sample of observations from a larger population. It would seem, therefore, that the hypothesis is invalid.

In terms of the tests of statistical significance associated with Wilks' *lambda*, it would seem that the function is not very good at discriminating between boroughs in terms of their size. Turning to the discriminant function itself, the loadings suggest that the main contribution to discriminating between the two groups of boroughs is made by variables X_4, X_3, X_2, X_8 and X_6. The positive signs for variables X_3, X_6, and X_8 suggest that the small boroughs (group A, which have the positive scores) tend to be the largest spenders per 1000 inhabitants and have most reference books; the negative signs for X_2 and X_4 suggest that the larger boroughs (group B, with the negative scores) have most books and most library points. The converses of these patterns also hold – small boroughs have fewest library points and books, etc. Comparison of this function with the principal components analysis of the same data set (Table 5.6) shows that the discriminant function is not the same as the principal component or factor, having been located to maximise a different function.

Table 8.2 Library provision in outer London boroughs: stepwise discriminant analysis

Step	Variables included	Wilks' lambda
1	X_4	0·522
2	X_4, X_2	0·451
3	X_4, X_2, X_6	0·403
4	X_4, X_2, X_6, X_3	0·372
5	X_4, X_2, X_6, X_3, X_8	0·362
6	X_4, X_2, X_6, X_3, X_8, X_7	0·349
7	X_4, X_2, X_6, X_3, X_8, X_7, X_1	0·348
8	X_4, X_2, X_6, X_3, X_8, X_7, X_1, X_5	0·348

Some of the variables may contribute little to the discriminant function, as in multiple regression, and so instead of fitting the function over all n variables, a stepwise procedure can be employed. This enters variables sequentially according to their contribution to some index of their contribution to a 'good result'. In our example, we use Wilks' *lambda*, so that the variables are added in the order with which they make the greatest contribution to reducing the ratio of within-groups to total variation. This, of course, is a similar procedure to that employed in stepwise multiple regression analysis (p. 84), although note that it is the contribution of variables to the function which is being studied here, not the contribution of different functions to the overall variance. Table 8.2 outlines the eight steps in such an analysis of the London library data, showing clearly that the last two variables to be entered – X_1 and X_5 – make virtually no contribution to an effective discrimination between loadings. A more parsimonious discrimination could be performed ending at stage 6 of the stepwise procedure, therefore.

Discriminant scores for the members of groups A and B on the eight-variable discriminant function are in Fig. 8.10. The two groups are almost completely 'segregated' along that continuum, there being only two 'over-

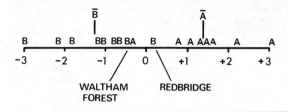

Fig. 8.10   Showing the misclassification of two boroughs in a discriminant analysis of the London data, using two groups of boroughs.

laps'. Waltham Forest is in group A but is clearly closer to $\overline{B}$ than to $\overline{A}$, whereas one borough in group B (Redbridge) is closer to $\overline{A}$ than to $\overline{B}$.

Evaluating a classification

The last point raises an interesting relationship between discriminant analysis and classification, and suggests another way of assessing the 'success' of a discriminant analysis. The observations have been allocated to two groups prior to the analysis, to form the dependent variable: to what extent does the discriminant function allocate the observations to their original groups? To investigate this, we regress the discriminant scores on the groups, using the equation

where $X_0 = 1$ if borough is small, 0 otherwise

$$X_0 = f(D_I) \tag{8.7}$$

The predicted values of X_0 from these equations are, as we have seen in the first part of the chapter, probabilities that the observation has a value of $X_0 = 1$.

The discriminant scores and the probabilities obtained from fitting formula (8.7) are given in Table 8.3, along with the actual values of X_0 (i.e. the group memberships). For two places — those whose discriminant score is not closest to their group mean — the probability that $\hat{X}_0$ equals the actual value of X_0 is smaller than the probability that it has the opposite value. Thus Waltham Forest is in the small boroughs group, but according to the discriminant function it has a probability of only 0·244 of being in that group; similarly Redbridge is the large borough group, but the function gives it a probability of only 0·487 of being in that group. As summarised at the foot of Table 8.3, this means two 'misclassifications' out of seventeen, or an 88·23% success rate.

Detailed interpretation of the probabilities in Table 8.3 depends on the purpose of the analysis. The real meaning is that although Waltham Forest is a relatively small borough, in terms of its library provision (or those elements of its library provision which contribute to the discriminant function), it is more like a large one, whereas Redbridge is in the group of larger boroughs but its library provision is more akin to that in the smaller

Table 8.3   Evaluation of a classification by discriminant scores

Place	X_0	Probability $X_0 = 1$ small boroughs (i.e. in group A)	Probability $X_0 = 0$ large boroughs (i.e. in group B)	Discriminant Score
Kingston	1	1·000	0·000	3·158
Barking	1	0·958	0·042	1·290
Sutton	1	0·996	0·004	2·197
Richmond	1	0·965	0·035	1·369
Harrow	1	0·930	0·070	1·080
Hounslow	1	0·968	0·032	1·404
Waltham Forest	1	0·244	0·756	−0·363
Haringey	1	0·855	0·145	0·766
Hillingdon	0	0·037	0·963	−1·193
Redbridge	0	0·513	0·487	0·095
Havering	0	0·147	0·853	−0·608
Enfield	0	0·003	0·997	−2·247
Brent	0	0·009	0·991	−1·763
Newham	0	0·220	0·780	−0·417
Barnet	0	0·141	0·859	−0·625
Bromley	0	0·000	1·000	−3·009
Croydon	0	0·043	0·957	−1·134

Misclassifications

	Classified into group	
Original group	A	B
A	7	1
B	1	8
Percentage correctly classified	88.23	

boroughs. Overall, however, the 88·23% success rate indicates that patterns of library provision clearly discriminate between large and small boroughs with but two relatively minor deviations. The method is therefore providing an evaluation of a classification of the observations by size in terms of the independent variables.

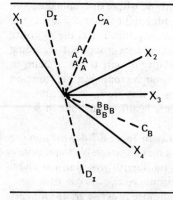

Fig. 8.11   The classification functions associated with a discriminant function.

Another way of evaluating classifications which is frequently used is to derive classification functions for each group. These are equivalent to multiple regression equations for each group of observations. Figure 8.11 illustrates their nature, as an extension of the geometrical argument in Fig. 8.8. We have two groups — A and B — in a four-variable space. The discriminant function — D_I — is located as the vector which provides the best F-ratio dividing groups A and B; the classification functions — C_A and C_B — are the best predictors of scores on the discriminant function for the respective groups.

The classification functions are usually expressed in unstandardised form, just as multiple regression equations are. For the London library data, excluding the insignificant variables, X_1 and X_5, they are for Group A (the smaller boroughs)

$$C_i = -83 \cdot 42 + 3 \cdot 77\, X_2 + 0 \cdot 53\, X_3 - 0 \cdot 02\, X_4 + 0 \cdot 06\, X_6 - 0 \cdot 54\, X_7 + 0 \cdot 04\, X_8$$

for Group B (the larger boroughs)

$$C_i = -82 \cdot 51 + 4 \cdot 32\, X_2 + 0 \cdot 46\, X_3 + 0 \cdot 003\, X_4 + 0 \cdot 05\, X_6 - 0 \cdot 37\, X_7 + 0 \cdot 04\, X_8$$

where, in each case, C_i is the classification score for observation i. The largest differences between the two functions are in the coefficients for X_2, X_4 and X_7, suggesting that these are the variables on which the groups are most different.

The purpose of the classification functions is to determine which group an observation should be in. For each observation we obtain a score for each group, and the larger the score, the closer it is to the classification function described for that score. Thus in Fig. 8.11, places with high values on variables X_1 and X_2 should be in group A; those with high values on X_3 and X_4 should be in group B.

Classifying new observations

Either the discriminant function or the classification functions can be used to allocate new individuals to existing groups, assuming that the observations used to produce the functions are random samples of the population. Thus, having conducted the discriminant analysis on the 17 London boroughs, we might later want to classify another borough, Merton. Its values on the eight variables are:

	X_1	X_2	X_3	X_4	X_5	X_6	X_7	X_8
Raw data	101	9	75	436	1590	443	15·5	2163
Standardised data	−1·49	−1·32	1·24	−0·66	2·37	−0·63	−0·20	−1·16

Fitting the standardised data into the discriminant function, we get a discriminant score of 1·56, which is clearly closer to the mean of group A than to that of group B (Fig. 8.10). Applying the classification functions, we get for group A a score of −87·63 and for group B, −87·58. Clearly, then, Merton should be in the small boroughs group according to its library provision. (Its population is 177 000.)

Three-group analysis

For this analysis, the 17 boroughs in Table 8.1 are divided into 3 groups: the 6 smallest (group A), the 6 largest (group C), and the 5 of intermediate size (group B). With three groups, two discriminant functions are possible, and in standardised form they are:

$$D_I = 0.89\ X_1 + 0.52\ X_2 - 0.12\ X_3 + 1.68\ X_4 - 0.01\ X_5 - 0.33\ X_6 - 0.09\ X_7 - 0.48\ X_8$$

canonical correlation 0.95 Λ 0.029

$$D_{II} = 2.30\ X_1 - 0.68\ X_2 - 1.90\ X_3 - 0.68\ X_4 - 0.12\ X_5 - 0.71\ X_6 - 0.10\ X_7 - 0.86\ X_8$$

canonical correlation 0.85 Λ 0.281

As these functions, like components, are extracted iteratively, the correlation and lambda for D_I refer to the total between-group variance whereas those for D_{II} refer to the residual variance after D_I has been held constant. Interpreting the functions, the first clearly emphasises library size, as indexed by staff (X_1) and by books (X_4) whereas the second contrasts staff (X_1) with the reference collection (X_3), as the independent variables which clearly discriminate between boroughs of different population sizes.

Discriminant scores for each vector are shown in univariate and bivariate space in Fig. 8.12. On the first function, the groups are clearly separated into size categories, with the smallest boroughs (A) having the largest negative scores (i.e. low values on X_1 and X_4) and the largest (C) having the largest positive scores. The second function discriminates the medium-sized boroughs (B) as having large staffs (discriminant function I being held constant) relative to groups A and C, between which there is apparently no difference in this function. The bivariate distribution (Fig. 8.12C) shows the clear separation between the groups; this is so marked that in fact all 17 boroughs are correctly classified and are closer to their own group centroid in the two-dimensional space than to any other. (Waltham Forest, the smallest in group B, is nearest to being misclassified. The probability of it being in group B is 0.594 and in group C 0.406.)

With a single discriminant function and two groups, the value of Wilks' *lambda* indicates whether the two groups are significantly different in the distributions of their discriminant scores. With two or more groups, differences between any pair are not indicated. Between-group analyses of variance can be conducted, however, either on a single function or on all functions. For example, the F-ratio comparing groups A and C on discriminant function II is 1.603, indicating no significant difference between the two distributions on that function. The F-ratio for their distances in the two-dimension space is 61.24, however, indicative of the clear spatial separation shown in Fig. 8.12C.

New observations can be allocated to groups in exactly the same ways as before, using either the discriminant functions or the classification func-

A   DISCRIMINANT FUNCTION I

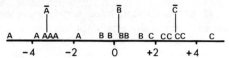

B   DISCRIMINANT FUNCTION II

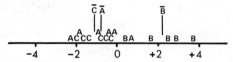

C   BOTH FUNCTIONS

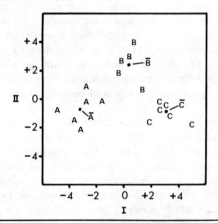

Fig. 8.12   A discriminant analysis requiring two functions to isolate three groups of London boroughs.

tions. For Merton (data on p. 243) the predicted scores from the two discriminant functions are:

D_I −1·51 D_{II} −4·76

The centroids for the three groups are:

	D_I	D_{II}
A	−3·26	−0·80
B	0·31	2·24
C	3·01	−1·06

so the distance from Merton to each are

A 4·33   B 7·23   C 5·84

and it should be allocated to group A − the smallest boroughs.

Some examples of discriminant analyses in geography

Discriminant analysis has not been employed widely in geographical research, but examples of each of the three main uses are outlined here.

Testing and generating hypotheses

The studies in this category are primarily inductive in character, addressing themselves to the question 'which independent variables discriminate between these groups of observations?'. Nevertheless, the selection of independent variables will have been guided by some prior theoretical consideration or speculation. For example, Roseman (1971) hypothesised that variables such as family size, income and education — known to be collinear — would discriminate between male workers according to their migrations after a change of job. The dependent variable comprised a sample of employees categorised into first 9 and then 3 groups according to the length of their journey-to-work (1) before they changed job, (2) after they changed job, and (3) after they had moved home as well. But the discriminant analyses were not very successful and he was unable to predict which commuting category workers would be in according to the selected variables.

A somewhat similar, but more successful, study was Newton's (1975) investigation of intra-urban migration in Newcastle, N.S.W. He had samples of 40 households who had moved to each of four suburban areas and hypothesised that which suburb that they had moved to (a four-group situation) should be predictable by such variables as occupation, income, family size, etc. Nine independent variables were selected, and two discriminant functions extracted which correctly predicted 66% of the group memberships. The first function was the best discriminator; its largest coefficients were for variables representing socio-economic status, indicating that this was the prime determinant of where movers were able to afford a home. The second function had its main weight for a variable representing the length of the journey to work, differentiating the groups according to the importance of this factor in their residence choice. Thus Newton's general hypotheses were confirmed, as a prelude to more constrained, predictive methodologies.

As an example of the use of discriminant analysis in physical geography, Norris and Barkham (1970) studied the ground flora at each of 880 sites in 13 different beechwoods on the Cotswold Hills. The woods were selected to represent different environmental conditions (aspect; physical conditions of site; age of trees; soils; and slope angle); for each site, the percentage cover of each of 50 species formed the variables; discriminant analysis was used as it met their 'aim of generating hypotheses about differences between woods' (Norris and Barkham, 1970, p. 604). Three discriminant functions were extracted; interpretation of loadings on each function identified the species contributing most to discrimination between the sites and interpretation of the mean scores for each of the 13 woods identified the environmental conditions associated with the particular groups of species. Of the three functions, the first two were easiest to interpret; the third seemed to be related to management of woods and the amount of recent disturbance of the floristic composition. Group centroids for the 13 woodlands on the scores for the first two functions are shown in Fig. 8.13, along with the interpretations which related them to characteristics of the soils -- factors leading to clear differences in floristic composition for the four 'extreme' woodlands. Thus Norris and Barkham were able to develop the hypothesis from this analysis that differences in floristic composition between the 13 beechwoods were related to the soil texture variations which affect moisture availability to plants. As they concluded (p. 618), discriminant analysis 'can be a useful primary analytical technique in displaying differences between groups of sites and may be used as the basis for rejection of peripheral or surplus information for later more detailed studies'.

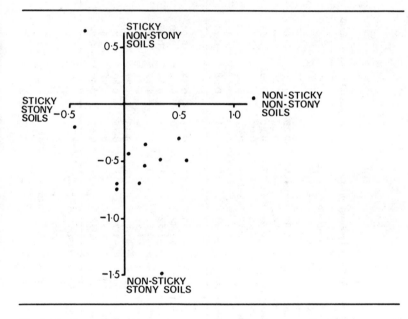

Fig. 8.13   Group centroids for 13 groups of woodlands on two discriminant functions. Source: Norris and Barkham (1970); reproduced with permission.

Further investigations were possible from Norris and Barkham's analysis. They could, for example, have tested whether each of the sites was closer to its group centroid than to any other in the three-dimensional discriminant space. For those that were not, further inquiry might have indicated micro-scale factors accounting for the deviations, such as local aspect or variation between soils within the woods. Similarly, they could have tested for differences between woods in terms of their group centroids, thereby

Table 8.4   Reallocation in classification by discriminant analysis

City	Score on component									
	I	II	III	IV	V	VI	VII	VIII	IX	X
Group 6										
Kanpur	−0·87	1·15	−0·28	1·38	0·00	−0·03	0·92	−0·14	0·70	2·00
Lucknow	−0·84	0·67	0·26	0·26	0·03	0·13	0·78	0·33	1·26	0·38
Allahabad	−0·30	0·27	0·85	0·60	0·21	0·53	0·86	−0·52	0·46	0·17
Varanasi	−0·28	0·01	0·02	0·42	0·32	0·94	1·29	−0·10	0·74	1·26
Mirzapur	0·27	−0·03	0·47	0·65	−0·42	1·51	1·87	−0·53	−0·21	0·47
GWALIOR	−0·45	0·17	−0·53	0·98	−0·24	0·59	0·80	0·69	0·94	−1·04
Group 8										
Agra	−1·63	0·15	0·11	0·34	0·54	1·05	0·65	1·44	−0·63	0·99
Suhranapur	−1·88	−0·08	−0·10	−0·42	−0·20	0·90	0·44	1·08	−0·31	0·38
Aligarh	−1·52	−0·14	−0·27	0·56	0·15	0·78	0·67	0·42	−0·37	0·03
Amritsar	−1·85	−0·66	0·42	−1·17	0·40	0·64	0·37	0·05	1·44	0·55
Bareilly	1·51	−0·38	0·34	−0·71	0·18	0·48	1·54	0·16	0·58	−0·98
Moradebad	−1·78	−0·43	−0·40	−1·77	−0·38	0·88	1·34	0·98	0·24	0·30
Mathura	−1·22	0·13	0·75	−0·80	−0·82	0·71	0·78	0·77	−0·25	0·65
Shahjanapur	−1·37	−0·22	0·98	−0·91	−1·62	1·32	2·32	−0·23	−0·01	0·54
Rampur	−1·32	−0·13	−0·53	−0·49	−0·74	1·53	1·77	0·47	0·18	−2·49

Source Ahmed (1965, pp. 79—81).

producing a classification of woodlands according to differences in their floristic composition.

This use of discriminant analysis is very similar to most of the applications of principal components analysis, factor analysis, and canonical correlation analysis in geographical research. It is essentially a search procedure, looking for anticipated general relationships that can be used to generate more precise hypotheses. This does not mean that they are entirely atheoretical, for the selection of independent variables is guided by the researcher's notions of what patterns are likely to occur. But, as is only to be expected in a subject much of whose theory is relatively immature, no precise hypotheses can be stated and researchers are still seeking guidelines, among their various vague ideas, as to the best possible paths to follow in their investigations.

The use of discriminant analysis to answer a preliminary research question (of the form specified in Cattell's I.H.D. spiral: Fig. 1.5) rather than to test a precise hypothesis is well illustrated by a paper of Massam's (1973). His aim was to identify whether any groups of variables successively discriminated between those municipalities in the Montreal metropolitan area which had opted for a city-manager government ($X_0 = 1$; this is considered the more 'professional' approach) from those which had retained rule by an elected mayor and council ($X_0 = 0$). Discriminations were conducted for 1921, 1931, 1941, 1951 and 1961, and indicated very good differentiating power. For 1961, for example, the single discriminant function obtained had the following 'significant' variables after a stepwise analysis

$$X_0 = -0.037\ X_1 + 0.027\ X_2 + 0.422\ X_3 - 0.00001\ X_4 + 0.00037\ X_5$$

where X_0 is 1 if a city manager, 0 if a mayor-council;
   X_1 is proportion who speak English only;
   X_2 is proportion who speak French only;
   X_3 is proportion earning $6000+;
   X_4 is value of taxable land *per capita*; and
   X_5 is municipal expenditure *per capita*.

Six of the 66 municipalities were misclassified (a 91% success rate), compared to 2 of the 32 analysed for 1951, none in either 1941 or 1931, and 2 in 1921. In general, therefore, the discriminant analyses were extremely successful, suggesting, within the constraint of the chosen data, that municipalities comprising above average proportions of French-speaking, high-income earners are the most likely to have adopted city-manager government; such results are of interest in themselves, as well as being extremely valuable as pointers to more precise hypothesis-testing in later research.

The evaluation of prior classifications

We saw in the previous chapter how classifications on the basis of the analysis of variance model may not be optimal, because, once formed, groups cannot be broken up. Distance to group centroids was then used at the selected grouping to test for optimality (p. 208). If the classification were based on orthogonal variables (e.g. component scores) then discriminant analysis could be used to test for optimality.

As a simple example of this, we have the two-group situation in Fig. 8.4. Is the classification of the sites optimal in terms of the two independent variables? Discriminant analysis indicates that one sandy beach is closer to the centroid of the shingly group than it is to its own group's, whereas two of the shingly beaches are closest to the sandy beach group centroid. It could be claimed that these are mis-classifications, and so the three samples were reallocated and a further discriminant analysis indicated that all were now correctly classified.

Because of the problem of non-optimal classifications, many researchers have included discriminant analysis to check for misclassifications as the final stage of their procedure (see Barker, 1976). Thus Ahmed (1965) classified Indian cities, using the method outlined in Chapter 7, into 18 groups, and then checked the optimality of this classification using discriminant analysis. Two changes only were made, one of which is illustrated in Table 8.4. The city of Gwalior was allocated to group 8 in the original classification but the discriminant analysis showed that it was closer to the group centroid of group 6. It was reallocated to the latter group, and a further discriminant analysis indicated that the classification was now optimal. The reason for the change can be quite clearly deduced from the table. Gwalior is not very similar to either group over the full range of ten components (nor to any other, according to the full data set). Individually, it is closer to Bareilly in group 8 than it is to most of the towns in group 6, but the centroid for group 8 is further from Gwalior than is the centroid for group 6. (Figure 8.14 illustrates this for a hypothetical example. The observation marked 0 is closer to one of those marked · than to any of those marked X and would be grouped with the former. In a two-group solution, however, it is clearly closer to the centroid for the group of Xs than to that of the other group to which it was initially allocated.)

Estimation of group membership for new observations

Discriminant functions can be used, as we saw with a brief example earlier (p. 243), to allocate new observations to the existing groups. This is a very valuable predictive tool and it is widely used in marketing research, in which data for a sample of individuals are used, for example, to discriminate between buyers of different types of commodities; the discriminant functions are then applied to predict the likely markets for the commodities in other samples from the assumed populations (districts in which a certain commodity has not previously been available, etc.). There has been little

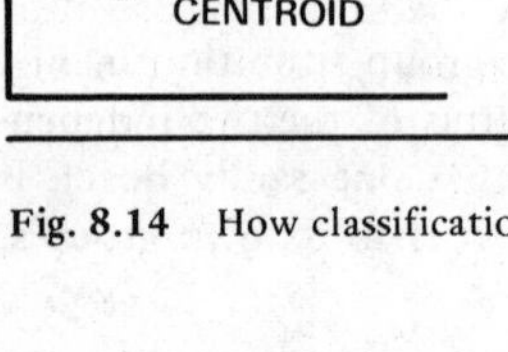

Fig. 8.14   How classifications become sub-optimal.

development of such predictive methodologies in geography, however, although this is clearly an aim of scientific research. Newton's analyses, for example (see p. 246), could be used to predict, on the basis of their characteristics, where households would move to within a city.

One way in which the predictive power of discriminant analysis has been used in geography is in the development of classifications for large data sets. In producing a map of spatial patterns of socio-economic structure in India, Horton, McConnell and Tirtha (1970) had data on 15 variables for 295 districts. The variables were reduced to 5 by a principal components analysis but attempts to classify the 295 districts according to their scores in this five-dimensional orthogonal space failed because of the size of the problem relative to the size of their computer. Thus they classified only a random sample of 248 of the districts (using Ward's method) and then tested for the optimality of the result by a discriminant analysis using the five components as the variables. (The original classification was 91·94% correct, and between-pairs-of-groups F-tests indicated that all group centroids were significantly different from all others.) Classification functions were then developed for each group and the other 47 districts were allocated to the closest group centroid.

This method clearly is one of research pragmatics only, using discriminant analysis as a means of circumventing the problem of insufficient computer space for the data set to be classified. Estimation of group membership in a predictive sense, using discriminant analysis as a means of anticipating results on a nominal scale, should be a major aim of geographical research, however. If Norris and Barkham's findings regarding relationships between soil texture and floristic composition are valid, for example, then their discriminant functions should accurately predict the type of woodland at comparable sites. Only if such predictions prove correct will research using techniques such as discriminant analysis proceed beyond the descriptive stage.

Conclusions

This chapter has dealt with another method whose use in geographical research is likely to increase in the future. Its flexibility allows it to be employed in a number of situations relating nominal dependent variables to interval- or ratio-scale independent variables, in the generation of hypotheses concerning group differences, in the evaluation of classifications, and in the prediction of behaviour. Other aspects of the method are likely to be adopted also. It is possible, for example, to rotate discriminant functions to aid interpretation (see an attempt at this by Norris and Barkham, 1970, for example), and no doubt it will soon be possible to have 'target rotations', as in factor analysis (p. 171), so that more direct hypothesis-testing can be undertaken.

This is the last of the chapters on particular statistical methods. As with the previous three, the method outlined is largely one that is best used in exploratory work, producing hypotheses rather than testing them. The latter function is feasible with all of these methods, but in general principal components analysis, factor analysis, canonical correlation, classification, and discriminant analysis have all been used by geographers as exploratory tools, isolating the general patterns within data sets rather than testing the viability of certain well-founded hypotheses of causal relationships. Thus it is somewhat paradoxical that the more complex methods discussed in this book are those with the least precise uses. Those discussed in Chapters 2–4, of which the methods in Chapters 5–8 are generalisations, are much more precise and valuable in the testing of the clear hypotheses which characterise a mature science.

Chapter 9

Multivariate analysis and geographical data

All of the examples in this book have been 'geographical', either taken from published studies or 'invented' to provide simple illustrations of methods in the context of geographical research. Apart from the relatively brief mention of problems of spatial autocorrelation in the introductory chapter on regression analyses (p. 43), the implicit assumption throughout has been that there are no particular problems with geographical data which raise difficulties with regard to the use of the various methods. This was certainly the general view when multivariate techniques were first introduced to geography (e.g. Garrison, 1956), but increasingly researchers have realised that to a considerable degree geographical applications violate one of the basic assumptions of the general linear model, that concerning independence among the observations. Because of this, considerable effort has been expended by some workers in recent years on ways of measuring and circumventing this problem (Cliff and Ord, 1973). Indeed, some now apparently believe that the problem is insurmountable, and therefore that in most situations geographers cannot validly use these methods, for the various coefficients and estimates that they produce are hopelessly biased (see, for example, Berry, 1973). Spatial autocorrelation is not the only problem of geographical data sets, however, and others are discussed here.

Spatial autocorrelation

As we saw in Chapter 2, autocorrelation exists when the value of a variable at one observation is not independent of the value at adjacent observations. This is particularly clear in time series analysis, which uses some measure of time as the independent variable. The value of the dependent variable at time t_2 may be very much dependent on the value at t_1, perhaps because the time-scale of the phenomenon differs from the time-scale used as the independent variable. Regressing the amount of pollution in the air against time with measurements being made daily, for example, can introduce temporal autocorrelation since some of today's pollution may still be here tomorrow, and so will be double-counted: for industrial pollution, the reduction in supply at weekends would aggravate the autocorrelation problem.

With time series, the problem of autocorrelation can be fairly easily tackled, since time moves in one direction only (at least in most operational research!). Similarly with some spatial series which refer to phenomena along a line, such as soil structure down a slope profile or downstream pollution in a river (see p. 44), the autocorrelation is unidirectional. But most spatial data sets are not unidirectional in terms of interpedependence among observations, which introduces problems of much greater complexity.

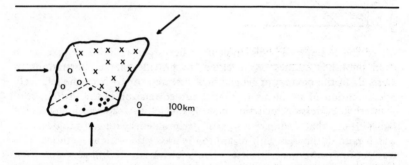

Fig. 9.1 An imaginary island, showing its three 'rainfall regions' and the location of rain gauges.

The major problem which spatial autocorrelation introduces is a biasing of statistical extimates, such as regression coefficients, when two variables are correlated over space. A major reason for this is 'multiple-counting' or the recording of the same thing, perhaps many times at different observations. As an example of this, take the imaginary large island of Fig. 9.1, in which we want to study the relationship between summer rainfall amount (X) and crop yields (Y), hypothesising a positive relationship between the two. Our data refer to the rainfall gauges which are maintained on the island, and crop yields, which have been measured in a field adjacent to each gauge.

On the island, summer rain is brought by three main climatic systems. The main one emanates from the north-east, bringing a similar amount of rain in each of the six months of the crop-growing season: rain-gauges marked by an X in Fig. 9.1 receive virtually all of their rain from this source. The west of the island receives its summer weather from further west and the rainfall at stations affected by this system (marked by 0) is characterised by long drought periods punctuated by very heavy storms. Finally, in the south is an area of recording stations (marked by ·) affected by a different regime, which is characterised by plentiful rainfall early in the growing season followed by a period of semi-drought. On the map (Fig. 9.1) these three areas have been represented as separate regions, although occasionally places in one area receive rainfall from storms penetrating from one of the other two.

Let us suppose for the moment that in each area the amount of rainfall is the same at every station, save for a small amount of measurement error. This gives us a scattergram relating rainfall in the growing season to crop

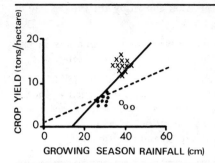

Fig. 9.2 Regressions of crop yields on rainfall for the island of Fig. 9.1.

yield (Fig. 9.2) for which the regression equation (the solid line in the figure) is

$$Y = -7.68 + 0.501\ X \qquad r_{YX} = 0.608$$

From this equation, we would infer that rainfall accounts for 37% of the variance in crop yields, and that every 10 extra inches result in just over 5 more metric tons per hectare. Or does it? What we have is an island divided into three regions, in each of which there is no variation in rainfall and crop yields; in other words, in the north-eastern region, for example, each storm brings the same amount of rainfall to each place, and has the same effect on crop yields. For the north-eastern region we have taken twelve readings of the same 'events', however, whereas for the western and southern regions we have taken three and ten respectively, and so our regression equation is biased towards the first of these three regions. If we regressed the three regional means (the broken line in Fig. 9.2) we would get

$$Y = 0.36 + 0.23\ X \qquad r_{YX} = 0.277$$

which tells us a very different story about the function $Y = f(X)$.

Which of the two regression equations in the preceding paragraph is the correct one? It could be argued that our initial hypothesis referred to the whole island, and not to the three regions, and so we are right in having more observations for the larger region (i.e. the number of observations per region should be a function of the region's area). Perhaps this means that we should be more precise with our hypotheses. Instead of postulating

> There is a positive relationship on the island between rainfall amounts in the growing season and crop yields

we should state either

> There is a positive relationship between rainfall amounts in the growing season and crop yields, among the various rainfall regions of the island

(which is the hypothesis for the regression shown by the broken line in Fig. 9.2) or

> There is a positive relationship between rainfall amounts in the growing season and crop yields over the surface of the island

(which is the hypothesis for the regression shown by the solid line in Fig. 9.2). To test the last hypothesis, however, we would need a random sample of locations with rain-gauges, which is a rare event. Even on our hypothetical island, there is a dense concentration of recording sites in the south-eastern corner, around the island capital and its airport.

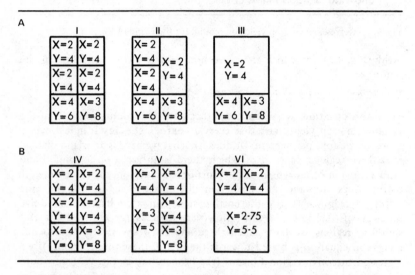

Fig. 9.3   Different 'regions' in an area for correlation analysis (after Thomas and Anderson, 1965).

This problem of the weighting of different regions was introduced to the geographical literature by Robinson (1956), using the example shown in Fig. 9.3A. His basic data set referred to the six 'counties' — each with the same area — of diagram I in Fig. 9.3A; in each, values of an independent variable X (annual rainfall in tens of centimetres, perhaps) and a dependent variable Y (population density as farmsteads per square mile) were measured. As shown in Table 9.1, there is a strong positive correlation between Y and X over these six counties. Robinson then proceeded to amalgamate some of the counties, producing observation units with different areas, so that the values for X and Y in the 'super-counties' in diagrams II and III (Fig. 9.3A) are averages. The resultant regression and correlation coefficients are substantially different from that for the counties in diagram I (Table 9.1).

The cause of these variations in the regression coefficients, Robinson argued, was that unequal weight was being given to the various parts of the

Table 9.1 Regression analyses of the data in Fig. 9.3

	Data set	N	a	b	r
			Regression parameters		
A	I	6	1·429	1·429	0·715
	II	5	1·625	1·375	0·687
	III	3	3·000	1·000	0·500
B	IV	6	1·429	1·429	0·715
	V	5	−1·000	2·500	0·829
	VI	3	0·000	2·000	1·000
Results with weighted data (for area)					
A	I	6	1·429	1·429	0·715
	II	5	1·429	1·429	0·715
	III	3	1·429	1·429	0·715
B	IV	6	1·429	1·429	0·715
	V	5	0·000	2·000	0·707
	VI	3	0·000	2·000	1·000

Source: after Thomas and Anderson (1965)

study area. To counter this, he reasoned, all values of X and Y should be weighted by being multiplied by the area of the county to which they referred, prior to calculation of the regression and correlation coefficients. As shown by the information in the lower part of Table 9.1, this resulted in a common set of results for each of the three counting systems (I, II and III).

In a subsequent paper, Thomas and Anderson (1965) extended Robinson's analysis and showed that his solution by weighting for area only applied in the particular case that he analysed, where all of the amalgamated counties had the same values for X and Y. They presented two alternative county systems (Fig. 9.1B) for which the regression and correlation coefficients differed from that for the basic system both before and after weighting to take account of areal variations (Table 9.1). Thomas and Anderson then proceeded to argue that the different findings reported in Table 9.1 may merely reflect random variations about the 'true parameters' of the data set. They tested whether this was so by assuming that each of the county systems in Fig. 9.1 was a sample from the same population (i.e. all the possible county systems which could be designed from that set of six basic counties) and tested whether differences between the values of a, b and r were statistically significant. They were not, either in Robinson's data or in some larger data sets which were simulated.

The implications of Thomas and Andersons' work are that this aspect of the spatial autocorrelation problem is not a particularly important issue; whatever the actual configuration of areas used, the regression and correlation coefficients will not differ significantly from those of other configurations. Further work by Openshaw (1976) denies this, however, and shows that for a county system it is possible to reorganise the boundaries to produce any value of r between +1·0 and −1·0. Further, Thomas and Anderson dealt only with exhaustive coverage of an area and not with the uneven sampling of points to represent an area, which is an allied (Fig. 9.2) though not exactly similar problem. And finally, their data had a basic set of building blocks — the 'true' counties — which is not the case in most studies. Multiple counting of the contents of different regions will affect the results of regression analyses, therefore, and the greater both the range in region size and the degree of multiple counting (ratio of observations to regional area in Fig. 9.2), the greater the problem of interpretation is likely to be.

Spatial processes and the autocorrelation problem

The examples discussed so far with regard to multiple counting and autocorrelation have concentrated on the unequal representation of regions. (Regions have been used because of their geographical relevance; the examples could just as easily be social classes, age groups, etc.) The problem of spatial autocorrelation is usually confounded, however, by the operation of spatial processes of spread and diffusion. Most geographic phenomena do not have precise boundaries; regions gradually merge into each other; rain storms gradually die out as they move over a land mass; the further a person lives from a place, the less he tends to know about it; and so on. Thus adjacent places are probably similar, but not exactly so: the rainfall at a station somewhere in the centre of our imaginary island (Fig. 9.1) is probably similar to that at a neighbouring station, but not exactly the same since the stations are differentially located relative to the rainfall source and to the process of decay in intensity as storms move westwards. Using both stations in a regression analysis will not involve double-counting, since each station has a unique component to its rainfall pattern, but there will be some multiple counting, its extent depending on the degree of similarity between the two. Instead of sampling two identical stations within a region, therefore, we would be sampling at two points on a planar surface (which itself is similar to a regression line).

Returning to our imaginary island, therefore, let us now suppose that in each of its three regions rainfall decreases in amount away from the source of the storm, giving the scattergram relating rainfall to crop yields in Fig. 9.4. Here we have, in each region, several samples of the same process, but these sample observations are not independent. If rainfall decreases in amount within the north-eastern region by about 20 centimetres for every 100 kilometres away from the north-eastern extremity of the island, and there is a standard relationship between rainfall and crop yields, then all we have for that region are twelve representatives at different points on the single distance—rainfall—crop yield function. And if at the same time our sample points are neither randomly nor uniformly distributed, as is the case in the southern region of the island, then we have a biased representation of the various stages of the process.

The closer we bring our example to a 'real world' situation, therefore, the greater the number of problems that we introduce. In Fig. 9.4 we have: unequal representation of three different 'events' — the rainfall

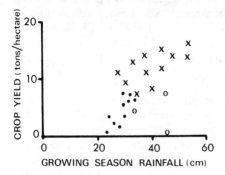

Fig. 9.4 Further regression of crop yields on rainfall for the island of Fig. 9.1.

regions (defined by rainfall source); unequal representation of different parts of the processes within these events; and the processes themselves differ (there is a more rapid decrease of rainfall away from the source in the southern region than in the north-eastern). Unravelling all of these to produce an unbiased regression equation of Y = f(X) for such an example is a difficult task.

There are many examples of such problems in geography. In the studies of rainfall trends cited in Chapter 5 on components analyses (p. 181), Gregory (1975) was forced to use those rainfall stations in the United Kingdom which had a sufficiently long run of records. There was a cluster of these in north-west England, and so the correlations on which Gregory's component and factor analyses are based were, as he indicated, undoubtedly biased by the 'double-counting' in that part of the country. Perry's (1970) analysis of precipitation anomalies over the North Atlantic used a regular grid of sampling points, but this does not necessarily mean that he therefore had an equal representation of different 'climatic regions'. In human geography, too, very similar problems can arise, for it is a basic tenet of, for example, spatial diffusion theory that dissemination of a wide range of phenomena has a regular distance-decay pattern away from a node or set of nodes, as with the spread of an idea or a disease. Again, this is a single process, which may be sampled many times at non-independent observations (Berry, 1973).

Spatial autocorrelation: a summary

The problem of spatial autocorrelation presents a paradoxical situation to geographers in terms of their use of statistical methods based on the general linear model. For the two reasons identified here — the division of regions and sampling from a spread or diffusion process — many geographical data sets violate the requirement of the general linear model that observations are independent of all others (p. 43). Can, then, the model be used?

Answers to this question depend on the nature of the problem being tackled, both its substance and whether the aim is description or prediction. Much work has been done on methods of quantifying the degree of spatial autocorrelation for single variables only, as in descriptions of the spread of measles through south-western England (Cliff *et al.*, 1975) and of the prices paid for beef cattle at various markets (Martin and Oeppen, 1975). From these, it may be possible to predict future trends. It is much more difficult to make multiple part measurements of the same phenomenon in different places, however, and then attempt to account for these by multiple regressions with other data sets containing similar problems. Much more complex methods than those described in this book may be needed (Bennett, 1975), especially if the aim is to produce unbiased regression coefficients and standard errors to allow reasonable predictions of future trends and patterns.

To some geographers (e.g. Gould, 1970) spatial autocorrelation is the basic subject matter of their discipline. We expect similar types of households to be clustered in particular parts of a town; the 'frictions of distance' ensure spatial biases in the flows of people and goods, ideas and messages, diseases and information; storm clouds, streams, and birds carrying seeds all follow spatial trajectories, and places in their paths are likely to be affected in similar ways. Geographers exist to describe and account for such interdependencies, and should adopt techniques such as those in the general linear model so as to achieve these ends. One way of achieving this has been suggested by Reynolds (1974) who: (1) tests to see whether there is spatial autocorrelation in the pattern for the dependent variable; (2) tests for spatial autocorrelation in the independent variables; (3) runs the regression; and (4) tests for spatial autocorrelation in the residuals. He then quotes Geary (1954) that if the original values for the dependent variable were highly autocorrelated, but that those for the residuals were not, then this would indicate that the independent variables had entirely accounted for the former (i.e. that the two patterns of autocorrelation were similar): other variables could account for some of the residual, non-autocorrelated pattern, of course. If the residuals were spatially autocorrelated, this would suggest the existence of spatial explanations for the pattern in the dependent variable, assuming that all of the relevant independent variables had been selected.

Clearly there are many problems still to be solved regarding the use of the general linear model with geographical data because of the existence of spatial autocorrelation. The nature of these problems depends on the particular use and whether its aim is description, explanation or prediction. The final conclusion may be that the existence of spatial interdependencies is such that many pieces of research using the techniques outlined in this book provide very biased reports from which few generalisations of note can be drawn (as is the view in Haggett, Cliff and Frey, 1977). In the meantime, however, it is necessary to be able to appreciate that great volume of research.

Geographical individuals

One of the problems identified by Robinson's research concerns the nature of the geographical observation unit or individual. Many geographical data sets have areas as their observations, and these introduce several other problems, somewhat related to that of autocorrelation.

Size and shape

The nature of some of these problems was explored in a published exchange in 1960. In an earlier paper, Dickinson (1959) had mapped the percentages of in- and out-commuters from each administrative area in West Germany, Belgium and the Netherlands, showing considerable regional variations in these values. Chisholm (1960, p. 187) pointed out that 'much of the geographical incidence of commuting shown by such data is illusory' because: (1) the administrative areas studied were not uniform in size and shape; (2) the population was not evenly distributed within each area; and (3) the distance and direction of movement were undoubtedly non-random. The spatial variations mapped could well reflect nothing more than regional differences in the size and shape of administrative areas. Recently Ord and Cliff (1976) have estimated, from Dickinson's data, that,

Country	% Commuters crossing a boundary	Average area of district (hectares)	Mean journey-to-work length (km)
Belgium	40·0	1880	1·10–1·13
Netherlands	15·2	6670	1·51–2·17

As the above data show, although Belgium has more people officially designated as commuters (i.e. they cross an administrative boundary) Dutch commuters probably travel the longer distances to work.

The problems introduced by variations in the size and shape of areas are undoubtedly crucial when the variable being studied concerns movements across their boundaries, but other problems, some of them perhaps more subtle, are also introduced by this factor to the study of a wide range of variables. The arguments made by Figs. 9.1–9.4 with respect to inter-dependent point patterns are relevant, for example. Take a town divided into 10 districts of equal population (Fig. 9.5A), in each of which we have measured the percentage of people who are aged under 5 and the number of children's playgrounds per 1000 homes. Our hypothesis is that there is a positive relationship between density of playgrounds and proportion of children in the population; the regression equation (Fig. 9.5B — solid line) testing this for the 10 areas is

$$Y = 0.56 + 0.11 X \qquad r_{YX} = 0.85$$

which clearly supports our proposal. But two related objections can be

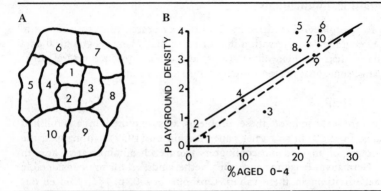

Fig. 9.5 Regressions of supply and demand for playgrounds in various 'regions' of a town.

made to this regression. The first is that the observations are probably not independent. Study of Figs. 9.5A and B suggests that in fact the city comprises three 'regions' in terms of these two variables — the inner city (districts 1 and 2); the central suburbs (3 and 4); and the outer suburbs (5 to 10) — but that the last of these three is given greater weight in the regression than the other two. (If the regression were run on the means for the three 'regions', it would read

$$Y = 0.08 + 0.134 \, X \qquad r_{YX} = 0.99$$

which is shown by the broken line in Fig. 9.5B.) As a counter to this argument, it could be claimed that the 10 districts each have the same population, so their use is giving equal weight to each unit of population; the clustering of 6 districts in the top right-hand corner of the graph in Fig. 9.5B comes about because 60% of the town's districts have that character. But what if all of the 6 outer suburban districts were built by the same developer during the same decade, to the same design? In this case, clearly there is autocorrelation in a substantive sense, as all are part of the same unit. Such an argument could be applied to the work of Morrison, Scripter and Smith (1968, p. 148), for many of their counties are part of the same industrial areas.

The two regressions in Fig. 9.5B are not very different, but whether they are or not the definition of the geographical individual raises a paradoxical problem for much geographical work, as pointed out by Harvey (1969). Many studies have aimed to produce regionalisations — of social areas, perhaps, or of type-of-farming areas — and have approached this through (1) a principal components analysis, collapsing the variables to a smaller number, and (2) a classification of the observations on the basis of their component scores. This procedure is based on correlation coefficients, whose computation rests on an assumption that the observations are independent. If our 'theory' about regions is correct, then they are not independent. And so we are trying to prove that adjacent observations are interdependent, using a method which does not allow us to do that, since it presumes they are independent!

Ecological correlations

In one of the examples of canonical correlation analysis, we saw how rates for violent crimes in districts of Cleveland were positively related to levels of poverty in those districts (p. 191). The correct interpretation of this finding is that high crime rates are recorded in the areas of greatest poverty, but it is easy to transfer this group (or ecological) correlation to the individual level and conclude that poorer people commit more crimes of violence than do wealthier people. This would be an incorrect inference, for there is no evidence in the data which suggests such a relationship.

This difficulty of inferring individual characteristics from group data is widely recognised, and is usually known as the *ecological fallacy*. It is a common problem in geographical study dealing with the characteristics of areas, and it can lead to very wrong interpretations. This was demonstrated in a classic paper by Robinson (1950). He showed that using the nine Census divisions of the United States as the observations the correlation between percentage of the population aged over 10 who were Negro (X) and percentage of the population aged over 10 who were illiterate (Y) in 1930 was $r_{YX} = 0.946$. For the forty-eight states $r_{YX} = 0.773$, but at the individual level for the 97 million Americans aged over 10 the correlation (using dummy variables) was $r_{YX} = 0.203$. In other words, there was less than a 5% chance (0.203^2) that a black person was also an illiterate, despite the fact that black people were spatially concentrated in the same areas as illiterates.

The need for caution in the interpretation of correlations using areal data is clearly indicated by Robinson's second example. Again using the population aged over 10 as his base, he found a correlation of $r_{YX} = -0.619$ at the Census division level and $r_{YX} = -0.526$ at the state level when regressing percentage illiterate (Y) against percentage foreign-born (X). At the individual level, the correlation was $r_{YX} = 0.118$!

Ecological correlations are very valuable in many circumstances, of course, as long as we are careful in their interpretation. They often offer strong clues as to individual relationships, for which more detailed data are unavailable (as with voting behaviour: Crewe and Payne, 1976), and this is especially so where well-developed theory provides precise hypotheses as to the expected form of the relationships. Nevertheless, geographers and others who use data on population and other aggregates by area always need to be careful in what they interpret from the results of their analyses, in translating results from one geographical individual (a population) to another (a person).

Closed number sets

By far the most frequently used ratio scale in geographical work is the percentage. Given that so much research is concerned with areas of different sizes and shapes, this is not surprising, for the use of percentages (and of proportions, of course) brings each area or population to a common scale. If we correlated the number of arable farms in each country of the world against the number of tractors, we would really just be relating two different measures of the country's size, but if we regressed percentage of farms with tractors against percentage of farms which are arable farms we could get (1) from the regression and correlation, measures of the relationship between mechanisation and types of farming, and (2) from the residuals, indicators of 'developed' and 'underdeveloped' countries in terms of farm mechanisation.

The range of values

Two problems in the use of percentages are widespread in geographical research. (The problems are exactly the same for proportions; merely divide every figure in the next paragraphs by 100.) First, the range of the

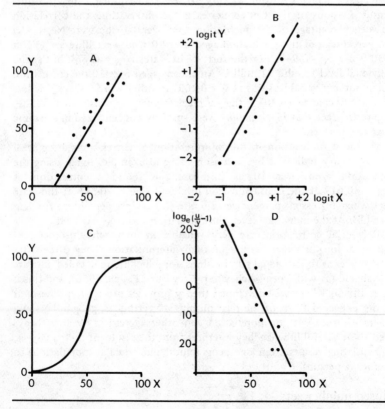

Fig. 9.6 Problem of extrapolating a regression using precentage data (A): solutions include (B) the logit transformation, and (C, D) the logistic curve.

numbers is fixed, which may make some interpretations of regression equations difficult. This is illustrated in Fig. 9.6A, which shows, for a sample of 12 towns, a regression between the percentage of the households which have a total annual income exceeding £2000 (X) and the percentage of the households with television sets (Y): the regression equation is

$$Y = -29 \cdot 18 + 1 \cdot 49 \, X \qquad r_{YX} = 0 \cdot 90$$

Using this equation, it is possible to estimate or predict nonsensical values of Y. A town with less than 29% of its households earning more than £2000 p.a., for example, will have a negative percentage of its households owning television sets, whereas a town with more than 80% of its households in the given income bracket will have more than 100% of its households with television sets!

Three methods can be used to circumvent this problem. The first is merely to state clearly that the equation obtained refers only to the range of values shown — i.e. to the *domain* of the independent variable. For the example in Fig. 9.6A, then, we would state that

$$Y = -29 \cdot 18 + 1 \cdot 49 \, X \qquad r_{YX} = 0 \cdot 90 \text{ when } 25 < X < 85$$

thereby limiting interpretation of the equation to values of X between 25 and 85%.

The second method is to transform the percentage values into an infinite ratio scale. Such a transformation is the *logit* (Wrigley, 1973), for which the formula is

$$L_i = \log_e \frac{PC_i}{(100 - PC_i)} \tag{9.1}$$

where PC_i is the percentage value at observation i; and
L_i is the logit for observation i.

The ratio $PC_i/(100 - PC_i)$ is the odds of being in the category expressed as percentages. If the percentage of households in place i with televisions is 20, then

$$PC_i/(100 - PC_i) = 20/(100 - 20) = 0 \cdot 25$$

The range of these odds is 0 to infinity. The natural logarithm is

$$\log_e \frac{20}{(100 - 20)} = \log_e 0 \cdot 25 = \bar{1} \cdot 9163$$

which ranges from minus infinity to plus infinity (i.e. $\log_e \frac{100}{0}$ = infinity and $\log_e \frac{0}{100}$ = minus infinity). If written for proportions rather than percentages

$$L_i = \log_e \frac{P_i}{(1 \cdot 0 - P_i)} \tag{9.2}$$

and the ratio is the probability of being in the category, so that if $P_i = 0 \cdot 20$

for households with a television set the ratio 20/80 = 0·25 is the probability of a household having a television set.

Using the logit transformation for the data of Fig. 9.6A (i.e. L_y = logit Y, etc.) we get the equation (Fig. 9.6B)

$$L_Y = -0·163 + 1·653 \ L_X \qquad r_{YX} = 0·903$$

which in terms of its goodness-of-fit differs very little from the regression using the raw data (Fig. 9.6A). This is not surprising, since the transformation was not to change the shape of the relationship (Fig. 9.6B) but to remove the problems of estimating or predicting irrelevant values of Y for given values of X. Thus, if X = 90 we would predict from the logit equation that Y = 93·10, but from the equation for the raw data that Y = 104·92. Use of the logit transformation means that predicted values of Y will never be less than 0 or greater than 100·0.

The final method is really an alternative transformation which forces the regression line through the point where X = Y = 100, as well as through the intersection of $\overline{X}$ and $\overline{Y}$. Such a regression is a special case of a more general formulation known as the *logistic curve* which has a characteristic S-shape (Fig. 9.6C) and meets the constraints set in the previous sentence. The main use of this curve is in studies of the diffusion of an innovation, in which there is a ceiling − U − of people who can adopt it, and in biological studies of population growth which also set a maximum level (i.e. that which an area's food resources can support). The formula for the logistic curve is

$$Y = \frac{U}{1 + ae^{-bX}} \qquad (9.3)$$

where X, Y are the independent and dependent variables;
     U is the upper limit of values for Y;
     a is the value of Y when X = 0 (i.e. the intercept);
     e is the natural logarithmic base (see p. 8); and
     b is the slope coefficient which, since we are dealing in natural logarithms, is the rate of change of Y with X.

This equation can be rewritten as

$$\log_e \left(\frac{U}{Y} - 1 \right) = \log_e a - b \ X \qquad (9.4)$$

and has the benefit of using logarithms which range from minus infinity to plus infinity. For the data in Fig. 9.6A, the logistic relationship is expressed as

$$\log_e \left(\frac{U}{Y} - 1 \right) = 4·486 - 0·085 \ X \qquad r_{YX} = 0·910$$

the form of which is given in Fig. 9.6D. In transforming the smooth S-shaped curve of Fig. 9.6C, by expressing each value of the dependent variable as a ratio to the upper limit it can take, and thus straightening the regression, what was formerly a positive relationship is re-expressed as a negative one. According to this, if X = 90, Y = 81·06.

Logistic curves ensure that regression relationships do not exceed an upper limit on the dependent variable. Their particular use is in diffusion studies, relating, for example, the percentage of households with television sets to time from the introduction of television (e.g. Berry, 1971) but they can be used more widely to ensure that no more than 100% of a population indulge in any activity (Johnston, 1976b).

Closed number sets and independence

Very frequently in geographical work, a population is divided into groups and the membership of each group is expressed as a percentage of the population: factorial ecologies of residential area characteristics in cities, for example, often study occupation characteristics, age structures, or ethnic origins in this way. Davies and Lewis (1973) in their study of Leicester (p. 171) examined households in each area according to the socio-economic status of their heads. Three mutually exclusive groups (1 and 2; 3; 4 and 5) were used, to one of which every household was allocated. The population in each area was also divided into five age groups (0—14; 15—24; 25—44; 45—59; 60+). All eight variables were included in their component and factor analyses. Yet, as we saw in Chapter 4 when discussing the use of dummy variables in regression, if you have three categories in a classification once the values of two are known the other is fixed, and so once the percentages of households in social classes 1 and 2 and in social class 3 are known, the percentage in social classes 4 and 5 must be fixed. By including all three variables in an analysis, therefore, the correlation structure is being biased, by recording the same thing more than once.

The nature of this bias can be indicated by a simple example. We have four variables measured over a set of areas to index aspects of their population structure:

X_1 is percentage of persons aged over 65;
X_2 is percentage of persons who own their home;
X_3 is percentage of persons who vote Conservative;
X_4 is percentage of persons who are retired;

to which we add indices of the sex ratio,

X_5 is percentage of population who are male; and
X_6 is percentage of population who are female.

A little thought will tell us that X_5 and X_6 must be negatively correlated, with $r_{56} = -1·00$; if 51% of the population is male, 49% must be female, and so on.

The correlation matrix for these six variables is shown in Fig. 9.7. A components analysis produces the following loadings on the first com-

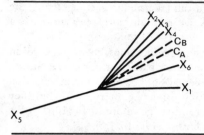

Fig. 9.7   The effect of variable selection on the location of principal components in a correlation matrix.

ponent (C_A in the figure):

X_1	X_2	X_3	X_4	X_5	X_6
0·887	0·924	0·954	0·976	−0·976	0·976

If we omit X_5, we get the component C_B in Fig. 9.7, with loadings

X_1	X_2	X_3	X_4	X_6
0·864	0·941	0·967	0·985	0·965

The result of removing the variable has been that the component has moved closer to the group X_2, X_3 and X_4. This is not unexpected. By including both X_5 and X_6 we are in fact measuring the same thing twice, since $X_5 = 100 - X_6$, and by doing this we bias the location of the components towards that 'double-counting' (Johnston, 1977).

Of course, both percentage male and percentage female should not be included in a principal components analysis, but closed number sets with more than two categories are frequently used, as shown with the Davies and Lewis example. These, too, will introduce biases to the correlation structure and hence to the component structure − and even more to a factor structure, since for every variable in a closed number set, the communality (h^2: p. 142) must equal 1·0, which is otherwise a rare occurrence in factor analysis. (These biases refer to the interpretation, which is a function of the data input. The component and factor solutions are not biased in a mathematical sense, of course, since they accurately represent the correlations in the matrix.)

The nature of these biases is illustrated by the small data set in Table 9.1, referring to the percentage of votes received by each major political party in Liverpool's eight parliamentary constituencies at the October 1974 General Election. From this we could derive the equation for the relationship between percentage Conservative (X) and percentage Labour (Y) as

$$Y = 88·57 - 1·057 X \qquad r_{YX} = -0·872$$

Labour and Conservative do not form a closed number system, as the Liberal Party achieved between 5·15 and 27·32% of the vote. But the

Table 9.2   Voting in Liverpool at the October 1974 General Election

Constituency	Percentage voting* Conservative	Labour	Liberal
Edge Hill	20·76	51·91	27·32
Garston	42·14	44·80	10·06
Kirkdale	28·49	61·41	10·10
Scotland Exchange	12·19	82·66	5·15
Toxteth	30·37	57·67	11·96
Walton	30·16	57·95	11·89
Wavertree	45·85	39·19	14·97
West Derby	28·88	60·48	10·64

* Of the votes cast for these three parties

system imposes many constraints, as Fig. 9.8 illustrates. In Edge Hill constituency, Liberal won 27·32% of the votes, and so the most Conservative and Labour could get was (100 − 27·32) = 72·68. Thus if one of them got 50·00%, the other must have got 22·68%. All possible divisions of this 72·68% between Labour and Conservative are shown by the diagonal line in Fig. 9.8A, where the value a is the percentage of the vote won by the

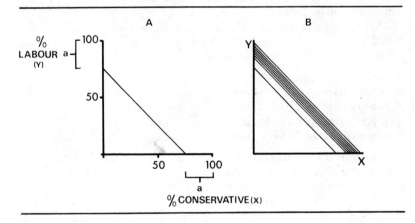

Fig. 9.8   The 'range of freedom' for observations when using the percentage data in Table 9.2.

Liberal Party. A similar line can be drawn for each of the eight constituencies, producing a band within the graph outside which no observation will lie. In Fig. 9.8B, the lowest line is for Edge Hill (27·32% Liberal) and the highest is for Scotland Exchange (5·15%). All of the observations must be between these. It is possible that within that area the points may be so distributed that there is a negligible correlation between percentage Conservative and percentage Labour, but on a random allocation procedure such a result is highly unlikely (Johnston, 1977). Thus although one is not measuring the same thing twice, as in Fig. 9.7, one is getting fairly close to it with a three-variable closed number set.

The larger the number of classes in a closed number set, the less the degree to which any one correlation between two of them is fixed, especially if the range of percentages covered by every variable is considerable. Nevertheless, without detailed investigation of the data, it is never clear when such correlations exist, or to what extent they are influencing the results, and so closed number sets should be avoided. This can be done by omitting some of the classes, or by transforming the data. With the Liverpool data, for example, instead of correlating percentage Conservative with percentage Labour, we could transform the latter to Labour as a percentage of the non-Conservatives, i.e.

$$\% \text{ Lab} \longrightarrow (\text{Lab}/(\text{Lab} + \text{Lib})) \times 100\cdot0 \qquad (9.5)$$

which gives the equation

$$Y = 91\cdot22 - 0\cdot35 \text{ X} \qquad r_{YX} = -0\cdot133$$

where X is percentage voting Conservative; and
    Y is percentage not voting Conservative who voted Labour.

In other words, there is no relationship of any strength between the percentage of the votes won by Conservative and the percentage of the remainder won by Labour.

This 'percentage of the remainder' transformation gets around the closed number set problem, but with four or more categories it may cause interpretative problems. If there are five classes.

X_1 is percentage aged 0—14;
X_2 is percentage aged 15—24;
X_3 is percentage aged 25—44;
X_4 is percentage aged 45—64; and
X_5 is percentage aged 65+

then there is a large number of ways in which transformations could be achieved, the substantive results of which would be different. For example, one could regress X_1 on X_2 as a percentage of $(X_2 + X_3 + X_4 + X_5)$; X_2 against X_3 as a percentage of $(X_3 + X_4 + X_5)$ or against X_3 as a percentage of $(X_1 + X_3 + X_4 + X_5)$; and so on. The problem can be a tricky one, therefore. If closed number sets must be used in the research then perhaps analyses based on the general linear model should not be; if such analyses are to be undertaken, then closed number sets are best avoided.

Percentages and proportions are not the only examples of closed number sets in geographical research. Distances, for example, do not form a closed set in that they all sum to the same total, but the configuration of the area in which they are measured determines the nature of the distribution of all possible distances (Taylor, 1971). This is important for research in which distance forms an independent variable — such as studies of migration and of trade flows (Johnston, 1976a) — since it influences the range and distribution of values on the independent variable, and from these the functional relationships which may be derived (Johnston, 1976d).

Conclusions

The issues outlined in this chapter have been raised here because readers are likely to find them discussed with increasing frequency in the literature. To some writers already referred to, they are sufficiently damning to suggest that geographers should not use methods based on the general linear model, since their data too frequently, if not always, violate the basic assumptions of that model. Clearly that is not the view advanced here, or this book would not have been written. If geographers are aiming to make precise statements about their subject matter, they must adopt precise methods, using them correctly in the light of their data.

As will have been deduced, many of the problems raised here, and particularly those concerned with spatial autocorrelation, are of greater importance to inferential statistical work then they are to descriptive statistics. But this is no reason to ignore them. Although much geographical research in the past has been concerned more with description than with prediction, any fully-developed scientific study will want to make predictive statements generalising to future populations from past and present samples. Advances in geographical methodology, then, will have to be based on overcoming the sorts of problems discussed here.

References

Ahmed, Q. (1965) *Indian Cities: Characteristics and Correlates*, Univ. Chicago, Dept. Geogr. Res. Pap. 102, Chicago.

Barker, D. (1976) 'Hierarchic and non-hierarchic grouping methods: an empirical comparison of two techniques', *Geogr. Annlr.* B, 42–58.

Bayliss, B. T. and Edwards, S. L. (1970) *Industrial Demand for Transport*, H.M.S.O., London.

Bell, W. (1955) 'Economic, family and ethnic status: an empirical test', *Amer. Sociol. Rev.*, **20**, 45–52.

Bennett, R. J. (1975) 'The representation and identification of spatio-temporal systems: an example of population diffusion in North-West England', *Trans. Inst. Brit. Geogr.*, **66**, 73–94.

Berry, B. J. L. (1964) 'Approaches to regional analysis: a synthesis', *Ann. Assoc. Amer. Geogr.*, **54**, 2–11.

Berry, B. J. L. (1966) *Essays on Commodity Flows and the Spatial Structure of the Indian Economy*, Univ. Chicago, Dept. Geogr. Res. Pap. 111, Chicago.

Berry, B. J. L. (1967) 'Grouping and regionalizing: an approach to the problem using multivariate analysis', in W. L. Garrison and D. F. Marble (ed.), *Quantitative Geography Part I Economic and Cultural Topics*, Northwestern University, Studies in Geography, **13**, Evanston, 219–51.

Berry, B. J. L. (1968) 'A synthesis of formal and functional regions using a general field theory of spatial behaviour', in B. J. L. Berry and D. F. Marble (ed.) *Spatial Analysis*, Prentice-Hall, Englewood Cliffs, New Jersey, 419–30.

Berry, B. J. L. (1971) 'The geography of the United States in the year 2000', *Trans. Inst. Brit. Geogr.*, **51**, 21–54.

Berry, B. J. L. (1973) 'A paradigm for modern geography', in R. J. Chorley (ed.), *Directions in Geography*, Methuen, London, 1–22.

Berry, B. J. L. and Garrison, W. L. (1958) 'The functional bases of the central-place hierarchy', *Econ. Geogr.*, **34**, 145–54.

Black, W. R. (1973) 'Towards a factorial ecology of flows', *Econ. Geogr.*, **49**, 59–67.

Blalock, H. M. (1960) *Social Statistics*, McGraw-Hill, New York.

Brown, L. A. and Horton, F. E. (1970) 'Social area change: an empirical study', *Urban Studies*, **7**, 271–88.

Cant, R. G. (1971) 'Changes in the location of manufacturing in New Zealand 1957–68: an application of three-mode factor analysis', *N.Z. Geogr.*, **27**, 38–55.

Cant, R. G. (1973) 'The Philippines: spatial dimensions of livelihood and society', *Proc. Seventh N.Z. Geogr. Conference*, Hamilton, 101–12.

Cant, R. G. (1975a) 'Three-mode factor analysis as applied to industrial location data', in L. Collins and D. F. Walker (ed.), *Locational Dynamics of Manufacturing Activity*, Wiley, London, 201–26.

Cant, R. G. (1975b) 'Territorial socio-economic indicators in development plans in the Asian region', *Intern. Soc. Sci. J.*, **27**, 53–77.

Casetti, E., King, L. J. and Jeffrey, D. (1971) 'Structural imbalance in the U.S. urban economic system', *Geogr. Anal.*, **3**, 239–55.

Cattell, R. B. (1966) *Handbook of Multivariate Experimental Psychology*, Rand McNally, Chicago.

Chisholm, M. D. I. (1960) 'The geography of commuting', *Ann. Assoc. Amer. Geogr.*, 50, 187–8.

Chorley, R. J. and Haggett, P. (1965) 'Trend surface mapping in geographical research', *Trans. Inst. Brit. Geogr.*, 37, 47–67.

Chorley, R. J. and Haggett, P. (1967) *Models in Geography*, Methuen, London.

Clark, D. (1973a) 'Urban linkage and regional structure in Wales: an analysis of change, 1958–68', *Trans. Inst. Brit. Geogr.*, 58, 41–58.

Clark, D. (1973b) 'The formal and functional structure of Wales', *Ann. Assoc. Amer. Geogr.*, 63, 71–84.

Clark, W. A. V. (1967) 'The use of residuals from regression in geographical research', *N.Z. Geogr.*, 23, 64–66.

Cliff, A. D. and Ord, J. K. (1973) *Spatial Autocorrelation*, Pion, London.

Cliff, A. D. *et al.* (1975) *Elements of Spatial Structure*, Cambridge University Press, Cambridge.

Clout, H. D. and Salt, J. (1976) *Migration in Post-War Europe: Geographical Essays*, Oxford University Press, London.

Corsi, Th. and Harvey, M. E. (1975) 'The socio-economic determinants of crime in the city of Cleveland; the application of canonical scores to geographical processes', *Tijdschr. Econ. Soc. Geogr.*, 66, 323–36.

Court, A. (1972) 'All statistical populations are estimated from samples', *Prof. Geogr.*, 24, 160–1.

Cox, K. R. (1968) 'Suburbia and voting behavior in the London metropolitan area', *Ann. Assoc. Amer. Geogr.*, 58, 111–27.

Crewe, I. and Payne, C. (1976) 'Another game with nature: an ecological regression model of the British two-party vote ratio in 1970', *Brit. J. Polit. Sci.*, 6, 43–81.

Davies, W. K. D. and Lewis, G. J. (1973) 'The urban dimensions of Leicester', *Inst. Brit. Geogr. Special Publication*, 5, 71–85.

Davis, J. C. (1973) *Statistics and Data Analysis in Geology*, John Wiley, New York.

Dickinson, R. E. (1959) 'The geography of commuting in West Germany', *Ann. Assoc. Amer. Geogr.*, 49, 443–56.

Duncan, O. D. (1966) 'Path analysis: sociological examples', *Amer. J. Sociol.*, 72, 1–16.

Duncan, O. D. (1975) *An Introduction to Structural Equation Models*, Academic Press, New York.

Everitt, B. (1974) *Cluster Analysis*, Heinemann, London.

Farmer, B. H. (1973) 'Geography, area studies and the study of area', *Trans. Inst. Brit. Geogr.*, 60, 1–16.

Fox, K. A. (1968) *Intermediate Economic Statistics*, Wiley, New York.

Freeman, D. B. (1973) *International Trade, Migration, and Capital Flows*, Univ. Chicago, Dept. Geogr. Res. Pap. 146, Chicago.

Freeman, T. W. (1961) *A Hundred Years of Geography*, Duckworth, London.

Fuller, G. (1974) 'On the spatial diffusion of fertility decline: the distance-to-clinic variable in a Chilean community', *Econ. Geogr.*, 50, 324–32.

Garrison, W. L. (1956) 'Applicability of statistical inference to geographical research', *Geogrl. Rev.*, 46, 427–9.

Garrison, W. L. and Marble, D. F. (1964) 'Factor-analytic study of the connectivity of a transportation network', *Pap. Proc. Reg. Sci. Assoc.*, 12, 231–8.

Gauthier, H. L. (1968) 'Transportation and the growth of the Sao Paulo economy', *J. Reg. Sci.*, 8, 77–94.

Geary, R. C. (1954) 'The contiguity ratio and statistical mapping', *The Incorporated Statistician*, 5, 115–41.

Goheen, P. (1970) *Victorian Toronto, 1850 to 1900*, Univ. Chicago, Dept. Geogr. Res. Pap. 137, Chicago.

Gould, P. R. (1967) 'On the geographical interpretation of eigenvalues', *Trans. Inst. Brit. Geogr.*, 42, 53–86.

Gould, P. R. (1969) 'Methodological developments since the fifties', *Progress in Geography*, 1, 1–50.

Gould, P. R. (1970) 'Is *Statistix inferens* the geographical name for a wild goose?' *Econ. Geogr.*, 46, 439–48.

Gould, P. R. and White, R. (1974) *Mental Maps*, Penguin Books, Harmondsworth.

Greer-Wootten, B. (1971) 'Some reflections on systems analysis in geographic research', in H. M. French and J.-B. Racine (ed.), *Quantitative and Qualitative Geography: la necessite d'un dialogue*, University of Ottawa Press, Ottawa, 151–74.

Greer-Wootten, B. (1972) *A Bibliography of Statistical Applications in Geography*, Association of American Geographers, Commission on College Geography, Technical Paper 9, Washington.

Gregory, S. (1978) *Statistical Methods and the Geographer* (4th ed.), Longman, London.

Gregory, S. (1975) 'On the delimitation of regional patterns of recent climatic fluctuations', *Weather*, 30, 276–87.

Guelke, L. (1971) 'Problems of scientific explanation in geography', *Canad. Geogr.*, 15, 38–53.

Haggett, P. (1961) 'Land use and sediment yield in an old plantation tract of the Serro do Mar, Brazil', *Geogr. J.*, 127–50–62.

Haggett, P. (1965) *Locational Analysis in Human Geography*, Edward Arnold, London.

Haggett, P. (1968) 'Trend surface mapping in the interregional comparison of intra-regional structures', *Pap. Reg. Sci. Ass.*, 20, 19–28.

Haggett, P., Cliff, A. D. and Frey, A. (1977) *Locational Analysis in Human Geography*, Edward Arnold, London.

Hammond, R. and McCullagh, P. S. (1974) *Quantitative Techniques in Geography: An Introduction*, Clarendon Press, Oxford.

Hart, J. F. and Salisbury, N. E. (1965) 'Population change in Middle Western villages: a statistical approach', *Ann. Assoc. Amer. Geogr.*, 55, 140–60.

Hartigan, J. A. (1975) *Clustering Algorithms*, John Wiley, New York.

Harvey, D. W. (1969) *Explanation in Geography*, Edward Arnold, London.

Hauser, D. P. (1974) 'Some problems in the use of stepwise regression techniques in geographical research', *Canad. Geogr.*, 18, 148–58.

Hay, A. M. (1975) 'On the choice of methods in the factor analysis of connectivity matrices: a comment', *Trans. Inst. Brit. Geogr.*, 66, 163–7.

Herbert, D. T. (1976) 'Social deviance in the city: a spatial perspective', in D. T. Herbert and R. J. Johnston (eds.), *Social Areas in Cities. Volume 2: Spatial Perspectives on Problems and Policies*, John Wiley, London, 89–122.

Horton, F. E., McConnell, H. H. and Tirtha, R. (1970) 'Spatial patterns of socio-economic structure in India', *Tijd. Econ. Soc. Geogr.*, 61, 101–13.

Jardine, N. and Sibson, R. (1971) *Mathematical Taxonomy*, John Wiley, London.

Jeffrey, D. (1974) 'Regional fluctuations in unemployment within the U.S. urban economic system: a study of the spatial impact of short term economic change', *Econ. Geogr.*, 50, 111–23.

Johnston, R. J. (1970) 'Grouping and regionalising: some technical and methodological observations', *Econ. Geogr.*, 46, 293–305.

Johnston, R. J. (1971) *Urban Residential Patterns*, G. Bell, London.

Johnston, R. J. (1973a) 'Possible extensions to the factorial ecology method: a note', *Environ. Plann.*, 5, 719–34.

Johnston, R. J. (1973b) 'Social area change in Melbourne, 1961–1966: a sample exploration', *Austr. Geogr. Stud.*, 11, 79–98.

Johnston, R. J. (1973c) 'Residential differentiation in major New Zeland urban areas: a comparative factorial ecology', in B. D. Clark and M. B. Gleave (eds.), *Social Patterns in Cities*. Institute of British Geographers, Special Publication 5, London, 143–68.

Johnston, R. J. (1974) 'Local effects in voting at a local election', *Ann. Assoc. Amer. Geogr.*, 64, 418–29.

Johnston, R. J. (1976a) *Classification in Geography*, CATMOG 6, Geoabstracts, Norwich.

Johnston, R. J. (1976b) 'Contagion in neighbourhoods: a note on problems of modelling and analysis', *Environ. Plann. A*, **8**, 581—6.

Johnston, R. J. (1976c) 'On regression coefficients in comparative studies of the friction of distance', *Tijds. Econ. Soc. Geogr.*, **67**, 15—28.

Johnston, R. J. (1976d) *The World Trade System*, G. Bell, London.

Johnston, R. J. (1977) 'Principal components analysis and factor analysis in geographical research: some problems and issues', *S. Afric. Geogr. J.*, **59**, 30—44.

Joshi, T. R. (1972) 'Toward computing factor scores', in W. P. Adams and F. Helleiner (eds.), *International Geography*, **2**, University of Toronto Press, Toronto, 906—9.

Kariel, H. G. (1963) 'Selected factors areally associated with population growth due to net migration', *Ann. Assoc. Amer. Geogr.*, **53**, 210—23.

Keeble, D. E. and Hauser, D. P. (1972) 'Spatial analysis of manufacturing growth in outer south-east England', *Reg. Stud.*, **6**, 11—36.

King, C. A. M. (1969) 'Trend surface analysis of Central Pennine erosion surfaces', *Trans. Inst. Brit. Geogr.*, **47**, 47—59.

King, L. J. (1961) 'A multivariate analysis of the spacing of urban settlements in the United States', *Ann. Assoc. Amer. Geogr.*, **51**, 222—33.

King, L. J. (1969) *Statistical Analysis in Geography*, Prentice-Hall, Englewood Cliffs, New Jersey.

King, L. J. and Jeffrey, D. (1972) 'City classification by oblique-factor analysis of time-series data', in B. J. L. Berry (ed.), *City Classification Handbook*, John Wiley, New York, 225—46.

Lankford, P. M. (1974) 'Testing simulation models', *Geogr. Anal.*, **6**, 294—302.

Magee, A. (1971) 'Problems of economic development and migration in Southern Europe, with special reference to Spain', in R. J. Johnston and J. M. Soons (eds.), *Proceedings of the Sixth New Zealand Geography Conference*, Christchurch, 179—85.

Martin, R. L. and Oeppen, J. (1975) 'The identification of regional forecasting models using space-time correlation functions', *Trans. Inst. Brit. Geogr.*, **66**, 95—118.

Massam, B. H. (1973) 'Forms of local government in the Montreal area, 1911—71: a discriminant approach', *Canad. J. Polit. Sci.*, **6**, 243—53.

Meyer, D. R. (1971) 'Factor analysis versus correlation analysis', *Econ. Geogr.*, **47**, 336—43.

Meyer, D. R. (1972a) 'Geographical population data: statistical description not statistical inference', *Prof. Geogr.*, **24**, 26—8.

Meyer, D. R. (1972b) 'Classification of U.S. metropolitan areas by the characteristics of their nonwhite populations', in B. J. L. Berry (ed.) *City Classification Handbook*, John Wiley, New York, 61—94.

Monmonier, M. S. and Finn, F. E. (1973) 'Improving the interpretation of geographical canonical correlation models', *Prof. Geogr.*, **25**, 140—2.

Moore, E. G. (1969) 'The structure of intra-urban movement rates: an ecological model', *Urban Studies*, **6**, 17—33.

Morrill, R. L. (1965) *Migration and the Spread and Growth of Urban Settlement*, Lund Studies in Geography, B26, C. W. K. Gleerup, Lund.

Morrison, J., Scripter, M. W. and Smith, R. H. T. (1968) 'Basic measures of manufacturing in the United States, 1958', *Econ. Geogr.*, **44**, 296—311.

Murdie, R. A. (1969) *Factorial Ecology of Metropolitan Toronto, 1951—1961: An Essay on the Social Geography of the City*, Univ. Chicago, Dept. Geogr. Res. Pap. 116, Chicago.

Murdie, R. A. (1976) 'Spatial form in the residential mosaic', in D. T. Herbert and R. J. Johnston (eds.), *Social Areas in Cities, Volume I Spatial Processes and Form*, Wiley, London, 237—72.

Newton, P. W. (1975) *Choice of Residential Location in Urban Environments*, Univ. Newcastle, Res. Papers in Geogr. 5, Newcastle, N.S.W.

Norris, J. M. and Barkham, J. P. (1970) 'A comparison of some Cotswold beechwoods using multiple-discriminant analysis', *J. Ecol.*, **58**, 603—19.

Openshaw, S. (1976) 'A general method for identifying scale and aggregation effects on any statistical model of pattern and process in a spatial domain', *Adv. Appl. Prob.*, **8**, 656—7.

Ord, J. K. and Cliff, A. D. (1976) 'The analysis of commuting patterns', *Environ. Plann.*, A, **8**, 941—6.

Palm, R. and Caruso, D. (1972) 'Labelling in factor ecology', *Ann. Assoc. Amer. Geogr.*, **62**, 122—33.

Perry, A. H. (1970) 'Filtering climatic anomaly fields using principal component analysis', *Trans. Inst. Brit. Geogr.*, **50**, 55—72.

Pocock, D. C. D. and Wishart, D. (1969) 'Methods of deriving multi-factor uniform regions', *Trans. Inst. Brit. Geogr.*, **47**, 73—98.

Poole, M. A. and O'Farrell, P. N. (1971) 'The assumptions of the linear regression model', *Trans. Inst. Brit. Geogr.*, **52**, 145—58.

Pyle, G. F. (1971) *Heart Disease, Cancer and Stroke in Chicago*, Univ. Chicago, Dept. Geogr. Res. Pap. 134, Chicago.

Ray, D. M. (1971) 'From factorial to canonical ecology: the spatial interrelationships of economic and cultural differences in Canada', *Econ. Geogr.*, **47**, 344—55.

Ray, D. M. and Lohnes, P. R. (1973) 'Canonical correlation in geographical analysis', Discussion Paper B.73.8, Ministry of State, Urban Affairs, Canada, Ottawa.

Rees, P. H. (1970) 'The urban envelope: patterns and dynamics of population density', in B. J. L. Berry and F. E. Horton (eds.) *Geographic Perspectives on Urban Systems*, Prentice-Hall, Englewood Cliffs, New Jersey, 276—305.

Rees, P. H. (1972) 'Problems of classifying sub-areas within cities', in B. J. L. Berry (ed.), *City Classification Handbook*, John Wiley, New York, 265—330.

Reynolds, D. R. (1974) 'Spatial contagion in political influence processes', in K. R. Cox, D. R. Reynolds and S. Rokkan (eds.), *Locational Approaches to Power and Conflict*, John Wiley, New York, 233—74.

Riddell, J. B. (1970) 'On structuring a migration model', *Geogr. Anal.*, **2**, 403—9.

Robinson, A. H. (1956) 'The necessity of weighting values in correlation analysis of areal data', *Ann. Assoc. Amer. Geogr.*, **46**, 233—6.

Robinson, G. and Fairbairn, K. (1969) 'An application of trend surface mapping to the distribution of residuals from regression', *Ann. Assoc. Amer. Geogr.*, **59**, 158—70.

Robinson, W. S. (1950) 'Ecological correlation and the behavior of individuals', *Amer. Sociol. Rev.*, **15**, 351—7.

Roseman, C. C. (1971) 'Migration, the journey to work, and household characteristics: an analysis based on non-areal aggregation', *Econ. Geogr.*, **47**, 467—74.

Rummel, R. J. (1967) 'Understanding factor analysis', *J. Conflict Resolution*, **11**, 444—80.

Schwind, P. M. (1971) *Migration and Regional Development in the United States, 1860—1960*, Univ. Chicago, Dept. Geogr. Res. Pap. 133, Chicago.

Siegel, S. (1956) *Nonparametric Statistics for the Behavioral Sciences*, McGraw-Hill, New York.

Smith, D. M. (1973) *The Geography of Social Well-Being in the United States*, McGraw-Hill, New York.

Smith, D. M. (1975) *Patterns in Human Geography*, David and Charles, Newton Abbott.

Smith, P. H. A. and Sokal, R. R. (1973) *Numerical Taxonomy*, Freeman and Company, San Francisco.

Society of County Treasurers (1975a) *Education Statistics 1973—74*, Society of County Treasurers, Reading.

Society of County Treasurers (1975b) *Public Library Statistics 1973—74*, Society of County Treasurers, Reading.

Taaffe, E. J. and Gauthier, H. L. (1973) *Geography of Transposition*, Prentice-Hall, Englewood Cliffs, New Jersey.

Tarrant, J. R. (1969) 'Some spatial variations in Irish agriculture', *Tijds. Econ. Soc. Geogr.*, **60**, 228—37.

Tarrant, J. R. (1970) 'Comments on the use of trend-surface analysis in the study of erosion surfaces', *Trans. Inst. Brit. Geogr.*, **51**, 221–2.

Taylor, P. J. (1969) 'Causal models in geographic research', *Ann. Assoc. Amer. Geogr.*, **59**, 402–5.

Taylor, P. J. (1971) 'Distances within shapes: an introduction to a new family of finite frequency distributions', *Geogr. Annlr. B*, **53**, 40–53.

Thomas, E. N. (1960) 'Areal associations between population growth and selected factors in the Chicago Urbanized Area', *Econ. Geogr.*, **36**, 158–70.

Thomas, E. N. and Anderson, D. L. (1965) 'Additional comments on weighting values in correlation analysis of areal data', *Ann. Assoc. Amer. Geogr.*, **55**, 492–505.

Timms, D. W. G. (1970) 'Comparative factorial ecology: some New Zealand examples', *Environ. Plann.* **2**, 455–68.

Timms, D. W. G. (1971) *The Urban Mosaic*, Cambridge University Press, Cambridge.

Tinkler, K. J. (1972) 'The physical interpretation of eigenfunctions of dichotomous matrices', *Trans. Inst. Brit. Geogr.*, **55**, 17–46.

Unwin, D. J. (1975) *An Introduction to Trend Surface Analysis*, CATMOG 5, Geoabstracts, Norwich.

Ward, J. H. (1963) 'Hierarchical grouping to optimize an objective function', *J. Amer. Stat. Assoc.*, **58**, 236–44.

Willis, K. G. (1972) 'The influence of spatial structure and socio-economic factors on migration rates. A case study: Tyneside 1961–1966', *Reg. Studs.*, **6**, 69–82.

Winsborough, H. H. (1962) 'City growth and city structure', *J. Reg. Sci.*, **4**, 35–49.

Wolpert, J. (1964) 'The decision process in spatial context', *Ann. Assoc. Amer. Geogr.*, **54**, 537–58.

Wrigley, N. (1973) 'The use of percentages in geographical research', *Area*, **5**, 183–6.

Wrigley, N. (1976) *Introduction to the Use of Logit Models in Geography*, CATMOG 10, Geoabstracts, Norwich.

Yeates, M. H. (1965) 'Some factors affecting the spatial distribution of Chicago land values', *Econ. Geogr.*, **41**, 57–70.

Yeates, M. H. (1974) *An Introduction to Quantitative Analysis in Human Geography*, McGraw-Hill, New York.

Index